FINANCIAL REPORTING
AND ANALYSIS

ICSA STUDY TEXT

FINANCIAL REPORTING AND ANALYSIS

YOUSUF KHAN

icsa.
Publishing

First published 2012
Reprinted 2013
Published by ICSA Information & Training Ltd
16 Park Crescent
London W1B 1AH

Designed and typeset by Paul Barrett Book Production, Cambridge
Printed by Hobbs the Printers Ltd, Totton, Hampshire

British Cataloguing in Publication Data
A catalogue record for this book is available from the British Library.

ISBN 978 1860 724855

Acknowledgements

I would like to thank all those who, in a variety of ways, supported me in this academic and professional endeavour. In particular I would like to express my gratitude to Michael Knight, Head of Department of Accounting and Finance, London South Bank University, for his support and encouragement and allowing me the time and space required to complete this undertaking. I would also like to thank Mr Iain Boatman and Mr Joe Adomako for their kind assistance in reviewing the material in the book.

I would also like to express my great appreciation to Prof Dr Kenneth D'Silva, Prof Andrew Chambers and Prof Jeffery Ridley for providing advice and support throughout the writing of this book.

Last, but not least, I would like to thank my wife, Razia Khan, for her understanding, patience and support.

Yousuf Khan

Contents

How to use this study text

ICSA study texts developed to support ICSA's Chartered Secretaries Qualifying Scheme (CSQS) follow a standard format and include a range of navigational, self-testing and illustrative features to help you get the most out of the support materials.

Each text is divided into three main sections:

- introductory material
- the text itself, divided into Parts and Chapters
- additional reference information

The sections below show you how to find your way around the text and make the most of its features.

Introductory material

The introductory section of each text includes a full contents list and the module syllabus which re-iterates the module aims, learning outcomes and syllabus content for the module in question.

The text itself

Each **part** opens with a list of the chapters to follow, an overview of what will be covered and learning outcomes for the part.

Every **chapter** opens with a list of the topics covered and an introduction specific to that chapter. Chapters are structured to allow students to break the content down into manageable sections for study. Each chapter ends with a summary of key content to reinforce understanding, as well as end of chapter examination-standard questions to test your knowledge further.

Part opening

Chapter opening

Features

The text is enhanced by a range of illustrative and self-testing features to assist understanding and to help you prepare for the examination. Each feature is presented in a standard format, so that you will become familiar with how to use them in your study.

The texts also include tables, figures and checklists and, where relevant, sample documents and forms.

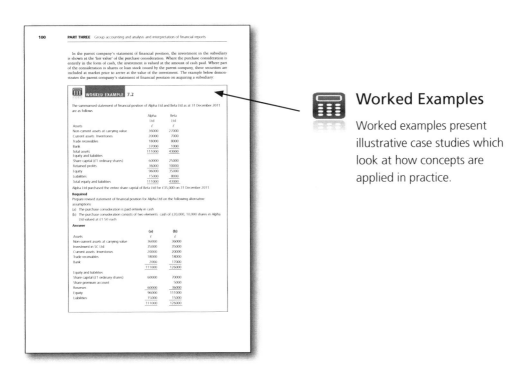

Worked Examples

Worked examples present illustrative case studies which look at how concepts are applied in practice.

Test your Knowledge

Short, revision-style questions to help you re-cap on key information and core concepts.

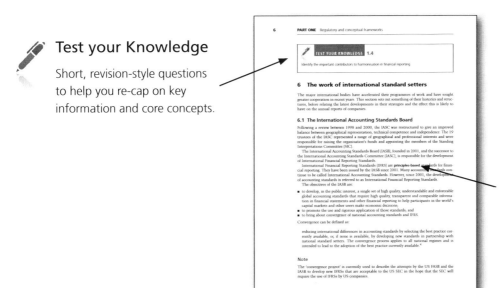

Definitions

Key terms are highlighted in bold on first use and defined in the end of book glossary.

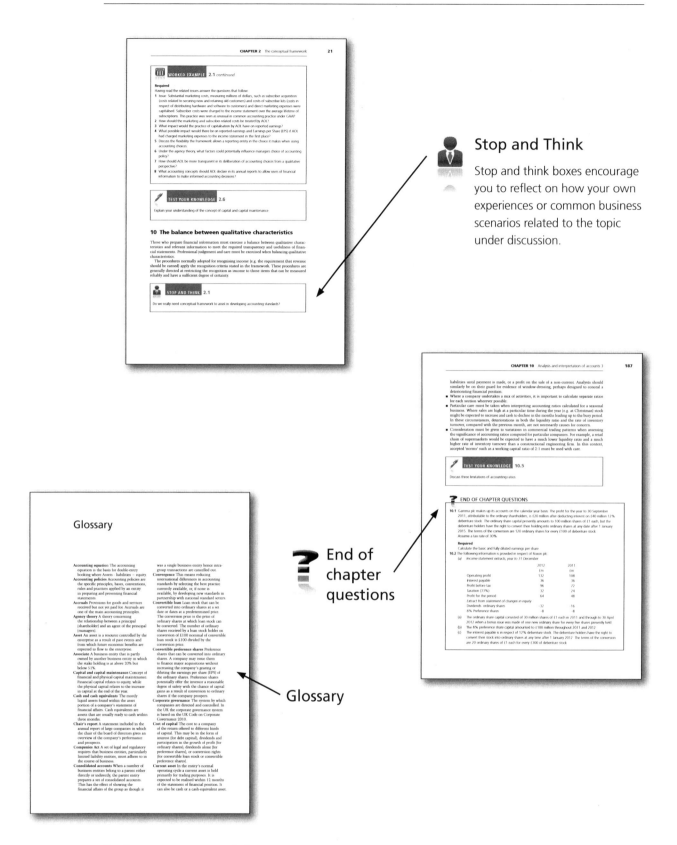

Stop and Think

Stop and think boxes encourage you to reflect on how your own experiences or common business scenarios related to the topic under discussion.

Glossary

End of chapter questions

Reference material

The text ends with a range of additional guidance and reference material.

Most texts will include Appendices which comprise additional reference material specific to that module.

Other reference material includes a glossary of key terms, a directory of further reading and web resources and a comprehensive index.

Financial Reporting and Analysis syllabus

Module outline and aims

In professional practice, the Chartered Secretary has to be competent in financial accounting and reporting. In public practice and in some other organisations, the Chartered Secretary can also be called upon to fulfil the role of corporate accountant. There, the emphasis is normally on accounting for purpose rather than on detailed accounting techniques.

Chartered Secretaries need to understand the significance and relevance of accounting information and the process by which it is acquired. Core responsibilities also include compliance with legal and stakeholder requirements, including financial statements. In the boardroom, Chartered Secretaries contribute to the analysis, presentation and interpretation of corporate financial performance and results, including the implications for the organisation, shareholders and stakeholders and for effective corporate governance.

The aim of the module is to develop the knowledge and skills necessary for you to understand and supervise the execution of these professional responsibilities.

Learning outcomes

On successful completion of this module, you will be able to:

Describe and explain the language, concepts and use of financial accounts and reports.
- Demonstrate a sound understanding of the significance of accounting information systems for both effective financial reporting and good corporate governance and demonstrate a systematic understanding and thorough appreciation of the regulatory framework for the preparation and presentation of financial statements.
- Apply the skills necessary for the preparation and presentation of financial statements for different forms of organisation in compliance with legal and regulatory requirements.
- Interpret and critically analyse corporate financial accounts and reports reflecting on the limitations of both published accounts and standard analytical techniques.
- Describe and explain the relationship between financial reporting and corporate governance.
- Show an understanding of selected current issues in financial reporting and analysis.
- Prepare reports and presentations relating to financial matters for the board and senior officers of organisations.

Syllabus content

The regulatory and conceptual frameworks for the preparation and presentation of financial statements – weighting 15%

The regulatory framework for the preparation and presentation of financial statements

National differences in financial reporting practices
Reasons for national differences in financial reporting practices
Classification of national accounting systems
Attempts to reduce national differences
The work of international standard setters
Arguments for and against accounting standards

The conceptual framework for the preparation and presentation of financial statements

The Framework for the Preparation and Presentation of Financial Statements issued by the International Accounting Standards Board (IASB) sets out the concepts that underlie the preparation and presentation of financial statements for external users.

The Framework deals with:

- the objective and users of financial statements;
- the reporting entity;
- the qualitative characteristics that determine the usefulness of information in financial statements;
- the definition of the elements of financial statements;
- the recognition of the elements from which financial statements are constructed;
- the measurement of assets and liabilities reported in financial statements; and
- concepts of capital and capital maintenance.

The preparation and presentation of financial statements in compliance with legal and regulatory requirements for single companies, groups, not for profit and public sector entities – weighting 40%

The preparation and presentation of financial statements for single companies in compliance with legal and regulatory requirements, including the relevant International Accounting Standards

Criteria for information appearing in a published income statement and balance sheet
Income statement
Balance sheet
Statement of changes in equity
Reporting comprehensive income
Segmental reporting
Accounting policies
Fair view treatment
Chairman's statement and directors' report
Notes to the accounts
Cash flow statements
Preparation of published accounts complying with accounting standards

The preparation and presentation of financial statements for groups in compliance with legal and regulatory requirements, including the relevant International Accounting Standards

Requirements for preparation of consolidated financial statements
Consolidated balance sheet
Consolidated income statement
Investment in associates
Interest in joint ventures
Consolidated cash flow statement

Analysis and interpretation of accounts, the limitations of published accounts, and current issues – weighting 45%

Analysis and interpretation of accounts

Trend or horizontal analysis
Common size statements

Accounting ratios and ratio analysis
Primary investment, operative and liquidity level ratios
Subsidiary ratios including investment performance indicators such as price/earnings ratio
Pyramid of ratios
Segmental analysis
Inter-firm comparisons and industrial averages
Analysing a cash flow statement
Earnings per share
Limitations of analytical and interpretative techniques

Limitations of published accounts

Creative accounting including the treatment of inventories
Off-balance sheet finance and leasing
Reporting the substance of transactions
Corporate governance and the external audit process

Current issues

Financial reporting on the internet
Environmental and social reporting
Ethics for accountants

Commentary on the syllabus

There are seven main areas in the Financial Reporting and Analysis syllabus. What follows is an overview of each of these areas, indicating what students need to achieve in order to prepare effectively for this examination.

The regulatory framework

Candidates need to be able to demonstrate an understanding of international differences in financial reporting practices that accounting standards are designed to address, and the economic consequences of such differences. They must be familiar with the history and potential of the convergence project and be able to explain and evaluate the case for international accounting standards.
The candidate will be expected to be able to:

- Explain how national characteristics may produce differences in financial reporting practices.
- Identify and discuss the specific reasons for variation in financial reporting practices.
- Show an awareness of the existence of different ways of classifying national accounting systems.
- Demonstrate familiarity with initiatives designed to reduce international differences in financial reporting systems.
- Identify and discuss the contribution of major international bodies to the harmonisation and standardisation of financial reporting.
- Outline the current state of the convergence project and be aware of planned future developments.
- Demonstrate an understanding of the economic consequences of different accounting practices.
- Identify and evaluate the main arguments for and against the imposition of standard accounting practice.

The conceptual framework

Candidates need to be fully familiar with the content and significance of the Framework for the Preparation and Presentation of Financial Statements issued by the International Accounting Standards Board.

The candidate will be expected to be able to:

- Explain the objective of financial statements.
- Identify and distinguish between the users of financial statements.
- Explain when an entity should report its affairs and how it decides which activities to include.
- List and explain the significance of each of the qualitative characteristics of financial information.
- Identify and distinguish between the elements of financial statements.
- Show an understanding of the conditions that must be met to justify the recognition of assets and liabilities.
- Be aware of the significance of the concepts of sufficient evidence and sufficient reliability for the recognition of assets and liabilities.
- Describe how entity managers decide which measurement basis to adopt for financial reporting purposes.
- Demonstrate an understanding of the concept of value to the business and of how the concept is given operational effect.
- Reveal an understanding of the existence of different concepts of capital and capital maintenance.

The preparation and presentation of financial statements

Candidates are expected to be able to prepare and present financial statements for single companies in compliance with legal and regulatory requirements, including the relevant international accounting standards.

The candidate will be expected to be able to:

- Identify the criteria which must be met for information to appear in the published income statement and balance sheet.
- Construct the income statement in accordance with prescribed format 1.
- Understand the effect of adopting different accounting policies on the content of the income statement and balance sheet.
- Report in the income statement the impact of discontinued operations.
- Account appropriately for 'non-recurring' items requiring separate disclosure in the income statement.
- Construct the balance sheet in accordance with prescribed formats.
- Show an understanding of the appropriate methods for valuing assets and liabilities.
- Demonstrate familiarity with the notes that accompany financial statements.
- Prepare the statement of changes in equity and explain why it must be published.
- Show an awareness of developments concerning the publication of a statement of comprehensive income.
- Explain the importance of segmental reporting and be able to prepare accounts on that basis.
- Demonstrate familiarity with the nature of accounting policies and the significance of differences between them.
- Reveal an understanding of the concepts of fair presentation, true and fair and the true and fair override.
- Explain the purpose of the directors' report and chairman's statement and give examples of the type of information each contains.
- Show an understanding of the reasons why entities are today required to publish a cash flow statement.
- Prepare a cash flow statement in accordance with standard accounting practice.

Group accounting

Candidates need to be able to prepare and present consolidated financial statements in compliance with legal and regulatory requirements, including the relevant international accounting standards.

The candidate will be expected to be able to:

- Define a reporting group in accordance with standard accounting practice.
- Explain why parent companies are required to publish consolidated accounts and the circumstance in which this obligation does not apply.

- Outline the circumstances in which a subsidiary company may be excluded from the consolidated accounts and the further disclosures required in such circumstances.
- Explain how the idea of control is applied to decide whether another entity must be included in the consolidated accounts.
- Prepare a consolidated balance sheet in accordance with the purchase method, making appropriate adjustments for fair value.
- Compute goodwill and minority interest for inclusion in the consolidated balance sheet.
- Distinguish between pre- and post-acquisition profits when preparing consolidated accounts.
- Make appropriate adjustments for inter-company balances and unrealised profits on inter-company sales.
- Show an appreciation of the need for uniform accounting policies and reporting dates.
- Explain how an investment in subsidiaries should be reported in the parent's own balance sheet.
- Prepare a consolidated income statement in accordance with standard accounting practice.
- Demonstrate knowledge of the definitions of an associate and of significance influence.
- Make calculations to enable an associate to be reported in accordance with the equity method.
- Identify the circumstances in which a joint venture exists.
- Describe the approved methods of accounting for a joint venture.
- Show familiarity with the content of a consolidated cash flow statement.

Analysis and interpretation of accounts

Candidates need to know how to calculate the percentages and ratios used to analyse entity performance. They must also be able to display expertise in interpreting the significance of such calculations.

The candidate will be expected to be able to:

- Undertake horizontal analysis of accounts between two periods based on percentage changes.
- Take account of the effect of exceptional items on comparability.
- Apply trend analysis to the results of a series of accounting periods.
- Undertake vertical analysis based on common size statements.
- Understand the nature of accounting ratios and the use that can be made of them.
- Calculate and interpret the significance of primary investment, primary operative and primary liquidity level ratios.
- Calculate and interpret subsidiary ratios: gearing, liquidity, asset utilisation, investment and profitability.
- Construct and understand the pyramid of ratios.
- Explain the reasons for and importance of segmental accounting.
- Undertake statement analysis based on segmental accounts.
- Outline sources of data available for inter-firm comparisons.
- Analyse and interpret the information contained in the cash flow statement.
- Display an understanding of the importance of earnings per share (EPS) and its relationship with the price/earnings ratio.
- Explain the calculation of the basic and diluted EPS.
- Compare and contrast the uses and limitations of EPS.
- Make calculations of EPS that require adjustments to the number of shares used in the basic EPS calculation.
- Calculate the EPS where there has been a rights issue.
- Compute and explain the significance of the fully diluted EPS.
- Show familiarity with the disclosure requirements applying to the EPS.
- Explain the limitations of accounting ratios computed on the basis of the information financial statements contain.

Limitations of published accounts

Candidates are required to demonstrate a thorough awareness of the limitations of published accounts as reliable indicators of entity progress and position. They are required to display such expertise in the context of creative accounting, off-balance sheet finance, the issue of substance versus form, and the effectiveness of the external audit process.

The candidate will be expected to be able to:

- Demonstrate an awareness of the steps entities might take to improve their accounts (e.g. to reduce the reported gearing ratio, increase the published EPS, and strengthen the balance sheet).
- Reveal a full understanding of the opportunities for subjectivity and creative accounting when measuring inventory for inclusion in published financial reports.
- Show familiarity with the role of the audit in countering creative accounting practices.
- Explain what is meant by off-balance sheet finance and understand its significance.
- Demonstrate the way in which leasing arrangements may be exploited to access the advantages of off-balance sheet finance.
- Outline and evaluate proposals designed to counter opportunistic behaviour by management when accounting for leases.
- Distinguish between the economic substance and the legal form of a business transaction.
- Examine the concept of substance over form in the context of consignment stocks, sale and repurchase agreements and debt factoring.
- Explain the principal qualities required of external auditors if they are to contribute to effective corporate governance.
- Evaluate the corporate governance implications of auditors providing consultancy services.

Current issues

Among the issues with which entity managers need to be fully familiar are the power of the internet, environmental and social reporting and the importance of complying with ethical standards.

The candidate will be expected to be able to:

- Reveal an awareness of the existence of online subscription databases that reformat company accounts in standardised form for comparative purposes.
- Explain what XBRL is and how it can be used.
- Describe the accountant's role in capitalist society.
- Trace the main steps in the evolution of stand-alone environmental reports and be aware of the economic consequences of environmental reporting.
- List the main elements of the Eco-Management and Audit Scheme for environmental disclosure in Europe.
- Reveal familiarity with the activities involved in an environmental audit.
- Outline the main features of social accounting.
- Demonstrate awareness of the history of social accounting in Britain – the Corporate Report.
- Outline recent developments in corporate social responsibility (CSR) reports and triple bottom line reporting.
- Discuss the nature of business ethics.
- Explain and evaluate the positivist and normative approaches in addressing ethical issues.
- Examine the role of ethics in modern business.
- Demonstrate familiarity with guidelines and regulations developed to help accountants in practice and in business to address ethical issues.

Overview

Financial accounting and reporting is central to modern entity management 'by the numbers'. The Chartered Secretary is regularly required to fulfil the following 'accounting' functions during their career:

- Analyse and interpret the outputs from an entity's accounting system.
- Initiate and participate in decision-making based on accounting information.
- Initiate and suggest improvements to the entity's accounting system and its output.
- Provide advice on the significance for the entity of contemporary accounting developments including regulatory changes.
- Counsel senior management on the significance of (proposed) published information for external user groups.

Acronyms and abbreviations

AGM	annual general meeting
ASB	Accounting Standards Board
ASC	Accounting Standards Committee
BIS	Department for Business, Innovation and Skills
CA 2006	Companies Act 2006
CFO	chief finance officer
CS	Chartered Secretary
CSR	corporate social responsibility
EC	European Commission
EPS	earnings per share
ESG	environmental social governance reporting
EU	European Union
FCA	Financial Conduct Authority
FRC	Financial Reporting Council
FRS	Financial Reporting Standards
FRSSE	Financial reporting standard for smaller entities
FSA	Financial Services Authority
GAAP	Generally Agreed Accounting Practices
GMM	gross margin method
GRI	global reporting initiative
HMRC	Her Majesty's Revenue and Customs
IAS	International Accounting Standards
IASB	International Accounting Standards Board
IASC	International Accounting Standards Committee
IESBA	International Ethics Standards Board for Accountants
IFAC	International Federation of Accountants
IFRS	International Financial Reporting Standards
IPC	integrated pollution control
IPR	intellectual property rights
KPI	key performance indicators
NDAC	non-discretionary accruals
NEDs	non-executive director
NGOs	non-governmental organisations
NPV	net present value
NRV	net realisable value
OCI	other comprehensive income
OFR	Operating and Financial Review
OROE	Operating Return on Equity
RIM	retail inventory method
ROCE	return on capital employed
ROE	return on equity
SAN	Social Audit Network
SEC	Securities and Exchange Commission
SIC	standing interpretations committee
SME	small and medium-sized enterprises
SOFP	statement of financial position
TBL	triple bottom line framework
WTO	World Trade Organization
XBRL	eXtensible Business Reporting Language

The regulatory and conceptual frameworks for the preparation and presentation of financial statements

■ LIST OF CHAPTERS

1   The regulatory framework for the preparation and presentation of financial statements
2   The conceptual framework for the preparation and presentation of financial statements

Chapters 1 and 2 in Part 1 cover the syllabus section entitled 'The Regulatory and Conceptual Frameworks for the Preparation and Presentation of Financial Statements'.

■ OVERVIEW

The IFRS Frameworks describe the basic concepts that underlie the preparation and presentation of financial statements for external users.

The regulatory and conceptual frameworks appear to be somewhat difficult to grasp, particularly as they are not financial reporting standards. However, the frameworks are the basis for which guidance is sought in reviewing and developing new standards.

Chapters 1 and 2 introduce the various terminologies used and build upon various frameworks from around the globe and related accounting issues that are pervasive and contemporary in nature.

To put things in context, the two chapters discuss historical issues to the development of financial reporting standards and the difficulties faced in their global acceptability.

Part 1 contains a Worked Example on America Online (AOL)

Having reviewed material, please attempt to answer the questions that follow the AOL scenario.

1

The regulatory framework for the preparation and presentation of financial statements

■ CONTENTS

1 Introduction
2 The regulatory framework
3 National differences in financial reporting practices
4 Reasons for national differences in financial reporting practices
5 The classification of national accounting systems
6 The work of international standard setters
7 The theoretical framework of accounting
8 Arguments for and against accounting standards

■ LEARNING OUTCOMES

Chapter 1 covers the syllabus section entitled 'The Regulatory Framework for the Preparation and Presentation of Financial Statements'. After reading and understanding the contents of the chapter, working through all the Worked Examples and Practice Questions, you should be able to:

■ explain national differences in financial reporting practices;
■ explain the reasons for national differences in financial reporting practices;
■ describe the basis for classification of national accounting systems;
■ explain the attempts to reduce national differences;
■ discuss the work of international standard setters; and
■ argue for and against accounting standards.

1   Introduction

The past decade has witnessed an ever-increasing volume of cross-border trade and cross-listing on the world's capital markets, due to the breakdown of trade barriers and the formation of international trade bodies such as the World Trade Organization (WTO). This, in turn, has resulted in the demand for quality cross-border financial information. International Financial Standards are the mechanism that attempt to provide a platform for financial reporting consistency and reliability to help stakeholders to make informed economic decisions.

The International Financial Reporting Standards (IFRS) are the remit of the International Accounting Standards Board (IASB) which seeks to achieve, as its objective, global comparability and consistency in financial reporting. In developing the IFRSs, the IASB, relies on the regulatory and conceptual frameworks for preparing and presenting financial statements. This chapter discusses the relevant issues that underpin these frameworks.

2   The regulatory framework

International Financial Reporting Standards (IFRS) for listed companies have been used in the UK and the European Union (EU) since 2002. Students need to be aware of their relevance and the importance attached to their use and application. The IFRS Framework is fundamental to the development and application of IFRSs.

The IFRS Framework refers to a principle-based approach to developing a common set of financial reporting standards. It provides a platform for accounting and financial reporting to help demonstrate to the users of general purpose financial statements the appropriate accounting treatment of common accounting matters on the basis of International Accounting Standards

(IASs) and International Financial Reporting Standards (IFRSs). The former International Accounting Standards Committee (IASC) issued IASs. However, standards issued since the formation of the IASB in April 2001 are referred to as IFRSs.

The objective of the framework is to set out the concepts that underlie the preparation and presentation of financial statements for external users as set out in the 'Framework for the Preparation and Presentation of Financial Statements'. It is important at the outset to understand that the framework itself is not a standard. Its primary purpose is to help the IASB to develop new or revised accounting standards and to assist those who prepare financial statements to apply accounting standards and to deal with any issues that they do not cover.

The framework covers:

- the objectives of financial reporting;
- the underlying assumptions;
- the qualitative characteristics;
- the elements of financial statements; and
- the concepts of capital and capital maintenance.

These are covered in the sections on the Conceptual Framework in chapter 2.

The IASB Framework was approved by the IASC Board in April 1989 for publication in July 1989 and was adopted by the IASB after its formation in April 2001. The section on the regulatory aspect of the framework discusses some important themes to have emerged during its development.

3 National differences in financial reporting practices

National differences in accounting and corporate reporting continue despite IFRSs. Countries in which the accounting profession has developed over a long period of time (i.e. the UK or the US) have generally led the evolution of accounting principles. Regulations influenced by local issues have given rise to particular accounting procedures. These rules and regulations are referred to as Generally Accepted Accounting Principles (GAAP).

There are many reasons for differing financial reporting practices. Some of these may emanate from cultural, economic, political, religious and other internal influences.[1] However, the speed of change in the global business environment and the pressure for change and the convergence of national GAAP to the IFRS system has resulted in many countries adopting the IFRS.

Nevertheless, national implementation of IFRSs differs in the degree of convergence.

Hopwood suggests that '[at] the very time when there are enormous pressures for convergence of forms of financial accounting, our insights into the factors resulting in earlier differences in such practices are still poorly developed'.[2]

The basis for accountability through corporate financial reporting (annual accounts) is fundamental to the dissemination of financial information relevant to the economic performance of the corporation. One view of the firm (corporation) is to look at it as a 'nexus of contracts' in which the firm has legal and ethical obligations to those who provide resources (e.g. banks and creditors) and other stakeholder groups (e.g. employees and the government).

TEST YOUR KNOWLEDGE 1.1

Describe two national characteristics that may lead to differences in financial reporting practice.

4 Reasons for national differences in financial reporting practices

The classification of national accounting systems has generally taken the form of 'Anglo-Saxon' and 'Continental Europe' models. However, other models have been developed by researchers trying to understand national accounting systems from differing perspectives.

Differences in national accounting systems can generally be explained by economic, legal, political, and cultural factors. Meek and Saudagaran (1990)[3] identify five external environmental and institutional factors for which there is a general consensus:

- the legal system affecting the accounting standardisation process (common law countries versus code law countries);
- business financing practices (whether financing is obtained via the stock market or from financial institutions);
- the tax system, and particularly its connection with accounting;
- the level of inflation likely to influence valuation methods; and
- the political and economic relationships between countries, for example links from colonisation.

 TEST YOUR KNOWLEDGE 1.2

Consider two national characteristics that may cause differences in financial reporting practice under a common IFRS.

5   The classification of national accounting systems

The purpose of any accounting classification system is to show the similarities and differences in various countries' accounting systems, based on a study of either domestic regulations or business practices.

Much of the debate on international accounting has revolved around the classification of countries with similar accounting procedures and processes. This has, to a certain extent, reduced the complexity in describing accounting differences and explaining similarities.

Researchers on international accounting have tried to divide countries into groups with similar features based either on common practices, or the national regulations in force. The differences observed in information disclosure and/or application methods undermine the understanding and comparability of financial statements. This has resulted in a comparative review of national practices for work on convergence, standardisation and harmonisation.

Classifying national accounting systems is a useful exercise to identify areas of concern and helps to address such differences. However, changing and converging accounting principles has been a long and difficult process which has given rise to new issues and problems in accounting that require constant monitoring.

Assuming that the standardisation exercise by the IASB will eventually lead to a common set of globally applicable standards for all economic entities, will, in turn, allow a departure from national GAAP. This will itself mean that accounting information should be easier to understand from an international viewpoint and will extend the cross-border flow of capital. Nevertheless, national differences on the basis of culture, national company law and different taxations systems etc, may be a barrier to complete global harmonisation. Issues relating to the interpretation of standards will be hampered by individual interpretation of accounting treatments at a local level. For example, the Coalition Government in the UK, led by David Cameron, has announced changes to the banking system whereby UK banks will be required to keep their retail arms separate from their more risky investment activities, thereby protecting certain investments. These changes, which are to come into force in 2013, may create financial reporting difficulties in the future for UK banks (e.g. how would banks be required to report financial information about. issues relating to group accounting?).

 TEST YOUR KNOWLEDGE 1.3

Explain how the application of a common IFRS may reduce national differences in financial reporting.

The ever-increasing use of global accounting and financial information has made it necessary to reduce the differences in the way accounting information is prepared and reported in different countries. In reducing accounting differences, standard setters use two particular approaches to standards development:

- standardisation; and
- harmonisation.

5.1 Standardisation

Standardisation is the process by which rules are developed to set standards for similar items on a global basis. Through standardisation, many technical issues relating to the treatment of accounting information have been resolved (e.g. the preparation of information relating to earnings per share (EPS IAS 33) is now recognised globally and is applied consistently using appropriate measures and stated on the statement of comprehensive income).

5.2 Harmonisation

Harmonisation reconciles national differences and provides those who prepare accounting information with a common framework to deal with major issues in a similar manner.

As efforts to improve comparability of financial statements have increased, the two approaches have come closer together. Attempts have been made to standardise, or at least harmonise, financial reporting to satisfy the needs of a number of different stakeholders. To make informed economic decisions, investors need clear and comparable information to assess a company's past or potential investment performance and its underlying economic reality.

Government agencies such as tax and customs authorities also have an interest in greater compatibility of information between countries to trace transactions. International accountancy firms have large numbers of multinational clients, whose accounts frequently need to be adjusted to common accounting principles before consolidations can be prepared. A reduction in national accounting differences would reduce the training costs of these firms and increase staff mobility (however, it would also limit the fees they could charge).

Companies seeking capital through cross-border listings may currently need to prepare financial statements under more than one set of regulations to meet the needs of different stock exchanges. This is both costly and time-consuming. However, almost every stock exchange will accept accounts prepared under IFRS. A number of international bodies are involved in the processes of harmonisation or standardisation. These include organisations that may not immediately be associated with accounting, such as the United Nations and the Organization for Economic Cooperation and Development (OECD). However, the most influential have probably been the International Accounting Standards Board and the European Union.

The process of standardisation and harmonisation through accounting standards has created an accounting environment which places an obligation on companies to disclose the accounting policies they have used to prepare their accounts.

This inevitably helps those who use accounts to better understand the information presented. Additionally, standards allow entities to be compared due to the consistency of accounting procedures used in the reporting of accounting information on the basis that accounting standards:

- require companies to disclose information in the financial statements which they otherwise would not if the standard did not exist;
- reduce the number of choices in the method used to prepare financial statements and therefore they should reduce the risk of creative accounting. This should help the users of financial statements to compare the financial performance of different entities;
- provide a platform in the accounting profession for discussion about accounting practice and to lobby the accounting setting bodies such as the IFRS and FRC (UK); and
- should increase the credibility of financial statements with the users by improving the amount of uniformity of accounting treatment between companies.

TEST YOUR KNOWLEDGE 1.4

Identify the important contributors to harmonisation in financial reporting.

6   The work of international standard setters

The major international bodies have accelerated their programmes of work and have sought greater cooperation in recent years. This section sets out something of their histories and structures, before relating the latest developments in their strategies and the effect this is likely to have on the annual reports of companies.

6.1 The International Accounting Standards Board

Following a review between 1998 and 2000, the IASC was restructured to give an improved balance between geographical representation, technical competence and independence. The 19 trustees of the IASC represented a range of geographical and professional interests and were responsible for raising the organisation's funds and appointing the members of the Standing Interpretations Committee (SIC).

The International Accounting Standards Board (IASB), founded in 2001, and the successor to the International Accounting Standards Committee (IASC), is responsible for the development of International Financial Reporting Standards.

International Financial Reporting Standards (IFRS) are **principles-based** standards for financial reporting. They have been issued by the IASB since 2001. Many accounting standards continue to be called International Accounting Standards. However, since 2001, the development of accounting standards is referred to as International Financial Reporting Standards.

The objectives of the IASB are:

- to develop, in the public interest, a single set of high quality, understandable and enforceable global accounting standards that require high quality, transparent and comparable information in financial statements and other financial reporting to help participants in the world's capital markets and other users make economic decisions;
- to promote the use and rigorous application of those standards; and
- to bring about convergence of national accounting standards and IFRS.

Convergence can be defined as:

> reducing international differences in accounting standards by selecting the best practice currently available, or, if none is available, by developing new standards in partnership with national standard setters. The convergence process applies to all national regimes and is intended to lead to the adoption of the best practice currently available.[4]

Note

The 'convergence project' is currently used to describe the attempts by the US FASB and the IASB to develop new IFRSs that are acceptable to the US SEC in the hope that the SEC will require the use of IFRSs by US companies.

TABLE 1.1: Factors causing differences in accounting practices across countries in the pre-convergence and post-convergence period

Pre-convergence period	Post-convergence period
Environmental factors	**Dominant factors**
Nature of business ownership	Nature of business ownership and financial system
Financing system	**Culture**
Colonial inheritance	Level of accounting education and experience of
Invasions	professional accountants
Taxation system	
Inflation	
Level of education	
Age and size of the accounting profession	
Stage of economic development	
Legal systems	
Other factors	
History	
Geography	
Language	
Influence of theory	
Political systems	
Social climate	
Accidents	
The individual characterisitics of accountants	
Experience	
Knowledge	
Ability	

Source: Libby and Luft (1993),[5] Bonner (1994),[6] Nobes (1998).[7]

The International Accounting Standards Board (IASB) is responsible for all technical matters including the preparation and implementation of International Accounting Standards (IASs).

The process of producing a new IFRS is similar to that of national accounting standard setters. Once the need for a new (or revised) standard has been identified, a steering committee is set up to identify the relevant issues and draft the standard. Drafts are produced at various stages and are exposed to public scrutiny. Subsequent drafts take account of comments obtained during the exposure period.

The final standard is approved by the board and an effective date agreed. IFRSs and IASs currently in effect are referred to throughout the rest of this book. This process assists in the development of future accounting standards and improves harmonisation by providing a basis for reducing the number of accounting treatments permitted by IASs. Professional accountancy bodies have prepared and published translations of IASs, making them available to a wide audience. The IASC has itself set up a mechanism to issue interpretations of the standards.

IASs and IFRSs (referred to below simply as 'IASs') may be applied in one of the following ways:

■ an IAS may be adopted as a national accounting standard. This can be useful where there are limited resources and an 'off the peg' solution is required (e.g. in Botswana, Cyprus and Zimbabwe). The disadvantage is that the standard may not meet specific local needs, due to the influence of the larger industrialised nations on the IASs;

■ an IAS may be used as a national requirement but adapted for local purposes (e.g. in Fiji and Kuwait); and

■ national requirements may be derived independently, but are adapted to conform to an IAS. This is currently the procedure in the UK, although the programmes of the IASB and ASB converged almost 14 years ago and developed IAS 37 and FRS 12 jointly.

It is important to note that if a company wishes to describe its financial statements as complying with IAS, IAS 1 requires the financial statements to comply with all the requirements of each applicable standard and each applicable interpretation of the SIC. This clearly outlaws the practice of 'partial IAS' reporting, where companies claim compliance with IAS while neglecting some of their more onerous requirements.

The old IASC had a large number of members, so it was difficult to achieve a consensus on many of the issues that the committee has addressed. Consequently, many IASs initially permitted a range of treatments. Whilst this was an improvement on not having a standard at all, it was still far from ideal. In response to this criticism, the IASC began its comparability/improvements project in 1987, which resulted in the revision of ten standards. The IASB adopted all IASs in issue, but soon identified the need for further improvement.

TEST YOUR KNOWLEDGE 1.5

(a) Outline the current state of the convergence project.
(b) What developments are planned for the future?

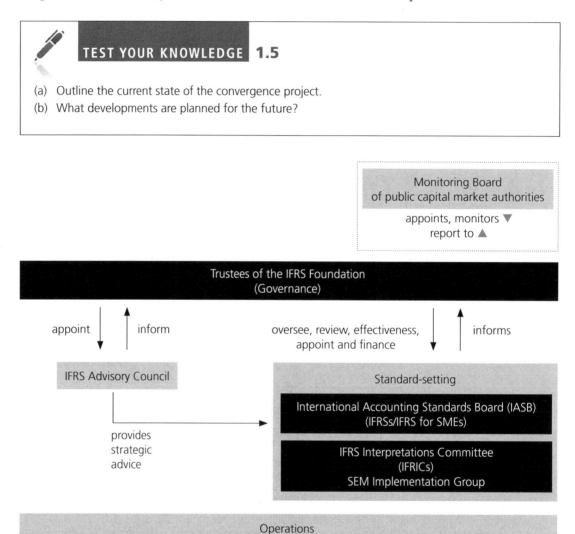

FIGURE 1.1 The revised structure of the IFRS/IASB

6.2 The revised structure of the IFRS/IASB

6.2.1 The Trustees of the IFRS Foundation

- The IFRS Foundation (until 2001, known as the IASC Foundation) appoints members of the IASB.
- It is responsible for raising funding for the standards setting process.

6.2.2 The IFRS Advisory Council

- IFRS Advisory Council (previously the Standards Advisory Council) liaises with individuals who have an interest in financial reporting.
- It advises the IASB regarding its agenda and priorities.

6.2.3 The IASB

- The International Accounting Standards Board was formed in 2001. It succeeded the IASC (International Accounting Standards Committee) and inherited accounting standards already issued.
- It is responsible for issuing International Financial Reporting Standards (IFRSs).

6.2.4 The IFRS Interpretations Committee

- The IFRS Interpretations Committee provides practical guidance on the application of IFRSs.
- Its interpretations are known as IFRICS. It replaced the Standards Interpretation Committee (SIC) in April 2001.

6.3 The European Commission

The European Commission (EC) has worked extensively in the past few years to promote IFRSs particularly amongst member states. The work of the EC is directed towards promoting the quality, comparability and transparency of the financial reporting by companies.

In 2005 the EC took a significant step and made the use of IFRSs obligatory for the consolidated financial statements of EU companies which are listed on the EU's stock markets.

In relation to listed companies, the Commission's work extends beyond the EU's borders and goes towards promoting the use of IFRS as the worldwide financial reporting language, thus enhancing the efficiency and transparency of capital markets throughout the globe.

6.4 UK GAAP

Accounting standards have their roots in various sources. In the UK, the principal standard-setting body is the Accounting Standards Board (ASB), which issues standards called **Financial Reporting Standards** (FRS). The ASB is part of the Financial Reporting Council (FRC) that took over from the Accounting Standards Committee (ASC) which was disbanded in 1990.

The principal legislation governing reporting in the UK is found in the Companies Act 2006, which incorporates the requirements of European law. The Companies Act dictates certain minimum reporting requirements for companies (e.g. it requires limited companies to file their accounts with the Registrar of Companies, which are then available to the general public).

From 2005, this framework changed as a result of European law requiring that all listed European companies report under IFRSs. In the UK, companies which are not listed have the option to report either under IFRSs or under UK GAAP. However, the ASB has put out a discussion paper to consider abandoning UK GAAP in favour of IFRS and the International FRSSE.

6.5 US GAAP

Accounting standards in the USA are typically referred to as **US GAAP** (**Generally Accepted Accounting Principles**). US GAAP are a set of accounting standards used to prepare and present financial reports for a range of entities, including public and private enterprises, not-for-profit organisations, and government departments. US GAAP is usually limited to the USA.

Currently, the Financial Accounting Standards Board (FASB) is the highest authority to establish GAAP for public and private companies, as well as for non-profit entities. However, listing requirements by the SEC require companies to follow IFRSs.

Some differences persist between US GAAP and IFRS. Christopher Cox, the former SEC chairman, set out a timetable for all US companies to adopt IFRS by 2016, but the new chair, Mary L. Shapiro, did not adopt the timetable. The decision was to be made by June 2011, but the FASB and ISAB agreed to continue their convergence project. Some of the largest listed companies (e.g. Tesco, BT) had switched to IFRS by 2008. Overseas companies quoted on the US exchanges could use IFRS without the need to convert/reconcile to US GAAP.

> **STOP AND THINK** **1.1**
>
> Why do you think we have so many national GAAPs?

7 The theoretical framework of accounting

Research in various areas of accounting and finance, particularly during the past five decades, has greatly influenced standard setting and development. Most notable is the agency theory which defines the characteristics of a public limited company (a company which may be listed on a capital market).

Jensen and Meckling (1976)[8] developed the notion of agency theory and suggested that the modern corporation exists on the basis of the principal–agent relationship, where the owner (shareholder) is the principal and the manager is the agent. It is envisaged that, as the custodian over the assets of the firm, the manager will act in the best interests of the owner and, hence, look to maximise the owner's wealth. However, due to a misalignment of common interests, the manager may pursue his own interests at the expense of the principal. In such circumstances the principal will incur monitoring costs to keep a check on the agent's activities and take corrective action where necessary.

The idea of a conflict of interests between the two contracting parties (principal and agent) is the cornerstone of the agency theory. The two parties will enter into contracts that facilitate their interests and minimise agency costs (costs incurred by the principal in monitoring the agent). Since the agent has superior knowledge of the principal, in relation to the underlying economic reality of the company, at any given time, a difference of information (information asymmetry) will exist between the principal and the agent. To mitigate and minimise such differences, the contracting parties will seek to optimise their relationship.

The monitoring processes take many forms; however, corporate governance is the mechanism by which control is exercised by the board of directors over the activities of the managers. Internally adopted mechanisms of corporate governance seek to enhance financial reporting and give a measure of confidence to accounting information users. The UK Code on Corporate Governance (2010) is a principles-based set of guidelines that require listed companies on the London Stock Exchange to 'comply or explain' in their financial reporting.

The UK Code on Corporate Governance is overseen by the Financial Reporting Council (FRC) and its relevancy is derived through the Financial Services Authority's (FSA) listing requirements. The FSA is being replaced by Financial Conduct Authority (FCA) in 2013 and many of its responsibilities will pass to the Bank of England. UK listings rules have a statutory authority under the Financial Services and Marketing Act 2000.

7.1 Other theoretical considerations

7.1.1 Public interest theory

- Proponents of public interest theory argue that regulation is needed to correct market failure.
- Market failure occurs when there is a failure of one or more of the conditions required for the smooth functioning of the market.

7.1.2 Market failure

Examples of situations that can lead to market failure:

- lack of competition;
- some market players do not have perfect information about the market (information asymmetry); and
- the product is a public good.

7.1.3 Capture theory

Proponents of capture theory believe that regulations are initially put in place in the public interest. However, the regulators are eventually controlled (captured) by the regulated parties.

7.1.4 Economic interest group theory

■ This theory assumes that groups will form to serve their own economic interests. In turn, these groups will lobby governments and regulators to act in their interests. Regulation serves the private interests of well organised political groups, while groups without political clout will be at a disadvantage.

8 Arguments for and against accounting standards

8.1 The arguments for

The corporate collapse of some well known major international companies such as Enron (2001), Worldcom (2002), Parmalat (2003), and recently Satyam (2009) highlighted the need for transparency in financial reporting. These corporate collapses necessitated the need for standardisation, harmonisation and convergence to protect stakeholder interests. However, these corporate collapses in large part were due to fraud, with irregularities in accounting procedures being pervasive and regulators being told untruths about the state of affairs of the various companies.

Accounting standards oblige companies to disclose the accounting policies they have used to prepare their published financial reports. This should make the financial information easier to understand and allow both shareholders and investors to make informed economic decisions.

Accounting standards require companies to disclose information in the financial statements which they might not disclose if the standards did not exist.

Accounting standards reduce the risk of creative accounting. This means that financial statements can be used to compare either the financial performance of different entities or the same entity over time.

Accounting standards provide a focal point for discussion about accounting practice. They should increase the credibility of financial statements by improving the uniformity of accounting treatment between companies.

Various EU accounting directives have sought to create minimum reporting standards so as to develop a common approach to financial reporting. The accounting directives commonly referred to are: the Fourth (Annual Accounts of Limited Companies, 1978), Seventh (Consolidated Accounts of Limited Companies, 1983) and the Eighth (Company Law, 1984). Each directive gives separate accounting guidance on the preparation and reporting of accounting information and various elements that must be shown on the face of financial statements. The aim of the accounting directives is to facilitate the commonality and hence the transparency of accounting information across the EU member states to help the flow of capital.

Due to the global nature of capital movement, stakeholders demand quality financial reports and accounting information which can be relied upon for consistency, commonality, and overall transparency. Accounting standards try to achieve that aim and the IASB is constantly working to reduce accounting differences.

8.2 The arguments against

It is acknowledged that standards fulfil a valuable short-term role by ensuring that all companies adopt the best procedures, but some quarters believe that they may prove to be detrimental in the long term. Over the years, considerable improvements have been made in the form and content of published accounts and much of this has occurred as the result of free market experiment and innovation. To place financial reporting procedures in a standardised straitjacket might, it is argued, therefore be to the longer-term detriment of those who use financial statements. In a nutshell, a major potential hazard of standards is that, although they may be intended as a floor, they end up as a ceiling.

A second problem is that, as industry itself is not standard, it seems unlikely that the figures they produce are amenable to a large degree of standardisation. The tendency is therefore to enforce standards that are suitable for the average firm (the majority) but not for those on the margins. Many areas disagree about which method should be used (e.g. whether to use average weighted cost, LIFO or FIFO to value inventories, or whether to use the deferral method or the flow through method to account for deferred taxation). The choices made by accounting standard setters, although often based on sound reasoning, can remain somewhat arbitrary.

Standards remove the need for accountants to exercise their judgement – a crucial feature of their status as professionals. Accountants are concerned that their role will be relegated to that of a mere technician who does no more than slot figures, calculated in accordance with accounting standards, into their appropriate location. This concern seems to be exaggerated because, although numerous matters are standardised, there is still plenty of scope for accountants to exercise their professional judgement. Indeed, an important drawback of standardisation is that it gives an illusion of precision and comparability which is totally unjustified in view of the wide range of subjective decisions which still have to be made.

A final criticism directed at the standard-setting process is that there are too many regulations. Forty-nine international standards have been issued and, although several have been withdrawn, more are in the pipeline. One suggestion is that a 'plethora of Principles' has been replaced by a 'surfeit of Standards'.

TEST YOUR KNOWLEDGE 1.6

(a) Give two examples of arguments in favour of and against accounting standards.
(b) How will they impact on financial accounting reporting?

END OF CHAPTER QUESTIONS

1.1 Should we have rules on how transactions should be processed?

1.2 Who determines the quantity and quality of information that firms should produce?

1.3 How can the production of accounting information be regulated?

1.4 Would firms provide the optimum level of information to users in the absence of regulation? Discuss.

1.5 Who should regulate? The State? Professional bodies?

1.6 What are the theories of regulation?

1.7 What are the arguments for and against the regulation of financial reporting?

1.8 What is public interest? (This is a normative issue).

1.9 Can regulators act in the public interest? Discuss.

1.10 Are regulators really disinterested parties?

Endnotes

1 Hopwood, A. J. (2000) Understanding financial accounting practice. *Accounting, Organizations and Society*, 25(8) 763.

2 *Ibid*. 764.

3 Meek, G. K. and S. M. Saudagaran (1990) A survey of research on financial reporting in a transnational context. *Journal of Accounting Literature*, Vol. 9 45–182.

4 Whittington, G. (2005) The adoption of international accounting standards in the European Union. *European Accounting Review*, 14(1) 127–53.

5 Libby, R., and J. Luft (1993) Determinants of judgment performance in accounting settings: Ability, knowledge, motivation and environment. *Accounting, Organizations and Society*, 18(5) 425–50.

6 Bonner, S. E. (1994) A model of the effects of audit task complexity. *Accounting, Organizations and Society*, 19(3) 213–44.

7 Nobes, C. W. (1998) Towards a general model of the reasons for international differences in financial reporting. *Abacus*, 34(2), 162–87.

8 Jensen, M. C. and W. H. Meckling (1976) Theory of the Firm: Managerial Behavior, Agency Costs, and Ownership Structure. *Journal of Financial Economics* 3, No. 4 (October) 305–60.

The conceptual framework for the preparation and presentation of financial statements

■ CONTENTS

■ LEARNING OUTCOMES

Chapter 2 covers the syllabus section entitled 'The Conceptual Framework for the Preparation and Presentation of Financial Statements'. After reading and understanding the contents of the chapter, working through all the Worked Examples and Practice Questions, you should be able to:

- identify the users of financial information and their objectives;
- explain the concept of the reporting entity;
- describe the qualitative characteristics that determine the usefulness of information in financial statements;
- identify the definition of the elements of financial statements;
- explain and describe the recognition of the elements from which financial statements are constructed;
- explain the concept of measurement of assets and liabilities reported in financial statements; and
- describe and explain the concepts of capital and capital maintenance.

1   Introduction

The development of the Conceptual Framework has its genesis in the set of guidelines primarily constituted by the American Financial Accounting Standards Board (FASB) and the Securities and Exchange Commission (SEC) since the early 1970s. Additionally, the UK's ASC 'The Corporate Report 1976' and the ASB's 'Statement of Principles of Financial Reporting 1999' contributed to the development of the conceptual framework. These set of guidelines form the basis of the conceptual framework developed by the IASB.

The Conceptual Framework forms the reference point by which new standards are developed and new challenges and/or issues in accounting are reviewed to offer practitioners and those who prepare accounts information on how to present financial data that is most suitable for users and reflects reality.

The IASB's Conceptual Framework for the Preparation and Presentation of Financial Statements 1989

1 This Framework sets out the concepts that underlie the preparation and presentation of financial statements for external users. The purpose of the Framework is to:

(a) assist preparers of financial statements in applying Accounting Standards and in dealing with topics that have yet to form the subject of an Accounting Standard;

(b) assist the International Accounting Standards Board in the development of future Accounting Standards and in its review of existing International Accounting Standards;

(c) assist the International Accounting Standards Board in promoting harmonisation of regulations, accounting standards and procedures relating to the preparation and presentation of financial statements by providing a basis for reducing the number of alternative accounting treatments permitted by Accounting Standards;

(d) assist auditors in forming an opinion as to whether financial statements conform with Accounting Standards;

(e) assist users of financial statements in interpreting the information contained in financial statements prepared in conformity with International Accounting Standards; and

(f) provide those who are interested in the work of the International Accounting Standards Board with information about its approach to the formulation of Accounting Standards.

2 This Framework is not an International Accounting Standard and hence does not define standards for any particular measurement or disclosure issue. Nothing in this Framework overrides any specific Accounting Standard.

3 The International Accounting Standards Board recognises that in a limited number of cases there may be a conflict between the Framework and an International Accounting Standard. In those cases where there is a conflict, the requirements of the International Accounting Standard prevail over those of the Framework. As, however, the International Accounting Standards Board will be guided by the Framework in the development of future Standards and in its review of existing Standards, the number of cases of conflict between the Framework and International Accounting Standards will diminish through time.

4 The Framework will be revised from time to time on the basis of the experience of the International Accounting Standards Board of working with it.

2 Scope of the conceptual framework

The Framework for the Preparation and Presentation of Financial Statements issued by the International Accounting Standards Committee in 1989 and adopted by the International Accounting Standards Board (IASB) in 2001 sets out the concepts that underlie the preparation and presentation of financial statements for external users. The Framework deals with:

- the objective and users of financial statements;
- the reporting entity;
- the qualitative characteristics that determine the usefulness of information in financial statements;
- the definition of the elements of financial statements;
- the recognition of the elements from which financial statements are constructed;
- the measurement of assets and liabilities reported in financial statements; and
- concepts of capital and capital maintenance.

The conceptual framework can be considered as a constitution and can be further defined as a systematic organisation of interconnected objectives and basic principles. The framework determines the nature, limits and purpose of financial accounting and also deals with the theoretical and conceptual issues surrounding financial accounting, building a logical and consistent foundation that justifies accounting standards. It outlines the grounds for determining how a transaction should be represented to its intended users (e.g. an asset should be recorded at historical cost or market value).

TEST YOUR KNOWLEDGE 2.1

Describe the role of the conceptual framework in the development of accounting standards.

2.1 Future developments

At the IASB board met on 28 September 2010 to consider improvements in the framework. The board made the following announcement:

> The objective of the conceptual framework project is to create a sound foundation for future accounting standards that are principles-based, internally consistent and internationally converged. The new framework builds on existing IASB and FASB frameworks. The IASB has revised portions of its framework; while the FASB has issued 'Concepts Statement 8' to replace 'Concepts Statements 1 and 2' (US GAAP).

However, the main drawback of a conceptual framework is that it can be too general in nature and the principles may not actually help when the financial statements are being prepared. In addition, there may be further disagreement as to the content of the framework and the contents of standards.

3 Users of financial information

To ensure the framework provides useful information it identifies a range of user groups. These include:

- **Investors** The providers of risk capital are concerned with the risk inherent in, and return provided by their investments. They need information to help them determine whether they should buy, hold, or sell. They are also interested in information which enables them to assess the ability of the enterprise to pay dividends.
- **Lenders** Lenders are interested in information which enables them to determine whether their loans, and the interest attaching to them, will be paid when due.
- **Employees** Employees and their representative groups are interested in information about the stability and profitability of their employers. They are also interested in information which enables them to assess the ability of the enterprise to provide remuneration, retirement benefits and employment opportunities.
- **Suppliers and other trade creditors** Suppliers and other creditors are interested in information which enables them to determine whether amounts owing to them will be paid when due. Trade creditors are likely to be interested in an enterprise over a shorter period than lenders (unless they are a major customer).
- **Customers** Customers have an interest in information about the continuance of an enterprise, especially if they have a long-term involvement with, or are dependent on, the enterprise.
- **Government agencies** Governments and their agencies are interested in the allocation of resources and, therefore, the activities of enterprises. They also require information to regulate the activities of enterprises, determine taxation policies and to serve as the basis for determining national income and similar statistics.
- **The public** Enterprises affect members of the public in a variety of ways. For example, they may make a substantial contribution to the local economy in many ways including the number of people they employ and their patronage of local suppliers. Financial statements may assist the public by providing information about the trends and recent developments in the prosperity of the enterprise and the range of its activities.

4   Objectives of financial statements

Published financial statements should provide information to a wide range of users informing on:

- financial position;
- financial performance; and
- changes in financial position.

Financial statements should also provide the results of stewardship of management and the user should be able to assess the accountability of management, which may influence the users' decision-making process.

Information on financial position is primarily provided in a statement of financial position (SOFP) that of performance in the income statement and changes in financial position through the presentation of a cash flow statement (IAS 7). IAS 1 also requires a statement of changes in equity.

The statements should be viewed as a whole (e.g. an income statement provides an overview of performance that is incomplete without its link with the SOFP). It is important that financial statements should show corresponding information for preceding periods. The statements should also be supplemented with notes and schedules to provide additional information.

 **TEST YOUR KNOWLEDGE** 2.2

State the objectives of financial statements and identify and distinguish between users of financial statements.

4.1   Underlying assumptions

The framework identifies two underlying assumptions:

- **Accruals basis** To meet their objectives, financial statements are prepared on an accruals basis. Transactions and events are simply recognised at the point when they occur, rather than when cash or its equivalent is received or paid and are reported in the financial statements of the periods to which they relate.
- **Going concern** Financial statements are usually prepared on the assumption that the reporting entity is a going concern and is likely to operate for the foreseeable future. The assumption here is that the reporting entity has no intention to liquidate or to adversely curtail its scale of activities. If this is the case then a different basis of reporting may be necessary and the basis disclosed.

5   Qualitative characteristics of financial statements

The revised IASB Framework identifies two *fundamental* qualitative characteristics of useful accounting information:

- Accounting information should be able to influence the economic decisions of users.
- Relevant accounting information should have a predictive and/or confirmatory value.

Amongst other issues, reported financial figures must convey to the user the underlying economic reality of the business entity. Information, both in quantitative and qualitative form, should allow users to make informed economic decisions by representing faithfully aspects of the business that are reported.

Attributes that make information useful to users further include:

- comparability;
- verifiability;
- timeliness; and
- understandability.

A fundamental characteristic of financial information is that it should be readily understandable by the user. This assumes the user has knowledge of the business, its economic activity, and accounting concepts. However, this should not deter the reporting entity from including complex matters in its financial reports.

Information possesses the attribute of relevance when it influences the economic decisions of users by helping to evaluate past, present and future events in both a predictive and a confirmatory way.

For information to be useful it must be reliable. It must therefore be free from error or bias and be a faithful representation of the facts. Information could, in certain circumstances, be relevant but unreliable.

Those who prepare financial statements need to address uncertainty (e.g. the collection of receivables and the provision for bad and doubtful debts). In such instances there is a need for prudence when preparing financial statements. (Prudence is the inclusion of a degree of caution in the judgement required to raise a provision to cover elements of uncertainty.)

Comparability allows the performance of the reporting entity to be compared over time. The performance of different entities can also be compared and analysed.

Financial statements must be prepared by applying the fundamental concept of consistency. The user should be informed of the accounting policies employed.

In summary, the *fundamental* qualities of financial statements are relevance, materiality and faithful representation. *Enhancing* qualities are identified by comparability, verifiability, timeliness and understandability.

5.1 Enhancing qualities

Enhancing qualities are **comparability** and **consistency**.

5.1.1 Comparability

Accounting information that has been measured and reported in a similar manner for different enterprises is considered comparable. Those who use financial reports require information that can be compared over time and between different entities on a consistent basis.

5.1.2 Verifiability

In essence, verifiability simply means that two different and independent observers of a set of financial reports would more or less reach the same conclusions. The conclusion may be a consensus and not a total agreement. However, the observers' perspective would be to arrive at a decision that the financial reports depict faithful representations of facts.

5.1.3 Timeliness

To facilitate effective decision-making, financial information needs to be available on a timely basis to allow economic decision makers to plan their economic strategy. For instance, financial reports would be enhanced if they are released within a timeframe that is still effective for financial and economic decision making. This can be complemented by the periodic release of financial information (e.g. management's expectation of meeting earnings targets).

5.1.4 Understandability

To facilitate understanding, those who prepare financial information should produce financial reports that classify, characterise and present financial information in a way that is easily understood. Information that is of a complex nature must not be excluded, rather disclosed in a manner that offers some level of utility.

 TEST YOUR KNOWLEDGE 2.3

List and explain the role of qualitative characteristics in the preparation of financial reports.

6 Elements of financial statements

The elements that relate to the financial position of an entity are those that comprise the statement of financial position: assets, liabilities and equity.

Those relative to financial performance comprise income and expenses.

The elements relating to financial position are defined in paragraph 49 of the Conceptual Framework, as:

1 An asset is a resource controlled by the entity as a result of past events and from which future economic benefits are expected to flow to the entity.
2 A liability is a present obligation of the entity as a result of past events the settlement of which is expected to result in an outflow from the entity of resources embodying economic benefits.
3 Equity is the residual interest in the assets of the entity after deducting all its liabilities.

The above form the accounting equation:

$$\text{assets} - \text{liabilities} = \text{equity}.$$

Income is defined as 'encompassing both revenue and gains'.

Revenue arises in the course of ordinary activities (e.g. sales, fees, etc). Gains may or may not arrive in the course of ordinary activities and include those arising on the disposal of non-current assets, unrealised gains on the revaluation of marketable securities, or an increase in the carrying value of long-term, non-current, assets.

Expenses arise in the course of ordinary activities of the entity (e.g. sales, wages, and salaries etc). They also include losses (e.g. those arising on the disposal of non-current assets and those arising from disasters (as in the case of the tsunami in Japan in 2011)).

TEST YOUR KNOWLEDGE 2.4

Identify and distinguish between the elements of financial statements.

7 Recognising the elements of financial statements

For an item to be recognised it must meet one of the definitions listed above together with a further two criteria. Paragraph 83 of the framework states:

- It is probable that any future economic benefit related to the item will flow to or from the reporting entity.
- The item has cost or value that can be measured reliably.

The concepts of probability and uncertainty are used in the above criteria. In assessing whether an item meets these criteria and therefore qualifies for recognition in the financial statements, regard needs to be given to the considerations of *materiality* discussed in paragraph 30 of the framework. The interrelationship between the elements means that an item that meets the definition and recognition criteria for a particular element (e.g. an asset) automatically requires the recognition of another element (e.g. income or a liability).

Materiality Materiality is a concept in accounting and finance relating to the importance or significance of an amount, transaction, or discrepancy. As such it is a measure of the estimated affect that the presence or absence of an item of information may have on the accuracy or validity of a statement. Materiality is judged in terms of its inherent nature, impact (influence) value, use value, and the circumstances (context) in which it occurs.

8   Measuring the elements of financial statements

Once an item has been recognised, a decision has to be made as to how it will be measured. To be included in the financial statements a monetary value must be attached to it. Paragraph 100 of the framework lists a number of bases. These include:

- *Historical cost* Assets are recorded at the amount of cash or cash equivalents paid or the fair value of another consideration given at the time of their acquisition. Liabilities are recorded at the proceeds received in exchange for the obligation, or in some circumstances (e.g. income tax) as the amounts of cash or cash equivalents expected to be paid to satisfy the liability in the normal course of business.
- *Current cost* Assets are carried at the amount of cash or cash equivalents that would have to be paid if the same, or an equivalent, asset was acquired. Liabilities are carried at the undiscounted amount of cash or cash equivalents that would be required to settle the obligation.
- *Realisable value* Assets are carried at the amount of cash or cash equivalents that could currently be obtained by selling the asset. Liabilities are carried at their settlement values (i.e. the undiscounted amount of cash or cash equivalents expected to be required to settle the liabilities in the normal course of business).
- *Present value* Assets are carried at the present value of the future net cash inflows that the item is expected to generate in the normal course of business. Liabilities are carried at the present value of the future net cash outflows that are expected to be required to settle the liabilities in the normal course of business.

The measurement basis most commonly adopted is historical cost (usually in combination with other measurement bases). For example, inventories are usually carried at the lower of cost and net realisable value and pension liabilities are carried at their present value. The current cost basis may be used as a response to the inability of the historical cost accounting model to deal with the effects of changing prices of non-monetary assets.

 **TEST YOUR KNOWLEDGE** **2.5**

Explain the economic consequences of different accounting practices under current cost, realisable cost and present value approaches.

9   Concepts of capital and capital maintenance

The framework focuses on two concepts of capital: the financial concept and the physical concept.

This is linked to investment and is synonymous with net assets or equity as highlighted in the accounting equation. The physical concept is relative to its operating capability or productive capacity (e.g. as shown in the ratio of value added to non-current assets).

A profit has been made if the value of net assets at the end of a period is greater than that at the start of the period (after any distributions to or from the owners have been deducted). This process is known as financial capital maintenance.

Physical capital maintenance acknowledges that a profit is made only if the physical capacity (or operating capacity) of the entity (or resources or funds needed to achieve that capacity) at the end of the period is greater than that at the start of the period (after distributions to or contributions from the owners have been deducted).

WORKED EXAMPLE 2.1

The following example relates to two American listed companies, America Online (AOL) and Time Warner. AOL was engaged in internet services (i.e. provision of internet-based applications). Time Warner was an entertainment company engaged in films and other entertainment products. It is not typical of an examination in financial reporting and analysis, however, its purpose is to highlight how larger companies can make detrimental mistakes.

In 2000, the merger between AOL and Time Warner (TW) was seen as one of the biggest corporate collaboration in recent times. The TW's strategy for the future seemed clear and straightforward; by tapping into AOL, Time Warner would have an established customer base of millions of home subscribers. AOL and TW could merge each other's resources in a marriage of convenience with high-speed cable lines to deliver to the new companies. This would have created 130 million subscription relationships.

With the advent of the worldwide web and upcoming dot.com companies and the steep demand for online services, the growth and profitability of the AOL division sharply declined due to advertising and subscriber slowdowns in mainly due to the burst of the dot.com bubble and the economic recession after September 2001. The value of the America Online division dropped significantly, not unlike the market valuation of similar independent internet companies that drastically fell. This forced a goodwill write-off, causing AOL Time Warner to report a loss of $99 billion in 2002; at the time, the largest loss ever reported by a company. The total value of AOL stock subsequently fell from $226 billion to about $20 billion.

Consequently there followed great upheaval within AOL with internal politics being played out amongst competing executives.

When the AOL-Time Warner merger was announced in January 2000, the combined market capitalisation was $350 billion. It has subsequently fallen dramatically. Even by the time the merger was approved by the relevant supervisory bodies, a year later on 11 February 2001, the company's market capitalisation had plummeted to $208.6 billion. By 2009, the company's value had tumbled even further, to just $65.7 billion, or approximately one-sixth of its value at the height of the dot. com bubble era when the deal was announced.

The expected synergies between AOL and Time Warner divisions never materialised, as most Time Warner divisions were considered to be independent companies that had rarely cooperated prior to the merger. A new incentive programme that granted options based on the performance of AOL Time Warner, replacing the cash bonuses for the results of their own division, caused resentment among Time Warner division heads who blamed AOL for failing to meet expectations and dragging down the combined company. AOL Time Warner Chief Operating Officer (COO) Pittman, who expected to have the divisions working closely towards convergence instead found heavy resistance from many division executives, who also criticized him for adhering to optimistic growth targets for AOL Time Warner that were never met.

For fiscal year 2002 the company reported a $99 billion loss on its income statement because of $100 billion in non-recurring charges, almost all from a write-down of the goodwill (intangible asset) from the merger in 2000. This loss is one of the largest in corporate history. The value of the AOL portion of the company had dropped sharply with the collapse of the Internet boom, in the early 21st century. On 4 February 2009, Time Warner posted a $16.03 billion loss for the final quarter of 2008, compared with a $1.03 billion profit for the same three months of 2007.

AOL-Time Warner was criticised by analysts for its aggressive accounting methods and the quality of its reported earnings figures. This was mainly related to the capitalisation of certain marketing costs, these marketing costs, which were substantial in size, should have been expensed and hence impacted upon the earnings figures.

WORKED EXAMPLE 2.1 *continued*

Required

Having read the related issues answer the questions that follow:

1 Issue: Substantial marketing costs, measuring millions of dollars, such as subscriber acquisition (costs related to securing new and retaining old customers) and costs of subscriber kits (costs in respect of distributing hardware and software to customers) and direct marketing expenses were capitalised. Subscriber costs were charged to the income statement over the average lifetime of subscriptions. This practice was seen as unusual in common accounting practice under GAAP.

2 How should the marketing and subscriber-related costs be treated by AOL?

3 What impact would the practice of capitalisation by AOL have on reported earnings?

4 What possible impact would there be on reported earnings and Earnings per Share (EPS) if AOL had charged marketing expenses to the income statement in the first place?

5 Discuss the flexibility the framework allows a reporting entity in the choice it makes when using accounting choices.

6 Under the agency theory, what factors could potentially influence managers choice of accounting policy?

7 How should AOL be more transparent in its deliberation of accounting choices from a qualitative perspective?

8 What accounting concepts should AOL declare in its annual reports to allow users of financial information to make informed accounting decisions?

TEST YOUR KNOWLEDGE 2.6

Explain your understanding of the concept of capital and capital maintenance.

10 The balance between qualitative characteristics

Those who prepare financial information must exercise a balance between qualitative characteristics and relevant information to meet the required transparency and usefulness of financial statements. Professional judgement and care must be exercised when balancing qualitative characteristics.

The procedures normally adopted for recognising income (e.g. the requirement that revenue should be earned) apply the recognition criteria stated in the framework. These procedures are generally directed at restricting the recognition as income to those items that can be measured reliably and have a sufficient degree of certainty.

STOP AND THINK 2.1

Do we really need conceptual framework to assist in developing accounting standards?

END OF CHAPTER QUESTIONS

2.1 Name the constituent elements in a set of financial statements that should be included in published annual reports.

2.2 The resources controlled by a firm as a result of past transactions or events and from which future economic benefits are expected to flow to the firm are the.........of the firm.
   (a) assets
   (b) liabilities
   (c) equity
   (d) retained earnings.

2.3 The residual interest in the resources of an entity that remains after deducting its liabilities is called:
   (a) assets
   (b) liabilities
   (c) equity
   (d) retained earnings.

2.4 Statements of financial position prepared in compliance with IAS 1 reflect a mixture of:
   (a) historical cost and future cash values.
   (b) current value and discounted future cash flows.
   (c) discounted cash flows and future values.
   (d) historical cost, fair value, and recoverable amounts.

2.5 Identify any three intangible non-current assets reported by firms.

2.6 Under what circumstances would the net realisable value of firm's inventory be lower than its cost?

The preparation and presentation of financial statements in compliance with legal and regulatory requirements for single companies, groups, not for profit and public sector entities

■ LIST OF CHAPTERS

3   Financial accounting and the preparation of financial reports
4   Income statement analysis and accounting policies
5   Valuing assets and liabilities, differences in accounting policies, fair presentation and the directors' report
6   Purpose of the cash flow statement

Part 2 covers the syllabus section entitled 'Preparation and Presentation of Financial Statements for Single Companies in Compliance with Legal and Regulatory Requirements'.

■ OVERVIEW

Chapters 3, 4, 5 and 6 together deal with:

- Understanding and applying rules relating to the presentation of information in financial statements contained in IAS 1 'Presentation of Financial Statements'.

- Distinguishing between recurring and non-recurring transactions and demonstrating the application of relevant accounting regulations to the content of the income statement.

- Distinguishing between continuing and discontinued operations and demonstrating the significance of relevant accounting regulations for the content of the income statement.

- Preparing segmental financial reports and explaining the purpose of analysing published financial data in this manner.

- The importance of being able to differentiate between recurring and non-recurring transactions and between continuing and discontinued operations.

- The main limitations of published financial reports.

- Understanding and being able to prepare the statement of cash flows on the basis of IAS 7.

Each chapter ends with practice questions that require application of the knowledge gained.

3

Financial accounting and the preparation of financial reports

■ **CONTENTS**

■ **LEARNING OUTCOMES**

Chapters 3 covers the syllabus section entitled 'Financial statements for single companies in compliance with legal and regulatory requirements'. After reading and understanding the contents of the chapter, working through all the Worked Examples and Practice Questions, you should be able to:

■ understand and explain the purpose of financial information and accountability;
■ understand the purpose and uses of financial information and the role of accountability;
■ explain financial accounting and name the principal reporting entities;
■ identify and explain the purpose of the principal accounting statements;
■ understand and explain the users of accounting information;
■ demonstrate both how financial statements are presented and the prescribed format for the financial reports;
■ understand and apply the concept of measurement and recognition of revenue, expenses assets and liabilities; and
■ use additional information in the financial reports.

1   Introduction

Numerous definitions of accounting persist; however, most definitions attempt to describe the same basic purpose of accounting. The American Accounting Association (1966) defines accounting as follows:

> the process of identifying, measuring, and communicating economic information to permit informed judgements and decisions by users of the information.

For the purposes of further discussion, it would be useful to analyse the terminology used in the above definition:

- It suggests that accounting is about providing information to others. Accounting information is economic information – it relates to the financial or economic activities of the business or organisation.
- Accounting information needs to be identified and measured in a systematic manner. This is done by way of a set of accounts, based on a system of accounting known as double-entry bookkeeping. The accounting system identifies and records accounting transactions.
- The measurement of accounting information is not a straightforward process. Accounting involves making judgements about the value of *assets* and *liabilities* owed by a business. It is also about accurately measuring how much profit or loss has been made by a business in a particular period. As we will see, the measurement of accounting information often requires subjective judgement to come to a conclusion
- The above definition identifies the need for accounting information to be communicated. The way in which this communication is achieved may vary. There are several forms of accounting communication (e.g. annual report and accounts, management accounting reports) each of which serve a slightly different purpose. The communication need is about understanding *who* needs the accounting information and *what* they need to know!

1.1 What is the purpose of a financial statement?

Accounting information is communicated using financial statements. Financial statements have two main purposes:

(a) to report on the financial position of an entity (e.g. a business, an organisation);
(b) to show how the entity has performed (financially) over a particularly period of time (an 'accounting period').

The most common measurement of 'performance' is profit. It is important to understand that financial statements can be historical or relate to the future.

TEST YOUR KNOWLEDGE 3.1

(a) What is meant by 'Accounting'?
(b) Demonstrate the purpose of financial statements.

2 Accountability

Accounting is about *accountabilty*. Most organisations are externally accountable in some way for their actions and activities. They produce reports on their activities that will reflect their objectives and the people to whom they are accountable.

The table below provides examples of different types of organisations and how accountability is linked to their differing organisational objectives:

TABLE 3.1 Accountability of different types of organisation

Organisation	Objectives	Accountable to (examples)
Private or public company (e.g. Barclays Bank, Tesco)	Profit Creation of wealth	Shareholders Other stakeholders (e.g. employees, customers, suppliers)
Charities (e.g. Age Concern)	Achievement of charitable aims Maximise spending on activities Value for money	Charity commissioners Donors Volunteers
Local Authorities (e.g. Liverpool City Council)	Provision of local services Optimal allocation of spending budget	Local electorate Government departments
Public services (e.g. transport, health) (e.g. NHS, Prison Service)	Provision of public service (often required by law) High quality and reliable services	Government ministers Consumers
Quasi-governmental agencies (e.g. Data Protection Registrar, Scottish Arts Council)	Regulation or instigation of some public action Coordination of public sector investments	Government ministers Consumers

All of these organisations have a significant role to play in society and have multiple stakeholders to whom they are accountable. All require systems of financial management to enable them to produce accounting information.

3 How accounting information helps businesses to be accountable

As described in the introductory definition, accounting is essentially an 'information process' that serves several purposes. It:

- provides a record of assets owned, amounts owed to others and monies invested;
- provides reports showing the financial position of an organisation and the profitability of its operations;
- helps management to manage the organisation;
- provides a way of measuring an organisation's effectiveness (and that of its separate parts and management);
- helps stakeholders to monitor an organisation's activities and performance; and
- enables potential investors or funders to evaluate an organisation and to make any necessary decisions.

There are many potential users of accounting information, including shareholders, lenders, customers, suppliers, government departments (e.g. HMRC), employees and their organisations, and society at large. Anyone with an interest in the performance and activities of an organisation is traditionally called a **stakeholder**.

For a business or organisation to communicate its results and position to stakeholders, it needs a language that is understood by all in common. Hence, accounting has come to be known as the 'language of business'. There are two broad types of accounting information:

- *Financial accounts*: geared toward external users of accounting information.
- *Management accounts*: aimed more at internal users of accounting information.

Although there is a difference in the type of information presented in financial and management accounts, the underlying objective is the same; to satisfy the information needs of the user. These needs can be described in terms of the following overall information objectives:

TABLE 3.2 Information objectives

Collection	Collection in money terms of information relating to transactions that have resulted from business operations.
Recording and classifying	Recording and classifying data into a permanent and logical form. This is usually referred to as **book-keeping.**
Summarising	Summarising data to produce statements and reports that will be useful to the various users of accounting information – both external and internal.
Interpreting and communicating	Interpreting and communicating the performance of the business to the management and its owners and users of financial information.
Forecasting and planning	Forecasting and planning for future operation of the business by providing management with evaluations of the viability of proposed operations. The key forecasting and planning tool is the **budget.**

The process by which accounting information is collected, reported, interpreted, and actioned is called **financial accounting.** Taking a commercial business as the most common organisational structure, the key objectives of financial management would be to:

■ create wealth for the business;
■ generate cash; and
■ provide an adequate return on investment bearing in mind the risks that the business is taking and the resources invested.

In preparing accounting information, care should be taken to ensure that the information presents an accurate and true view of the business performance and position. To impose some order on what is a subjective task, accounting has adopted certain conventions and concepts which should be applied when preparing accounts.

For financial accounts, the regulation or control of the kind of information that is prepared and presented goes much further. UK and international companies are required to comply with a wide range of accounting standards. These define the way in which business transactions are disclosed and reported. These are applied by businesses through their accounting policies.

 TEST YOUR KNOWLEDGE **3.2**

(a) On what basis is accounting information prepared?
(b) Summarise the five principals for whom accounting information is prepared.

4   What is financial accounting?

A conventional division of the discipline of 'accounting' is into what are labelled '*financial accounting*' and '*management accounting*'. Under the two classifications, the following explanation is used to describe both types of approaches to accounting:

■ *Financial accounting*: Accounting information prepared for external users such as investors and lenders. Financial accounting information may influence the economic decisions external users make and are prepared under International Financial Reporting Standards (IFRS) or Generally Agreed Accounting Practice (GAAP).
■ *Management accounting*: Accounting information for internal users. Accounting information for management use is prepared for internal monitoring and control in making the most efficient use of limited resources.

5   Reporting entities

Suppliers of accounting information include the following entities (these are listed in no particular order of priority).

5.1 Sole traders

These are businesses that have a single owner, who also takes all the major managerial decisions. Operations are usually on a small scale. Typical examples would be an electrician, local newsagent, or milkman. Accounts are prepared for the sole trader to help establish the amount of income tax due to HMRC. The sole trader makes little use of accounting statements for business decisions, which are instead based on knowledge obtained as a result of direct contact with all aspects of business activity.

5.2 Partnerships

These exist where two or more individuals join together to undertake some form of business activity. The partners share ownership of the business and the obligation to manage its operations between them. Professional people, such as accountants, solicitors and doctors, commonly organise their business activities in the form of partnerships. Accounting statements are required as a basis for allocating profits between the partners and, again, for agreeing tax liabilities with HMRC.

5.3 Clubs and societies

There are many thousands of clubs and societies in Britain, organised for recreational, educational, religious, charitable, and other purposes. Members pay an annual subscription and management powers are delegated to a committee elected by the members. The final accounts prepared for (usually large) societies are often controlled by statute. For a local club or society, the form of the accounts is either laid down in the internal rules and regulations or decided at the whim of the treasurer. Conventional accounting procedures are sometimes ignored in a small organisation. Reasons for this are lack of expertise, the meagre quantity of assets belonging to the organisation and the fact that the accounts are of interest only to the members.

5.4 Limited companies

A limited company is usually formed by registering with the Registrar of Companies under the provisions of the Companies Act 2006 and complying with certain formalities. The company may be private, indicated by the letters Ltd at the end of its name, or public, in which case the designatory letters are 'plc'. The main significance of the distinction is that only the latter can make an issue of shares to the general public. In the case of public companies, there is a further distinction between quoted companies, whose shares are listed and traded on the stock exchange, and unquoted companies. In general, public companies are larger than private companies and quoted companies larger than unquoted.

The directors of all limited companies are under a legal obligation to prepare and publish accounts, at least once in every year, which comply with the requirements of the Companies Act 2006 (CA 2006). A limited company may, alternatively, be formed by either a private Act of Parliament or a Royal Charter. Before registration under the Companies Act became possible (prior to 1844) these were the only methods of incorporation available, but they are rarely used today. Companies formed in this way are called statutory and chartered companies, respectively. The form of their accounts may be regulated by their charter or statute and they normally comply with the general requirements of the CA 2006. Additionally, the CA 2006 may also applies to charities that trade, public sector bodies such as hospital trusts and universities, local authorities and quasi-government agencies (companies that are private yet supported by the government). These types of organisations can be considered as reporting entities.

(a) Define financial accounting.
(b) Distinguish between partnerships and sole traders.

6   Principal accounting statements

International Accounting Standard 1 (IAS 1 'Presentation of Financial Statements') is the basis by which the primary financial statements are prepared. Limited liability companies prepare annual reports consisting of a complete set of financial statements that include narratives which help to further explain the financial figures. IFRS prescribed standard formats, including IAS 1.10 'Complete Set of Financial Statements', are used to prepare financial reports. These include:

- a statement of comprehensive income;
- a statement of financial position;
- a statement of change in equity;
- a statement of cash flows; and
- explanatory notes.

The narrative expands upon particular aspects of the financial reports and helps users to make a further qualitative review of the underlying economic reality of the company.

The purpose of financial accounting statements is mainly to show the financial position of a business at a particular point in time and to show how that business has performed over a specific period of time.

A statement of financial position shows what resources are owned by a business (assets) at a particular point in time and what it owes to other parties (liabilities). It also shows how much has been invested in the business and what the sources of that investment finance were.

It is often helpful to think of a statement of financial position as a snapshot of the financial position of the business at a specific point in time. However, while this is a useful picture to have, every time an accounting transaction takes place, the snapshot will also change.

By contrast, the income statement provides a perspective on a longer time-period. If the statement of financial position is a snapshot of the business, then the income statement account is the 'summary measure of 12 months of business activity'. It illustrates what financial transactions took place in a particular period and (most importantly) what the overall result of those transactions was. Not surprisingly, the income statement account measures **profit**. Profit is the amount by which sales revenue (also known as turnover or income) exceeds expenses (or costs) for the period being measured.

The range of financial information published by reporting entities varies according to the nature and purpose of their operations. We will now consider the practice of limited companies.

6.1 The statement of comprehensive income (income statement)

Revenues are generated and costs are incurred as a result of undertaking business activity. These are summarised in the income statement, which may be prepared to cover a week, a month, a year, or other chosen interval. If total revenue exceeds total expenses the business has made a profit; otherwise the business suffers a loss. The advantages of the income statement are that it provides the following information: whether a profit has been made; how much profit has been made; how the profit figure has been arrived at; the taxation payable; and the amount available for the shareholders.

6.2 The statement of financial position (the balance sheet)

This sets out the financial position of the business at a particular point in time. It is the date to which the income statement is made up. The most common accounting dates are the calendar year end (31 December) and the tax year end (31 March). An obvious difference between the income statement and balance sheet is that, whereas the former reports inflows and outflows of resources over a period of time, the latter sets out the assets and liabilities at a particular point in time.

It is for this reason that the statement of financial position has been likened to a financial photograph of a business. Like all photographs, the position just before or just afterwards may be entirely different. This provides scope for management to undertake cosmetic exercises that present the company's position in the best possible light. For example, it might borrow money just before the year end in order to inflate the cash balance and then repay it on the first day of the next accounting period. Such devices are called 'window dressing' and it is part of the auditor's job to ensure that decision makers are not misled by such procedures.

6.3 The statement of changes in equity

The **statement of changes in equity** is an important component of financial statements since it explains the composition of equity and how has it changed over the year. Typical information we can get from a statement of changes in equity include:

The statement of changes in equity summarises the movement in the equity accounts during the year namely: share capital, share premium, retained earnings, revaluation surplus, unrealised gains on investments, issue and redemption of share capital, transfers between reserves, as well as profit after tax and dividends.

6.4 The statement of cash flows

This lists all cash inflows and outflows that have occurred during the accounting period under review (this is normally a year). Chapter 12 shows that the cash flows are classified under headings designed to maximise their informative value. Because it is based on 'hard cash', the cash flow statement is considered to be less susceptible to manipulation than the other main financial reports. As a result, it is likely to provide important insights concerning business performance during a particular accounting period (e.g. whereas the income statement may show a healthy figure for operating profit, the cash flow statement could cast doubt on the quality of reported profit if it communicates a decline in the actual cash flow from operating activities).

7 Users and uses of accounting information

Financial statements are important reports. They show how a business is doing and are very useful internally for a company's shareholders, board of directors, its managers and some employees, including labour unions. Externally, they are important for prospective and existing investors, to government agencies responsible for taxing and regulating and to lenders such as banks and credit rating agencies. Other users not mentioned in the framework include investment analysts and stockbrokers.

We have seen that people who use accounting information can be classified into those within the firm and those outside. Those within the firm are managers, at any level of responsibility ranging from the shop floor to the board of directors, who use information for one or more of the following purposes:

- *Planning* – to assess the financial effects of possible alternative courses of future action.
- *Decision making* – for example, to decide which project to undertake or whether to reallocate resources from one use to another.
- *Assessment and control* – to monitor the performance of personnel, departments, and products.

External users require information for these purposes too, but in a rather different sense. In the case of an investor, for example, he or she may use financial reports to assess past performance and predict future performance to help decide whether to make an initial investment in the business, purchase more shares or dispose of an existing holding. Historically, the principal external users of accounting information were seen as comprising only the shareholder and the creditor groups, but for some time this has been recognised as too narrow a view.

We can, therefore, see that external users require accounting information for a range of purposes. The principal accounting statements are of interest to both internal and external users but, when presented to the latter, they will normally be in a condensed form. The main factor affecting the amount of detail contained in the accounts is the requirements of the user group. In general, external users wish to assess the overall performance of the entity, so an enormous amount of detail is inappropriate, both because it is of little interest and because it is likely to obscure important trends. It is mainly for this reason that information is presented in a highly summarised form in the published accounts. However, disclosing too much detail may be useful to competitors when analysing a company's strengths and weaknesses.

Financial statements prepared for management contain much more detail. Shareholders base their decision to sell shares, retain their investment, or buy more shares mainly on the level of reported profit and dividends declared. Management, in contrast, has a keen interest in the costs and revenues that make up the profit figures. They are responsible for taking the following kinds of decisions:

- whether to expand or contract production;
- whether to substitute one material for another, or one type of worker for another;
- whether to replace labour-intensive production methods by machinery;
- whether to acquire property instead of renting it; and
- which type of power supply to use.

These decisions influence individual items of revenue and expenditure. In many instances reports must be specially prepared to help reach these decisions, and appraisal techniques have been developed to help the management process. After the decisions have been made, the outcome is monitored to see the extent to which expectations have been fulfilled.

TEST YOUR KNOWLEDGE 3.4

(a) Define the seven external users of financial reports identified by the 'Framework for the Preparation and Presentation of Financial Statements'.
(b) State and explain the nature of and purpose of the principal financial statements.

8 Presentation of financial statements

This is the subject of IAS 1 'Presentation of Financial Statements'.

8.1 Objectives of IAS 1

IAS 1 prescribes the basis for the presentation of general purpose financial statements, to ensure comparability with: the entity's financial statements of previous periods; and the financial statements of other entities.

8.2 Concepts and guidelines

IAS 1 sets out some of the basic concepts and other guidelines that that should be complied with when preparing and presenting statements. These concepts have been covered above when considering the content of the framework, namely: going concern; accruals; consistency; and materiality.

8.3 Offsetting

It is important that both assets and liabilities and income and expenses, when material, are reported separately so that users can make a proper assessment of the progress and financial position of the entity. It is for these reasons that IAS 1 states that assets and liabilities and income and expenses are not to be offset unless required or permitted by an IFRS.

Offsetting in either the income statement or the statement of financial position is required or permitted where it reflects the substance of the transaction or event. The reporting of assets net of valuation allowances (e.g. obsolescence allowances on inventories and doubtful debts allowance on receivables) is therefore permitted.

8.4 Comparative information

Comparative information is disclosed for all amounts reported in the financial statements, unless an IFRS requires or permits otherwise.

8.5 Criteria for items that must be reported

The financial statements that constitute the annual reports of a company, prepared on the basis of IFRS, must declare a minimum number of items. The prescribed format in the presentation of the statement of comprehensive income and the accompanying financial statements must include items that are included in the various standards. These items must also be calculated in a consistent and recommended manner.

Once a company has selected the manner and format in which it will report its financial figures it must use that format consistently. In the UK, companies that do not follow the IFRS system of accounting must comply with CA 2006 as well as with UK GAAP. These give comprehensive guidance on what items must be reported on the face of the financial statements with appropriate set of narratives. The table below shows the items that must be recorded on the face of the income statement:

TABLE 3.3 Items to be presented on the face of the income statement – IAS 1

IFRS Accounting	UK GAAP Accounting
■ Revenue	■ Turnover
■ Finance costs	■ Cost of sales
■ Share of profit/loss of associates and joint ventures on the basis of the equity method	■ Gross profit
■ Tax expenses	■ Distribution costs
■ Additionally a single amount totalling:	■ Administrative expenses
– After-tax profit or loss of discontinued operations and	■ Other operating income
– After-tax gain or loss recognised on disposal of the discontinued operation	■ Income from shares in group undertakings
■ Profit or loss	■ Income from participating interests (excluding group undertakings)
■ Where relevant include:	■ Income from other fixed asset investments
– Income or loss attributable to ordinary shareholders of the company	■ Other interest received and similar income
– Income or loss attributable to minority shareholders	■ Amounts written off investments
■ Earnings per share (EPS)	■ Interest payable and similar charges
	■ Tax on profit or loss of ordinary activities
	■ Profit or loss on ordinary activities after taxation
	■ Extraordinary income
	■ Extraordinary charges
	■ Extraordinary profit or loss
	■ Tax on extraordinary profit or loss
	■ Other taxes not shown under the above items
	■ Profit or loss for the financial year

Note: No items may be presented in the statement of comprehensive income (or in the income statement, if separately presented) or in the notes as 'extraordinary items' (IAS 1.87).

The income statement is the first part of the statement of comprehensive income.

9 Prescribed format for the statement of comprehensive income

IAS 1 allows entities to choose between two formats for reporting income and expenses. All items of income and expense recognised in a period must be included in profit or loss unless a standard or an interpretation dictates otherwise (IAS 1.88).

Some differences exist between the US GAAP understanding of revenue and IFRS version. In the UK, for listed companies, the IFRS version takes precedence. As an example of interpretation and understanding, here is the distinction in revenue recognition between US GAAP and IFRS:

■ *Earned*: The earnings process must be complete and the value of the transaction can be measured.
■ *Realisation*: The revenue must have been collected OR there must be some assurance that it will be collected.

The most popular method of reporting on the face of the income statement in the EU is format 1. Format 1 analyses expenses by function (i.e. by cost). Format 2 analyses expenses by type (i.e. employee benefits, similar type of operating expenses etc). For the purposes of this manual, we will illustrate income and expense using Format 1.

WORKED EXAMPLE 3.1

NRG plc – Statement of comprehensive income for the years ended 31 December

	Notes	2012 £'000	2011 £'000
Income from continuing operations			
Revenue	1	550000	470000
Cost of sales	2	420000	370000
Gross profit		130000	100000
Distribution costs	3	12000	8000
Administrative expenses	4	24000	18000
Other expenses	4	9000	6000
Profit from operations	5	85000	68000
Interest payable	6	500	300
Profit before tax		84500	67700
Tax	7	25350	20310
Profit for the period from continuing operations		59150	47390
Discontinued operations			
Loss for the period from discontinued operations	8	6200	4500
Comprehensive income		52950	42890
Attributable to ordinary equity holders		42360	34312
Attributable to minority interest		10590	8578
Earnings per share	9	11	9

10 Measurement and recognition of revenue

IAS 18 'Revenue' prescribes the steps towards revenue recognition. IAS 18 describes revenue as:

> The gross inflow of economic benefits (cash, receivables, other assets) arising from the ordinary operating activities of an entity (such as sales of goods, sales of services, interest, royalties, and dividends).

As such, IAS 18 further describes two crucial elements in revenue recognition to enhance transparency and aid in reporting. The two elements are:

10.1 Measurement of revenue

IAS 18 explains measurement of revenue as:

> Revenue should be measured at the fair value of the consideration received or receivable. An exchange for goods or services of a similar nature and value is not regarded as a transaction that generates revenue. However, exchanges for dissimilar items are regarded as generating revenue.

10.2 Recognition of revenue

All revenues and expenses arising due to an entity's business activities must be recorded and calculated using the accruals methods. Similarly, revenue is recognised in the income statement as cash received for goods and services plus any credit sales made in the same period. IAS 18 explains recognition of revenue as:

> Recognition, as defined in the IASB Framework, means incorporating an item that meets the definition of revenue (above) in the income statement when it meets the following criteria:
> - it is probable that any future economic benefit associated with the item of revenue will flow to the entity, and
> - the amount of revenue can be measured with reliability.

IAS 18 further explains the process of recognising revenue. The following are IAS 1 rules for the preparation of the statement of comprehensive income:

1   Comprehensive income for a period includes profit or loss for that period plus other comprehensive income (OCI) recognised in that period. As a result of the 2003 revision to IAS 1, the standard is now using 'profit or loss' rather than 'net profit or loss' as the descriptive term for the bottom line of the income statement.
2   The amendments to IAS 1 'Presentation of Financial Statements' (June 2011) require companies preparing financial statements in accordance with IFRSs to group together items within OCI that may be reclassified to the profit or loss section of the income statement. The amendments also reaffirm existing requirements that items in OCI and profit or loss should be presented as either a single statement or two consecutive statements.
3   All items of income and expense recognised in a period must be included in profit or loss unless a Standard or an Interpretation requires otherwise (IAS 1.88).
4   Some IFRSs require or permit that some components to be excluded from profit or loss and instead to be included in other comprehensive income (IAS 1.89). The components of other comprehensive income include:
    (a) changes in revaluation surplus (IAS 16 and IAS 38); and
    (b) actuarial gains and losses on defined benefit plans recognised in accordance with IAS 19.
5   Gains and losses arising from translating the financial statements of a foreign operation (IAS 21).
6   Gains and losses on re-measuring available-for-sale financial assets (IAS 39).
7   The effective portion of gains and losses on hedging instruments in a cash flow hedge (IAS 39).

Additionally, certain items must be disclosed separately either in the statement of comprehensive income or in the notes, if material, including (IAS 1.98):

- write-downs of inventories to net realisable value or of property;
- plant and equipment to recoverable amount, as well as reversals of such write-downs;
- restructuring of the activities of an entity and reversals of any provisions for the costs of restructuring;
- disposals of items of property, plant and equipment;
- disposals of investments;
- discontinuing operations;
- litigation settlements; and
- other reversals of provisions.

Expenses recognised in the income statement should be analysed either by nature (raw materials, staffing costs, depreciation, etc.) or by function (cost of sales, selling, administrative, etc) (IAS 1.99). If an entity categorises by function, then additional information on the nature of expenses; at a minimum depreciation, amortisation and employee benefits expense; must be disclosed (IAS 1.104).

 WORKED EXAMPLE 3.2

NRG plc is in the business of supplying electricity to commercial customers. NRG plc typically enters into contracts that are worth at least £1million and last for a minimum of two years. NRG recently acquired two new customers. Customer 'A' entered into a contract with NRG for the supply of electricity for four years at a contract price of £5 million. Customer 'B' had a similar arrangement, but with a contract price of £8 million over eight years. The annual contract values are paid in advance by both customers.
NRG plc has a policy to give discounts to longer running contracts.

Required
State the values of the annual charge to revenue for each customer and show the workings and explain the basis for the calculations.

Answer
The calculated charge to revenues for customers A and B are as follows:

Customer A
£5m/4 years = £1.25 million (annualised charge to revenue)

Customer B
£8m/8 years = £1.00 million (annualised charge to revenue)
Total annualised charge to revenue for customers A and B are:
£1.25 million Customer A
£1.00 million Customer B
£2.25 million

Under IFRS rules and IAS 1, the above calculations are measurable and reliable. The calculations will meet the criteria for prescribed revenue recognition whereby 'the gross inflow of economic benefits arising from the ordinary operating activities of an entity' would have been met. Additionally, the recognition to revenue would have met the criteria for revenue measurement at 'fair value of the consideration'.

Further, revenue is being recognised on an *accruals basis*. NRG is being paid in advance of the annualised contract value; hence it will defer revenue recognition to the statement of financial position and introduce monthly charge to revenues. The proportion of annualised contract not yet expended will be a liability to NRG plc.

11 Reporting comprehensive income

The Financial Accounting Standards Board (USA) describes comprehensive income as:

> the change in equity (net assets) of a business enterprise during a period from transactions and other events and circumstances from non-owner sources. It includes all changes in equity during a period except those resulting from investments by owners and distributions to owners.

As such, comprehensive income is the total of profit or loss and other items that are not recorded through the income statement due to their nature and include items such as unrealised holding gain or loss from available-for-sale securities and foreign currency translation gains or losses. Since these items are not part of profit or loss, nevertheless if they are material they should be included in comprehensive income, thus allowing users a more comprehensive understanding of organisational performance.

Items included in comprehensive income, but not profit or loss are reported under the accumulated other comprehensive income section of shareholder's equity. Comprehensive income paints a better picture when measured on a per-share basis. This in turn reflects the effects of events such as dilution and options. Comprehensive income mitigates the effects of equity transactions for which shareholders would be indifferent; dividend payments, share buy-backs and share issues at market value.

12 Prescribed format for the statement of financial position

IAS 1 (paragraph 54) specifies the minimum line item disclosures on the face of, or in the notes to, the statement of financial position, the income statement, and the statement of changes in equity.

12.1 General format

Both current and non-current assets and current and non-current liabilities are presented as separate classifications on the face of the statement of financial position. These distinctions are required because the extent into the future that assets and liabilities are to be realised has clear implications for an assessment of the financial position and solvency of an entity. Any assets and liabilities not falling within the definitions of 'current', as indicated below, are to be classified as non-current.

A current asset is one which:

- is expected to be realised, or is intended for sale or on consumption, in the entity's normal operating cycle;
- is held primarily for trading purposes;
- is expected to be realised within 12 months of the statement of financial position date; or
- is cash or a cash equivalent asset.

A current liability is one which:

- is expected to be settled in the normal course of the entity's operating cycle; or
- is due to be settled within 12 months of the statement of financial position.

A format which covers most of the information that one might expect to appear in an entity's statement of financial position, is given below.

 TEST YOUR KNOWLEDGE **3.5**

(a) What is meant by a current asset and current liability?

(b) Explain the process of recognising revenue under IAS 18

WORKED EXAMPLE 3.3

NRG plc – Statement of financial position at 31 December

	Notes	2012	2011
Assets		£'000	£'000
Non-current assets			
Property, plant AND equipment	10	607000	602000
Accumulated depreciation	11	134000	119000
		473000	483000
Goodwill	12	11000	11000
Accumulated impairment	13	5000	4000
		6000	7000
Other intangible assets	14	13000	9000
Investments in associates	15	9000	9000
Available-for-sale investments	16	13000	6000
Total non-current assets		35000	24000
Current assets			
Inventories	17	34000	24000
Trade receivables	18	24000	18000
Cash and cash equivalents	19	22000	21000
Total current assets		80000	63000
Total assets		594000	577000
Equity and liabilities			
Share capital		50000	50000
Other reserves		63000	63000
Retained earnings		225000	172050
		338000	285050
Minority interest		103000	92410
Total equity		441000	377460
Non-current liabilities			
Long-term borrowings	20	52000	56000
Deferred tax	21	11000	9000
Long-term provisions	22	5000	5000
Total non-current liabilities		68000	70000
Current liabilities			
Trade and other payables	23	13000	26540
Short-term borrowings	24	36000	68000
Current portion of long-term borrowings	25	6000	6000
Taxation	26	25000	20000
Short-term provisions	27	5000	9000
Total current liabilities		85000	129540
Total liabilities		153000	199540
Total equity and liabilities		594000	577000

13 Additional information on the statement of financial position

IAS 1 paragraph 54 provides the minimum line items to be included on the face of the statement of financial position.

Additional line items, headings, and subtotals shall be presented on the face of the statement of financial position if these are relevant to understanding the entity's financial position. There is no prescribed order or format in which items are to be presented; however, the guidelines are as follows:

- line items are included when the size, nature or function of an item or aggregation of similar items is such that separate presentation is relevant to an understanding of the entity's financial position; and
- the descriptions used and the ordering of items or aggregation of similar items may be amended according to the nature of the entity and its transactions, to provide information that is relevant to an understanding of the entity's financial position.

14 Statement of changes in equity

Changes in shareholders' equity between statement of financial position dates are, of course, equal to the increase or decrease in net assets during that period. The change comprises two basic elements:

- capital injections by the shareholders or withdrawals in the form of repayment of capital and dividends; and
- gains and losses.

The general rule, as noted above, is that gains and losses should go through the statement of comprehensive income. The reasons for this are two-fold:

- gains and losses, whatever their source, have an identical impact on the financial position of the enterprise; and
- the impact of a gain, or perhaps more likely a loss, is not 'played down' by relegating it to a position outside the primary financial statements.

We have noted in section 11, however, that accounting standards require a restricted range of gains and losses to be excluded from the income statement, but shown as other comprehensive income such as gains and losses on sale of an asset. These, together with the profit for the year reported in the income statement are reported in the statement of changes in equity. The content of this report will depend on the nature of gains and losses arising during the year, but the following pro forma covers the more common possibilities.

14.1 Other items appearing in the statement of change in equity

Transactions that are material in nature may also be reported through the statement of changes to equity and may include items such as transfer between reserves (e.g. revaluation reserve) and issue of shares and prior period adjustments (discussed in chapter 4).

- *Transfers from reserves*: When an asset held for sale is eventually disposed of any gain that transpires may be transferred to the equity. Any such transfer will simply be shown in the statement by a minus in one column and a plus in another.
- *Share issues*: companies often issues shares in various forms that have a material impact on the capital structure. These include bonus shares, rights issues, new shares issues (seasoned offering) and occasionally companies will buy back their own shares (in the US these are known as treasury shares). Any share issue below the market price will have a dilutive effect on shareholder wealth.
- *Prior period adjustment*: If prior period mistakes or errors are material, IAS 8 'Accounting Policies, Changes in Accounting Estimates and Errors' allows such misstatements to be included in the statement of changes as adjusting item(s) brought forward from those years. For instance, a research and development expense wrongly capitalised will have a subsequent reducing impact on retained earnings and assets (see below).

WORKED EXAMPLE 3.4

Statement of changes in equity for the year ended 31 December 2010

	Share capital	Other reserves	Translation reserve	Retained earnings	Total
	£'000	£'000	£'000	£'000	£'000
Balance at 1 January 2010	x	x	x	x	x
Change in accounting policy (IAS 8)				x	x
Restated balance at 1 January 2010				x	x
Changes in equity during the year					
Other comprehensive income					
Gain/loss on property revaluation (IAS 16)		x			x
Exchange differences (IAS 21)					x
Available for sale investments (IAS 39)		x			x
Tax on above items (gains or losses) recognised directly in equity		x			
Total other comprehensive income		x	x		x
Profit for the period				x	x
Total recognised income and expenses for the period	x	x	x	x	x
Dividends				(x)	(x)
Issued share capital	x				x
Balance at 31 December 2010	x	x	x	x	x

WORKED EXAMPLE 3.5

	Share capital	Share premium	Revaluation reserve	Retained earnings	Total
	£m	£m	£m	£m	£m
Balance at 1 January 2010	350	50	20	640	1060
Change in accounting policy (IAS 8)				10	10
Restated balance at 1 January 2010				650	1070
Changes in equity during the year					
Other comprehensive income					
Gain/loss on property revaluation (IAS 6)		–	10		10
Transfer on realisation		–	–7	7	0
Tax on above items (gains or losses) recognised directly in equity		–	–3		–3
Total other comprehensive income	350	50	20	7	7
Profit for the period				20	20
Total recognised income and expenses for the period				27	27
Dividends				–6	–6
Issued share capital					
Balance at 31 December 2010	350	50	20	671	1091

STOP AND THINK 3.1

Do we really need a defined and constantly evolving standard setting process?

END OF CHAPTER QUESTIONS

3.1   Briefly discuss the principal statements and their purpose that constitute a complete set of financial statements.

3.2   The statement of changes in equity includes reconciliation between:
   (a)   the carrying amount of retained earnings at the beginning and the end of the period.
   (b)   the carrying amount of total equity at the beginning and the end of the period.
   (c)   the carrying amount of each component of equity at the beginning and the end of the period separately disclosing changes resulting from:
     ■   profit or loss;
     ■   each item of comprehensive income; and
     ■   the amounts of investments by, and dividends and other distributions to, owners.

   From the above statements select which answer best reflects the statement of changes in equity.

3.3   The following items were extracted from the records of Sigma plc on 31 December 2011.

	£'000
Goodwill	400
Capitalised development expenditure	200
Brand	100
Property, plant and equipment	900
Trade and other receivables	950
Inventories	300
Cash and cash equivalent	200
Trade and other payables	300
Derivative financial assets (short term)	100
Other receivables (due to be received 2014)	300
Investments in subsidiaries	200
Deferred tax liabilities	100
Current tax payable	100
10% bond payable 2015	60
Provision for decommissioning of nuclear plant in 2015	50
Revaluation reserve	150
Retained earnings	300
Retirement benefit obligations	120
Capital redemption reserve	80
Share capital – £1 ordinary shares (balancing item)	?

Required

Prepare the statement of financial position of Sigma plc on 31 December 2011. The statement should be prepared in accordance with IAS 1.

END OF CHAPTER QUESTIONS

3.4 Opal Ltd is a company which operates a number of retail shops, some of which it owns and others it rents. The following is the company's trial balance at 31 December 2012:

	£'000	£'000
Sales revenue		5100
Purchases	2500	
Accounts payable		212
Accounts receivable	208	
Inventories at 1 January 2012	250	
6% debenture loan		200
Administration expenses	924	
Equipment at cost	600	
Accumulated depreciation at 1 January 2012		120
Distribution costs	540	
Ordinary shares		2200
Share premium account at 1 January 2012		250
Retained profit at 1 January 2012		850
Bank		15
Final dividend for 2011 paid in July 2012	35	
Freehold property at cost	3890	
	8947	8947

You are given the following additional information:
1   The company does not depreciate its freehold property.
2   The equipment was purchased on 1 January 2012, at which time they were expected to have a ten-year life and a zero residual value.
3   Six months' rent of £26,000, included in administration expenses, was paid in advance on 1 October 2012.
4   An invoice of £5,000 for advertising during 2012 was received in January 2013 and is not reflected in the above trial balance.
5   The debenture interest due for 2012 has not yet been paid or accrued.
6   The value of inventories at 31 December 2012 was £270,000.
7   The company has an authorised share capital of 2 million ordinary shares of £1 each and had an issued share capital of 1.75 million ordinary shares of £1 each at 31 December 2011.
8   On 30 June 2012 the company issued, for cash, 250,000 shares. The entire proceeds of this issue have been recorded as part of the balance of £2.2 million on the ordinary shares account.
9   It is estimated that the corporation tax charge for 2012 will be £300,000 and has not been paid.
10   The directors intend to declare an ordinary dividend of 4 pence per share on each share in issue at 31 December 2012.

Required
Prepare the following financial statements of Opal Ltd for 2012 in accordance with the provisions of IAS 1 'Presentation of Financial Statements':
1   Statement of comprehensive income using function of expense format.
2   Statement of financial position.
3   Statement of changes in equity.
4   Provide definitions for the following concepts/terminologies:
   (a)   Fair value in accordance with IFRS 3 'Business Combinations' (Past ICSA question).
   (b)   Measurement and recognition of revenues in accordance with IAS 18 'Revenues'.
   (c)   Other comprehensive income.
   (d)   Reporting entities.

4

Income statement analysis and accounting policies

■ CONTENTS

■ LEARNING OUTCOMES

Chapter 4 covers the syllabus section entitled 'Financial Statements for Single Companies in Compliance with Legal and Regulatory Requirements'. After reading and understanding the contents of the chapter, working through all the Worked Examples and Practice Questions, you should be able to:

- analyse the statement of comprehensive income;
- explain changes in accounting estimates and their impact on current and past events;
- understand the role of accounting policies;
- appreciate the impact of prior period errors and misstatements on the financial statements due to new and discontinued operations and the disclosure requirements;
- explain how non-recurring profit/losses should be reported on financial statements;
- explain the role and purpose of segmental reporting and its limitations; and
- appreciate the limitations of published accounts.

1   Introduction

The general purpose of financial reports is to convey information to people who are interested in assessing the past performance and future progress of business entities. Income statements can be used to:

- understand past performance;
- predict future profit and losses; and
- forecast the resulting cash flows.

2   Income statement analysis

Decision-makers are interested in potential future earnings, but those who use accounting information have to rely principally on past accounts to reach commercial decisions. It is therefore part of the purpose of IAS 8 'Accounting Policies, Changes in Accounting Estimates and Errors', IFRS 5 'Non-current Assets Held for Sale and Discontinued Operations' and IFRS 8 'Operating Segments' to help improve the interpretative value of published accounts, principally through additional analyses of the information reported in the income statement. There are three aspects to this:

- It is necessary to highlight the impact of non-recurrent transactions to help users better assess current progress and estimate future profits or losses (IAS 8).
- It is important to be able to identify the contribution of separate segments of business activity to enable users to carry out a detailed comparison of this year's results with those of previous years and other companies (IFRS 8).
- The impact of discontinued operations must be isolated in order to ensure that like is being compared with like when comparing actual reported results with last year's results or with the forecasts made for the current period (IFRS 5).

3   Impact of change in accounting estimates

Because the true value of assets and liabilities depends, at least to some extent, on events that have not yet taken place, the information reported in financial statements often cannot be measured with precision, it can only be estimated. The estimation process involves making judgements that are based on the latest information available. Estimates may be required (e.g. for bad debts, the provision for doubtful debts, the useful lives of non-current assets, the appropriate method for writing off non-current assets to reflect the expected pattern of future benefit and warranty liabilities).

A change in an accounting estimate occurs when the carrying amount of an asset or liability or the amount to be written off an asset's value in an accounting period needs to be revised because new information has become available. As IAS 8 states:

> A change in accounting estimate is an adjustment of the carrying amount of an asset or a liability, or the amount of the periodic consumption of an asset, that results from the assessment of the present status of, and expected future benefits and obligations associated with, assets and liabilities.

An example of a situation where a revised estimate would be needed is where a company decides that the remaining life of an office building is 30 years rather than the 40 years previously anticipated. If it becomes evident during an accounting period that prior estimates were materially inaccurate, the accounts must be revised and the amount involved should be disclosed. The effect of a change in an accounting estimate is recognised *prospectively* (a likely or expected occurrence of an event) in the profit and loss in the period of the change; it must also be listed in future income statements if the change affects future periods.

 WORKED EXAMPLE 4.1

A company has a computing system which was purchased on 1 January 20X0 for £2 million. The system was initially depreciated on the diminishing-balance basis at 20% per annum. During 20X2, management reaches the conclusion that use of the straight-line basis more fairly reflects the pattern of expected benefit. It also estimates that the system has a further useful economic life at 1 January 20X2 of four years. The asset has a zero residual value at the end of four years.

Required

(a) Calculate the carrying value of the computer system in the statement of financial position prepared at 31 December 20X1.

(b) Calculate the depreciation charge for 20X2 and carrying value at 31 December 20X2.

Note: Make calculations to the nearest £'000.

Answer

(a)

	£'000	£'000
Computer system at cost		2,000
Accumulated depreciation	$(2,000 \times 0.2) + (1,600 \times 0.2)$	720
		1,280

WORKED EXAMPLE 4.1 *continued*

(b) Depreciation charge	1,280/4	<u>320</u>
Computer system at cost		2,000
Accumulated depreciation	720 + 320	<u>1,040</u>
Net book value		960

Changes in estimates need only be disclosed if the amount is material. IAS 8 defines an item as material in the following circumstances:

> Omissions or misstatements of items are material if they could, by their size or nature, individually or collectively, influence the economic decisions of users taken on the basis of the financial statements. Materiality depends on the size and nature of the omission or misstatement judged in the surrounding circumstances. The size or nature of the item, or a combination of both, could be a determining factor.

4 Accounting policies

Accounting policies are dealt with in IAS 8 'Accounting Policies, Changes in Accounting Estimates, and Errors'. The important issue of changes in accounting policies is discussed below. Here we are concerned with the nature and purpose of accounting policies. We start with a definition.

Accounting policies are the specific principles, bases, conventions, rules, and practices applied by an entity in preparing and presenting financial statements. The following are important features concerning the choice and application of accounting policies:

- An entity should adopt accounting policies for valuing assets and liabilities most appropriate for the purpose of ensuring that the accounts give a true and fair view.
- The accounting policies adopted should be reviewed regularly to ensure that they remain appropriate and are changed when a new policy becomes more appropriate to the entity's particular circumstances.
- Sufficient information must be disclosed in the financial statements to enable users to understand the accounting policies adopted and how they have been implemented.

It is the task of many other accounting standards to identify the range of acceptable accounting policies from which particular entities make their selection. The following amended extracts from the accounts of the 2011 Annual Report of Vodafone plc are typical examples of how companies disclose the accounting policies used for inventories (IAS 2) and property, plant and equipment (IAS 16).

4.1 Inventories

Inventory is stated at the lower of cost and net realisable value. Cost is determined on the basis of weighted average costs and comprises direct materials and, where applicable, direct labour costs and those overheads that have been incurred in bringing the inventories to their present location and condition.

4.2 Property, plant and equipment

Land and buildings held for use are stated in the statement of financial position at their cost, less any subsequent accumulated depreciation and subsequent accumulated impairment losses.

Equipment, fixtures and fittings are stated at cost less accumulated depreciation and any accumulated impairment losses.

Assets in the course of construction are carried at cost, less any recognised impairment loss. Depreciation of these assets commences when the assets are ready for their intended use.

The cost of property, plant and equipment includes directly attributable incremental costs incurred in their acquisition and installation.

Depreciation is charged to write off the cost or valuation of assets, other than land and properties under construction, using the straight-line method, over their estimated useful lives, as follows:

Freehold buildings	25–50 years
Leasehold premises	The term of the lease
Network infrastructure 3–25 years	3–25 years
Other	3–10 years

Depreciation is not provided on freehold land.

5 Impact of change in accounting policies

An entity can change its accounting policy only if the change is:

■ required by standard accounting practice; or
■ results in the financial statements providing more relevant and reliable information about the entity's financial position, financial performance or cash flows.

Usually, a change in accounting policy is applied *retrospectively* to all periods presented in the financial statements. This means that the brought-forward carrying value of the asset or liability and retained profits must both be appropriately adjusted. The following is an extract from Vodafone plc's (2011 annual report) changes to accounting policies.

> **Amendment to IAS 27 'Consolidated and Separate Financial Statements'**
> The Group adopted the amendment to IAS 27 on 1 April 2010 … The adoption of this standard has resulted in a change in presentation within the statement of cash flows of amounts paid to acquire non-controlling interests in Group entities that do not result in a change in control. In the year ended 31 March 2011 £137 million related to such transactions was classified as 'Other transactions with non-controlling shareholders in subsidiaries' within 'Net cash flows from financing activities', whereas these amounts would have previously been recorded in 'Purchase of interests in subsidiaries and joint ventures, net of cash acquired' within 'Cash flows from investing activities'.

 **WORKED EXAMPLE** 4.2

The following balances relating to 2012 have been extracted from the books of Oldham plc:

	£'000
Turnover	11,170
Cost of sales	7,721
Profit on the sale of shares in Preston Ltd	500
Administration expenses	621
Distribution costs	133
Interest payable	26
Final dividend paid in respect of 20X0	600
Interim dividend paid for 20X1	250
Retained profit at 1 January 20X1	3,875

The following additional information is provided:

1 Shares in Preston Ltd were sold during the year. These shares were purchased ten years ago and were the only investments owned by the company. It is estimated that attributable tax payable will be £150,000.

WORKED EXAMPLE **4.2** *continued*

2 The company's cost of sales includes a £200,000 write-off of uninsured inventories damaged by fire.
3 After the above balances were extracted, the directors decided to adopt the policy of depreciating the company's freehold building that has been owned for some years. This decision requires the opening carrying amount of the building to be reduced by £700,000, and a charge for 2011 of £114,000 must be added to cost of sales.
4 Corporation tax on profits from normal trading operations is estimated at £1.2 million.
5 Oldham plc's issued share capital amounted to £10 million throughout 2011.

Required
The income statement and statement of changes in equity of Oldham plc for 2011 in 'good form' and complying with standard accounting practice so far as the information permits.
Note: Assume all amounts are material.

Answer
Workings

Cost of sales	7721
Add: Additional depreciation	114
Adjusted cost of sales	7835

Income statement for Oldham plc 2011	£'000
Turnover	11170
Cost of sales (Note 1)	−7835
Gross profit	3335
Distribution costs	−133
Administration expenses	−621
Operating profit	2581
Other income (Note 2)	500
Finance costs	−26
Profit before tax	3055
Taxation (1,200 + 150)	−1350
Profit for the year 2011	1705

Statement of changes in equity of Oldham plc for 2011

	Share capital £'000	Retained earnings £'000	Total £'000
Balance at 1 January 2011	10000	3875	13875
Change in accounting policy (Note 3)		−700	−700
Balance at 1 January 2011 as restated	10000	3175	13175
Changes in equity during the year			
Profit for the year 2011		1705	1705
Dividends		−850	−850
Balance at 31 December 2011	10000	4030	14030

Cost of sales includes a £200,000 write-off of uninsured inventories damaged by fire. Material amount requires disclosure.

During the year the company realised a profit of £500,000 on the sale of its shareholdings in Preston Ltd purchased some years ago and also requires disclosure in view of the material amount involved.

The directors have decided to change Oldham's accounting policies so as to depreciate the company's freehold building, purchased some years ago, in order to give a fairer presentation of the results and financial position of the company.

6 Prior period errors

These are omissions from, and misstatements in, the entity's financial statements for one or more prior periods arising from the failure to use, or to misuse, information that was available at the time the financial statements were being issued. Such errors must be taken directly to equity and reported in the statement of changes in equity. They include the effects of:

- mathematical mistakes;
- mistakes in applying accounting policies;
- oversights and misinterpretation of facts; and
- fraud.

IAS 8 makes it clear, however, that any adjustments to incorrect estimates made in earlier years must not be accounted for as prior year items and must be shown on the face of the income statement. For example, a major customer may go into liquidation owing £1 million and the company may make a bad debt provision of £600,000 in anticipation of an ultimate payment of 40 pence in the pound to unsecured creditors. This optimism may prove to be unfounded, in which case the remaining balance of £400,000 has to be written off in the following year.

When this happens, the additional write-off is not accounted for as a prior year item despite the fact that it was caused by a liquidation that occurred in a previous year. Instead, it must be accounted for during the current accounting period, with the amount disclosed if material.

7 New and discontinued operations

A **discontinued operation** is a component of an enterprise that has either been disposed of, or is classified as 'held for sale', and:

- represents a separate major line of business or geographical area of operations; and
- is part of a single, coordinated plan to dispose of this separate major line of business or geographical area of operations; or
- is a subsidiary acquired exclusively with a view to resale.

(IFRS 5: 'Non-current Assets Held for Sale and Discontinued Operations').

If there is any gain or loss from the sale of assets they should be recognised in the statement of comprehensive income.

Financial reporting regulations require that continuing operations are reported separately in the income statement from discontinued operations, and that any gain or loss from the disposal of a segment (an entity whose activities represent a separate major line of business or market segment) be reported along with the operating results of the discontinued segment.

The results of operations of a component of a company that either has been disposed of, or is classified as being held for sale are reported in discontinued operations only if *both* of the following conditions are met:

- the operations and cash flows of the component have been (or will be) eliminated from the ongoing operations as a result of the disposal decision, and
- the company will not have any significant continuing involvement in the operations of the component after the disposal decision.

A component, as described under IFRS 5, consists of operations and cash flows that can be clearly distinguishable, operationally and for financial reporting purposes from the rest of the entity. However, due to the subjectivity of the above definition, the IASB has aligned the definition with that used in IFRS 8 'Operating Segments'.

The importance of understanding changes over time in the various segments of activity which make up the whole of the company is illustrated in Figure 4.1.

Segment	20X0	20X1
1	Operational	Discontinued
2	Operational	Operational
3	Operational	Operational

FIGURE 4.1 Changing activities over time

This shows that in 20X0 the company had three main segments of activity – 1, 2 and 3 and in 20X1 segment 1 was discontinued. Any predictions made for 20X2 based on the results of 20X1 would be wrong to the extent that activity 1 no longer contributes towards the overall performance of the enterprise.

Similarly, comparisons between the actual results for 20X2 and those of the previous year should take account of the fact that the business has downsized. As the name indicates, IFRS 5 'Non-current Assets Held for Sale and Discontinued Operations', deals with a number of issues. Here we are concerned with the last-mentioned item.

7.1 Disclosure – statement of comprehensive income

The impact of accounting for discontinued operations is that regulations require separate disclosure from continuing operations on the face of the income statement. Business entities are required to show, as a minimum, the following items on the face of the income statement:

- the post-tax profit or loss of discontinued operations;
- the post-tax gain or loss recognised on the measurement to fair value less cost of sale of the discontinued component(s).

Additionally, the quality of disclosure can be enhanced through further analysis of discontinued operations either in the income statement or in the narratives to the financial reports:

- the revenue, expenses and pre-tax profit or loss of discontinued operations;
- the related income tax expense as required under IAS 12;
- the gain or loss recognised on the measurement to fair value less cost of sale of the discontinued component(s); and
- the related income tax expense, subject to IAS 12.

The following example of disclosures required for Vodafone is given below.

Income statement and segmental analysis of discontinued operations		
	2007	2006
	£m	£m
Service revenue	376	5264
Equipment and other revenue	144	2004
Segment revenue	520	7268
Inter-segment revenue	–	–2
Net revenue	520	7266
Operating expenses	–402	–5667
Depreciation and amortisation	–	–1144
Impairment loss	–	–4900

Operating profit/(loss)	118	–4445
Non-operating income and expense	–	–
Net financing costs	8	–3
Profit/(loss)	126	-4448
Taxation relating to performance of discontinued operations	–15	7
Loss on disposal	–747	–
Taxation relating to classification of the discontinued operations	145	–147
	–491	–4588
Loss per share from discontinued operations	2007	2006
	*pps	*pps
Basic (loss)/earnings per share	–0.90	–7.35
Diluted (loss)/earnings per share	–0.90	–7.35
* pps = pence per share		

7.2 Disclosure – statement of cash flows

Cash flows arising out of discontinued operations requiring separate disclosure. Additional information must be made similar to the requirement for the statement of comprehensive income either on the cash flow statement or the narratives. The example below comes from a discontinued operation by Vodafone.

Cash flows from discontinued operations	2007	2006
	£m	£m
Net cash flows from operating activities	135	1651
Net cash flows from investing activities	–266	–939
Net cash flows from financing activities	–29	–536
Net increase in cash and cash equivalents	–160	176
Cash and cash equivalents at the beginning of the financial year	161	4
Exchange loss on cash and cash equivalents	–1	–19
Cash and cash equivalents at the end of the financial year	–	161

 TEST YOUR KNOWLEDGE 4.1

(a) What do you understand by the term 'discontinued operation'?
(b) What constitutes a 'discontinued operation' under IFRS 5?

8   Non-recurring profits and losses

The profits earned and losses suffered by a business arise from normal operating activities or accrue as a result of non-recurrent transactions or events outside the normal scope of a company's trading activities. Transactions that occur due to normal business activities of an entity are called **recurring** items. Profits and losses incurred due to normal business activities are stated under 'profits from continuing operations' in the statement of comprehensive income.

Unusual or infrequent transactions, outside the normal business activities of a firm are referred to as **non-recurring** items and reported separately in the income statement. The problem is how to account for these non-recurring transactions (e.g. an unusually large bad debt causing the removal of the debtor from the total receivables shown in the statement of financial position and an equivalent charge in the income statement). A case can be made that non-recurring transactions should be excluded from the income statement as their inclusion distorts the true trend of operating results and allows incorrect conclusions to be drawn regarding a company's past performance and likely future prospects.

 WORKED EXAMPLE 4.3

Inclusion of the non-recurring gain might cause individuals examining the accounts for 2010 to assume that annual profits are still rising, whereas in reality, recurring profits have begun to fall. On the other hand, there are strong arguments for including non-recurring transactions in the income statements as:

- non-recurring transactions have exactly the same effect on the financial position of a business as normal operating transactions; for this reason they should be given equal prominence;

- allocating individual transactions either to the income statement or directly to equity is a matter of judgement; this provides scope for both error and the manipulation of financial information. In either case, the result may be that the wrong conclusions are drawn regarding a company's performance;

- exclusion could cause users to overlook the effect of a non-recurrent transaction when assessing corporate performance;

- it is the directors' job to manage all aspects of business activity, whether they give rise to recurrent or non-recurrent profits and losses; the reported profit figure should therefore measure management's overall performance.

These arguments led to the introduction of the requirement for almost all non-recurrent profits and losses to be reported in the income statement with full disclosure of their effect. This treatment ensures that readers do not overlook the financial effect of important transactions.

A further question is the extent to which such items should be the subject of separate classification and disclosure. This issue has been the subject of considerable controversy over the years, with non-recurring items sometimes being designated as 'exceptional' or 'extraordinary'. However, concern that some companies used such terms to imply that the items – usually losses – were not events that users should be unduly worried about (because they were non-recurring) has led to such captions being banned.

The treatment of items of a non-recurring nature is currently regulated by IAS 8 'Accounting Policies, Changes in Accounting Estimates and Errors'. The objective of IAS 8 is stated as follows:

> The objective of this Standard is to prescribe the criteria for selecting and changing accounting policies, together with the accounting treatment and disclosure of changes in accounting policies, changes in accounting estimates and corrections of errors. The Standard is intended to enhance the relevance and reliability of an entity's financial statements and the comparability of those financial statements over time and with the financial statements of other entities.

TEST YOUR KNOWLEDGE 4.2

(a) Why is it important to disclose non-recurring items?
(b) Identify the circumstances in which prior-period adjustments are required.

9 Segmental reporting

In the distant past the single-product firm dominated, but such specialisation gradually gave way to horizontal integration (e.g. to eliminate competition) and vertical integration (e.g. to safeguard supplier inputs or consumer outputs).

The move towards diversification (i.e. the increasing engagement in different types of business) gained pace during the 1960s with the growth of the multinational enterprise. The result is that companies today, or more usually groups of companies, engage in a wide range of activities, where:

- there are significant variations in rates of profitability;
- the activities involve different degrees of risk (e.g. different geographical areas raise problems of movements in exchange rate, political upheaval, expropriation of assets, and high inflation rates); and
- there are differential opportunities for growth.

These are, of course, often the very reasons for diversifying. However, the result is that aggregated performance data are of limited use for decision making. Empirical research has shown that, for such companies, segmental data improves the shareholders' ability to make effective assessments of past results that can be used to predict future enterprise profits and developments. Disaggregated data is also of greater use to the government for planning purposes. It enables the accumulation of industry statistics that can be used for policy-making, (e.g. to encourage inward investment to certain industries, or to provide financial assistance for depressed areas). Equally, more detailed information on the profitability of various parts of the business may be helpful to trade unions and employees for wage and salary bargaining purposes. The move towards segmental reporting in Britain started with the Companies Act 1967. This required the directors' report to provide turnover and profit by 'class' of activity. Today, the Companies Act 2006 requires this information to be given in the notes to the accounts so that it is specifically covered by the audit report. In addition, disclosure of turnover by geographical area is required.

Segmental reporting is the subject of IFRS 8 'Operating Segments'. The objective of this standard is to establish principles for reporting financial information. This helps users of financial statements to:

- better understand the enterprise's past performance;
- better assess the enterprise's risks and returns; and
- make more informed judgements about the enterprise as a whole.

9.1 Identification of reportable segments

A business or geographical segment can be identified as reportable if a majority of its revenue is earned from sales to external customers and:

- its revenue is 10% or more of total revenue, external and internal, of all segments; or
- its result (either profit or loss) is 10% or more of the combined result of all segments in profit or the combined result of all segments in loss, whichever is the greater in absolute amount; or
- its assets are 10% or more of the total assets of all segments.

9.2 Disclosures

The following must be disclosed for each primary reportable segment:

- revenue (disclosing separately sales to external customers and inter-segment revenue);
- the basis of inter-segment pricing;
- results (before interest and taxes) from continuing operations and, separately, the result from discontinued operations;
- carrying amount of segment assets;
- carrying amount of segment liabilities; and
- cost incurred in the period to acquire property, plant and equipment, and intangibles.

9.3 Nature of reportable segments

There are two types of reportable segments:

- A business segment (one based on supply of products or services) is a distinguishable component of an enterprise that is engaged in providing an individual product or service or a group of related products or services and that is subject to risks and returns that are different from those of other business segments.
- A geographical segment is a distinguishable component of an enterprise that is engaged in providing products or services within a particular economic environment and that is subject to risks and returns that are different from those of components operating in other economic environments.

Segmental information must be prepared for both business and geographical segments, with one treated as the primary segment and the other as the secondary segment. The primary segment is determined on the basis of whether particular products or services or particular geographical areas are more important in affecting the entity's risks and rates of return. Rather more information must be published in the primary segmental reports, but the differences are minor and are not considered further here.

Figure 4.2 below sets out the treatment of inter-segment sales, which must be cancelled as they do not represent transactions with external parties.

Income statement

Revenue	Paper products 20X1	Paper products 20X0	Office products 20X1	Office products 20X0	Publishing 20X1	Publishing 20X0	Other operations 20X1	Other operations 20X0	Eliminations 20X1	Eliminations 20X0	Consolidated 20X1	Consolidated 20X0
External sales	55	50	20	17	19	16	7	7				
Inter-segment sales	15	10	10	14	2	4	2	2	−29	−30		
Total revenue	70	60	30	31	21	20	9	9	−29	−30	101	90
Results												
Segment result	20	17	9	7	2	1	0	0	−1	−1	30	24
Unallocated corporate expenses											−7	−9
Operating profit											23	15
interest expense											−4	−4
interest income											2	3
Share of net profits of associates	6	5					2	2			8	7
Income taxes											−7	−4
Profit on ordinary activities											22	17
Uninsured earthquake damage to factory		−3									0	−3
Net profit											22	14

Income statement

	Paper products		Office products		Publishing		Other operations		Eliminations		Consolidated	
	20X1	20X0	20X1	20X0	20X1	20X0	20X1	20X0	20X1	20X0	20X1	20X0
Segment assets	54	50	34	30	10	10	10	9			108	99
Investment in equity methods associates	20	16					12	10			32	26
Unallocated corporate assets											35	30
Consolidated total assets											175	155
Segment liabilities	25	15	8	11	8	8	1	1			42	35
Unallocated corporate liabilities											40	55
Consolidated total liabilities											82	90
Capital expenditure	12	10	3	5	5		4	3				
Depreciation	9	7	9	7	5	3	3	4				
Non-cash expenses other than depreciation	8	2	7	3	2	2	2	1				

FIGURE 4.2 Pro-forma statements for business with multiple segments

The presentation of all the above information in a single statement may not work well in terms of improving the readability of annual reports. Sometimes companies will use a number of tables, each focusing on a different item to be reported. The following segmental information in respect of turnover is taken from the 2010 Annual Report of Alliance Boots Group plc (Figure 2).

The Group's external revenues for groups of similar products and services were:

	2011 £million	2010 Re-presented £million
Health & Beauty Division		
Dispensing and Related Income	2,829	2,763
Retail	4,420	4,412
Optical	329	320
Other	48	–
	7,626	7,495
Pharmaceutical Wholesale Division		
Wholesale and Related Services	13,942	11,283
	13,942	11,283
All other segments and eliminations	(1,350)	(1,207)
	20,218	17,571

FIGURE 4.3 Alliance Boots – Group revenues by segments

9.4 Limitations of segmental reporting

A major problem associated with the preparation of segmental reports is the treatment of common costs relating to more than one segment. Entities often apportion some of their common costs for the purpose of internal reporting (perhaps based on sales). In such cases, it may be reasonable for these costs to be treated in the same way for external reporting purposes. If the apportionment would be misleading, however, common costs should not be apportioned to the segments, but should be deducted from the total segment result (see the total charges to revenues for post-tax earnings of associates and joint ventures, net finance costs and tax charge in Figure 4.4 below).

2011	Health & Beauty Division £million	Pharmaceutical Wholesale Division £million	All other segments £million	Eliminations £million	Total £million
External revenue	7,621	12,478	119	–	20,218
Intra-group revenue	5	1,464	134	(1,603)	–
Total revenue	7,626	13,942	253	(1,603)	20,218
EBITDA	962	364	(26)	–	1,300
Underlying depreciation and amortisation	(195)	(44)	(10)	–	(249)
Trading profit/(loss)	767	320	(36)	–	1,051
Share of underlying post tax earnings of associates and joint ventures					74
Underlying net finance costs					(381)
Underlying tax charge					(137)
Underlying profit					607

FIGURE 4.4: Alliance Boots segmental reporting – revenues and expenses

A similar situation arises in the case of assets and liabilities which cannot be directly linked with the activities of individual segments. The arbitrary allocations of such items would distort the financial information published, and undermine the usefulness of any accounting ratios that make use of figures for assets and/or liabilities (e.g. rate of return on capital employed). Common assets and liabilities must also, therefore, remain unallocated and be reported at the level of the group (see Figure 4.5). At the same time, it must be realised that common costs, assets, and liabilities do benefit the individual segments, so their true segmental values will inevitably be understated. This bias in reported data should be borne in mind when comparing segmental results with other companies, particularly those entities undertaking no other activities with the consequence that their reported results will take account of *all* costs, assets and liabilities.

			2011
	Assets £million	Liabilities £million	Net £million
Health & Beauty Division	10,864	(1,374)	9,490
Pharmaceutical Wholesale Division	7,506	(3,794)	3,712
All other segments	290	(108)	182
Eliminations	(281)	281	–
Allocated segment assets/(liabilities)	18,379	(4,995)	13,384
Unallocated:			
Investments in associates and joint ventures	838	–	838
Available-for-sale investments	67	–	67
Retirement benefit obligations	–	(223)	(223)
Assets classified as held for sale	3	–	3
Net current and deferred tax	17	(1,119)	(1,102)
Net cash/(borrowings)	950	(8,793)	(7,843)
	20,254	(15,130)	5,124

FIGURE 4.5: Alliance Boots segmental reporting – assets and liabilities

One further factor affecting the reliability of segmental data arises where inter-segment sales take place. Here, there is the possibility of creative accounting if, for some reason, management wishes to inflate the reported results of one segment and deflate those of another. Even where best efforts are made to use realistic transfer prices, the possible error resulting from the subjective nature of this exercise should be borne in mind. Transfer prices should be fixed for this purpose.

TEST YOUR KNOWLEDGE 4.3

(a) What is segmental accounting?

(b) What are the two segmental bases for reporting segments?

10 Limitations of published accounts

Over the years the content of the accounts published by companies has been the subject of substantial modification in response to changes in regulatory requirements. The result is that many of the earlier limitations of published accounts have been rectified. Those that remain include the following:

1 A fundamental criticism of the published accounts of a company is that they are principally a record of past events, whereas users want to know what is likely to happen to in the future. Some modifications are made to published accounts to improve their predictive potential (e.g. non-recurring transactions are the subject of separate identification to help users compute to results that have occurred in the past that might be expected to be repeated in the future). Nevertheless, the accounts remain essentially backward-looking. There has always been a strong lobby in favour of the publication of forecast information, but this has always been resisted on the grounds that its content would be subjective and subject to potential manipulation.

2 A mixed measurement system exists in Britain with some assets and liabilities reported in the accounts at historical cost and others reported at current value. Historical cost has been the traditional basis for financial reports but there has been a significant move towards the adoption of current values under the leadership of the standard setters. Current or fair values must be used in certain circumstances (e.g. when another company is acquired and when an impairment review is undertaken). However, in many other cases, particularly in relation to the valuation of fixed assets, companies retain the option to compute these figures on the basis of historical cost. Alternatively, they may choose to use the current value basis. There is little doubt that the standard setters have shied away from *enforcing* the widespread use of current values, in anticipation of resistance from the business community, but the consequence is continued inconsistency in the valuation basis adopted both within the company (e.g. some classes of non-current assets may be stated on the basis of historical cost and others at current value) and between companies.

3 Despite the ever-increasing number of accounting standards, there remain available a number of choices concerning the accounting treatment of particular items in the accounts (e.g. in the case of non-current assets, it is permissible to use the straight-line basis, the diminishing balance basis, the sum of the digits method and any other established method for depreciating non-current assets).

4 The information is out of date. A period of three to four months typically elapses between the end of the accounting period and the point the annual accounts are circulated to members. Circumstances may have changed significantly between the period covered by the accounts and the date when members examine them. It must also be remembered that the accounts cover a 12-month period and some of the information being reported will relate to events that have occurred round about 15 months before they are reported in the published accounts.

TEST YOUR KNOWLEDGE 4.4

(a) Discuss the limitations and usefulness of published financial reports.
(b) Outline and describe two main criticisms often attributed to the limitations of published financial reports.

STOP AND THINK 4.1

Do you think the markets should be left to develop their own accounting standards?

END OF CHAPTER QUESTIONS

4.1 Describe, with an example of what is meant by 'statement of comprehensive income'.

4.2 How should companies determine an entity's reportable segments?

4.3 Radar plc has always depreciated its plant and equipment over 15 years. Recently, the board of directors have determined that due to advancements in technology, the useful life of the assets should only be for ten years. Radar plc's year-end is 31 December 2010.

At 1 January 2010 the company's statement of financial position extract had the following amount:

	£'000
PPE at cost	50000
Accumulated depreciation	(20000)
Carrying amount	30000

Required

Determine the Radar plc's net asset value at the end of 2010.

4.4 Buffalo Ltd runs a chain of stationary stores providing three main products, namely, copiers, paper, and printing services to its business customers. The current financial statements contain the following:

Statement of financial position of Buffalo Ltd as at 31 December 2010

Assets	
Non-current assets at book value	2443
Current assets	
Inventories	57
Receivables	44
Bank	225
Total assets	2769

Equities and liabilities	
Equity	
Share capital	1000
Retained earnings	1449
Non-current liabilities	
Long-term borrowing	210
Current liabilities	
Payables	78
Short-term borrowing	32
Total equities and liabilities	2769

Statement of comprehensive income of Buffalo Ltd as at 31 December 2010

	£'000	£'000
Revenue		1110
Less: Cost of sales	574	
Administration expenses	96	
Distribution costs	142	
Finance costs	10	–822
Net profit		288

The table below contains a breakdown of the company's financial results:

	Copiers	Paper	Printing	HO
Revenue	611	395	104	–
Cost of sales	384	146	44	–
Administration expenses	47	9	18	22
Distribution costs	101	17	24	–

END OF CHAPTER QUESTIONS

Finance costs	6	1	1	2
Non-current assets at book value	1012	767	432	232
Inventories	31	14	12	–
Receivables	23	12	9	–
Bank	148	46	31	–
Payables	32	20	16	10
Short-term borrowing	13	7	4	8
Long-term borrowing	210	–	–	–

Required

Prepare a segmental statement of comprehensive income for Buffalo Ltd complying, so far as information permits, with the provisions of IFRS 8 'Operating Segments' indicating revenues and expenses for each segment and the business as a whole:

(a) revenue;

(b) profit; and

(c) net assets

4.5 Identify the circumstances in which IAS 8 enables a company to change its accounting policy and indicate how the change must be treated in the accounts.

4.6 The issued share capital of Hawkestone Ltd at 1 July 2011 consisted of 20 million ordinary share of £1 each issued at par. On 1 January 2012, the directors made a rights issue of one share for every two shares held at £2.80 per share. The following further information is provided for Hawkestone Ltd for the year to 30 June 2012:

	£'000
Turnover	74400
Cost of sales (Note 1)	49200
Loss on closure of manufacturing division (Note 2)	14600
Distribution costs	7200
Administrative expenses	12400
Bad debts write off arising from prior period error (Note 3)	4280
Retained profit at 1 July 2011	25200

Notes

The cost of sales figure includes closing inventories of finished goods valued at £4.74 million. The company's auditors have drawn attention to the fact that £1.04 million of these inventories is obsolete and should be written off.

In the past the company's activities consisted of a manufacturing division and a service division. The service division has been making healthy profits in recent years but the manufacturing division has been making losses. The manufacturing division was closed down during the year to 30 June 2012.

It has been discovered that last year's accounts were wrongly prepared. Owing to a clerical error, a debt due to Hawkestone of £4,280,000 that was known to be bad was wrongly classified as cash at bank.

Required

(a) Define a material item in accordance with the provisions of IAS 8.

(b) Prepare the income statement and statement of changes in equity of Hawkestone Ltd in accordance with good accounting practice and complying with standard accounting practice so far as the information permits.

Note: Ignore taxation.

4.7 Explain the nature of a non-recurring item and how it should be reported in the financial statements.

4.8 State and explain the conditions that need must be met for and asset to be classified as being held for sale.

4.9 IFRS 5 explains the criteria for determining a discontinued operation. Explain the criteria.

4.10 What is an operating segment? Explain the criteria in identifying an operating segment?

5 Valuing assets and liabilities, differences in accounting policies, fair presentation and the directors' report

■ CONTENTS

■ LEARNING OUTCOMES

Chapter 5 covers the syllabus section entitled 'Financial Statements for Single Companies in Compliance with Legal and Regulatory Requirements'. After reading and understanding the contents of the chapter, working through all the Worked Examples and Practice Questions, you should be able to:

- explain how assets and liabilities are valued and recognised;
- understand and demonstrate the nature and differences of accounting policies and their impact on financial reporting;
- develop an understanding of various types of accounting;
- understand the nature of accounting assumptions;
- explain how companies face accounting constraints;
- explore the concepts of 'fair presentation', 'true and fair' and the 'true and fair override'; and
- appreciate the role of the director's report and the chair's statement.

1 Introduction

Central to the theme of fair presentation of financial results is the measurement of assets and liabilities. IAS 1 states: 'An entity shall present separately each material class of similar items. An entity shall present separately items of a dissimilar nature or function unless they are immaterial.' Typically, items on the face of the statement of financial position are presented as 'assets' or 'liabilities' in the form of current and non-current assets and liabilities. IAS 1 further states that it is not permitted to offset assets or liabilities or income and expenses unless required or permitted by an IFRS.

2 Methods for valuing assets and liabilities – initial recognition of an asset or liability

2.1 Asset

An asset is recognised in the statement of financial position when 'it is probable that the future economic benefits will flow to the entity and the asset has a cost or value that can be measured reliably'. As such, an asset is defined as 'a resource controlled by an entity as a result of past events and from which future economic benefits are expected to flow to the entity'.

2.2 Liability

A liability is defined as a 'present obligation of the entity arising from past events, the settlement of which is expected to result in an outflow from the entity of resources embodying economic benefits'.

When an asset is acquired or a liability is assumed in an exchange transaction for that asset or liability, the transaction price is the price paid to acquire the asset or received to assume the liability (often referred to as an entry price). In contrast, the fair value of the asset or liability represents the price that would be received to sell the asset or paid to transfer the liability (an exit price).

 **WORKED EXAMPLE** **5.1**

Required

A manufacturer imports a piece of machinery from France. What total costs should be recognised in the property, plant and equipment?

	£
Purchase price	250,000
Import duties	5,600
Delivery costs	6,800
Installation costs	7,600
Cost of function to celebration new production line	3,800

Answer

The cost of function to celebrate the new production line is not ancillary to the cost of procurement of the machinery. These costs will be excluded in the overall cost of purchase of the asset. The total cost of procurement of the asset is £270,000.

Similarly, the present obligation of a liability can be demonstrated as per the example below.

 **WORKED EXAMPLE** **5.2**

Required

Havent plc entered into a three-year lease for a plant that had a fair value of £25,379 on 1 January 2009. The implicit rate of interest applied half yearly is 5%. The terms of the lease are as follows:

(a) Primary lease period: Three years

(b) Frequency of rental payments: Six monthly in arrears.

(c) Amount of each rental: £5,000.

(d) First payment: 30 June 2009.

The estimated useful life of the plant is three years. Havent plc depreciates all non-current assets using the straight-line basis.

Required

1 Prepare a schedule of lease payments for Havent plc.

2 Show how the lease would be reported in the statement of comprehensive income for the years ended 31 December 2009 and 2010 and the statements of financial position as at 31 December 2009 and 2010.

WORKED EXAMPLE **5.2** *continued*

Answer

Lease Table

Period	Bal o/s at beg	Interest	Rental	Bal o/s at end
1/1/2009–31/06/2009	25379	1269	–5000	21648
1/7/2009–31/12/2009	21648	1082	–5000	17730
1/1/2010–30/06/2010	17730	887	–5000	13617
1/7/2010–31/12/2010	13617	681	–5000	9298
1/1/2011–30/6/2011	9298	465	–5000	4763
1/7/2011–31/12/2011	5000	237	–5000	0

Statement of comprehensive income for the year ended 31 December 2010

	2009	2010
	£	£
Depreciation	8460	8460
Interest	2351	1567

Havent plc statement of financial position as at 31 December 2010

Non-current assets	2009	2010
	£	£
Property, plant and equipment-cost	25379	25379
Accumulated depreciation	8460	16920
	16919	8459
Non-current liabilities		
Lease obligation	9298	0

2.2.1 Historical cost

■ The amount of cash or cash equivalent paid to purchase an asset (plus any cost of acquisition and/ preparation).

■ If the asset was not bought for cash, historical cost is the fair value of whatever was paid to purchase the asset.

■ For liabilities, the historical cost basis of measurement is the amount of proceeds received in exchange for the obligation.

2.2.2 Current cost

■ For assets, current cost is the amount of cash or cash equivalents that would have to be paid to buy the same, or an equivalent, asset today.

■ For liabilities, the current cost basis of measurement is the undiscounted amount of cash or cash equivalents that would be required to settle the obligation today.

2.2.3 Realisable (settlement) value

■ For assets, realisable value is the amount of cash or cash equivalents that could currently be obtained by selling the asset in an orderly disposal.

■ For liabilities, the equivalent to realisable value is called the 'settlement value' (ie **settlement value** is the undiscounted amount of cash or cash equivalents expected to be paid to satisfy the liabilities in the normal course of business).

2.2.4 Present value

■ For assets, present value is the present discounted value of the future net cash inflows that the asset is expected to generate in the normal course of business.

■ For liabilities, present value is the present discounted value of the future net cash outflows that are expected to be required to settle the liabilities in the normal course of business.

WORKED EXAMPLE 5.3

Edgar Ltd is evaluating an investment opportunity and expects the future cash flows arising as in the table below. Edgar expects a return of 10% on its investment and the expected life of the investment is expected to be five years with no residual value.

Year	Cash flow
0	−250,000
1	80000
2	80000
3	72000
4	68000
5	45000

Required

Calculate the net present value of all future cash flows.

Answer

	Year	Cash flow	Calculation of PV	Discount factor	PV
Investment in year 0	0	−250000	250,000/(1+0.1)^0	1.00	−250000
Cash inflow in year 1	1	80000	80,000/(1+0.1)^1	0.91	72727
Cash inflow in year 2	2	80000	80,000/(1+0.1)^2	0.83	66116
Cash inflow in year 3	3	72000	72,000/(1+0.1)^3	0.75	54095
Cash inflow in year 4	4	68000	68,000/(1+0.1)^4	0.68	46445
Cash inflow in year 5	5	45000	45,000/(1+0.1)^5	0.62	27941
Net Present Value (NPV)					17324

Since the net present value of the initial investment and future cash inflows is £17,324, this represents a good investment based on an expected return rate of 10%.

 WORKED EXAMPLE 5.4

Infonet Ltd is a small provider of online services to business clients. It enters in to a loan agreement with its bank to borrow £20,000 over five years starting 1 January 2011. The repayments include capital and interest at £5,000 per annum paid at the end of each year. The company can comfortably borrow money at an interest rate of 8%.

Required

Calculate the net present value of all future cash outflows.

WORKED EXAMPLE 5.4 *continued*

Answer

	Year	Cash flows	Repayments	calc of PV	PV
Loan	0	20000		20,000/(1+0.8)^0	20000
	1		−5000	−5,000/(1+0.8)^1	−4630
	2		−5000	−5,000/(1+0.8)^2	−4287
	3		−5000	−5,000/(1+0.8)^3	−3969
	4		−5000	−5,000/(1+0.8)^4	−3675
	5		−5000	−5,000/(1+0.8)^5	−3439
Net present value					**0**

The net present value indicates interest rate is suitable for the company to discharge its obligation over the five-year loan period.

2.2.5 Fair value

■ Is the amount at which an asset could be exchanged or a liability settled, between knowledgeable, willing parties in an arm's length transaction, which may involve either market measures or present measure (see Worked Example 5.5 below):

WORKED EXAMPLE 5.5

Tanner Ltd runs a nationwide convenient store business with many stores around the country. Recently the company re-valued its chain of stores on a fair value basis. The fair value assessment revealed an increase in the value of land and building by £40 million in 2010. See extract of statement of financial position for 2009 below:

	2009
	£m
Non-current assets	
PPE	412
Land and buildings	602
Equities and liabilities	
Equity	1200
Revaluation reserve	0

Required

Assuming all other assets and liabilities remain the same, reflect the amended information in the extract of the balance sheet for Tanner Ltd.

WORKED EXAMPLE **5.5** *continued*

Answer

Extract from the statement of financial position for Tanner Ltd as amended to reflect the changes in value to land and buildings. Land and buildings would increase by £40 million while a revaluation reserve would be created in equity and liabilities:

	2009	2010
	£m	£m
Non-current assets		
PPE	412	412
Land and buildings (602 + 40)	602	642
Equities and liabilities		
Equity	1200	1200
Revaluation reserve	0	40

2.2.6 Value in use

IAS 36 deals with impairment of assets and aims 'to ensure that assets are carried at no more than their recoverable amount, and to define how recoverable amount is determined'. IAS 36 further states that *value-in-use* is the discounted present value of the future cash flows expected to arise from the continuing use of an asset, and from its disposal at the end of its useful life.

The standard gives further guidance on testing assets for impairment in relation to their carrying amount. The calculation of value in use should reflect the following elements:

- an estimate of the future cash flows the entity expects to derive from the asset;
- expectations about possible variations in the amount or timing of those future cash flows;
- the time value of money, represented by the current market risk-free rate of interest;
- the price for bearing the uncertainty inherent in the asset; and
- other factors, such as illiquidity, that market participants would reflect in pricing the future cash flows the entity expects to derive from the asset.

This suggests that, particularly in the absence of a market price, the carrying amount is the value-in-use if the present value of all future cash flows is greater than the book value of the asset.

WORKED EXAMPLE **5.6**

Solar Ltd suspects its printing press, with a net book value (after depreciation) of £280,000, is impaired. However, in the absence of a market price, Solar carries out value-in-use exercise. Its cost of capital is 10%. Solar has determined the future cash flows arising from the continued use of the asset as:

Year	Cash flow
1	100000
2	86000
3	76000
4	68000
5	52000

Required

Determine if the asset is impaired based on current book value of the asset and its value-in-use.

WORKED EXAMPLE **5.6** *continued*

Answer

Year	Cash flow	Calc of PV	PV
1	100000	100,000/(1+0.1)^1	90909
2	86000	86,000/(1+0.1)^2	71074
3	76000	76,000/(1+0.1)^3	57100
4	68000	68,000/(1+0.1)^4	46445
5	52000	52,000/(1+0.1)^5	32288
Net present value			297816
Value-in-use of the asset:			297816
Net book value of the asset (NBV)			280000
Carrying amount = NBV			280000

Since the value-in-use of the asset is greater than the book value, the asset is deemed not to be impaired and the book value remains at £280,000 net of depreciation.

TEST YOUR KNOWLEDGE **5.1**

Describe three ways in which an asset or a liability can be measured.

3 Nature of accounting policies and the significance of differences between them

3.1 Nature of accounting policies

Accounting policies (IFRS and IAS) essentially refer to specific accounting principles and the methods of applying those principles adopted by a business entity in the preparation and presentation of financial statements. However, there is no single list of accounting policies that applies to every situation.

Companies operate in a diverse and complex marketplace. Choosing the appropriate accounting bases and the methods of applying those principles requires a certain degree of judgement on the part of management.

Regulatory requirements together with IFRS guidance on preparing and presenting financial statements have reduced the number of options available to management. With the level of convergence set to increase further, particularly between IFRS and US GAAP, these alternatives will be further eroded, with the result that greater transparency will be achieved in financial statements. Nevertheless, the availability of alternative accounting practices of applying those principles is not likely to be eliminated altogether in view of the differing circumstances faced by the enterprises that may transpire over time or because of regional issues.

TEST YOUR KNOWLEDGE 5.2

Explain what is meant by the nature of accounting policies and how different companies can treat assets and liabilities differently.

3.2 Accounting assumptions

Business entities are required to prepare financial information with regard to certain fundamental accounting assumptions that underlie the preparation and presentation of financial statements. They are usually not specifically stated because their acceptance and use are assumed. Disclosure is necessary if they are not followed. The following three fundamentals are necessary to represent a true and fair view:

- *Going concern* The enterprise is normally viewed as a going concern (i.e. continuing in operation for the foreseeable future). It is assumed that the enterprise has neither the intention nor the necessity to liquidate or materially curtail the scale of its operations.
- *Consistency* It is assumed that accounting policies are consistent from one period to another.
- *Accrual revenues* and costs are accrued, that is, recognised as they are earned or incurred (and not as money is received or paid) and recorded in the financial statements of the periods to which they relate. (The considerations affecting the process of matching costs with revenues under the accrual assumption are not dealt with in this Standard.)
- *Qualitative characteristics of financial reports* The qualitative aspect of financial reports are those attributes that render the information provided in financial reports useful to users. The principal qualitative characteristics are relevance and faithful representation.

TEST YOUR KNOWLEDGE 5.3

(a) Discuss, briefly, what is meant by accounting assumptions.
(b) Give at least one example of for each case.

3.3 Accounting constraints

While exercising diligence in the preparation and presentation of financial reports on the basis of the items above, business entities will nevertheless face accounting constraints. Principally there are six types of accounting constraints that may have a material impact on the preparation of financial information:

3.3.1 Estimates and judgements

Certain measurements cannot be performed completely accurately, and must therefore be calculated using conservative estimates. For example, a company cannot fully predict the amount of money it will lose in bad debts (when customers purchase goods on credit and then do not pay). Instead, a company must make a conservative estimate based on its past experience. IAS 1 'Presentation of Financial Statements' requires further that '... an entity must disclose, in the summary of significant accounting policies or other notes, the judgements, apart from those involving estimations, that management has made in the process of applying the entity's accounting policies that have the most significant effect on the amounts recognised in the financial statements'.

3.3.2 Materiality

Inclusion and disclosure of financial transactions in financial statements depends on their size and the effect on the company performing them. Note that materiality varies across different entities; a material transaction for a small outlet (e.g. taking out a £1,000 loan) is likely to be immaterial for British Petroleum, whose financial information is reported in millions of pounds. IAS 1 addresses the issue of materiality by stating 'each material class of similar items must be presented separately in the financial statements. Dissimilar items may be aggregated only if they are individually immaterial'.

3.3.3 Consistency

For each company, the preparation of financial statements must utilise measurement techniques and assumptions that are consistent from one period to another. Companies can use several different accounting methods to measure the monetary value of their inventory. However, the principal is that a company should consistently apply the same acceptable inventory method across consecutive fiscal years. IAS 1 states 'the presentation and classification of items in the financial statements shall be retained from one period to the next unless a change is justified either by a change in circumstances or a requirement of a new IFRS'.

3.3.4 Conservatism

Financial statements should be prepared on the basis of sound judgement. Assets and revenues should not be overstated, while liabilities and expenses should not be understated.

3.3.5 Offsetting

Assets and liabilities, and income and expenses, may not be offset unless required or permitted by an IFRS.

3.3.6 Comparative information

IAS 1 requires that comparative information should be disclosed in respect of the previous period for all amounts reported in the financial statements, both on the face of financial statements and in the notes, unless another standard requires otherwise. If comparative amounts are changed or reclassified, various disclosures are required.

 TEST YOUR KNOWLEDGE 5.4

(a) Discuss, briefly what is meant by accounting constraints.
(b) Give at least one example of for each case.

4 Significance of differences in accounting policies

The following are examples of the areas in which different accounting policies may be adopted by different business entities:

- impairment of assets;
- methods of depreciation, depletion and amortisation;
- treatment of expenditure during construction;
- conversion or translation of foreign currency items;
- valuation of inventory;
- treatment of goodwill;
- valuation of investments;
- treatment of retirement benefits;
- recognition of profit on long-term contracts;
- valuation of fixed assets; and
- treatment of contingent liabilities.

TEST YOUR KNOWLEDGE 5.5

(a) Discuss how difference in accounting policies can arise.
(b) How can directors mitigate discrepancies in accounting policies?

Changes to accounting and measuring procedures of assets and liabilities from one period to the next may blur reality and present misinformation for users. Business entities must ensure that economic reality is faithfully represented and that accounting and reporting principles are followed.

As an example, if a company changes its accounting policy on the way it measures depreciation on assets, this must be declared in the narratives and an explanation provided as to why the changes have occurred. The change may have a material impact on the book value of the assets:

WORKED EXAMPLE 5.7

Potter Ltd is engaged in the mining of coal. It has a plant which originally cost £300,000. This is depreciated over five years on a straight-line basis. In year 4 Potter Ltd decides to switch to the reducing-balance method to calculate depreciation.

Required
Calculate the impact of Potter Ltd switching to the reducing-balance method and its impact on the financial statements assuming a depreciation rate of 20%.

Calculation for depreciation on straight-line basis:

Year	Cost	Depn	NBV
0	300000		
1		60000	240000
2		60000	180000
3		60000	120000
4		60000	60000
5		60000	0
NBV of asset after five years			Nil

Calculation for depreciation on reducing-balance basis:

Year	Cost	Depn	NBV
0	300000		
1		60000	240000
2		60000	180000
3		60000	120000
4		24000	96000
5		19200	76800
NBV of asset after five years			76800

NBV = Net Book Value

On a reducing-balance basis, Potter Ltd would report a depreciation charge of £60,000 per annum in the statement for comprehensive income and a reduction in the same amount on the carrying value of the asset in each subsequent year. After five years the asset will have a nil residual value. The net book value of the asset in Year 4 would be £96,000 in the statement of financial position.

If Potter Ltd switches to the reducing balance method in Year 4, the depreciation charge to the statement for comprehensive income would only be £24,000, thus inflating income for Year 4 by £36,000. Similarly, the asset would have a carrying amount in the statement of financial position of £76,800.

The directors of Potter Ltd would have to declare the change in accounting policy for depreciation and demonstrate why the change was necessary in the narratives.

IAS 8 'Accounting Policies, Changes in Accounting Estimates and Errors' states that the effect of a change in an accounting estimate should be recognised prospectively by including it in profit or loss in:

- the period of the change, if the change affects that period only; or
- the period of the change and future periods, if the change affects both.

IAS 8 further states that entities that exercise a change in accounting estimates must further disclose:

- the nature and amount of a change in an accounting estimate that has an effect in the current period, or is expected to have an effect in future periods; or
- if the amount of the effect in future periods is not disclosed because estimating it is impracticable, an entity shall disclose that fact.

5   Concepts of fair presentation, 'true and fair' and the 'true and fair override'

5.1 Fair presentation and the 'true and fair' view

Fair presentation and the 'true and fair' concept may appear to be similar; however, there is a level of difference between them. The former concept is used in the United States, the latter is used in the UK, the EU, Singapore, Australia and New Zealand.

The IASB's job is to prepare a 'high quality global accounting standard that requires transparent and comparable information in general purposes financial statements'. According to the IASB, the concept of fair presentation should be used; however, in the UK, the Companies Act 2006 states that it should be the true and fair view. IAS 1 adopted both concepts requiring 'fair presentation and disclosure of compliance with IAS and a limited true and fair view override (explained below) if compliance is misleading'.

The concept of fair presentation first appeared in 1939. It can be defined as 'Presenting information, including accounting policies, in a manner which provides relevant, reliable, comparable, and understandable information'.

Fair presentation requires the faithful representation of the effects of transactions and other events, in accordance with the definitions and recognition criteria for assets, liabilities, income and expenses set out in the framework.

The principle of fair representation embodies all the principles, procedures and guidelines discussed in this and earlier chapters. The framework describes the basic concepts that underlie the preparation and presentation of financial statements for external users and serves as a guide to resolving accounting issues that are not addressed directly in a standard. However, IAS 1 'Presentation of Financial Statements', prescribes the basis for presentation of general purpose financial statements, to allow these to be compared both with the entity's previous financial statements and with the financial statements of other entities.

The expression 'true and fair' is one of the most common terminologies used in financial reporting. This principle is used in guidelines ranging from auditing and financial standards to the Companies Act 2006. It is primarily used to describe the required standard of financial reporting, but it is also used to justify decisions which require a certain amount of arbitrary judgement.

Under the IASB the term fair presentation is made in accordance with the International Financial Reporting Standards (IFRS). Under the Companies Act 2006 the true and fair view does not have to abide by IFRS standards, but UK law obliges companies to produce a true and fair view in agreement with international standards.

5.2 True and fair override

Sometimes a business entity does not wish to follow a particular accounting standard, considering that if it does so, the requirement of the basic accounting principle of 'fair presentation' may be compromised. The judgement exercised by management in this case is said to represent the 'fair presentation override'. A 'true and fair' override implies that a company can depart from the international accounting standards in extremely rare circumstances.

However, the true and fair requirement remains fundamentally important in both UK GAAP and IFRS. Section 393 of the Companies Act 2006 requires that the directors of a company must not approve accounts unless they are satisfied that they present a true and fair view. The true and fair requirement has been fundamental to accounting in the UK for many years. It is a requirement of both UK and EU law

True and fair is not something that is merely a separate add-on to accounting standards. Rather the whole essence of standards is to provide recognition, measurement, presentation, and disclosure for specific aspects of financial reporting in a way that reflects economic reality and hence provides a true and fair view.

In the rare circumstance that compliance with standards will result in misleading financial statements (i.e. financial statements which do not provide a true and fair view) management can disregard a standard or standards to make the statements true and fair, using such procedures that, in their opinion, will help to create a true and fair financial statement.

In circumstances when management recognises it has to depart from an IFRS, the business entity must disclose:

- that management has produced financial statements with a true and fair view;
- that it has complied with all the standards, except it has departed from a particular requirement to achieve fair presentation;
- the title of the IFRS from which the entity has departed;
- the reason for the departure from the IFRS;
- the treatment required by the IFRS and the alternative treatment adopted;
- why the treatment required by the IFRS may be misleading; and
- the financial effect of departure on each element of the financial statement.

 TEST YOUR KNOWLEDGE 5.6

(a) Explain what is meant by 'fair' presentation and 'true and fair' view.
(b) Explain what is meant by 'true and fair override' and give at least two examples of how this can occur.

---

6 The directors' report

6.1 The directors' report

The **directors' report** is an aspect of the annual financial report produced by the board of directors of a business entity. It details the state of the company and its compliance with a set of financial, accounting and corporate social responsibility (CSR) disclosures. The UK has a mandated requirement for a directors' report in the interests of greater transparency and accountability and it is required under UK company law.

6.1.1 The purpose the report

The need for a directors' report in a set of financial results arose because of the demand for greater transparency in corporate governance. The directors' report must contain a declaration that the directors are not aware of any other information that the auditors might need to prepare their audit report. In this regard the auditor will pay attention to matters in the director's report when assessing the financial information in the annual report.

The directors' report allows shareholders to assess the financial viability of a company, anticipate risks in the market and future growth, and whether the business has the necessary capacity to identify/expand new opportunities. In essence, it is a business review. The directors' report is further supported by information included in the directors' remuneration report and the financial information. The EU's Accounts Modernisation Directive for EU listed companies requires a director's report. Aspects of the directors' report touch upon conforming to IFRS standards. However, it mostly reviews the performance of the past year.

6.2 Legal requirements

Section 415 of the Companies Act 2006 places a duty on directors to produce an annual director's report. Under s. 416, the contents must include the directors' names and the company's principal activities. The critical requirement is found in s. 417(1), under which a business review must be carried out (for large companies). However, smaller companies with fewer employees and less turnover are exempt for this purpose by statutory instrument.

Under s. 417(2), directors must explain how they have fulfilled the directors' duty under s. 172 of the CA 2006 to 'promote the success of the company' with regard to all its stakeholders (including the long-term interests of shareholders, employees, the environment, the community) while maintaining a high business reputation.

Section 417(3) requires that a fair review of risks and uncertainties facing the company must be explained (a requirement of the Accounts Modernisation Directive). Section 417(4) requires a 'retrospective' analysis of the business' development in the last year, as required by the directive.

Under s. 417(5), public companies must state the main trends in the business, provide information about the company's effect on the environment and its employees, including any contractual arrangements (through supply chains) that are essential to the company. Public companies must either comply with this provision or explain why they have not complied.

All analysis, under s. 417(6) and mandated by the directive, must use key performance indicators (KPIs), unless the company is a small or medium-sized (SME) company. Where appropriate, s. 417(8) requires that accounts are explained.

Under s. 463(1) civil liability follows, for false or misleading statements in the director's report. Compensation must be paid for any loss caused to the company, but only the company (i.e. no groups except the board of directors or company members with the power to bring derivative claims) can sue. Liability only arises for an intentional or reckless act, or a dishonest omission.

According to s. 496, the company auditor must give its own brief report on the director's report. This only indicates a company's economic robustness and states whether the report is inconsistent with anything in the accounts.

Opening extract of the 2011 directors' report for Mothercare plc

The directors present their report on the affairs of the group, together with the financial statements and auditor's report for the 52-week period ended 26 March 2011. The corporate governance statement set out on pages 30 to 35 forms part of this report. The chairman's statement at page 4 gives further information on the work of the board during the period. The principal activity of the group is as a specialist multi-channel retailer and wholesaler of products for mothers-to-be, babies and children under the Mothercare and Early Learning Centre brands. It also owns and operates Gurgle. com, the social networking site for parents ....

TEST YOUR KNOWLEDGE 5.7

(a) What is the purpose of the directors' report?
(b) What major items/themes should be covered in a directors' report?

7 The chair's report

The chair's report is included in the annual report of large companies in which the chair of the board of directors gives an overview of the company's performance and prospects. The chairman's report further discusses changes in board personnel, initiatives and past and future activities of the company. A chair's report is more of a customary requirement rather than a legal obligation. In the UK, companies listed on the London Stock Exchange traditionally provide a chair's report which complements the director's report.

The chair's report also touches upon other factors that have a bearing on the company and its stakeholders. These may include:

7.1 Board development

The chair will usually discuss any changes to the board (e.g. if a director's tenure has lapsed or new director has been appointed). Director's duties and responsibilities will also be mentioned. The chairman will also outline any procedural processes followed after the appointment of new directors.

7.2 Board governance

Corporate governance is at the forefront of company matters. In this regard the chair will discuss important issues that are relevant to the good governance of the company and provide some insight into how the board has managed/improved corporate governance within the company.

7.3 Investor communications

Akin to good corporate governance is the issue of board communication with investors. Since investors provide the funding by which companies exist, it is important that their stakeholder interests are accounted for. The chair will report issues relating to investor communication and the roles and responsibilities allocated to particular board members in this regard.

7.4 Executive pay

Executive pay has gained much publicity of late, particularly that of bankers post the credit crunch in 2008. Executive pay will continue to attract attention from the public.

Shareholder concerns at levels of executive pay at AVIVA (one of UK's largest insurance companies) resulted in shareholders voting down executive pay at the 2012 Annual General Meeting (AGM). AVIVA's chief executive resigned soon after the AGM.

The chair's role is to explain how the remuneration committee has evolved the pay structure and what measures it has undertaken to ensure that bonus pay (in particular) is aligned to shareholder interests.

7.5 Strategy development

This is one of the most important aspects of the chair's report to shareholders. A typical analysis of business strategy may be reported by the chairman along the following lines:

Strategy development was a recurrent and important theme ... with investors. Our Board strategy reviews have progressed from being budget centred and informed by detailed management presentation to being driven by an agenda set by Board members themselves which looks to the longer-term direction and time horizon of the business ...'

Opening extract of Chairman's report of Mothercare plc 2011
This year marks the fiftieth anniversary of the founding of Mothercare by Selim Zilkha in September 1961. Since 2002, when Ben Gordon and I joined the Group, your board and management have made considerable progress in transforming Mothercare from a UK business into a globally recognised parenting company with brands that resonate with the consumer ...

Ian Peacock (Chair Mothercare plc)

 TEST YOUR KNOWLEDGE 5.8

(a) What is meant by fair presentation and true and fair view?
(b) What is meant by true and fair override? Give at least two examples of how this can occur.

 STOP AND THINK 5.1

Left to itself, do you think the board of directors could be transparent in reporting its financial accounts?

 END OF CHAPTER QUESTIONS

5.1 Give a definition of ASSET and LIABILITY. Give three examples of each. Why would they be classified as an asset or liability?

5.2 Demonstrate the meaning of 'recognition' in accounting.

5.3 What is impairment? Demonstrate the basis for an impairment test.

5.4 Explain each of the following terms:
(a) Going concern.
(b) Accruals.

5.5 Explain why companies should be deterred from overstating profits and understating liabilities.

5.6 Explain the responsibilities of directors of a company towards their shareholders in relation to published financial reports.

5.7 Alibi Ltd bought (and capitalised as a non-current asset) an 'off-the-shelf' computer system at a cost of £1 million. A few months afterwards the manufacturer dropped the price of the same system to £700,000.
What accounting action should Alibi Ltd take as a result of this action?

(a) Increase the depreciation of the computer system.
(b) Impair the carrying amount of the computer system.
(c) Recognise the reduction as an impairment indicator and carry out an impairment test.
(d) No action required.

5.8 Reporter plc, a newspaper publisher, entered into a four-year lease agreement with Admac plc for a printing machine on 1 January 2009 on which date the machine being leased was delivered and a deposit of £38,211 paid to the lessor. The initial direct cost incurred in negotiating the lease amounted to £4,000.
The lease agreement provides for four equal payments of £230,010 due on 31 December annually with the first payment due on 31 December 2009. The fair value of the machine on 1 January 2009 was £800,000. The estimated useful life of the machine is four years.
Ken Wood is expected to insure and maintain the printing machine over the lease period.

END OF CHAPTER QUESTIONS

Ken Wood's similarly owned assets are depreciated on a straight-line basis. The implicit interest rate within the lease is 8%.

Required

Using the information given above, calculate the amounts to be shown in the financial statements of Reporter Plc for the years ended 31 December 2009 and 2010.

5.9 The broad principles of accounting for tangible non-current assets involve distinguishing between capital and revenue expenditure, measuring the cost of assets, determining how they should be depreciated and dealing with the problems of subsequent measurement and subsequent expenditure. IAS 16 'Property, Plant and Equipment' seeks to improve consistency in these areas.

Required

Explain:

(a)   how the initial cost of tangible non-current assets should be measured; and

(b)   the circumstances in which subsequent expenditure on those assets should be capitalised.

5.10 If the directors' report or an aspect of it is inconsistent with the financial review of the external auditor, what duty is placed upon the directors to ensure that their report is consistent with the annual financial report?

5.11 Alphabet Ltd secures a long-term loan agreement from its bankers. The purpose of the loan is to invest in the land and buildings owned by the company to bring them within the requirements of the relevant health and safety legislation. The loan is for £1.5 million over 13 years with an annual payment (in arrears) of £170,000; however the final payment in year 13 will be a reduced amount of £154,396. The implied rate of interest is 5%.

Required

Prepare a schedule of repayments clearly showing capital and interest payments and the balance reducing after each annual payment.

6 Purpose of the cash flow statement

■ CONTENTS

1 Introduction
2 Purpose of the statement of cash flows
3 Cash and cash equivalents
4 Components of the statement of cash flows
5 Methods for preparation of statement of cash flows
6 Further guidance on statement cash flows
7 Interpretation of cash flow information and disclosures
8 Limitations of statement of cash flows

■ LEARNING OUTCOMES

Chapters 6: Statement of Cash Flows – covers the syllabus section entitled 'financial statements for single companies in compliance with legal and regulatory requirements'. Chapter 6 discusses in depth matters of regulatory nature and disclosure issues. After reading and understanding the contents of the chapter, working through all the Worked Examples and Practice Questions, you should be able to:

- appreciate the purpose of a statement of cash flows and its usefulness to users of financial information;
- discuss and explain the concept of cash and cash equivalents in light of IAS 7 and the limitations of classifying items under cash and cash equivalents;
- explain the components of a statement of cash flow statement under IAS 7;
- understand and prepare a statement of cash flow statement under both the direct and indirect methods as guided by IAS 7;
- be able to interpret a cash flow statement together with the other financial statements; and
- realise the limitations of a cash flow statement and what other useful information could be used to make comprehension clearer.

1 Introduction

The statement of cash flows is one of the principal financial statements that must be disclosed together with the other principal statements, namely, the statement of comprehensive income, the statement of financial position and the statement of changes in equity. IAS 7 'Statement of Cash Flows' provides the basis under which the cash flow statement is to be prepared and the items to be disclosed.

The statement of cash flows reports the *cash* generated and used during the reporting period. While the statement of cash flows is referred to in this chapter over a 12-month reporting period, companies can and do prepare an interim statement of cash flows for quarterly and half-yearly reporting. IAS 7 requires the disclosure of cash flows under three main headings: operating, investing and financing activities, plus any supplemental information supporting the statement:

- *Operating activities* Converts the items reported on the income statement from the accrual basis of accounting to cash.
- *Investing activities* Reports the purchase and sale of long-term investments and property, plant and equipment.

- *Financing activities* Reports the issuance and repurchase of the company's own bonds and stock and the payment of dividends.
- *Supplemental information* Reports the exchange of significant items that did not involve cash and reports the amount of income taxes paid and interest paid.
- The statement of cash flows explains the changes in cash and cash equivalents. Reporting entities can choose between the *'direct'* or *'indirect'* method of cash flows disclosure on the basis of IAS 7. The various terminologies used in preparing and presented the statement of cash flows will be discussed as they arise.

TEST YOUR KNOWLEDGE 6.1

Describe the four elements of a statement of cash flows and how they might be useful to users.

2 Purpose of the statement of cash flows

Because the income statement is prepared under the accruals basis of accounting, the revenues reported may not have been collected at the reporting date with outstanding trade receivables being reported in the statement of financial position. Similarly, the expenses reported on the statement of comprehensive income (income statement) might not have been paid with outstanding trade payables reported in the statement of financial position. The statement of cash flows facilitates an assessment of a company's liquidity as well as determining both the use of cash within a company and the ability of a company to generate cash. Movements in cash flows can impact the liquidity position of a company in various ways:

1 The cash from operating activities is compared to the company's net income. If the cash from operating activities is consistently greater than the net income, the company's net income or earnings are said to be of a 'high quality'. If the cash from operating activities is less than net income, this raises issues as to why the reported net income is greater than cash flows generated.
2 Typically investors believe that 'cash is king'. The cash flow statement identifies the cash that is flowing in and out of the company. If a company is consistently generating more cash than it is using, it will be able to increase its dividend, buy back some of its shares, reduce debt, or acquire another company/asset/investment. All of these are perceived to be good for shareholder value.
3 Some financial models are based upon cash flow. While in the short term, a company's performance is measured on a profit/profitability basis, in the long term, investors and stakeholders view the financial health of a company on the present value of all future cash flows.

3 Cash and cash equivalents

IAS 7 states that:

> The objective of IAS 7 is to require the presentation of information about the historical changes in cash and cash equivalents of an entity by means of a statement of cash flows, which classifies cash flows during the period according to operating, investing, and financing activities.

Cash equivalents are said to be highly liquid short-term assets that are readily convertible to known cash amounts (IAS 7 para. 7). Additionally, there must be little risk of change in value to cash equivalents. IAS 7 further suggests that, to qualify as cash equivalents, investments should normally have a maturity of three months or less.

Technically speaking, items that do not fall under the banner of operating, investing and financing activities do not get reported in the statement of cash flows. However, items that are deemed to be cash or cash equivalents are excluded since these items form part of the cash management of a business entity rather than the three reportable components. Cash management includes the investment of excess cash in cash equivalents.

 **WORKED EXAMPLE 6.1**

Exel Ltd's financial year end is 31 December 2011. The company purchased some high quality corporate bonds as a short-term investment. The bonds were purchased on 1 September 2011 with a maturity date of 31 December 2011.

Required

The CEO of Exel has included the corporate bonds in the cash and cash equivalent statement of financial position. Advise the CEO if this is correct.

Answer

At the date of purchase of the corporate bonds, 1 September 2011, the bonds had a maturity date of four months. However, this does not comply with the three months or less rule in on the basis of IAS 7, so the bonds should not be classified as cash equivalent.

---

4 Components of the statement of cash flows

4.1 Cash flows from operating activities

Cash inflow and outflow generated by the normal course of business activity comes under operating activities. These include the revenues generated through production and the expenses incurred due to delivery of the company's product(s) resulting in cash transactions. Cash inflows are generated by sales, while cash outflows are incurred by expenses. The expenses may include production costs and distribution costs, as well as expenses for administration and taxes. Under IAS 7, operating cash flows include:

- operating profit;
- receipts from the sale of goods or services;
- receipts for the sale of loans, debt or equity instruments in a trading portfolio;
- interest received on loans;
- dividends received on equity securities;
- payments to suppliers for goods and services;
- payments to employees or on behalf of employees; and
- interest payments (alternatively, this can be reported under financing activities in IAS 7).

Items which are added back to (or subtracted from, as appropriate) the net income figure (which is found on the income statement) to arrive at cash flows from operations generally include:

- depreciation (loss of tangible asset value over time);
- deferred tax;
- amortisation (loss of intangible asset value over time); and
- any gains or losses associated with the sale of a non-current asset, because associated cash flows do not belong in the operating section (unrealised gains/losses are also added back from the income statement).

The above adjustments are only necessary if the indirect method is used, in which case the following adjustments will also be required:

- any increases/decreases in inventory; and
- any increase/decrease in receivables and payables.

These will also need to be added back. Having regard to the above items, the net cash flows generated account for the cash used in normal business activity.

4.2 Cash flows from investing activities

Non-current assets purchased and cash payments made are reported in the investing activities. Cash receipts on disposal of non-current assets are also disclosed in this section. Non-current assets may include, but are not limited to, such items as:

- purchase or sale of an asset (assets can be land, building, equipment, securities, etc.);
- financial investments (equities and loans); and
- acquisition of other businesses.

Loans made outside the company will generate cash inflow in the form of interest received. Investment in other companies will generate cash inflow in the form of dividends received. In both cases the actual receipt of cash will be disclosed in the statement of cash flows.

4.3 Cash flows from financing activities

Financing activities typically include long-term bank loans and cash from investors such as new share issue, debentures and bonds. The company will also make cash payments to shareholders in the form of dividends representing an outflow of cash. Company taxes paid will be disclosed in this section and represent actual cash payments made by the reporting date. IAS 7 gives some guidance on what can be included under financing activities:

- proceeds from issuing short-term or long-term debt;
- payments of dividends;
- payments for repurchase of company shares;
- repayment of debt principal, including capital leases; and
- for non-profit organisations, receipts of donor-restricted cash that is limited to long-term purposes.

The reason for segregating how cash flows arise in a business is to create a level of transparency for users. It is expected that the finances of companies should be generated through normal day-to-day activities (i.e. operating activities). This indicates how the business is performing and its long-term prospects.

 **TEST YOUR KNOWLEDGE** 6.2

Explain why users of cash flow information would find it useful to have disclosure under the three headings of operating, investing and financing activities.

---

5 Methods for preparation of the statement of cash flows

IAS 7 also gives guidance on how the operating cash flows should be prepared. Basically, two methods are indicated: the 'direct' and 'indirect' methods. Companies should use these methods to prepare the operating cash flows.

5.1 Direct method

The direct method of operating cash flows disclosure shows cash receipts and cash disbursements from operating activities. The difference between these two amounts in the net cash flow from operating activates represents cash flows from operating activities. In other words, the direct method deducts the operating cash disbursements from the operating cash receipts. The direct method presents a condensed cash receipt and cash disbursement statement. IAS 7 states that the **direct method** should show each major class of gross cash receipts and gross cash payments. Under the direct method, the operating cash flows section of the statement of cash flows would look something like this:

Cash receipts from customers	xx,xxx
Cash paid to suppliers .	xx,xxx
Cash paid to employees	xx,xxx
Cash paid for other operating expenses	xx,xxx
Interest paid	xx,xxx
Income taxes paid	xx,xxx
Net cash from operating activities	**xx,xxx**

Under IAS 7, dividends received may be reported either under operating activities or investment activities. If taxes paid are directly linked to operating activities, they are reported under operating activities; if the taxes are directly linked to investment activities or financing activities, they are reported under investment or financing activities (see below).

WORKED EXAMPLE 6.2

	£	£
Cash flows from operating activities		
Cash receipts from customers (see note 1)	15500	
Cash paid to suppliers and employees (see note 2)	–7000	
Cash generated from operations	**7500**	
Interest paid	–2800	
Income taxes paid	–4200	
Net cash flows from operating activities		2500
Cash flows from (used in) investing activities		
Proceeds from the sale of equipment	8200	
Dividends received	2400	
Net cash flows from investing activities		10600
Cash flows from (used in) financing activities		
Dividends paid	-2200	
Net cash flows used in financing activities		–2200
Net increase in cash and cash equivalents		9,900
Cash and cash equivalents, beginning of year		–1800
Closing cash and cash equivalents		8100

WORKED EXAMPLE **6.2** *continued*

Note:

1 Cash receipts from customers – derived through sales adjusted by opening and closing receivables. By way of an example, this can be calculated as:

	£
	£
Opening receivables	6500
Sales	22000
	28500
Closing receivables	–13000
Cash received from customers	15500

Opening and closing receivables are simply made-up figures to demonstrate how cash received from customers is arrived at.

2 Cash paid to suppliers and employees – derived through expenses incurred in the period adjusted by opening and closing payables and accruals. By way of an example, this can be calculated as:

	£
Opening payables and accruals	3500
Expenses incurred in the period	12250
	15750
Closing payables and accruals	8750
Cash paid to suppliers and employees	7000

Opening and closing payables are simply made-up figures to demonstrate how cash paid to suppliers and employees is arrived at.

TEST YOUR KNOWLEDGE **6.3**

Explain the concept of the direct method of cash flow and which section of the statement of cash flow this method relates to.

5.2 Indirect method

The indirect method uses net income as a starting point and adjusts for all transactions for non-cash items (e.g. depreciation and taxes). Adjustments are then made for all cash-based transactions. An increase in an asset account is subtracted from net income, and an increase in a liability account is added back to net income. This method converts accrual-basis net income (or loss) into cash flow by using a series of additions and deductions.

5.3 Rules for calculating cash flows under operating activities

The example below describes how to calculate cash flows from operating activities when two-year comparative statement of financial position and the net income figures are given. Cash flows from operating activities can be calculated by adjusting net income relative to the change in start and end balances of cash at bank/overdraft, inventories/receivables and payables, and sometimes, non-current assets. When comparing the change in non-current assets over a year, we must be certain that these changes were caused entirely by their depreciation/devaluation rather than purchases or sales (i.e. they must be operating items not providing or using cash; or they are non-operating items).

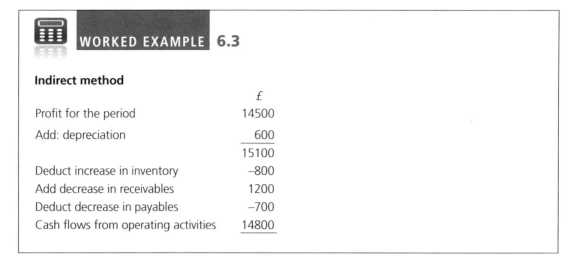

WORKED EXAMPLE 6.3

Indirect method

	£
Profit for the period	14500
Add: depreciation	600
	15100
Deduct increase in inventory	−800
Add decrease in receivables	1200
Deduct decrease in payables	−700
Cash flows from operating activities	14800

Rules for calculating operating cash flows are described below:

- **Depreciation**: Since depreciation represents an accounting expense and is a non-cash item, it has to be added back to net profit.
- **Inventory**: An increase in inventory means the business has used cash and hence represents a cash outflow. If inventory increases from one period to the next, cash is decreased in the business, however, when inventory decreases, cash increases.
- **Receivables**: Receivables represent goods and services sold to customers on credit. If receivables increase form one period to the next this has an effect of decreasing cash of the business. As such, if receivables decrease from one period to the next this has an effect of increasing cash inflow; hence these must be added to net profit.
- **Payables**: Conversely similar to receivables, payables represent payment outstanding to suppliers of the business. Likewise, if payables increase from one period to the next this represents an inflow of cash to the business and should be added to the net profits. However, if payables decrease we must deduct the difference from the net profit.
- **Other items**:
  - **Interest expense** an accounting figure which should be added back to net profit; if this is a positive figure in the income statement then it should be deducted. Interest actually paid in cash should be deducted from profits for the period.
  - **Tax expenses** shown on the face of income statement must be must be added back to the net profit as they represent an accounting tax estimate. However, taxes actually paid in cash must be deducted from the net profit figure.
  - **Dividends paid** will be deducted from the net profit as these represent cash outflow from a business. However, dividends can be shown under 'cash from financing activities'.

WORKED EXAMPLE 6.4

The following information is relevant to Gamma Ltd for the year ended 31 December 2011:

Notes:

1 During the year depreciation of £17,000 was charged to cost of sales and £23,000 to administrative expenses.
2 Plant and equipment disposed of during the year had an original cost of £90,000 and accumulated depreciation of £84,000. Cash received on disposal was £21,500. Additions to property, plant and equipment were purchased for cash.
3 The 2011 dividend of £50,000 was paid during the year ended 31 December 2011.
4 A cash issue of 20,000 £1 ordinary shares were made during the year for £2.10 per share.
5 All finance costs were paid in the year.

```
┌─────────────────────────────────────────────────────────────────────────────┐
```

WORKED EXAMPLE **6.4** *continued*

The financial statements of Gamma Ltd are given below:

Income statement for the year ended 31 December 2011

	£
Revenue	900000
Cost of sales (Note1)	−670000
Gross profit	230000
Administration expenses (Note 2)	−87800
Distribution costs	−1300
Operating profit	140900
Finance costs (Note 5)	−17600
Profit before taxation	123300
Taxation	−34000
Profit for the period	89300

Statement of financial position as at 31 December

	2011	2010
	£	£
Assets		
Non-current assets		
Property, plant and equipment at cost (Note 2)	350000	334000
Accumulated depreciation	−110,000	−154,000
	240000	180000
Current assets		
Inventory	82000	83900
Trade receivables	54500	68000
Cash and cash equivalents	43500	10000
	180000	161900
Total assets	420000	341900
Equity and liabilities		
Equity		
Ordinary share capital (£1 ord. shares – Note 4)	120000	100000
Share premium (Note 4)	72000	50000
Revaluation reserve	20000	10000
Retained earnings	55400	16100
Total equity	267400	176100
Non-current liabilities		
Long-term loans	90000	100000
Current liabilities		
Trade payables	38200	40000
Taxation	24400	7000
Bank overdraft	0	18800
	62600	65800
Total liabilities	152600	165800
Total equity and liabilities	420000	341900

Required

You are required to prepare a statement of cash flows for Gamma Ltd for the year ended 31 December 2011, using the indirect method in accordance with IAS 7.

WORKED EXAMPLE **6.4** *continued*

Answer:

Gamma Ltd – Statement of cash flows for the year ended 31 December 2011

Cash flows from operating activities	Item	£
Profit for the period		89300
Add: depreciation	1	40000
Gain on disposal of asset	2	−15500
Inventory	5	1900
Trade receivables	6	13500
Tax expense	7	34000
Payables	8	−1800
Tax paid	7	−16600
Net cash flows from operating activities		144800
Cash flows from investment activities		
Purchase of property, plant and equipment	4	−96000
Disposal of property, plant and equipment	Note 2	21500
Net cash flows from investment activities		−74500
Cash flows from financing activities		
Share issue	Note 4	42000
Dividends paid	Note 3	−50000
Repayment of long-term loan	9	−10000
Net cash flows from financing activities		−18000
Net increase/(decrease) in cash and cash equivalents		52300
Opening cash and cash equivalents		-8800
Closing cash and cash equivalents		43500

Notes 2, 3 and 4 are from the question

Calculation of cash flow items:

Item 1: Depreciation write-back

Depreciation charge	£	
Opening depreciation	154000	
Less: Depreciation on sale of asset	−84000	
	70000	
To operating activities	40000	Balancing figure
Closing depreciation	110000	

The sum of £40,000 will be added back to net profit in operating activities

---

[calc icon] **WORKED EXAMPLE** **6.4** *continued*

Item 2: Gain/(Loss) on disposal of assets write-back

Gain/(Loss) on disposal	£
BV of disposed assets	90000
Less: Accumulated depreciation	–84000
Net BV of disposed assets	6000
Cash received on disposal	21500
Gain on disposal of assets	15500

BV = Book value

The sum of £15,500 will be added back to net profit in operating activities

Item 3: Gain/(Loss) on revaluation of assets write-back

Gain/(Loss) on revaluation	£	
Opening revaluation reserve	10000	
Gain on revaluation of assets	10000	Balancing figure
Closing revaluation reserve	20000	

Item 4: Asset purchased for cash

Purchase of assets	£	
Opening PPE	334000	
Disposal of asset	–90000	
BV of assets before revaluation	244000	
Gain on revaluation of assets	10000	
BV of assets after revaluation	254000	
To operating activities	96000	Balancing figure
Closing PPE	350000	

PPE = Property, plant and equipment; BV = Book value

The sum of £96,000 will be deducted from investing activities

Item 5: Inventory adjustment

Inventory	£	
Opening inventory	83900	
Decrease in inventory	–1900	Balancing figure
Closing inventory	82000	

The sum of £1,900 will be added back to net profit in operating activities

WORKED EXAMPLE **6.4** *continued*

Item 6: Trade receivables adjustment

Trade receivables	£	
Opening trade receivables	68000	
Decrease in trade receivables	−13500	Balancing figure
Closing trade receivables	54500	

The sum of £13,500 will be added back to net profit in operating activities

Item 7: Tax expense and paid adjustments

Tax expense and tax paid	£	
Opening tax balance	7000	
Tax for the year	34000	From income statement
	41000	
Tax paid in the year	16600	Balancing figure
Closing tax balance	24400	

The sum of £34,000 will be added back to net profit in operating activities
The sum of £16,600 will be deducted from net profit in operating activities

Item 8: Payables adjustment

Payables	£	
Opening payables	40000	
Decrease in payables	−1800	Balancing figure
Closing payables	38200	

The sum of £1,800 will be deducted from net profit in operating activities

Item 9: Long-term loan adjustment

Long-term loan	£	
Opening long-term loan	100000	
Decrease in long-term loan	−10000	Balancing figure
Closing long-term loan	90000	

The sum of £10,000 will be deducted from financing activities

Item 10: Short-term borrowing adjustment

Short-term borrowing	£	
Opening short-term balance	18800	
Decrease in short-term balance	−18800	Balancing figure
Closing long-term loan	0	

6 Further guidance on statement cash flows

IAS 7 gives additional advice on the preparation of items disclosed on the face of the statement of cash flows. The additional guidance relates to specific treatment items and the way they should be presented:

- The exchange rate used for translation of transactions denominated in a foreign currency should be the rate in effect at the date of the cash flows (IAS 7.25).
- Cash flows of foreign subsidiaries should be translated at the exchange rates prevailing when the cash flows took place (IAS 7.26).
- Aggregate cash flows relating to acquisitions and disposals of subsidiaries and other business units should be presented separately and classified as investing activities, with specified additional disclosures (IAS 7.39). The aggregate cash paid or received as consideration should be reported net of cash and cash equivalents acquired or disposed of (IAS 7.42).
- Cash flows from investing and financing activities should be reported gross by major class of cash receipts and major class of cash payments except for the following cases, which may be reported on a net basis: (IAS 7.22–24).

Cash receipts and payments on behalf of customers (e.g. receipt and repayment of demand deposits by banks, and receipts collected on behalf of and paid over to the owner of a property).

Cash receipts and payments for items in which the turnover is quick, the amounts are large, and the maturities are short, generally less than three months (e.g. charges and collections from credit card customers, and purchase and sale of investments).

Cash receipts and payments relating to deposits by financial institutions.

Cash advances *and loans made to customers and repayments thereof.*

- Investing and financing transactions which do not require the use of cash should be excluded from the statement of cash flows, but they should be separately disclosed elsewhere in the financial statements (IAS 7.43).
- The components of cash and cash equivalents should be disclosed, and a reconciliation presented to amounts reported in the statement of financial position (IAS 7.45).
- The amount of cash and cash equivalents held by the entity that is not available for use by the group should be disclosed, together with a commentary by management (IAS 7.48).

Source: Deloitte IAS Plus[1]

7 Interpretation of cash flow information and disclosures

A company's cash flow can provide useful information on its ability to meet current and future commitments. The cash flow of some companies move much faster than others mainly due to the nature of their business and their business sector. Broadly speaking companies whose customers are the general public (e.g. Tesco, Sainsbury, Mothercare etc), tend to deal primarily in cash transactions, hence they have a faster cash cycle. If we were to compare the cash flow statements of these companies we would find trends in the cash cycle.

Analysis of cash flow trends and cycles allows managers to plan for difficult times and situations to ensure they can meet the company's short- and long-term commitments. Cash flow analysis can highlight when shortfalls in funding should be met with assistance from lenders and allow decision-makers to plan for either short-term or long-term borrowing.

Cash flow analysis can further help in cash flow management related to trade receivables and trade payables. In times of financial difficulty, management may need to review credit policy. When a company has a strong reputation, it can negotiate shorter credit terms with its suppliers. By the same token, a strong company can negotiate longer credit periods for payment of debt, enabling it to hold on to cash for longer periods.

The example below demonstrates how a statement of cash flows was reported by Sainsbury plc for the period ending March 2011.

WORKED EXAMPLE **6.5**

	Note	Group 2011 £m	2010 £m
Cash flows from operating activities			
Cash generated from operations	26	**1,138**	1,206
Interest paid		**(126)**	(111)
Corporation tax paid		**(158)**	(89)
Net cash generated from/(used in) operating activities		**854**	1,006
Cash flows from investing activities			
Purchase of property, plant and equipment		**(1,136)**	(1,036)
Purchase of intangible assets		**(15)**	(11)
Proceeds from disposal of property, plant and equipment		**282**	139
Acquisition of and investment in subsidiaries, net of cash acquired	12	**(1)**	–
Investment in joint ventures		**(2)**	(2)
Investment in financial assets		**(50)**	(10)
Interest received		**19**	18
Dividends received		**1**	2
Net cash (used in)/generated from investing activities		**(902)**	(900)
Cash flows from financing activities			
Proceeds from issuance of ordinary shares		**17**	250
Repayment of short-term borrowings		**(11)**	(36)
Proceeds from long-term borrowings		**45**	235
Repayment of long-term borrowings		**(61)**	(74)
Repayment of capital element of obligations under finance lease payments		**(3)**	(2)
Interest elements of obligations under finance lease payments		**(4)**	(3)
Dividends paid	10	**(269)**	(241)
Net cash (used in)/generated from financing activities		**(286)**	129
Net (decrease)/increase in cash and cash equivalents		**(334)**	235
Opening cash and cash equivalents		**834**	599
Closing cash and cash equivalents	26	**500**	834

7.1 A brief commentary on Sainsbury plc's statement of cash flows

The statement of cash flows for Sainsbury plc for the year ending 2011 more than suggests that the closing net cash flows were lower in 2011 (£500 million) as compared to the previous year (£834 million). The main reasons for this decline are discussed below:

- **Cash flows from operating activities:**
  - the interest paid in 2011 represents a 13.5% (£15 million) increase over 2010;
  - there was a substantial increase in the actual amount of corporation tax paid in 2011 (£158 million) as compared to 2010 (£89 million); and
  - the combination of taxes and interest paid resulted in 15% lower cash flows from operating activities. In the same period the company's statement of financial position (available from www.sainsburys.co.uk) shows higher inventory and receivables indicating that more cash left the company than it received.

■ **Cash flows from investing activities:**
  – Net cash outflows from investing activities changed very little in 2011 (£902 million) compared to 2010 (£900 million). However, £100 million more was used to purchase PPE in 2011 (£1,136 million) over the previous year (£1.036 million).
  – The higher expenditure on PPE was more or less cancelled out by the proceeds on disposal of assets in 2011 (£282 million) over 2010 proceeds of disposal (£139 million) amounting to £143 million cash inflow.
  – Cash outflow of £50 million represents investment in financial assets which is £40 million above that spent in 2010 (£10 million).
■ **Cash flows from financing activities:**
  – There was substantial outflow of cash in 2011 (£286 million) compared to an inflow of cash in 2010 of £129 million.
  – In 2010 proceeds of issuance of new shares of £250 million and further cash inflow of £235 million due to proceeds from long-term borrowings represented most of the 2010 cash movement under financing activities.
  – Higher dividend payments of £269 million in 2011 compared to 2010 dividend payments of £241 million was another factor that contributed to the net cash outflows under financing activities.

Of course are many other issues that can be discussed on Sainsbury's statement of cash flows. However, analysis can be made in conjunction with the other financial statements and narratives to give a clearer picture over the state of affairs of the company.

8 Limitations of statement of cash flows

One problem often stated in relation to IAS 7 is that the classifications used are too broad. It could be argued that if a company's expenditure was explained in more detail, it would give users of financial information much greater insight in to the underlying economic reality. Items such as research and development, mining and exploration costs and marketing expenditure should be disclosed in the cash flow statement. However, the issue arises as to where such expenditure should be disclosed (i.e. under operating or investing activities).

The indirect method causes confusion for some users as it is based on the statement of financial position movements and reconciliation. For this reason it has been argued that IAS 7 should only permit the direct method. However, companies could counter argue that new accounting procedures would need to be adopted to keep track of cash movements.

Another argument in favour of the indirect method is that a reconciliation of cash flows from operating activities from net profit allows users to see if profit figures are being manipulated; this would facilitate a greater degree of analysis and would allow users to make more informed economic decisions. Similarly, cash raised through financing instruments such as loans, should not form part of cash flows from operating activities, but should be shown separately from cash flows generated through business activity.

TEST YOUR KNOWLEDGE 6.5

(a) Discuss the potential limitations of the statement of cash flows.
(b) What other information could usefully be included?

STOP AND THINK 6.1

Do you think we should simply revert to accounting on a cash basis?

END OF CHAPTER QUESTIONS

6.1 In a statement of cash flows, which of the following items will NOT appear in the cash flow from investing activities section when using the indirect method?
   (a)   purchase of non-current assets;
   (b)   taxation paid;
   (c)   purchase of investments; and
   (d)   disposal proceeds of non-current assets.

6.2 In accordance with IAS 7 'Statement of Cash Flows', which of the following categories is NOT used to classify cash flows in a statement of cash flows?
   (a)   managing activities;
   (b)   financing activities;
   (c)   investing activities; and
   (d)   operating activities.

6.3 Why is reported profit different to a company's cash flow for a particular accounting period?

6.4 Explain the following events will impact cash flow movements:
   (a)   increase in inventory from one period to the next;
   (b)   decrease in payables;
   (c)   decrease in receivables;
   (d)   increase in the market value of a company's share price;
   (e)   gains made on disposal of a non-current asset; and
   (f)   issue of new shares at market price.

6.5 If credit sales for the year were £75 million and the trade receivables at start of the year were £20m and at the end of the year were £12 million, state how much cash was received from trade customers.

6.6 A company has made purchases of materials on credit £36 million during the year. At the beginning of the year the payables balance was £12 million. Closing payables balance was £18 million. State how much money was paid to suppliers during the year.

6.7 Give three examples of income statement items that do not involve cash payment and explain why.

6.8 The proceeds of cash sale of an item of plant amounted to £120,000. The item was originally purchased for £500,000 and had accumulated depreciation of £400,000. How will this information affect the cash flow statement?

Income statement for year ended 31 December 2011			
	£'000		
Revenue	949000		
Cost of sales	−442,000		
Gross profit	507000		
Administration expenses	−47000		
Distribution costs	−82000		
Operating profit	378000		
Finance costs	−26000		
Profit before taxation	352000		
Taxation	−36000		
Profit for the period	316000		
Extract from statement of changes to equity			
Dividends	137000		

END OF CHAPTER QUESTIONS

Statement of financial position as at 31 December	2011		2010
	£'000		£'000
Assets			
Non-current assets			
Property, plant and equipment at cost	470000		470000
Accumulated depreciation	230000		180000
	240000		290000
Current assets			
Inventory	75000		45000
Trade receivables	144000		120000
	219000		165000
Total assets	459000		455000
Equity and liabilities			
Equity			
Ordinary share capital (£1 ord. shares)	140000		100000
Share premium	8000		–
Retained earnings	121000		79000
Total equity	269000		179000
Non-current liabilities			
Long-term loans	66000		84800
Current liabilities			
Trade payables	87000		170000
Taxation	30000		18000
Bank overdraft	7000		3200
	124000		191200
Total liabilities	190000		276000
Total equity and liabilities	459000		455000

6.9 Capri Ltd has net profits of £20 million, which includes a charge of £500,000 for depreciation. During the year the inventory decreased by £800,000 and receivables increased by £200,000. Payables decreased by £400,000. You are asked to prepare a calculation of cash flows from operations.

6.10 Sarah Ltd is a manufacturer of a line of children's clothing. The information below is relevant to Sarah Ltd for the year ended 31 December 2011:

Notes:
Dividends relating to 2011 amounted to £137,000 and were paid in cash by the year end.
Issue of new shares were for 40 million ordinary £1 shares at the market price of £1.20.
There were no purchases of property, plant and equipment in the year.
Interest expense for 2011 has not been paid.

END OF CHAPTER QUESTIONS

Required

Prepare a statement of cash flows for Sarah Ltd for the year ending 31 December 2011.

Plumbus Ltd is a small engineering firm that manufactures various types of piping for industrial clients. The information below relates to 30 September 2011:

Income statement for the year ended 30 September 2011	
	£
Revenue	1200000
Cost of sales	–810000
Gross profit	390000
Administration expenses	–105000
Distribution costs	–87000
Operating profit	198000
Finance costs	–8000
Profit before taxation	190000
Taxation	–54000
Profit for the period	136000

Statement of financial position as at 30 September		
	2011	2010
Assets	£	£
Non-current assets		
Property, plant and equipment at cost	520000	418000
Accumulated depreciation	–260000	–188000
	260000	230000
Current assets		
Inventory	64000	68000
Trade receivables	38000	45000
Cash and cash equivalents	144000	54000
	246000	167000
Total assets	506000	397000
Equity and liabilities		
Equity		
Ordinary share capital (£1 ord. shares)	150000	120000
Share premium	24000	–
Revaluation reserve	18000	8000
Retained earnings	56000	33000
Total equity	248000	161000

END OF CHAPTER QUESTIONS

Non-current liabilities		
Long-term loans	224000	165000
Current liabilities		
Trade payables	12000	60000
Taxation	22000	11000
Total liabilities	258000	236000
Total equity and liabilities	506000	397000

Notes:

1 During the year a depreciation charge of £70,000 charge was made cost of sales and £32,000 to administration expenses in the income statement.

2 Plant and equipment (PPE) disposed of during the year had an original cost of £40,000 and accumulated depreciation of £30,000. Cash received on disposal was £8,000.

3 Additions to PPE were purchased for cash.

4 A cash issue of 30,000 ordinary £1 share issue were made during the year for £1.80 per share.

5 Finance costs were paid in the same year.

6 All dividends were paid in cash during the year.

Required

1 Prepare a statement of cash flows for Plumbus Ltd for the year ending 30 September 2011 using the indirect method under IAS 7.

2 Make a brief commentary on the statement of cash flows and discuss/recommend any remedial action the company should take.

Endnotes

1 Deloitte IAS Plus – IAS 7 'Statement of Cash Flows' (www.iasplus.com/standard/ias07.htm).

Group accounting and analysis and interpretation of financial reports

■ LIST OF CHAPTERS

Part 3 covers the syllabus section entitled 'Group Accounting' and 'Analysis and Interpretation of Accounts'.

■ OVERVIEW

The dismantling of international trade barriers and the ability of large corporations to be cross-listed in other countries facilitated the need for reporting that conveyed the economic reality of a business as an economic unit rather than just a legal entity within business combinations.

The ability of large corporations to unite several entities into one economic entity necessitated the need for changes to the way financial reports are prepared and presented in light of the relevant IFRS and IAS. Part 3 addresses the issues specific to this process. It looks at the different ways in which companies combine and consolidate and how this is reflected in accounts prepared for groups of companies. A separate chapter covers the impact of foreign currency transactions.

Part 3 also looks at and discusses, with relevant examples, the analysis and interpretation of financial reports. This allows users to make informed economic decisions and to evaluate emerging trends.

Each chapter ends with practice questions that require application of the knowledge gained.

7 Group accounting

■ LEARNING OUTCOMES

This chapter deals with the part of the syllabus section entitled 'Group Accounting'. After reading and understanding the contents of the chapter, working through *all* the worked examples and practice questions, you should be able to understand the group and consolidation process and:

- identify the existence of a group of companies;
- explain why parent companies are required to publish consolidated accounts and the circumstance in which this obligation does not apply;
- prepare a consolidated statement of comprehensive income and a consolidated statement of financial position that takes account of adjustments required for: goodwill; post-acquisition profits and minority interest;
- demonstrate and apply an understanding of the nature and significance of other consolidation adjustments;
- appreciate the value added to the accounting package available to external users by the existence of requirements to publish consolidated accounts;
- identify and account for associated companies and joint ventures in accordance with standard accounting requirements;
- show familiarity with the content of a consolidated cash flow statement; and
- explain the purposes and limitations of group accounts.

1 Introduction

This chapter discusses issues related to group accounting and the provisions of the IFRS and IAS that give guidance on how to disclose items in the financial statement. We start with a definition of a 'group' and explain the need for consolidated accounts and benefits to users of consolidated accounting information. The objectives of IFRS 10 'Consolidated Financial Statements' are 'to establish principles for the presentation and preparation of consolidated financial statements when an entity controls one or more other entities'.

We will discuss various terminology used in a group accounting context and give an explanation as to their meaning and application. While IFRS 10 gives guidance on preparation and presentation of consolidated accounts, IFRS 12 'Disclosure of Interests in Other Entities' sets out disclosure requirements for reporting entities that have an interest in a subsidiary, joint arrangement, associate or unconsolidated structured entity.

The need to develop an IFRS to deal specifically with issues of consolidated accounts arose due to inherent weaknesses in IAS 27. While recognising that the basic model for consolidated accounts was fine in IAS 27, inconsistency in applying the provisions of IAS 27 necessitated the need for a single combined model that met the needs of both those preparing accounts and end users of financial information in a consistent manner.

TABLE 7.1 Summary of relevant International Financial Reporting Standards

IFRS 10 (2011)	Consolidated financial statements
IAS 27	Separate financial statements
IFRS 3 (2008)	Business combinations
IAS 28	Investments in associates

1.1 Definition of key terms

- Consolidated financial statements are financial statements of a group of entities presented as those of a single economic entity.
- Consolidated financial statements are prepared when an entity *controls* another entity or entities.
- The process of consolidation involves *aggregating the amounts* shown in each of the individual accounts on a *line-by-line basis* and making appropriate adjustments to achieve *consistency of measurement* and to *eliminate double counting*.
- A group is made up of the parent entity and its subsidiaries.
- Parent entity – the entity that controls the other entities.
- A subsidiary is an entity controlled by another entity.
- According to IFRS10 *'control of an investee'* arises when an investor 'is exposed, or has rights, to variable returns from its involvement with the investee and has the ability to affect those returns through its power over the investee'.

According to IFRS 10, an investor controls an investee if and only if the investor has all of the following elements: [IFRS10:7]

- power over the investee (i.e. the investor has existing rights that gives it the ability to direct the relevant activities (the activities that significantly affect the investee's returns));
- exposure, or rights, to variable returns from its involvement with the investee; and
- the ability to use its power over the investee to affect the amount of the investor's returns.

1.2 Definition of a group

A business entity can exist in mutual relationship with other business entities in many ways. These relationships can be in the form of subsidiaries, associates, and joint ventures.

In the context of a group, IFRS 3 'Business Combinations' describes a group as a 'transaction or event in which an acquirer obtains control of one or more businesses. A business is defined as an integrated set of activities and assets that is capable of being conducted and managed for the purpose of providing a return directly to investors or other owners, members or participants'.

IFRS 10 gives a more definitive description of a group suggesting that a group exists where one enterprise (the parent) controls, either directly or indirectly, another enterprise (subsidiary). It follows that a group consists of a parent (owner) and subsidiary.

Additionally, an entity can have control over another entity or entities either directly or indirectly. The diagrams below demonstrate how direct or indirect control is achieved by a parent company:

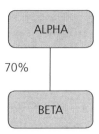

FIGURE 7.1 Direct control by a parent company

In the above figure, the parent company (Alpha) has direct control of the subsidiary company (Beta) due to its controlling rights. This is manifested through a majority shareholding in the subsidiary company of 70% of the ordinary shares.

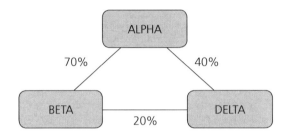

FIGURE 7.2 Indirect control by a parent company

Here, the parent company (Alpha) has an indirect control over Delta. Since Alpha has majority control over Beta (70%) and also has a 40% stake in Delta (due to the fact that Beta also has a 20% stake in Delta) Alpha has control over Delta (40% + 20%). Hence, both Beta and Delta will be regarded as subsidiaries of Alpha.

Linking together the various definitions, we can say that consolidated financial statements must be prepared where one company – the parent – controls the activities of another company – the subsidiary. So, how does one decide whether one entity is able to control another, giving rise to the obligation to prepare consolidated accounts? The basic rule, as we have seen above, is that a parent/subsidiary relationship exists where the first company owns a majority of the voting share capital of the latter company.

In a simple and straightforward world this would be enough, but the business world is neither simple nor straightforward. Over the years, various schemes were devised by managers, in conjunction with their professional advisers, with the objective of conducting a part of a company's business operations through another organisation that, although *in reality* a subsidiary, was not *in law* a subsidiary (e.g. the Special Purpose Entity (SPE)). It, therefore, became necessary to define the parent/subsidiary relationship more closely in order to prevent these abuses.

Today, control is presumed to exist (and consolidated financial statements must, therefore, be prepared) when the parent acquires more than half the voting rights of the enterprise. In the absence of a majority of voting rights, a subsidiary should be consolidated where the parent has power:

■ over more than one half of the voting rights by virtue of an agreement with other investors; or
■ to govern the financial and operating policies of the other enterprise under a contractual agreement; or
■ to appoint or remove the majority of the members of the board of directors; or
■ to cast the majority of votes at a meeting of the board of directors.

Often two or more of these tests produce the same result. For example, it is usually necessary to acquire more than half the voting shares to control the composition of the board of directors. In certain circumstances, a parent company/subsidiary company relationship may exist by applying one test but not the other.

 **WORKED EXAMPLE 7.1**

Alpha Ltd purchased 102,000 ordinary shares in Beta Ltd on 1 January 2011. The issued share capital of Beta Ltd consists of 200,000 ordinary shares of £1 each, which carry equal voting rights. Alpha Ltd is, therefore, the parent company of Beta Ltd, as from 1 January 2011 because:

- it holds more than half the voting power and is therefore able to control the composition of the board of directors; and
- it owns more than half the equity share capital, and the relationship between the two companies can be presented as follows:

51% Alpha Ltd (Parent) Beta Ltd (Subsidiary)

2 Combinations based on assets or shares

The combination of two or more businesses may be based on the purchase of assets or shares.

2.1 Combinations based on the purchase of assets

These occur where one company, A, acquires the assets of another company, B and ownership of B's assets is transferred to A. B then goes into liquidation and A carries on the activities formerly undertaken by two companies. Alternatively, company C may be formed to acquire the assets of both A and B.

Companies A and B may then be wound up and a single legal entity, C, emerges to carry on the activities previously undertaken by the two companies. In both cases it is necessary to value the assets transferred for inclusion in the acquiring company's books. Once this has been done, the assets are accounted for in the normal way and the reporting problems that arise when the combination is based on shares (see below) are avoided.

2.2 Combinations based on the purchase of shares

This is achieved by one company acquiring enough shares of another to give it control (e.g. company A acquires the entire share capital of company B). You should note that agreement is reached between A and the *shareholders* of B. The transaction does not affect B directly and it remains in existence as a separate legal entity. A combination based on shares may alternatively involve the formation of a new company, C, to acquire the shares of A and B. Again, A and B remain in existence as separate legal entities.

The reasons for basing a combination on an acquisition of shares rather than assets are as follows:

- *Economy* – It is not necessary to purchase all the target company's shares, merely enough to ensure effective control over its activities.
- *Continuity* – Where the acquired company maintains a separate identity, its goodwill is more likely to survive unimpaired.
- *Decentralisation* of both managerial and decision-making processes is facilitated where companies retain their own identity.

 **TEST YOUR KNOWLEDGE 7.1**

Identify three reasons for basing a business combination on the purchase of shares rather than the purchase of assets.

The remainder of this chapter deals with acquisitions based on the purchase of shares, which is the common business combination used today.

3 The group

3.1 Legal and economic forms

The external reporting requirements imposed by the Companies Acts, until 1948, applied only to separate legal entities. In Figure 7.1, for instance, Alpha and Beta each had to publish separate accounts, but these accounts were confined to the transactions directly affecting them as separate legal entities.

The accounts published by Alpha, therefore, included cash actually received from Beta in the form of dividends, but any profits earned and retained by the subsidiary were not reported by the parent company. This gave management an enormous amount of scope to publish misleading financial information if it was inclined to do so. For instance, when the parent company's profits were low, management was often able to conceal this by making large, undisclosed, transfers of dividends from profitable subsidiaries.

In different circumstances, management allowed subsidiaries to retain all their profits and even made generous provisions for actual or potential losses of subsidiaries to depress a highly favourable profit figure that might otherwise have become the basis for unwelcome wage demands or dividend claims. Admittedly, these are extreme examples, but they indicate the scope for potential abuse where accounting reports are confined to the legal entity.

Where such abuses occurred, the parent company's accounts were of little use for assessment purposes or as a basis for resource allocation decisions. The legislature's response, in 1948, was to require parent companies to supplement their legal entity-based accounts with financial statements based on the affairs of the entire economic entity.

In Figure 7.3 below, Alpha (parent) and Beta (subsidiary) are separate legal entities which continue to publish legal entity-based accounts. In addition, Alpha is required to publish group accounts dealing with the affairs of the overall economic entity formed by Alpha and Beta.

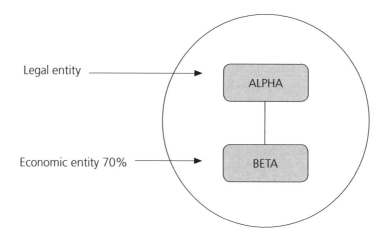

FIGURE 7.3 Separate legal entities

TEST YOUR KNOWLEDGE 7.2

Discuss the difference between a legal entity and an economic entity.

4   Consolidation

The concept underlying the preparation of **consolidated accounts** is extremely simple. The **objective** is to provide the shareholders of the parent company with full information concerning the activities of the entire economic unit in which they have invested. This is achieved by combining all the assets and liabilities of the parent company and its subsidiary into a single statement of financial position to disclose the overall financial position of the group. The effect of a share purchase on the statement of financial position of the separate legal entities is considered first. We then turn our attention to the preparation of the consolidated statement of financial position.

4.1   General rule and exceptions

All parent entities are required to prepare consolidated financial statements (parent entity's accounts combined with the subsidiary). A parent is exempted from the requirement to prepare consolidated accounts if all the following conditions are met:

- it is a wholly or partially owned subsidiary of another entity whose owners have been informed about the decision not to consolidate and they do not have any objection to the decision;
- the intermediate parent entity that has decided not to consolidate does not have any debt or equity instruments that are publicly traded; and
- its ultimate or intermediate parent prepares consolidated financial statements for public use that comply with IFRS.

4.2   Determining the cost of a business combination

The consideration given by the parent entity to acquire control in the investee firm must be measured at fair value.

In general, the consideration given by the parent entity can be split in to four categories:

- cash;
- shares in the parent company;
- deferred consideration; and
- contingent consideration.

4.2.1   Components of the purchase consideration

Direct costs of the acquisition, such as legal and other consultancy fees ARE NOT treated as part of the purchase consideration. They are EXPENSED!

- *Cash*. This is the most straightforward form of acquisition. The parent company acquires the control of a subsidiary through a cash settlement.
- *Shares in the parent company* The part of the purchase consideration settled in shares is valued at the market value of the parent entity's shares at the date of acquisition.
- *Deferred consideration* This refers to the part of the purchase consideration that is payable at a future date. The present value of the amount payable should be recorded as part of the consideration transferred at the date of acquisition. At the end of the financial year, debit the consolidated retained earnings and credit the deferred consideration account with the interest that has accrued on the deferred consideration.
- *Contingent consideration* This is payable in the future if, say, a target is met. Under revised IFRS3, contingent consideration must be included at its fair value, even if it is deemed unlikely to be paid.

4.2.2   Parent company's statement of financial position

A parent company may acquire the shares of a subsidiary for cash or in exchange for its own shares or loan stock. You should note that where consideration is entirely in the form of cash, former shareholders of the subsidiary no longer retain any financial involvement with the group. Where consideration is entirely in the form of shares, the former shareholders of the subsidiary combine with the shareholders of the parent company and have a joint interest in the activities of the group.

In the parent company's statement of financial position, the investment in the subsidiary is shown at the 'fair value' of the purchase consideration. Where the purchase consideration is entirely in the form of cash, the investment is valued at the amount of cash paid. Where part of the consideration is shares or loan stock issued by the parent company, these securities are included at market price to arrive at the value of the investment. The example below demonstrates the parent company's statement of financial position on acquiring a subsidiary:

WORKED EXAMPLE 7.2

The summarised statement of financial position of Alpha Ltd and Beta Ltd as at 31 December 2011 are as follows:

	Alpha Ltd	Beta Ltd
Assets	£	£
Non-current assets at carrying value	36000	27000
Current assets: Inventories	20000	7000
Trade receivables	18000	8000
Bank	37000	1000
Total assets	111000	43000
Equity and liabilities		
Share capital (£1 ordinary shares)	60000	25000
Retained profits	36000	10000
Equity	96000	35000
Liabilities	15000	8000
Total equity and liabilities	111000	43000

Alpha Ltd purchased the entire share capital of Beta Ltd for £35,000 on 31 December 2011.

Required

Prepare revised statement of financial position for Alpha Ltd on the following alternative assumptions:

(a) The purchase consideration is paid entirely in cash.

(b) The purchase consideration consists of two elements: cash of £20,000; 10,000 shares in Alpha Ltd valued at £1.50 each.

Answer

	(a)	(b)
Assets	£	£
Non-current assets at carrying value	36000	36000
Investment in SC Ltd	35000	35000
Current assets: Inventories	20000	20000
Trade receivables	18000	18000
Bank	2000	17000
	111000	126000
Equity and liabilities		
Share capital (£1 ordinary shares)	60000	70000
Share premium account	–	5000
Reserves	36000	36000
Equity	96000	111000
Liabilities	15000	15000
	111000	126000

WORKED EXAMPLE **7.2** *continued*

The investment in Beta Ltd is shown in each case at the fair value of the purchase consideration, namely £35,000. Under (a), the only change is a redistribution of Alpha Ltd's assets; £35,000 is transferred from 'Bank' to 'Investment in Beta Ltd'. Under (b) 'Bank' is reduced by £20,000; the remainder of the consideration is shares valued at £15,000. This gives rise to an increase in 'Share capital' of £10,000 and a balance on 'Share premium account' of £5,000. The statement of financial position of Beta remains unchanged in either case; the transaction is with shareholders of Beta Ltd and no resources transfer into or out of the subsidiary company as a result of the share purchase.

TEST YOUR KNOWLEDGE **7.3**

(a) Prepare a diagram showing the relationship between a parent company and a subsidiary company.

(b) Outline the conditions that must be met for one company to be considered, for financial reporting purposes, the subsidiary of another company.

5 Other consolidation adjustments

The preparation of consolidated accounts requires certain further adjustments to be made. On consolidation there is a need to ensure that inter-company balances agree before they are eliminated. Differences in balances may be due to:

- inventory in transit;
- cash in transit; and
- management fees not recorded by subsidiary entity.

5.1 Inter-company loans and transfers of goods

Quite often transfers of cash and goods are made between the members of a group of companies. Indeed, an important reason for takeovers and mergers is that they provide scope for achieving a more effective utilisation of available resources. Where, for instance, a public company with significant and readily available sources of finance acquires a controlling interest in a small family concern, which has good potential for expansion but finds it difficult to raise funds, a transfer of cash, via inter-company loan accounts, may follow almost immediately. The loan is, of course, reported respectively as an asset and liability in the separate accounts published for the parent company and subsidiary. Group accounts, however, regard these separate legal entities as a single undertaking and inter-company balances must be cancelled out on consolidation.

5.2 Inter-company unrealised earnings

The accounting convention that a transfer at arm's length must occur before profit is recognised must be applied on a group basis when preparing consolidated accounts. Intra-group transfers of inventories are quite common, particularly where the share purchase has resulted in an element of vertical integration designed to safeguard either sources of raw materials or consumer outlets. These transfers of inventories are often made at a figure that approximates market price, both to enable the performance of individual companies to be fairly assessed and to avoid unnecessary complications where minority shareholdings exist. Provided that the recipient company has resold the item transferred, either in its original form or incorporated in a different product, it is perfectly legitimate to recognise both elements of profit in the consolidated accounts (i.e. the profit arising on the intra-group transfer and the profit arising on the sale of the product to an external party). Where, however, the item transferred remains unsold by the transferee company at the end of the accounting period, consolidation adjustments must be made to reduce the value of the inventories to a figure which represents its original cost to the group and in order to eliminate the unrealised profit.

 **WORKED EXAMPLE** **7.3**

Small Ltd is a wholly-owned subsidiary of Large Ltd. During 2011, Small Ltd transferred inventories to Large Ltd, for £36,000. The transfer price was arrived at by adding 50% to the cost to Small Ltd of the inventories. At the year end, 31 December 2011, Large Ltd had resold three-quarters of the inventories for £31,000.

Required

Calculate the amount of unrealised profit and explain how it must be treated in the consolidated accounts.

Answer

The inventories which remain unsold by Large Ltd at the balance sheet date have not left the economic entity and must be restated at cost to that entity.

Unsold inventories – £36,000 × 1/4 =	£9000
Cost of unsold inventories = £9,000×(100%/ 150%)	£6000
Unrealised profit	£3000

The unrealised profit must be deducted from both profit and the value of inventories

Journal entry to record the adjustment:	*Debit*	*Credit*
Consolidated income statement	£3000	
Inventories		£3000

Note: Even if Large Ltd did not hold all the shares in Small Ltd, the entire unrealised profit should be removed as part of the consolidation exercise. The justification for this treatment is that the minority shareholders are outside the group and, so far as they are concerned, the profit has been realised and they should not therefore be affected by an adjustment designed to ensure that inventories are reported at cost.

5.3 Dividends out of pre-acquisition earnings

A controlling interest may be acquired after a new subsidiary has proposed a dividend payment but before it has been paid. The source of the dividend is therefore profits earned by the subsidiary before the combination took place. The dividend therefore represents a partial return of the capital cost and must be accounted for as a reduction in the value of the investment. The journal entry required to account for a dividend paid out of pre-acquisition profit is:

Journal entry to record the adjustment:	Debit	Credit
Cash	£xxxx	
Investment in subsidiary		£xxxx

WORKED EXAMPLE 7.4

The example below illustrates the calculations needed to give effect to the three secondary adjustments discussed above as well as the three principal calculations already considered.

The summarised statement of financial position of Quick plc and Silver Ltd at 31 December 2010 contained the following information.

	Quick	Silver
Non-current assets	£m	£m
Property, plant and machinery at carrying value	172	27
30 million shares in Silver Ltd	43	
Loan to Silver	7	
	222	27
Current assets		
Inventories	20	17
Receivables	39	18
Cash and cash equivalents	30	10
	89	45
Total assets	311	72
Equity and liabilities		
Share capital (£1 ordinary shares)	200	40
Retained earnings	75	20
	275	60
Non-current liabilities		
Loan from Quick plc		5
		5
Current liabilities		
Trade and other payables	36	7
	36	7
Total equity and liabilities	311	72

The shares in Silver Ltd were purchased on 31 December 2009 when the statement of financial position of that company included retained earnings amounting to £12 million. Silver Ltd paid a final dividend for 2009 of £4 million on 31 March 2010. Quick plc's share of the dividend is included in its retained earnings of £75 million in the above summarised statement of financial position. At 31 December 2010, the inventories of Silver Ltd include goods transferred from Quick plc, at cost plus a 50% mark-up, amounting to £3 million. On 29 December 2010, Silver despatched a cheque for £2 million to Quick plc, in part repayment of the loan, which was received by the latter company on 3 January 2011.

Required

The consolidated statement of financial position of Quick plc and its subsidiary company, on the basis of IFRS, at 31 December 2010.

Note: There were no differences between the carrying value and fair value of Silver's assets and liabilities at 31 December 2009.

WORKED EXAMPLE *7.4 continued*

Answer

The following journal entries give the appropriate treatment, for consolidation purposes, of the items covered in sections 1.5.1–1.5.3 above:

Dividends out of pre-acquisition earnings	Debit		Credit
	£m		*£m*
Retained earnings	3		
Investment in Silver			3

Inter-company unrealised profit – (see calculation below)	Debit		Credit
	£m		*£m*
Reserves	1		
Inventories			1

	%
Cost	100
Mark-up	50
Selling price	150

$$\frac{\text{Mark-up}}{\text{Selling price}} \quad \frac{50\%}{150\%} \times £3m = £1m$$

Inter-company loan	Debit		Credit
	£m		*£m*
Cash-in-transit	2		
Loan to Silver			2

	Total equity £m	At acquisition £m	Since acquisition £m	Minority interest £m
Share capital (see calculations below)	40	30		10
Retained earnings:				
At acquisition	12	9		3
Since acquisition	8		6	2
	60	39	6	15
Price paid (£43m – £3m [pre-acquisition])		40		
Goodwill		1		
Retained earnings of parent company (£75m – £3m [pre-acquisition] – £1m [unrealised profit on inventories])			71	
Group retained earnings			77	

Percentage of shares purchased – calculation:

	£m
Total share capital in Silver Ltd	40
Shares purchased by Quick plc	30
% of shares purchased by Quick plc:	
30m/40m × 100% = 75% (Hence NCI = 25%)	

WORKED EXAMPLE 7.4 *continued*

Statement of financial position as at 31 December 2010

	£m
Non-current assets	
Property, plant and equipment	199
Goodwill	1
(On consolidation inter-company loan is eliminated and does not appear on SOFP)	200
Current assets	
Inventories (£37m – £1m [unrealised profit on inventories])	36
Trade receivables	57
Cash and cash equivalents (£40m + £2m [cash-in-transit])	42
	135
Total assets	335
Equity and liabilities	
Parent company shareholders' equity	
Share capital	200
Retained earnings	77
	277
NCI	15
Total equity	292
Current liabilities	
Trade and other payables	43
Total equity and liabilities	335

TEST YOUR KNOWLEDGE 7.4

What adjustments need to be made to take account of inter-company unrealised earnings?

5.4 Interpreting consolidated statement of financial position

We have already drawn attention to the fact that the basic objective of consolidated accounts is to provide the shareholders of the parent company with detailed information concerning the activities of the entire economic unit in which they have invested.

We have examined the various procedures followed when preparing a consolidated statement of financial position and it is now possible to consider more fully what this statement means.

The parent company's legal entity-based accounts deal with the results of a single organisation, whereas group accounts set out the combined results of at least two, and perhaps a much larger number, of legally separate businesses. Therefore, it is not surprising that there are often significant differences between the two sets of accounts. Some important differences may well be clearly visible from a simple comparison of the totals appearing in the statement of financial position. For instance, the parent company's statement of financial position may contain a large overdraft, whereas the consolidated balance sheet shows a healthy cash surplus indicating that the subsidiaries are in possession of substantial amounts of cash.

A more searching comparison can be made of the information contained in economic entity- and legal entity-based accounts by using techniques such as ratio analysis and cash flow analysis.

For illustrative purposes, a comparison is made below of the information contained in Clubs Ltd's own statement of financial position (see Practice Question 7.3) and the statement of financial position of the group given in the solution to that question. The main points of interest are as follows:

1 Revenue reserves:

Clubs Ltd	£43000
Group	£38850

This shows that the two subsidiaries are not improving the overall profitability of the group; the post-acquisition profits of Diamonds Ltd are more than cancelled out by the post-acquisition losses of Hearts Ltd.

2 Fixed assets:

Clubs Ltd	£59000
Group	£488200

This shows that most of the group's non-current assets are owned by the subsidiary companies. This information would be of particular interest to prospective creditors of the parent company who might be keen to ensure that their advance is adequately secured. One option open to them would be to require subsidiaries to guarantee repayment of the loan.

3 Solvency:
Working capital ratio relates to the ability of a company to meets its day-to-day cash requirements. The ratio gives an indication of the liquidity of a company to meet its short-term cash requirements.

$$\text{Working capital ratio} = \frac{\text{Current assets}}{\text{Current liabilities}}$$

For Club Ltd:

$$\text{Working capital ratio} = \frac{£79000}{£65000} = 1.2:1$$

For the Group:

$$\text{Working capital ratio} = \frac{(79,000 + 62,500 + 29,500)}{(65,000 + 37,400 + 75,600)} = 0.96:1$$

The working capital position of Clubs Ltd is significantly better than that of the group as a whole. This would suggest that there are underlying financial difficulties which are not evident from examining the content of Clubs Ltd's own statement of financial position. An examination of the subsidiary companies' statement of financial position shows that the problem is at Hearts Ltd, where current liabilities significantly exceed current assets, which shareholders of the group would not see.

4 Gearing:
Gearing is a comparison between the amounts of borrowing a company has to its shareholders funds. The gear ratio indicates the proportion of capital available within the company in relation to that owed to sources outside the company.

Debt/equity ratio	Clubs Ltd	Zero (no loans)
	Group	105%

Inter-company shareholdings cancel out on consolidation, whereas the debentures all held outside the group, must be aggregated. Consequently, the consolidated statement reveals a much higher level of gearing than is evident from an examination of the individual statement of financial position of Clubs Ltd and the other companies within the group. The group pays annual interest to debenture holders totalling £37,500 (£250,000×15%). Annual profit figures are not given, but the interest charge is almost equal to the total retained profits. This would suggest that the group will find it difficult to meet its interest payments unless trading results improve.

The group accounts point to the existence of significant financial difficulties that are not evident from Clubs Ltd's own statement of financial position.

6 Consolidated statement of financial position

The reason for producing consolidated accounts is that the group of companies is in substance, though not in law, a single undertaking. It therefore follows that the essence of consolidation procedures is the cancellation of inter-company balances and the aggregation of any remaining balances. Following the acquisition, Alpha Ltd's revised statement of financial position contains an asset entitled 'Investment in Beta Ltd, £35,000', whereas Beta Ltd's Statement of Financial Position shows a similar mount 'owing' to its shareholders (i.e. the total of share capital and reserves and equity (assets minus liabilities) of Alpha Ltd). When preparing a consolidated statement of financial position, these inter-company balances cancel out (signified by ¢) and the remaining assets and liabilities are combined to produce total figures for the group.

 WORKED EXAMPLE 7.5

Prepare the consolidated statement of financial position of Alpha Ltd and its subsidiary, Beta Ltd, using the information given in Worked Example 7.2 and assuming that the purchase consideration is entirely in the form of cash.

Answer

Consolidated Balance Sheet of PC Ltd and Subsidiary Workings:

	Alpha Ltd		Beta Ltd		Group
Non-current assets	£		£		£
Fixed assets at carrying value	36000	+	27000	=	63000
Investment in Beta Ltd	¢ 35,000				
Current assets: Inventories	20000	+	7000	=	27000
Trade Receivables	18000	+	8000	=	26000
Bank	2000	+	1000	=	3000
	111000		43000		119000
Equity and liabilities					
Share capital (£1 ordinary shares)	60000		¢25,000		60000
Retained profits	36000		¢10,000		36000
Equity	96000		0		96000
Liabilities	15000	+	8000	=	23000
	111000		8000		119000

This illustrates the essence of consolidation procedures, but it is an oversimplification. It is very unlikely that the price paid on acquisition will exactly equal the figure for shareholders' equity in the subsidiary company's statement of financial position. Furthermore, a period of time usually elapses between the date when the shares are acquired and the consolidation date. Finally, the investing company may well take the opportunity, which this form of business combination permits, to achieve control while purchasing less than the entire share capital. Consequently, the preparation of consolidated accounts under the purchase method (the only method now allowed under IFRS as the Merger Method is no longer used) involves the following three principal calculations:

- goodwill;
- post-acquisition profits; and
- minority interest.

The calculation of these balances is now examined.

6.1 Goodwill

Often, the price paid for the shares in a subsidiary significantly exceeds the carrying value of the underlying net assets. Part of this surplus is attributable to the favourable trading connections, or goodwill, built up by the subsidiary company over the years. The residual difference is a consequence of the fact that a disparity exists between the *carrying* value and the fair value of the assets and liabilities of the subsidiary at the takeover date. Standard accounting practice, therefore, requires goodwill to be computed in two stages:

1   Restate the subsidiary company's assets and liabilities at their 'fair value'. Fair value is intended to reflect conditions at the time of acquisition which refers to the time of the company takeover and not the date of the acquisition of the assets by the subsidiary. They need not be written into the books of the subsidiary company and used for the purpose of its legal entity-based accounts, but they must be used for consolidation purposes. IAS 32, 'Financial Instruments: Disclosure and Presentation', provides guidance for the identification of fair value through the following definition: 'Fair value is the amount for which an asset can be exchanged, or a liability settled, between knowledgeable, willing parties in an arm's length transaction.'

2   Compute goodwill, in accordance with IFRS 3, as the excess of the price paid for the shares in the subsidiary over and above the net fair value of the identifiable assets, liabilities and contingent liabilities acquired. However, IFRS 3 prohibits the amortisation of goodwill. Instead, goodwill must be tested for impairment at least annually in accordance with IAS 36 'Impairment of assets'.

If the parent's interest in the fair value of the acquired identifiable net assets exceeds the cost of the business combination, that excess (sometimes referred to as negative goodwill) must be recognised immediately in the income statement as a gain. Negative goodwill is, of course, a very unusual occurrence. It reveals that the business has been sold as a going concern for less than might have been produced by selling assets off individually at their fair value. Before concluding that 'negative goodwill' has, in fact, arisen IFRS 3 requires that the parent *reassess* the identification and measurement of the subsidiary's identifiable assets, liabilities, and contingent liabilities and the measurement of the cost of the combination.

TEST YOUR KNOWLEDGE **7.5**

Explain the effect on the legal entity-based balance sheet of a holding company of acquiring the entire share capital of a new subsidiary for £350,000 in cash.

WORKED EXAMPLE **7.6**

The summarised statement of financial position of Tom Ltd and Jones Ltd at 31 December 2011 are as follows:

	Tom Ltd	Jones Ltd
Assets	£	£
Non-current assets at carrying value	60000	46000
Investment in Jones Ltd	75000	–
Current assets: Inventories	32000	13000
Trade receivables	27000	17000
Bank	1000	2000
	195000	78000
Equity and liabilities		
Share capital (£1 ordinary shares)	100000	50000
Retained profits	70000	12000
Equity	170000	62000
Liabilities	25000	16000
	195000	78000

 **WORKED EXAMPLE** **7.6** *continued*

Tom Ltd purchased the entire share capital of Jones Ltd on 31 December 2011. The non-current assets of Jones Ltd are considered to possess a fair value of £54,000, but there are no material differences between the carrying values and fair values of the remaining assets.

Required

(a) Calculate the goodwill arising on consolidation.
(b) Prepare the consolidated statement of financial position of Tom Ltd and its subsidiary at 31 December 2011.

Answer

Calculation of goodwill arising on consolidation (net asset approach):

	£	£
Price paid		75000
Less: value of business acquired:		
Non-current assets at fair value	54000	
Inventories	13000	
Trade receivables	17000	
Bank	2000	
Liabilities	−16000	
		70000
Goodwill		5000

Note

When solving examination questions, it is generally necessary to calculate the 'value of business acquired' using the equity components rather than the net asset approach above. The result is the same, but the former procedure is followed because, in most group accounting questions, a period of time will have elapsed between the dates of takeover and consolidation. Consequently, the figures for assets and liabilities may not be available, but sufficient information will be given to enable examinees to build up the figure for the shareholders' equity interest at that date. The calculation of goodwill applying the shareholders' equity approach is as follows:

(a) *Calculation of goodwill arising on consolidation (shareholders' equity approach):*

	£	£
Price paid		75000
Less: value of business acquired:		
Share capital	50000	
Revaluation surplus (W1)	8000	
Retained profits	12000	
		70000
Goodwill		5000

W1 £54,000 (fair value of Jones' Non-current assets) − £46,000 (book value)

WORKED EXAMPLE 7.6 *continued*

(b) *Consolidated statement of financial position of Tom Ltd at 31 December 2011*

Non-current assets	£	£
Goodwill arising on consolidation	5000	
Non-current assets (W2)*	114000	119000
Current assets		
Inventories	45000	
Trade receivables	44000	
Bank	3000	92000
Total assets		211000
Equity and liabilities		
Share capital (£1 ordinary shares)	100000	
Retained earnings	70000	170000
Non-current and current liabilities	41000	41000
Total equity and liabilities		211000

*W2 balance includes the non-current assets of Jones Ltd at their fair value.

The consolidated profit figure consists only of the retained profits of the parent company and includes no part of the retained profits of the subsidiary at the takeover date. Profits earned prior to the date of acquisition (pre-acquisition profits) accrue to the former shareholders of Jones Ltd and are paid for in the purchase price. They are, therefore, unavailable for distribution to the shareholders of Tom Ltd and are instead treated as part of the capitalised value of the business at the takeover date.

This is clearly demonstrated in the calculation of goodwill that uses the shareholders' equity approach. The retained profits at acquisition and revaluation surplus, which is also pre-acquisition, are added to share capital to produce a figure of £70,000 for shareholders' equity. This is offset against the price paid (£75,000) and results in a balance of £5,000 that is described as 'goodwill arising on consolidation' in the consolidated statement of financial position. Profits earned after the date of acquisition accrue to the parent company's shareholders, and their accounting treatment is examined in the next section of this chapter.

6.2 Post-acquisition profits

A period of time usually elapses between the acquisition of a controlling interest in a subsidiary company and the date of the consolidated accounts. The subsidiary company may have generated profits during the interim period. These profits accrue to the shareholders of the parent company and, when transferred, are available for distribution. Their accounting treatment is dealt with in Worked Example 7.7.

WORKED EXAMPLE 7.7

Use the same information as for Worked Example 7.6, except that a share acquisition date of 31 December 2010 is assumed, at which time the retained profits of Jones Ltd amounted to £9,500.

Required:

(a) Calculate
   (i)   goodwill; and
   (ii) post-acquisition profits of Jones Ltd.

(b) Prepare the consolidated balance sheet of the group at 31 December 2011.

Notes

Goodwill arising on consolidation is to be included in the accounts at 31 December 2011 at £6,000 based on an impairment at review date. Ignore depreciation of other non-current assets.

Answer:

(a) Calculations

		£	£
(i)	*Goodwill*		
	Price paid		75000
	LESS: Value of business acquired		
	Share capital	50000	
	Revaluation surplus	8000	
	Retained profits	9500	67500
			7500
(ii)	*Post-acquisition profits of Jones Ltd*		
	Retained profits at 31 December 2011		12000
	LESS: Retained profits at 31 December 2010		9500
			2500

The retained profit of the group therefore consists of the retained profit of Tom Ltd, £70,000, plus the post-acquisition profit of Jones Ltd, £2,500, *minus* goodwill impaired £1,500 (£7,500 – £6,000) = £71,000.

(b) Consolidated statement of financial position of Tom Ltd as at 31 December 2011

	£	£
Non-current assets		
Goodwill after impairment review	6000	
Non-current assets at carrying value	114000	120000
Current assets		
Inventories	45000	
Trade receivables	44000	
Bank	3000	92000
Total assets		212000
Equity and liabilities		
Share capital (£1 ordinary shares)	100000	
Retained profits	71000	171000
Current and non-current liabilities		
Liabilities		41000
Total equity and liabilities		212000

There are three further matters that require emphasis concerning the calculation of reported profits for inclusion in the consolidated statement of financial position:

1 Losses suffered by a subsidiary company since the acquisition date are attributable to the shareholders of the parent company in the same way as profit earned. Any post-acquisition losses must, therefore, be deducted from the parent company's balance of retained profits to compute the reported profit of the group.

2 We have seen that a subsidiary company's non-current assets must be stated at fair value in the consolidated accounts. Where the subsidiary chooses to retain non-current assets at historical cost for the purpose of its own accounts, a consolidation adjustment must be made equal to the difference between the historical cost-based charge for depreciation, already made, and an appropriate charge based on the re-valued amount.

3 To the extent that post-acquisition profits earned by a subsidiary are transferred to the parent company by way of dividends, the amount to be aggregated when consolidation takes place is correspondingly reduced. For instance, in Worked Example 7.5, assume Jones Ltd had paid an interim dividend of £800 during July 2011. Tom Ltd's retained profits increase to £70,800, the retained profit of Jones Ltd falls to £11,200 and the post-acquisition retained profits of Jones Ltd become £1,700 (£11,200 − £9,500).

The consolidated balance of reported profit remains unchanged at £71,000 (£70,800 + £1,700− £1,500 [goodwill impaired]).

TEST YOUR KNOWLEDGE **7.6**

(a) Explain the calculation of goodwill when shares are acquired in a subsidiary company.
(b) Why is it that only the post-acquisition profits of a subsidiary are consolidated under the purchase method?

6.3 Non-controlling interest

In many cases, the parent company may choose a controlling interest of less than 100% either in the interests of economy, or because of the obstinacy of certain shareholders. In these circumstances, the investment confers an interest in the subsidiary company's net assets based on the proportion which the number of equity shares acquired bears to the total number of equity shares then in issue. This must be taken into account when preparing the consolidated statement of financial position. The appropriate procedure is to include the full amount of the subsidiary's assets and liabilities in the consolidated statement of financial position, with the proportion financed by outside investors represented by a credit balance described as 'minority interest'. This is shown as a separate item, normally immediately following shareholders' equity. The non-controlling interest (NCI) consists of an appropriate proportion of the share capital plus reserves and any other credit balances that accrue to the equity shareholders at the consolidation date.

 **WORKED EXAMPLE** **7.8**

The summarised statement of financial position of Zen Ltd and Duff Ltd at 31 December 2011 are as follows:

	Zen Ltd £	Duff Ltd £
Non-current assets		
Non-current assets at carrying value	94000	58000
Investment in Duff Ltd	90000	–
	184000	58000
Current assets		
Inventories	103000	52000
Trade receivables	79000	25000
Cash and cash equivalents(West Bank)	35000	–
	217000	77000
Total assets	401000	135000
Equity and liabilities		
Share capital (£1 ordinary shares)	200000	80000
Retained profits at 1 January 2011	77000	7000
Add: Profit for 2011	18000	6000
Equity	295000	93000
Current liabilities		
Trade payables	106000	25000
Cash and cash equivalents (East Bank)	–	17000
Liabilities	106000	42000
Total equity and liabilities	401000	135000

Further information

1 The investment in Duff Ltd consists of 60,000 ordinary shares purchased on1 January 2011.
2 It may be assumed that there are no significant differences between the carrying value and fair value of Duff Ltd's assets.
3 Goodwill arising on consolidation remains unimpaired at 31 December 2011.

Required
(a) Calculate
    (i) goodwill;
    (ii) retained profits of the group; and
    (iii) minority interest.
(b) Prepare the consolidated statement of financial position at 31 December 2011.

Answer
When answering a question involving the preparation of consolidated accounts, the starting point is to determine the exact relationship between the members of the group.
    The relationship may be presented in the form of a diagram (below):

Zen Ltd

75% shareholding (see working below)
↓
Duff Ltd (pre-acquisition profit £6,000)

WORKED EXAMPLE **7.8** *continued*

(i)   Goodwill:

		£	£
Price paid			90000
LESS: Value of business acquired			
Share capital		80000	
Retained profits		7000	
Proportion of shares acquired 60,000/80,000×100% = 75% ×		87000	65250
			24750

(ii)   Retained profits: Zen Ltd   95,000
       Duff Ltd 6,000 (post-acquisition
       profit)×75%   4500
                                                                                                     99500

(iii)   NCI:
Total equity of Duff Ltd at the consolidation date
Share capital   80000
Retained profits   13000
                                                                                                     93000

Proportion attributable to minority shareholders:
    20,000/80,000×100% = 25%*×93,000   23250

*Since Zen purchased 75% of the shares in Duff, the NCI will hold the other 25% of the shares.

Note

The figures for goodwill, post-acquisition profit and NCI may be calculated in a convenient manner by constructing a table (see below) where:

1 The subsidiary's balance of total equity (including any revaluation reserve and consequential depreciation adjustment) is distributed between the parent company, distinguishing between the positions 'at' and 'since' acquisition, and the minority interest.
2 Goodwill is calculated by comparing the value of the subsidiary 'at acquisition' with the price paid.
3 The parent company's retained profits are added to the subsidiary's profits arising 'since acquisition' to arrive at group retained profits.
4 Goodwill may be subject of impairment, though not so in this case.
5 The balances for goodwill, if any, reported profit and minority interest are transferred to the consolidated statement of financial position.

Duff Ltd	Total equity	At acquisition	Since acquisition	Minority interest 25%
	£	£	£	£
Share capital	80000	60000	–	20000
Retained profits:				
At acquisition	7000	5250		
Since acquisition	6000	–	4500	1500
	93000	65250	4500	21500
Price paid		90000	–	
Goodwill on acquisition		24750	–	
Retained profits, Zen Ltd			95000	
Group retained profits		24750	99500	

An advantage of this presentation is that it is easy to check whether total equity has been fully allocated for the purpose of calculating goodwill, retained profits and minority interest. Also, provided the additions and cross-casts are checked, the possibility of arithmetical error is reduced.

	£	£
Non-current assets		
Goodwill at carrying value	24750	
Non-current assets at carrying value	152000	176750
Current assets		
Inventories	155000	
Trade receivables	104000	
Cash and cash equivalents (W1)	35000	294000
Total assets		470750
Equity and liabilities		
Share capital (£1 ordinary shares)	200000	
Retained profits	99500	299500
NCI		23250
Current and non-current liabilities		
Trade payables		131000
Cash and cash equivalents (W1)*		17000
Total equity and liabilities		470750

* W1 – the bank overdraft and bank balance are at different banks. Best accounting practice, therefore, requires these items to be shown separately and not offset against one another. If they were offset, current assets and current liabilities would both be understated. In large companies holding many bank accounts, a practical step might be to amalgamate and show all bank balances which are overdrawn and show as ONE overdrawn figure and amalgamate all bank balances that are not overdrawn to overcome the difficulty of reporting each individual bank balance(s).

7 Consolidated income statement

We have seen above that, for the purpose of preparing the consolidated statement of financial position, the investment in a subsidiary is replaced by the subsidiary's underlying net assets (and the minority interest if any). The same logic applies for the purpose of preparing the consolidated income statement where the dividend income from the subsidiary, if any, is replaced by the underlying income and expenditure of the subsidiary (less the minority interest if any). This method of consolidation is often described as *line-by-line consolidation*, or sometimes full consolidation. This name is derived from the fact that, on each line of the statement of financial position and the income statement, the figures of the subsidiary are aggregated with those of the parent. We have seen above that inter-company transactions must be eliminated on consolidation. Most of the possibilities relevant to the financial reporting and analysis examination have already been considered. We only need to draw attention here to the need to eliminate inter-company sales when preparing the consolidated income statement.

WORKED EXAMPLE **7.9**

The individual income statements of Fast plc and Loose plc contain the following information for the year ended 31 December 2011.

	Fast plc	Loose plc
	£'000	£'000
Revenue	6000	5000
Cost of sales	–4100	–3200
Gross profit	1900	1800
Dividends received	75	
Distribution expenses	–250	–500
Administration expenses	–900	–700
Profit before taxation	825	600
Taxation	–200	–160
Profit for the year	625	440
Note		
Dividends paid	0	–100
Retained earnings 2011	625	340

The retained earnings of Fast and Loose at 1 January 2011 amounted respectively to £500,000 and £1.1 million.

Fast acquired 150,000 shares (out of a total of 200,000 shares) of £1 each in Loose on 1 January 2011. During the year, goods which cost Fast £50,000 were sold to Loose for £68,000; however, none of these were in inventory at the end of the period. An interim dividend of £100,000 for 2011 was paid by Loose on 31 July 2011.

Required
The consolidated income statement of Fast plc and its subsidiary Loose plc for the year ended 31 December 2011, and an explanation of how the retained earnings of Loose plc at 1 January 2011 would be treated in the consolidated accounts.

Answer
Income statement for the year ended 31 December 2011

	Fast plc	Loose plc	adj.	Group
	£'000	£'000	£'000	£'000
Revenue	6000	5000	–68	10932
Cost of sales	–4100	–3200	50	–7250
Gross profit				3682
Dividends received	75	0	–75	0
Distribution expenses	–250	–500		–750
Administration expenses	–900	–700		–1600
Profit before taxation				1332
Taxation	–200	–160		–360
Profit for the year				972
Attributable:				
Equity holders of the parent				862
NCI 110				

(Loose plc profit for the year £440,000×25% = £110,000)

The retained earnings of Loose plc at 1 January 2011 have accrued during the period prior to acquisition and are treated as part of the shareholders' equity in the subsidiary for the purpose of computing goodwill arising on consolidation.

7.1 Summary of income statement consolidation procedures

Adjustment to profits:

1 Eliminate intra-group sales on consolidation.
2 Eliminate unrealised profit on intra-group sales of unsold goods still in closing inventory.
3 Aggregate the adjusted sales and cost of sales figures.
4 Aggregate expenses.
5 Deduct impairment loss.
6 Adjustment to intra-group dividends and interest:
   ■ eliminate dividends paid to parent by subsidiary; and
   ■ eliminate intra-group interest paid.
7 Aggregate the taxation figures (parent and subsidiary).
8 Allocate net profit to parent's shareholders and NCI.

TEST YOUR KNOWLEDGE 7.7

Discuss the accounting treatment of dividends and interest on consolidation.

8   Investment in associates

During the 1960s, companies increasingly began to conduct part of their activities through other companies in which they had acquired a less than 50% equity interest and which, consequently, escaped the group accounting provisions introduced in the Companies Act 1948 (now incorporated in the Companies Act 2006). Significant influence was exercised, however, either through the existence of some form of partnership agreement, or because of a wide dispersal of shares. Consequently, the directors of the investing company were able to influence both the commercial and financial policies of the company in which shares were held.

The growing demand for fuller disclosure was therefore fully justified:

(a) to remove obvious opportunities for the managers of investing companies to manipulate their company's reported results, for instance, by building up undisclosed profits in the accounts of the investee company which could, when required, be transferred to the investing company in the form of a dividend; and

(b) to provide more meaningful performance data concerning the activities of the entire economic unit over which some influence was exercised. In this context, the growing popularity of the price/earnings ratio emphasised the increasing significance attached to reported earnings as a performance indicator. It was therefore important to take steps to ensure that the investing company's published earnings fairly represented their actual performance.

The matter was referred to the Accounting Standards Committee (as it then was) which concluded that where management assumes a measure of direct responsibility for the performance of its investment by actively participating in the commercial and policy-making decisions of an associated company, it must present a full account to its members.

Accordingly, it was decided that group accounts, prepared in accordance with the Companies Act, should be extended to incorporate additional information concerning the activities of these associated companies.

This decision obliged the regulators to draft requirements covering two matters:

■ the identification of an associated company; and
■ the additional information to be published.

8.1 Definition of an associate

IAS 28 defines an associate as 'an entity over which the investor has significant influence and that is neither a subsidiary nor an interest in a joint venture'. Significant influence is defined as 'the power to participate in the financial and operating policy decisions of the investee but is not control or joint control over those policies'. Holding 20% or more of the voting power leads to the presumption of significant influence. (Note, however, that the carrying amount of the investment in the associate is tested for impairment.)

8.2 Indicators of significant influence

On the basis of IAS 28, and for the purposes of financial reporting, the following items will be indicators of significant influence by the investor company which may give rise to reporting for associates:

■ representation on the board;
■ participation in decisions about profit distribution and retention;
■ material transactions between the investor and investee; and
■ exchange of managerial staff.

8.3 Accounting for associates

IFRS 12 'Disclosure of Interests in Other Entities' gives guidance on reporting in relation to associate entities. The standard suggests that interests in unconsolidated structured entities shall be disclosed taking into account the following. IFRS 12:24 states that an entity shall disclose information that enables users of its financial statements to:

■ understand the nature and extent of its interests in unconsolidated structured entities; and
■ evaluate the nature of, and changes in, the risks associated with its interests in unconsolidated structured entities.

Associates are accounted for using the equity method-single line consolidation. The amount reported in the statement of financial position is arrived at as follows:

– Initial investment in associate	x
+/- share of associates post	x
–Impairment of goodwill	x
Acquisition profits	
+/- Share of post acquisition	x
Reserves e.g. revaluation reserves	x
Carrying amount of investment in associate	x

The accounting treatment for associates is not the same as for subsidiaries. Consideration must be given to the following issues:

■ Transactions between investor and associate – the investor's share of any unrealised profit must be adjusted against the share of associates profit for the period.
■ How do we account for unrealised profit on goods sold by associate to the parent company?
■ How do we account for unrealised profit on goods sold by parent to the associate company?
■ Intercompany balances are not eliminated.

8.4 Applying the equity method of accounting

The following are the key issues that require attention where an investment is accounted for in accordance with the equity method.

1   The investment must be recorded initially at cost of acquisition. Any difference (whether positive or negative) between cost and the investor's share of the fair values of the net identifiable assets of the associate is attributed to goodwill and accounted for in accordance with IFRS 3 'Business Combinations'.

2   At subsequent accounting dates, the investing company's share of the post-tax profits less losses of associated companies must be computed. This amount is then brought into the investing company's accounts as an addition:
    (a) to profit in the income statement (credit entry); and
    (b) to the value of the investment in the associated company reported in the statement of financial position (debit entry). The carrying value of the investment must of course be reduced to the extent that the profits of the associate have been transferred to the investor in the form of dividends.

3   Any goodwill shown as part of the carrying amount of the investment in an associate must be checked annually as normal for impairment in accordance with the provisions of IFRS 3.

4   Unrealised profits and losses resulting from upstream (associate to investor) and downstream (investor to associate) transactions should be eliminated to the extent of the investor's interest in the associate.

5   If the associate uses accounting policies that differ from those of the investor, the associate's financial statements should be adjusted to reflect the investor's accounting policies for the purpose of applying the equity method.

Investments accounted for in accordance with the equity method must be classified as non-current assets in the statement of financial position.

 WORKED EXAMPLE 7.10

On 31 December 2010, Investment plc purchased 25% of the equity share capital of Associated plc for £1 million. At the acquisition date, Associated plc possessed identifiable assets, net of liabilities, with a fair value of £3.6 million.

In 2011, Associated plc earns a profit of £300,000 of which £140,000 is paid out as a dividend during 2011 (ignore taxation).

Required

(a) Allocate the price paid for the shares in Associated plc between fair value and goodwill.

(b) For 2011, show the amounts which must be recognised in the accounts of Investment plc in respect of its shares in Associate plc.

Answer

(a)

		£'000
	Price paid	1000
	Fair value of net assets acquired: £3.6m ÷ 4	900
	Goodwill	100

(b)

		£'000
	Statement of financial position – Non-current assets	£'000
	Investment in associate	1000
	Share of undistributed profits ([300,000-140,000] ÷ 4)	40
		1040
	Income statement: £300,000 ÷ 4	75

The results of L plc and its subsidiaries for 2011 have already been consolidated. The results of K plc, an associated company, must now be incorporated by applying the requirements contained in IAS 28. The following information is provided.

WORKED EXAMPLE **7.10** *continued*

Income statement for year ended 31 December 2011

	L Group	K plc
	£m	£m
Revenue	51	290
All operating costs	−36	−170
Profit before tax	15	120
Taxation	−4	−20
Profit for the year	11	100

Statement of financial position at 31 December 2011

	L Group	K plc
	£m	£m
Non-current assets		
Property, plant and equipment	54	178
Investment in K plc at cost	80	
	134	178
Current assets	95	364
Total assets	229	542
Equity and liabilities		
Share capital	137	170
Retained earnings	21	192
	158	362
NCI	16	
	174	362
Current liabilities	55	180
Total equity and liabilities	229	542

L plc acquired 25% of the share capital of K plc on 31 December 2009, at which date the reserves of K plc stood at £40 million. At 31 December 2009, the statement of financial position of K plc contained net assets whose fair value and carrying value were identical at £260 million.

The goodwill attributable to the shareholding of the L Group in K plc was the subject of an impairment review after the above accounts were prepared. The impairment review revealed that a write off of £6 million was required. The amount of tax payable remains unaffected.

Required

The consolidated income statement of the L group of companies for 2011 and the consolidated statement of financial position as at 31 December 2011 incorporating the results of the associated company K plc.

WORKED EXAMPLE 7.10 *continued*

Answer

Income statement for year ended 31 December 2011

	£m	L Group £m
Revenue		51
All operating costs		−36
Profit for the period		15
Share of profit of associate (100 ÷ 4) − 6 (impairment review)		19
Profit before taxation		34
Taxation − L Group	−4	
Associate	−5	−9
Profit for the year		25

Statement of financial position at 31 December 2011

	£m	L Group £m
Non-current assets		
Property, plant and equipment		54
Investment in K plc at cost	80	
Add: post acquisition retained profit		
([192 − 40] ÷ 4) − 6	32	112
Current assets		95
Total assets		261
Equity and liabilities		
Share capital		137
Retained earnings (21 + 32)		53
		190
NCI		16
Total equity		206
Current liabilities		55
Total equity and liabilities		261

The table below indicates the likely categorisation of an equity investment, based on level of shareholding, as an investment, an associate or a subsidiary. Remember of course that the level of shareholding is not the definitive test.

Accounting for equity investments		
% of shares held	Classification	Accounting method
< 20%	Investment	Cash basis
> 20% < 50%	Associate	Equity method
> 50%	Subsidiary	Purchase method

9 Interest in joint ventures

A joint venture involves the pooling of resources and expertise by two or more businesses to achieve a particular goal. The risks and rewards of the enterprise are also shared. The reasons behind the formation of a joint venture often include business expansion, development of new products or moving into new markets, particularly overseas. Collaborating with another company for this purpose may be useful because, for example, it provides access to:

- more resources;
- greater capacity;
- increased technical expertise; and
- established distribution channels.

Joint ventures are particularly popular where cooperation between businesses in different countries is an advantage (e.g. in the areas of transport, tourism and hotels).

9.1 Relevant IFRS and IAS to joint ventures

IAS 28 'Investments in Associates and Joint Ventures' (effective 1 January 2013) (supersedes IAS 28 (2003) 'Investments in Associates') describes a joint venture as: 'A joint arrangement whereby the parties that have joint control of the arrangement have rights to the net assets of the arrangement.' The objective of IAS 28 is to prescribe the accounting treatment for joint ventures. Where a joint venture clearly exists, management shall report on the same under IAS 28.

IFRS 11 'Joint Arrangement' (effective January 2013) requires parties to a joint arrangement to determine the type of joint arrangement in which they are involved by assessing its rights and obligations and accounts for those rights and obligations in accordance with that type of joint arrangement.

IFRS 12 'Disclosure of Interests in Other Entities' prescribes the disclosure of information that enables users of financial statements to evaluate:

- the nature of, and risks associated with, its interests in other entities; and
- the effects of those interests on its financial position, financial performance and cash flows.

9.2 Disclosure requirements

There are no disclosures specified in IAS 28. Instead, IFRS 12 'Disclosure of Interests in Other Entities' outlines the disclosures required for entities with joint control of, or significant influence over, an investee.

9.3 Identifying a joint venture

IAS 28 describes three types of joint ventures:

- *Joint arrangement* – An arrangement of which two or more parties have joint control.
- *Joint control* – The contractually agreed sharing of control of an arrangement, which exists only when decisions about the relevant activities require the unanimous consent of the parties sharing control.
- *Joint venture* – A joint arrangement whereby the parties that have joint control of the arrangement have rights to the net assets of the arrangement.

9.4 Accounting for a joint venture

IAS 28 (effective from 1 January 2013) only allows accounting for joint ventures under the equity method and defines various aspects of accounting treatment as:

1 *Basic principle* Under the equity method, on initial recognition the investment in an associate, investment is above 20% but less than 50%, or a joint venture, a contractually agreed sharing of control, is recognised at cost and the carrying amount is increased or decreased to recognise the investor's share of the profit or loss of the investee after the date of acquisition.

2 *Distributions and other adjustments to carrying amount* The investor's share of the investee's profit or loss is recognised in the investor's profit or loss. Distributions received from an investee reduce the carrying amount of the investment. Adjustments to the carrying amount may also be necessary for changes in the investor's proportionate interest in the investee arising from changes in the investee's other comprehensive income (e.g. to account for changes arising from revaluations of property, plant and equipment and foreign currency translations).

3 *Potential voting rights* An entity's interest in an associate or a joint venture is determined solely on the basis of existing ownership interests and, generally, does not reflect the possible exercise or conversion of potential voting rights and other derivative instruments.

4 *Interaction with IFRS 9* IFRS 9 'Financial Instruments' does not apply to interests in associates and joint ventures that are accounted for using the equity method. Instruments containing potential voting rights in an associate or a joint venture are accounted for in accordance with IFRS 9, unless they currently give access to the returns associated with an ownership interest in an associate or a joint venture.

5 *Classification as non-current asset* An investment in an associate or a joint venture is generally classified as a non-current asset, unless it is classified as held for sale in accordance with IFRS 5 'Non-current Assets held for Sale and Discontinued Operations'.

 **WORKED EXAMPLE** **7.11**

Grumpy plc and Sleepy plc jointly established Dopey Ltd to operate a holiday business. Grumpy and Sleepy have equal shares in Dopey and share profits equally. The results of Grumpy plc and Dopey Ltd are set out below.

Income statement for year ended 31 December 2011

	Grumpy plc £m	Dopey Ltd £m
Revenue	300	170
All operating costs	−229	−86
Profit before tax	71	84
Taxation	−15	−18
Profits for the year	56	66

WORKED EXAMPLE **7.11** *continued*

Statement of financial position at 31 December 2011

	Grumpy plc £m	Dopey Ltd £m
Non-current assets		
Property, plant and equipment	111	100
Investment in Dopey Ltd at cost	60	
	171	100
Current assets	49	134
Total assets	220	234
Equity and liabilities		
Share capital (£1 ordinary shares)	50	120
Retained earnings	140	90
	190	210
Current liabilities	30	24
Total equity and liabilities	220	234

Required

The income statement and statement of financial position and notes showing movement on reserves of Grumpy plc for 2011 incorporating the results of Dopey on the equity method on the basis of IAS 28.

Answer

Income statement for year ended 31 December 2011

	Grumpy plc £m
Revenue	300
All operating costs	–229
Operating profit	71
Share of profit of joint venture (84 ÷ 2)	42
Profit before tax:	113
Grumpy plc	–15
Joint venture	–9
Profits for the year	89

Statement of financial position at 31 December 2011

	Grumpy plc £m
Non-current assets	
Property, plant and equipment	111
Investment in joint venture at cost	60
ADD: Post acquisition retained profit: (90 ÷ 2 = 45)	45
Current assets	49
Total assets	265
Equity and liabilities	
Share capital (£1 ordinary shares)	50
Retained earnings	185
	235
Current liabilities	30
Total equity and liabilities	265

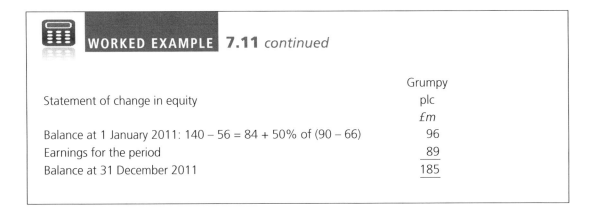

WORKED EXAMPLE **7.11** *continued*

Statement of change in equity	Grumpy plc £m
Balance at 1 January 2011: 140 − 56 = 84 + 50% of (90 − 66)	96
Earnings for the period	89
Balance at 31 December 2011	185

TEST YOUR KNOWLEDGE **7.9**

Why do companies enter into joint ventures?

10 Consolidated statement of cash flows

Issues related to the statement of cash flows are discussed in chapter 6. IAS 7 gives guidance on preparation of the statement of cash flows. Here we discuss the consolidated statement of cash flows. The consolidated statement of cash flows is prepared on the basis of the consolidated financial statement.

Accounting standards require the 'economic entity' to prepare a single set of consolidated statements, including a consolidated cash flow statement, which presents all of the entities within the group as one statement. It is also important to identify the different techniques that organisations use to manipulate their reporting of cash flows.

On consolidation, cash flows arising from the parent company, subsidiaries, associates and joint ventures will need to be consolidated. The process is a lot simpler than consolidating any of the other consolidated financial statements. However, IAS 7 provides further guidelines in relation to the consolidated statement of cash flows:

1 Foreign currency transactions – the exchange rate used for translation of transactions denominated in a foreign currency should be the rate in effect at the date of the cash flows.
2 Cash flows of foreign subsidiaries should be translated at the exchange rates prevailing when the cash flows took place.
3 As regards the cash flows of associates and joint ventures, where the equity method is used, the statement of cash flows should report only cash flows between the investor and the investee; where proportionate consolidation is used, the cash flow statement should include the venturer's share of the cash flows of the investee.
4 Aggregate (consolidated) cash flows relating to acquisitions and disposals of subsidiaries and other business units should be presented separately and classified as investing activities, with specified additional disclosures. The aggregate cash paid or received as consideration should be reported net of cash and cash equivalents acquired or disposed of.
5 The amount of cash and cash equivalents held by the entity that is not available for use by the group should be disclosed, together with a commentary by management.

STOP AND THINK **7.1**

Group accounting is a waste of money – what is your opinion?

END OF CHAPTER QUESTIONS

7.1 The summarised statement of financial position of Halesworth Ltd and Haverhill Ltd as at 31 October 2010 were as follows:

	Halesworth £'000	Haverhill £'000
Assets		
Investment in Haverhill	6000	
Other net assets at book Value	7200	3700
	13200	3700
Financed by:		
Ordinary share capital (£1 shares)	10000	1000
Retained profit at 1 October 2009	2940	1720
Net profit for 2009/10	260	980
	13200	3700

Halesworth purchased the entire share capital of Haverhill on 1 November 2009 for £6 million. The fair value of the net assets of Haverhill at that date was £1.2 million in excess of book value.

Required:

Prepare the consolidated statement of financial position of Halesworth and its subsidiary, as at 31 October 2010, based on the information provided. You should use the purchase method and comply as far as the information permits with standard accounting practice.

7.2 The following summarised balance sheet is provided for Twickenham Ltd as at 30 September 2011.

	£'000
Non-current assets at carrying value	2000
Net current assets	1600
	3600
Share capital (£1 ordinary shares)	2700
Retained profit at 1 October 2010	600
Profit for year to 30 September 2011	300
	3600

Wembley Ltd purchased 1.8 million shares in Twickenham Ltd on 1 October 2010 for £2.5 million. There were no differences between the carrying values and fair values of the Twickenham's assets and liabilities at that date and the company has paid no dividends for some years.

Required:

Based on the above information, calculate the balances to be included in the accounts of the Wembley Ltd group of companies for the year to 30 September 2011 in respect of the following items:

1 Goodwill.

2 NCI

3 Post-acquisition profits.

7.3 The summarised balance sheets of Clubs Ltd and its subsidiary companies Diamonds Ltd and Hearts Ltd at 31 December 2010 were as follows:

	Club Ltd £	Diamond Ltd £	Heart Ltd £
Non-current assets at carrying value	59000	299500	129700
80,000 shares in Diamond Ltd	126000	–	–
30,000 shares in Hearts Ltd	44000	–	–
	229000	299500	129700
Current assets	79000	62500	29500
Total assets	308000	362000	159200

END OF CHAPTER QUESTIONS

Equity and liabilities

Share capital (£1 shares)	200000	80000	40000
Retained earnings at 31 Dec 2009	36000	33200	7200
Profit/(Loss) for 2010	7000	11400	–13600
Non-current liabilities			
15% debentures	–	200000	50000
	243000	324600	83600
Current liabilities	65000	37400	75600
Total equity and liabilities	308000	362000	159200

Clubs Ltd acquired the shares in both subsidiaries on 31 December 2009. Neither subsidiary paid a dividend during the year.

Required

The consolidated balance sheet for the group at 31 December 2010 presented in vertical format so as to disclose the balance for net current assets.

Notes

1 Ignore taxation.
2 Assume no differences between the carrying values and fair values of the assets and liabilities of Diamonds Ltd and Hearts Ltd.
3 You should assume that any goodwill arising on consolidation suffers impairment equal to one-quarter of its initial value at the end of 2010.
4 Interest on debentures has been charged in arriving at the profit or loss for the year.

7.4 During the year ended 30 September 2011, Company A (the parent company) sells goods to Company B (the subsidiary) at cost plus a mark-up of 25%.

■ Explain the appropriate accounting treatment, for consolidation purposes, of the profit arising in the books of Company A on transfers of stock to Company B.
■ Also explain the logic behind the treatment.

7.5 Alpha paid £265,000 to acquire 70% of the equity shares of Beta on 1 January 2011. Beta's retained earnings at the date of acquisition were £50,000. The market price of Alpha's shares on 1 April 2010 was £4 each. The market price of Beta's shares was £2.50 each. The statements of financial position for the two companies at the close of business on 31 December 2011 were as follows:

	Alpha £	Beta £
Non-current assets		
Intangible non-current assets	–	30000
Tangible non-current assets	500000	70000
Investments	290000	60000
	790000	160000
Current assets		
Inventory	100000	50000
Trade receivables	150000	100000
Cash and cash equivalents	30000	20000
	280000	170000
Total assets	1070000	330000
Equity and liabilities		
Ordinary shares of £1 each	700000	100000
Share premium	140000	50000
Retained earnings	100000	100000
	940000	250000

END OF CHAPTER QUESTIONS

Current liabilities		
Trade payable	90000	60000
Accruals	40000	20000
	130000	80000
Total equity and liabilities	1070000	330000

Additional information
1 At the date of acquisition, 1 January 2011, Beta owned a piece of land that had a fair value of £20,000 in excess of its book value. The fair value adjustments have not been reflected in the individual financial statements of Beta.
2 One-half of goodwill arising on acquisition of Beta is impaired.
3 During the year to 31 December 2011, Alpha sold goods to Beta for £20,000 (at a mark up on cost of 20%). Beta had one-half of these goods in its inventory at 31 December 2011.
4 Intangible assets of Beta are all of a type whose recognition would not be permitted under IAS 38. IAS 38 is to be followed in preparing the consolidated financial statements. When Alpha made its investment in Beta on 1 January 2011, the intangible assets of Beta included £10,000 on that would not qualify for recognition under IAS 38.
5 Creditors reported by Beta include £10,000 owed to Alpha; whereas the corresponding amount in Alpha books is £15,000. The difference in inter-company balances is due to cash in transit.
6 It is group policy to value the non-controlling interest at the date of acquisition at its proportionate share of the fair value of the subsidiary's net assets. The non-controlling interest in Beta is to be valued at its (full) fair value. For this purpose, Beta's share price at that date of acquisition can be taken to be indicative of the fair value of the shareholding of the non-controlling interest at the date of acquisition.

Required
Prepare a consolidated statement of financial position for Alpha at 31 December 2011.
7.6   Explain what is meant by the parent entity concept and how the choice of this concept affects the preparation of consolidated financial statements.
7.7   The following information is provided in respect of Ronson plc.

	£m
Operating profit for 2011	26
Inventories:	
1 January 2011	107
31 December 2011	101
Receivables	
1 January 2011	86
31 December 2011	99
Payables	
1 January 2011	54
31 December 2011	72
Taxation charge, 2011	12
Depreciation charge, 2011	33
Purchase of non-current assets	111

Required
Calculate the 'Net cash generated from (or used in) operating activities' for Ronson plc for 2011 in accordance with the provisions of IAS entitled Statement of Cash Flows using the 'Indirect Method'.
7.8   In the preparation of the consolidated cash flow statement, should you include a joint venture that has been accounted for in the financial statements using the equity method of accounting?

Analysis and interpretation of accounts 1

■ CONTENTS

■ LEARNING OUTCOMES

This chapter deals with the part of the syllabus section entitled 'Analysis and Interpretation of Accounts'. After reading and understanding the contents of the chapter, working through all the Worked Examples and Practice Questions, you should be able to:

- understand the nature and principals of ratio analysis;
- the uses of ratio analysis and how managers and stakeholders can analyse published financial information;
- measure and interpret ratios as yardstick for company performance and comparison;
- carry out common size and trend analysis to give indication of company performance and efficiency;
- determine the primary ratios and their purpose using practical examples; and
- determine company performance on working capital and investment.

1 Introduction

Stakeholders that have a vested interest in the affairs of a business entity need to make informed decisions. Current and potential investors, creditors, customers and employees all have a vested interest in the financial performance and other aspects of a company. Financiers and credit providers need to gauge the creditworthiness of a company prior to any commitment of finances. This need for stakeholder servicing by companies is mostly enshrined in law, as well as in national and international guidelines.

Published financial reports provide stakeholders with financial information. Each stakeholder, having a different vested interest in a business entity requires access to financial information that serves their purposes. The information may be accessible in different forms allowing users of financial information to determine the current state of affairs of a company and to anticipate its future prospects.

Changes to company and related law and the development of, and considerable amendments to, International Financial Reporting Standards (IFRS) has placed a greater burden on companies to deliver additional and more detailed information, thereby facilitating a greater depth and quality of transparency particularly after the 2008 'credit crunch'.

This chapter will primarily evaluate company financial performance on the basis of published financial reports of listed companies. The nature of the modern corporation, being a limited liability entity, gives it a legal personality distinct from its owners. However, the nature of limited liability ensures that the liability of owners is limited to the extent of their ownership stake.

2   Stewardship and the role of managers

The principal–agent dichotomy (i.e. the separation of ownership from control) manifests in agency issues arising. Managers of companies are entrusted by the owners to maximise their investments; however, for various reasons, managers are presumed to work in their own interests at the expense of the owners. In this regard the owners will put mechanisms in place to monitor managerial behaviour. Shareholders entrust the board of directors with the responsibility for managing the affairs of the company by giving it direction, control, strategy and continuance. Typically, in modern corporations, the board of directors consists of non-executive and executive directors. Executive directors have a duty to implement the strategic vision of the board and report on progress, while the board as a whole monitors the conduct of executives.

The UK Code on Corporate Governance (2010) provides guidelines for board conduct, behaviour, duties and obligations. The UK Code is principle-based and requires directors to conduct business with integrity, responsibility and accountability. Corporate governance and ethical issues are more thoroughly covered in chapter 10. The remainder of this chapter discusses and analyses financial reports using various analysis techniques.

TEST YOUR KNOWLEDGE 8.1

What is meant by stewardship?

3   Horizontal and vertical analysis of accounts

3.1 Performing a horizontal analysis

The main point of performing a horizontal analysis on the financial statements is to see how things have changed from one period to the next. A horizontal analysis of the accounts is a comparison of two or more year's financial data. Horizontal analysis is facilitated by showing changes between years in both pound and percentage form (see Worked Example 8.1 below). Showing changes in pound form helps the analyst to focus on key factors that have affected profitability or financial position.

A horizontal analysis allows the user to compare the financial numbers from one period to the next, using financial statements from at least two distinct periods. Each line item has an entry in a current period column and a prior period column. Those two entries are compared to show both the pound difference and the percentage change between the two periods.

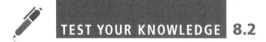

TEST YOUR KNOWLEDGE 8.2

(a) What is horizontal analysis is and how is it carried out?
(b) What useful information can the user extract by performing horizontal analysis?

WORKED EXAMPLE **8.1**

Comparative statement of financial Position of Jane plc as at 31 December

	011	2010	Increase/(Decrease)	
	£'000	£'000	Amount	%
Non-current assets				
Property and equipment:				
Land	4,000	4,000	0	0.0%
Building	12,000	8,500	3,500	41.2%
Total non-current assets	16,000	12,500	3,500	28.0%
Current assets				
Cash	1,200	2,350	−1,150	−48.9%
Accounts receivable	6,000	4,000	2,000	50.0%
Inventory	8,000	10,000	−2,000	−20.0%
Prepaid expenses	300	120	180	150.0%
Total current assets	15,500	16,470	−970	−5.9%
Total assets	31,500	28,970	2,530	8.7%
Equity and liabilities				
Share capital (£12 shares)	6,000	6,000	0	0.0%
Share premium	1,000	1,000	0	0.0%
6% preferred shares				
(£100 nominal value)	2,000	2,000	0	0.0%
Retained earnings	8,000	6,970	1,030	14.8%
	17,000	15,970	1,030	6.4%
Long-term liabilities:				
Bonds payable 8%	7,500	8,000	−500	−6.3%
Total long- term liabilities	7,500	8,000	−500	6.3%
Current liabilities				
Accounts payables	5,800	4,000	1,800	45.0%
Accrued payables	900	400	500	125.0%
Notes payables	300	600	−300	−50.0%
Total current liabilities	7,000	5,000	2,000	40.0%
Total liabilities	14,500	13,000	1,500	−11.5%
Total equity and liabilities	31,500	28,970	2,530	8.7%

Cash figure: Since we are measuring the change between 2009 and 2010, the £ amounts for 2009 become the base figure for expressing these changes in percentage form. For example, cash decreased by £1,150 between 2009 and 2010. This decrease expressed in percentage form is computed as follows: £1,150 ÷ £2,350 = 48.9%. Other percentage figures in this example are computed using the same formula.

WORKED EXAMPLE **8.1** *continued*

Comparative income statement and statement of changes in equity for the year ended 31 December

	2011	2010	Increase /(Decrease)	
	£'000	£'000	Amount	%
Sales	52,000	48,000	4,000	8.3%
Cost of goods sold	36,000	31,500	4,500	14.3%
Gross margin	16,000	16,500	−500	−3.0%
Operating expenses:				
Selling expenses	7,000	6,500	500	7.7%
Administrative expense	5,860	6,100	−240	−3.9%
Total operating expenses	12,860	12,600	260	2.1%
Net operating income	3,140	3,900	−760	−19.5%
Interest expense	640	700	−60	−8.6%
Profit before tax	2,500	3,200	−700	−21.9%
Income taxes (30%)	750	960	−210	−21.9%
Profit for the period	1,750	2,240	−490	21.9%

	Share capital £'000	Other reserves £'000	Translation reserve £'000	Retained earnings £'000	Total £'000
Balance at 1 January 20102011	6,000	3,000	–	6,970	15,970
Change in accounting policy (IAS 8)				–	–
Restated balance at 1 January 20102011				6,970	15,970
Changes in equity during the year					
Other comprehensive income					0
Total other comprehensive income	–	–	–	–	–
Profit for the period				1,750	1,750
Total recognised income and expenses for the period	0	0	0	1,750	1,750
Dividends				−720	−720
Issued share capital					0
Balance at 31 December 20102011	6,000	3,000	–	1,030	17,000

Notes:
1. Dividends to preferred shareholders, £6 per share (see statement of financial position above):
   2,000,000 x 6% = £120,000
2. Dividends to ordinary shareholders, £1.20 per share announced: £6,000,000 ÷ £12 x £1.20 = £600,000

Observe in the example that sales for 2011 were up £4 million over 2010, but that was more than negated by a £4.5 million increase in the cost of goods sold. Showing changes between years in percentage form helps the analyst to gain perspective and to get a feel for the significance of the changes that are taking place. For example, a £1 million increase in sales is much more significant if the prior year's sales were £2 million than if the prior year's sales were £20 million. In the first example, the increase would be 50% – undoubtedly a significant increase for any firm. In the second example, the increase would be 5%, which is just a reflection of normal progress and/or perhaps inflation.

3.2 Performing a vertical analysis

Another name for vertical analysis is a 'common size' analysis. For a business, particularly those in a growth cycle, a vertical analysis of the statement of income statement can be particularly enlightening. Looking at every item on the statement as a percentage of sales tells you where every penny of the company's revenue is going. Once you know that, it's easy to see which items are eating up too much of the profits. Those are the areas where managers can try to cut back. A two-year version of this analysis can show how components have changed, which may not be apparent until they are expressed in this manner. The following example demonstrates what a vertical analysis looks like for both a statement of profit and loss and a balance sheet.

 **WORKED EXAMPLE** 8.2

	2011	2011	2010	2010
	£'000	%	£'000	%
Sales	52,000	100.00%	48,000	100.00%
Cost of goods sold	36,000	69.23%	31,500	65.63%
Gross margin	16,000	30.77%	16,500	34.38%
Operating expenses:				
Selling expenses	7,000	13.46%	6,500	13.54%
Administrative expenses	5,860	11.27%	6,100	12.71%
Total operating expenses	12,860	24.73%	12,600	26.25%
Net operating income	3,140	6.04%	3,900	8.13%
Interest expenses	640	1.23%	700	1.46%
Net income before taxes	2,500	4.81%	3,200	6.67%
Less income taxes (30%)	750	1.44%	960	2.00%
Net income	1,750	3.37%	2,240	4.67%

Here, it can readily be seen that, although sales were up in 2011, gross margins were lower in 2011 than in 2010, because the cost of goods sold in 2011 was higher than in 2009. This needs to be investigated and reasons sought as to why this has happened. It could be that material was more expensive in 2011 than in 2010. Even though the rest of the expenses were comparatively higher in 2010 to sales, net profits were lower in 2011 due to the increased cost of sales.

TEST YOUR KNOWLEDGE 8.3

(a) Explain vertical analysis. How is it carried out?
(b) What useful information can the user extract by performing vertical analysis?

3.2.1 Dealing with exceptional items

At times exceptional items may arise – say a one-off gain made or loss incurred – that are not a regular occurrence in the ordinary course of business. These should be considered prior to any analysis being performed. The user is interested in the financial performance of a company in the ordinary course of events; hence, any exceptional items should be deleted prior to performing horizontal, or indeed any other analysis. By removing exceptional items from the calculations, the analyst can determine the rising trends using various analysis techniques. These will be considered in due course.

4 Trend analysis to a time series

Horizontal analysis of financial statements can also be carried out by computing trend percentages. Trend percentage states several years' financial data in terms of a base year. The base year equals 100%, with all other years stated in some percentage of this base.

 **WORKED EXAMPLE 8.3**

Consider a corporation that runs a multinational chain of fast-food outlets and restaurants, with thousands of outlets and restaurants worldwide. The corporation enjoyed tremendous growth in the years 2000–2010, as evidenced by the following data:

£'000	2010	2009	2008	2007	2006	2005	2004	2003	2002	2001	2000
Sales	14,200	13,300	12,400	11,400	10,700	9,800	8,300	7,400	7,100	6,700	6,400
Net income	1,980	1,950	1,550	1,640	1,570	1,430	1,220	1,080	960	860	800

By observing the data, it can be seen that sales increased every year. From the above table it is difficult to see how rapidly sales have been increasing and how the increases in net income have kept pace with the increase in sales. It is difficult to answer these questions by looking at the raw data alone.

The increases in sales and the increases in net income can be put into better perspective by stating them in terms of trend percentages, with 2000 as the base year. These percentages (all rounded) appear as follows:

£'000	2010	2009	2008	2007	2006	2005	2004	2003	2002	2001	2000
Sales	222%	208%	194%	178%	167%	153%	130%	116%	111%	105%	100%
Net income	248%	244%	194%	205%	196%	179%	153%	135%	120%	108%	100%

The trend analysis is particularly striking when the data are plotted as above. The chain's growth was impressive through the entire 11-year period, but it was outpaced by even higher growth in the company's net income. We will have to review the company's income statement and the statement of financial position to ascertain why there was a dip in the net income growth in 2008. One possible reason could be investment by the company in new plant and equipment which would lead to an increase in the depreciation charge. The expenditure in 2008 may be of exceptional nature and, for the purposes of analysis it may be prudent to write-back the expense to profits in determining the trend over the 11-year period.

The analysis presented in Worked Example 8.3 is a simple case of sales and income over an 11-year period. However, more powerful use can be made of trend analysis by analysing ratios (to be discussed later). By this means a picture will emerge that will indicate, using time-series, the growth, profitability and liquidity of a company. The table below is an example of a time-series of ratios depicting changes to prominent firm performance indicators:

TABLE 8.1: A time-series of ratios depicting changes to firm performance indicators

Ratio	2011	2010	2009	2008	2007
Profitability (Net profit to sales)	12.07	10.98	9.17	7.63	6.25
Rate of return (Return on capital employed)	5.40	5.10	5.20	1.70	4.10
Liquidity (Current ratio)	1.2 : 1	0.9 : 1	1.1 : 1	0.8 : 1	1.2 : 1
Asset usage (Total asset turnover)	1.5 times	1.1 times	1.4 times	1.3 times	1.2 times
Trade receivables turnover (Rate of turnover)*	40 days	43 days	57 days	53 days	49 days
Gearing	0.50 : 1	0.44 : 1	0.35 : 1	0.60 : 1	0.40 : 1

The firm performance indicators in the table show trends over an 11-year period using some important ratios. While all the indicators appear to show the company in good health, the dip in 2008 indicates the company may have incurred some exceptional expenditure. Nevertheless, the company returned to good financial position in the following year indicating it had taken the right steps in 2008.

5 Principles of ratio analysis

Ratios, as a tool of financial analysis, provide symptoms with the help of which an analyst is in a position to diagnose the financial health of a business. Financial analysis is similar to the diagnosis of a person by a doctor. As previously mentioned different groups of people are interested in different aspects of a business, therefore, *significance of ratio analysis* for various groups is different and may be discussed as follows:

5.1 Usefulness to management

5.1.1 Decision making

The management of a company will have easy access to financial information and hence can analyse trends more quickly. The mass of information contained in internal reports and financial statements may be unintelligible and confusing. Ratios help to highlight areas requiring attention and any corrective action needed, facilitating rapid decision making.

5.1.2 Financial forecasting and planning

Ratios help management to understand the history of the business. They also provide useful data on the existing strengths and weaknesses of the business. This knowledge is vital as it allows management to plan and forecast for the future.

5.1.3 Communication

Ratios can help to communicate information to interested parties in a way that they can easily understand. This enabling them to make informed economic decisions by using the existing situation to help them plan for the future.

5.1.4 Facilitate coordination

By being precise, brief and highlighting specific areas, ratios are likely to improve coordination between relevant quarters of management.

5.1.5 Control is more effective

Planning and forecasting systems establish budgets, develop forecast statements and lay down standards. Using ratios means that actual outturn (i.e. actual results), can be compared with these standards. Variances can be computed and analysed by managers, thereby administering an effective system of control.

5.1.6 Owners/shareholders

Existing, as well as prospective owners or shareholders, are fundamentally interested in the long-term solvency and profitability of the business. Ratio analysis helps them by analysing and interpreting both aspects of the business.

5.1.7 Creditors

Creditors can broadly be classified into short term and long term. Short-term creditors are trade payables etc. Trade creditors are interested in analysing the liquidity of the business to assess its creditworthiness.

Long-term creditors are financial institutions, debenture holders and mortgage creditors. They are interested in analysing the capacity of the business to repay its loans and any periodical interest on a timely basis. Ratio analysis provides answers to both type of creditors.

5.1.8 Employees

Employees are interested in fair wages and salaries, acceptable fringe benefits and bonuses linked with productivity/profitability. Ratio analysis can provide them with information regarding the efficiency and profitability of the business. This allows them to bargain more effectively for improved wages, bonuses and other aspects of their employment contracts.

5.1.9 The government

The government is interested in the financial information from businesses both at macro and micro levels. Information from businesses regarding production, sales, and profit is required for excise duty, VAT and income and corporation tax purposes. Group information from industry is required to formulate national policies and planning. In the absence of dependable information, government plans and policies may not achieve their desired results.

The accounts published annually by companies constitute an important source of information for external users and their form and content are carefully regulated with the intention of ensuring that they are a helpful and reliable guide to corporate progress (see chapters 1, 2 and 3). The amount of useful information that can be gleaned from the income statement and statement of financial position, however, is severely limited, even when a detailed breakdown of trading results is provided. For example, the income statement might show sales amounting to £500 million and the statement of financial position might disclose trade receivables totalling £21 million (sales to trade receivables ratio) but, taken in isolation, it is impossible to assess whether these amounts are satisfactory or unreasonable.

Ratio analysis has been developed to help translate the information contained in the accounts into a form more helpful and readily understandable to users of financial reports. The ratios do not appear in the accounts, however and users must calculate and interpret them themselves or employ someone with the necessary skills to do the job.

Accounting ratios are calculated by expressing one figure as a ratio or percentage of another with the objective of disclosing significant relationships and trends which are not immediately evident from the examination of individual balances appearing in the accounts. The ratio that results from a comparison of two figures possesses real significance only if an identifiable commercial relationship exists between the numerator and the denominator. For example, one would expect there to be a positive relationship between operating profit and the level of sales. Assuming that each item sold produces a profit, one would expect a higher sales figure to produce more profit. So, mere observation of the fact that profit is £5 million is not particularly illuminating. What is of greater interest is operating profit expressed as a percentage of sales. If sales are found to be £25million, the net profit percentage could be calculated as follows:

$$\text{Operating profit percentage} = \frac{\text{Operating profit}}{\text{Sales}} \times 100 \quad \frac{5}{25} = 20\%$$

The significance of an accounting ratio is enhanced by comparison with some yardstick of corporate performance. There are three options available, namely comparison with:

- results achieved during previous accounting periods by the same company (trend analysis);
- results achieved by other companies (inter-firm comparisons); and
- predetermined standards or budgets.

The advantage of making comparisons is that it enables users to classify a company's performance as good, average or poor in certain key areas. Sifting through the large volume of information contained in annual reports is cumbersome; reducing such information to a handful of important and very useful ratios enables the user to answer key questions on the economic reality of a company:

1   Does the profit being earned reflect good progress?
2   Is the company sufficiently cash-enabled?
3   Is there sufficient amount of capital on a long-term basis?
4   Are the resources of the company being used efficiently?
5   Are trade receivables and payables being managed efficiently?

Ratios are highly efficient way of determining the answers to the above questions, particularly if they are used on a time-series basis.

 **WORKED EXAMPLE** 8.4

For 2010, Bradford Ltd reported net profit and sales figures respectively of £50,000 and £400,000. In 2011, net profit increased to £90,000 and sales for the year amounted to £900,000. The net profit percentage earned by Bingley Ltd, a company that carries on trade in competition with Bradford, was 14% in 2011.

Required
Calculate and comment on the net profit percentages of Bradford for 2010 and 2011.

Answer

Net profit percentages	2010	2011
(50 ÷ 400,000) × 100 =	12.5%	
(90 ÷ 900,000) × 100 =		10.0%

The company's accounts report a significant *increase* in net profit, but the accounting ratios show that net profit expressed as a percentage of sales has *declined* and, moreover, is well below the return earned by a similar business. We cannot make a definitive assessment of Bradford's progress on the basis of a single accounting ratio, but it does point to the need for further investigation to determine why the ratio has fallen and why the margin earned by its competitor has not been achieved.

There are attractions and limitations attached to each of the three bases for comparison listed above. Last year's results are readily available, but observed changes over time are not necessarily significant. A comparison may show that there is an improvement in the net profit percentage, but last year's results may have been disastrous. Problems with inter-firm comparisons include the difficulty of finding a company engaged in a similar range of business activities, while differences in accounting policies might detract from the significance of any findings. It is, however, important to discover how a company is faring in relation to its competitors, as this should throw a great deal of light on its efficiency of management and its long-term prospects. A comparison of actual results with predetermined budgets should, in theory, be the best test of whether the workforce has achieved a reasonable level of efficiency. There is, however, the problem and cost of establishing standards. Also, it is little consolation to discover that work is being carried out efficiently if, due to the existence of a declining market, profit is falling. In practice, management rarely publishes forecasts of future results and so external users of accounting reports usually have to confine their attention to trend analysis and inter-firm comparisons.

 **TEST YOUR KNOWLEDGE** 8.4

Identify three appropriate yardsticks for comparing one or more accounting ratios prepared for a single company for a particular accounting period.

6 Nature of ratio analysis

Ratios, by themselves, are not an end, but only one of the means of understanding the financial health of a business entity. Ratio analysis is not capable of providing precise answers to all the problems faced by any business. Ratio analysis is basically a technique for establishing a meaningful relationship between significant variables of financial statements and interpreting the relationships to form a judgement regarding the financial affairs of a business.

6.1 Usefulness

Whether ratio analysis can be considered as useful depends upon:

- the objective of the analysis;
- selection of the relevant data;
- deciding the appropriate ratios to be calculated;
- comparing the calculated ratios with norms or standards or forecasts; and
- interpretation of the ratios.

6.2 Interpretation of accounting ratios

Calculating ratios is relatively simple. Interpreting them is a highly sophisticated and intricate phenomenon. The benefit of ratio analysis depends a great deal upon their correct interpretation. It needs skill, intelligence, training, farsightedness and intuition of a high order on the part of the analyst. The following are different ways in which ratios may be interpreted.

6.2.1 Individual ratio

An individual ratio may have its own significance (e.g. if the current ratio for a business continuously falls, it may indicate that the business may eventually become insolvent). Normally a single ratio does not convey any meaningful insight. However, it may be studied with reference to certain popular rules of thumb which can only give approximations. Care must be exercised here, because such comparison may be erroneous or unrealistic.

6.2.2 Group ratios

Ratios may be interpreted by considering several groups of related ratios. This kind of interpretation can be more meaningful as the current ratio can be studied alongside the liquidity ratio, or profitability ratios can be studied alongside return on investment.

6.2.3 Comparison with past ratios

Ratios may be interpreted by making comparisons over a period of time (i.e. the same ratio may be studied over a period of years). This will highlight any significant trends (e.g. use, decline, or stability). The average value of a ratio for the past number of years can serve as a standard against which current performance can be measured. When interpreting ratios for comparison over a period of time, any changes which might have taken place should be considered (e.g. price indexes, changes in managerial policy, or changes in accounting practices).

6.2.4 Projections

A business unit with a system of budgetary control and forecasts usually draws up projected financial statements. Any ratios based on these will act as the standard. Ratios calculated from the present financial statements will be compared to them. Variances will be calculated and analysed for specific purposes. This will enable corrective action to be taken wherever required.

6.2.5 Inter-firm or inter-industry

The ratios of one business may be compared with those of an identical business, or with the industry average at the same point in time. This type of comparison is useful to evaluate relative financial position of the business vis-à-vis other businesses or industries. When comparing businesses differences in accounting methods, policies, procedures and terminology must be taken into account.

6.2.6 Classification of accounting ratios

A meaningful accounting ratio is calculated by comparing balances between which there exists some identifiable economic relationship, but there are certain balances between which no apparent link exists (e.g. accumulated depreciation and trade payables). In many cases, however, a significant relationship does exist and the large number of financial totals appearing in the accounts produces numerous combinations that form the basis for the calculation of a relevant accounting ratio. Many of these ratios duplicate one another, whereas others are of limited significance and can probably be ignored without detracting from the value of the analysis. The author believes that the following representative list of 'traditional' accounting ratios is adequate for most purposes:

- working capital (current) ratio;
- liquidity (quick) ratio;
- proprietorship ratio;
- interest cover;
- rate of inventories turnover;
- rate of collection of trade receivables;
- rate of payment of trade payables;
- fixed (non-current) asset turnover;
- total asset turnover;
- gross profit margin;
- net profit percentage;
- rate of return on gross assets;
- rate of return on shareholders' equity (operating return on equity);
- debt: equity ratio; and
- return on capital employed (ROCE).

TEST YOUR KNOWLEDGE 8.5

Discuss and explain what is meant by the nature and classification of ratios.

6.3 Return on Capital Employed (ROCE)

The Return on Capital Employed (ROCE) ratio, expressed as a percentage of all capital (including non-current liabilities) reflects a company's total 'capital employed'. Capital employed can be defined in a number of ways. However, a common definition is all non-current liabilities (i.e. equity, reserves and non-current borrowings).

This measures a company's ability to generate returns from its available capital base. The ROCE ratio used to identify companies that offer good value, have the potential to grow and earn more relative to the price being paid.

6.3.1 The RoCE formula

The ROCE is a measure of the returns a company derives from its capital. It is calculated as profit after interest and taxes divided by tangible capital employed. The resulting ROCE ratio presents how efficiently capital is being used to generate post-tax profit. The ROCE formula is:

ROCE Ratio = Profit for the period/Shareholders fund + non-current borrowings.

In ratio analysis, analysts can use different terms in different ways. You should be aware of some of the different terminologies used for a particular ratio. ROCE, together with OROE, can give the user better insight as to a company's financial progress. On a time-series basis, ROCE and Operating Return on Equity (OROE) (see below) provide powerful techniques to understand a company's financial health. However, if there are no non-current borrowings, there will be no interest expenses, so in this situation ROCE and OROE would be the same.

WORKED EXAMPLE 8.5

Using the income statement and statement of financial position for Jane plc in Worked Example 8.1, calculate the ROCE ratio for 2009 and 2010. Make appropriate comments to the results.

Answer

ROCE Ratio = Profit for the year/Equity shareholders fund

	2010	2009
Return on Capital Employed =	1,750	2,240
	17,000	15,970
ROCE =	10%	14%

The ROCE calculations indicate that this ratio has declined from 14% in 2009 to 10% in 2010. It follows the trend by the calculated OROE ratio (see below) and suggests efficient use of company resources. Even though the sales revenue was slightly below 2009 level, the efficiency in the cost of goods sold has resulted in a lower ROCE figure, which is similar to that of the OROE.

6.3.2 Advantages of using ROCE

ROCE is used to indicate the value of the business gains (or losses) from its assets less its liabilities. The ratio is basically used to show how efficiently a business is using its resources.

For example, depending on the level of gearing, a business which owns substantial land but has little profit will have a smaller ROCE than a business which owns little land but makes the same profit.

6.3.3 Disadvantages of using ROCE

The main drawback of ROCE is that it measures return against the book value of assets in the business. As these depreciate, the ROCE will increase even though cash flow has remained the same. Thus, older businesses, with depreciated assets, will tend to have higher ROCE than newer, possibly more profitable businesses. In addition, while cash flow is affected by inflation, the book value of assets is not. Consequently revenue increases with inflation, while capital employed generally does not (as the book value of assets is not affected by inflation).

6.4 Operating Return on Equity (OROE)

The primary investment ratio, also known as Operating Return on Equity (OROE), is one of several measurements used in financial analysis. This ratio is used to assess the profitability of businesses and how well they make use of equity. For example, when investors place their money in a corporation, or consider doing so, the primary investment ratio enables them to determine if that decision is worthwhile. Since the ratio is implemented when assessing company value, it is more appropriately applied to businesses in operation for profit.

6.4.1 The OROE formula

To calculate the primary investment ratio a company's earnings before interest and tax (EBIT) are divided by total shareholder equity:

$$\text{Operating Return on Equity} = \frac{\text{EBIT}}{\text{Total equity}} \times 100$$

The first of these numbers is determined by subtracting business expenses from sales revenue, and the second number is the total book value of a company's shares plus all reserves. Worked Example 8.6 demonstrates how OROE is calculated and the meaning derived from the ratio:

WORKED EXAMPLE 8.6

From the statement of financial position and the income statement for Jane plc (Worked Example 8.1) calculate the Operating Return on Equity for 2009 and 2010.

Answer

$$\text{Operating Return on Equity} = \frac{\text{EBIT}}{\text{Total equity}} \times 100$$

	2010	2009
Operating Return on Equity =	3,140	3,900
	17,000	15,970
OROE =	18%	24%

Operating Return on Equity appears to have decreased in 2010 as compared to 2009. Reasons for this need to be investigated and answers found using other ratios.

6.4.2 Advantages of OROE

An important advantage of the primary investment ratio is that it allows analysts and lenders to quickly determine the level of a business' debt. Additionally, because the ratio does not subtract tax from earnings, it provides a better understanding of core corporate ability to generate income. The primary investment ratio also shows how well a company generates income and can be used within related formulas that also calculate a company's return on equity (ROE). The 'equity' aspect of ROE relates here to total assets – total liabilities.

6.4.3 Disadvantages of OROE

Without comparing the primary investment ratio against the same ratio from previous periods in the business cycle, a comprehensive and chronological financial evaluation cannot be determined. Financial ratios can also be manipulated by business decision making (e.g. share buybacks that reduce the number of existing shares and increase the primary investment ratio). Another limitation of the ratio is that it does not examine the influence of other accounting figures such as those that measure how well businesses utilise cash flow.

6.5 Primary operative ratio

Operating and gross profit margin ratios indicate the operating and gross profits as a percentage of the sales revenue in a particular period. The ratio is expressed as:

$$\frac{\text{Operating profit}}{\text{margin}} = \frac{\text{Operating profit}}{\text{Sales}} \times 100\%$$

$$\text{Gross profit margin} \frac{\text{Gross profit}}{\text{Sales}} \times 100\%$$

WORKED EXAMPLE **8.7**

Using the income statement and statement of financial position for Jane plc in Worked Example 8.1, calculate the primary operative ratios (i.e. operating profit margin and gross profit margin, for 2009 and 2010). Make appropriate comments as to the results.

				2010		2009	
Operating profit margin	=	Operating profit / Sales	=	3,140 / 52,00	= 6%	3,900 / 48,000	= 8%
Gross profit margin	=	Gross profit / sales	=	16,000 / 52,000	= 30%	16,500 / 48,000	= 34%

The operating profit figure is used in the operating profit margin ratio as this represents the business profit from trading operations. However, the gross profit margin ratio simply compares the margin profit to total sales. Comparing both sets of ratios, especially over time, can give an insight into the operating efficiency of a business. In the above example, it is quite clear that the business became highly efficient and achieved desirable margins in 2009 as compared to the figures for 2010.

6.6 Primary liquidity ratio

A business requires working capital to function in its day-to-day operations. Any pressure on working capital could lead to a business either defaulting on its obligations (e.g. to trade payables and employees) or, in the worst case scenario, lead to total business failure. Liquidity ratios measure the working capital employed in a business and a change in the amount of working capital over time will indicate if the business is facing short-term financial difficulties.

The ratios illustrated in this section may be further classified into those that examine short-term solvency and those that investigate the longer-term financial strength of the concern.

6.6.1 Working capital (current) ratio

Working capital is defined as the excess of current assets over current liabilities, and an adequate surplus is normally interpreted as a reliable indication of the fact that the company is solvent. The working capital ratio is calculated as follows:

$$\text{Working capital ratio} = \frac{\text{Current assets}}{\text{Current liabilities}}$$

The purpose of the ratio is to shed further light on the short-term solvency of the company and, more specifically, on its ability to pay its debts as they fall due. It does this by calculating the relationship between current assets and current liabilities. A question which students and business people often ask is, 'What is a correct working capital ratio?' Textbooks often quote a ratio of 2:1 but, although this is often a useful guideline, it must be used with care.

Analysts must familiarise themselves with the rate at which current assets are converted into cash and how quickly current liabilities must be paid. This very much depends on what is normal practice within a particular industry. For example, a retailer who sells goods for cash normally operates with a much lower ratio than a manufacturer who sells goods on credit. In the retail industry, resources are converted directly from inventories into cash, whereas in manufacturing, goods sold are probably tied up as debts outstanding for six to eight weeks before cash becomes available. The period for which inventories are held varies from one industry to another. A manufacturer of small metal products is likely to convert raw materials into finished goods and sell them much more quickly than a construction company where inventories are likely to comprise a much higher proportion of current assets to reflect the relatively slow rate of turnover.

For these and other reasons, you should be on your guard against always accepting accounting ratios at face value, and should assess their significance only after carefully considering the economic facts that lie behind them.

WORKED EXAMPLE 8.8

Ludlow Ltd (see draft internal financial statements below) is a firm of wholesale merchants and we can see from its accounts that most of its sales are made on credit and that the company also receives credit from its suppliers. The company, therefore, requires a working capital ratio sufficiently in excess of 1:1 to accommodate the large quantity of resources tied up in its inventory. This is because the company is likely to allow customers roughly the same amount of credit that it receives from suppliers, so resources tied up in inventory will not be converted into cash in time to pay trade payables as they fall due. It is on the assumption that one-half of all current assets are invested in inventory that a working capital ratio of 2:1 is often regarded as a reasonable rule of thumb.

Towards the end of 2010 the directors of Ludlow Ltd, a firm of wholesale merchants, decided to raise additional capital in the form of a debenture of £800,000 to facilitate expansion of the business.

The draft internal management accounts for the year ended 31 December 2011, together with corresponding figures for 2010, are set out below:

Income statement		2011		2010	
		£	£	£	£
Sales:	Credit		6,600,000		5,500,000
	Cash		400,000		500,000
			7,000,000		6,000,000
Less:	Opening inventories	1,360,000		1,340,000	
	Purchases (on credit)	5,670,000		4,700,000	
		–		–	
	Closing inventories	1,500,000		1,360,000	
	Cost of sales		5,530,000		4,680,000
	Gross profit		1,470,000		1,320,000
Expenses:	Administration	275,000		270,000	
	Selling	400,000		395,000	
	Distribution	325,000		280,000	
	Depreciation	35,000		30,000	
		1,035,000		975,000	
Operating profit		435,000		345,000	
Less: Debenture interest		80,000		–	
Profit before tax		355,000		345,000	
Income tax (tax rate 50%)		177,500		172,500	
Profit for the period		177,500		172,500	

Movement on Reserves	2011	2010
	£	£
Reserves at 1 January	750,000	655,000
Add: Profit after tax	177,500	172,500
	927,500	827,500
Less: Dividends	77,500	77,500
Reserves at 31 December	850,000	750,000

WORKED EXAMPLE **8.8** *continued*

Statement of financial position

	2011		2010	
	£	£	£	£
Non-current assets				
Cost		900,000		700,000
Accumulated depreciation		185,000		150,000
		715,000		550,000
Current assets				
Inventories	1,500,000		1,360,000	
Trade receivables	1,560,000		960,000	
Cash and cash equivalents	120,000	3,180,000	20,000	2,340,000
		3,895,000		2,890,000
Less: Current liabilities				
Trade payables	567,500		467,500	
Taxation	177,500		172,500	
	745,000		640,000	
Working capital		2,435,000		1,700,000
		3,150,000		2,250,000
Non-current liability:		800,000		–
10% debenture loan		3,950,000		2,250,000
Equity				
Share capital		1,500,000		1,500,000
Reserves		850,000		750,000
		2,350,000		2,250,000

The following additional information is provided:
1. At 1 January 2010 inventories amounted to £800,000, gross assets to £2,710,000 and shareholders' equity to £2,155,000.
2. The product range and buying prices were unchanged over the period 1 January 2010 to 31 December 2011.
3. The debenture loan was received on 1 January 2011 and additional warehouse facilities became available on that date at a cost of £200,000.
4. No non-current assets were purchased during 2010.

Note
This example will be used as a basis for calculations throughout the remainder of this chapter, so it is worth taking some time to familiarise yourself with these figures.

6.6.2 Current ratio

Calculations for Ludlow Ltd are:

$$2010 = \frac{345,000}{(2710,000 + 2890,000)} \times 100\% = 12.3\% \times 1/2$$

$$2011 = \frac{435,000}{(2890,000 + 3895,000)} \times 100\% = 12.8\% \times 1/2$$

We do not know what type of wholesaler Ludlow Ltd is, but a ratio of about 1.5:1 is quite common in that sector of the economy, and so the calculated figures suggest that the company is financially stable. The high ratio may have unfavourable implications for the profitability of the firm; however, since resources unnecessarily tied up in inventory, cash and receivables are not earning a return. In business there is often a conflict between profitability and financial stability and managerial policies that place an excessive amount of emphasis on financial stability may cause profits to be unduly depressed.

6.6.3 Liquidity (quick) ratio

The purpose of the liquidity ratio is also to examine solvency. It is calculated in a similar manner to the working capital ratio, but with one important difference: the liquidity ratio concentrates attention more directly on a company's prospect of paying its debts as they fall due by excluding current assets which will not be converted into cash within the next couple of months. It is for this reason that the calculation is often colourfully described as the 'quick ratio' or 'acid test of solvency'.

It is necessary to examine carefully current assets to decide which items should be included or omitted. Inventory should be excluded, unless it is expected to be sold quickly for cash, as should any trade debts not receivable within the next few months (e.g. because the sales price is payable on an instalment basis spread over a year). Marketable securities held as a temporary means of employing surplus funds should be included, whereas prepayments should technically be excluded though the amount involved is usually immaterial.

The normal approach is to include all current liabilities irrespective of their payment dates. Trade payables are, of course, usually payable within a relatively short time span, but this is not necessarily the case with taxation. It might also be argued that, for many companies, the bank overdraft is a revolving source of finance which is unlikely to be withdrawn without advance warning, though much may depend on the company's financial position and the general economic climate. It is probably because accountants are inclined to favour conservative measures of corporate progress that all current liabilities are usually included in the calculation of the liquidity ratio. We will comply with this convention, but bear in mind the limitation that this places on the significance of the ratio that results. Calculations for Ludlow Ltd (the fact that a small proportion of sales is for cash is ignored and all inventories are excluded) are:

$$2010 \ \frac{980,000}{640,000} = 1.5 : 1$$

$$2011 \ \frac{1,680,000}{745,000} = 2.3 : 1$$

A liquidity ratio of 1:1 is desirable; a ratio significantly below unity usually means that a company will have great difficulty in meeting its debts as they fall due, while a ratio in excess of unity indicates that the company has cash resources that are surplus to requirements. At the end of 2010, Ludlow Ltd's ratio is more than adequate and a year later it has improved still further. While there is no doubt that the company is solvent, there must be some doubt as to whether it is making the best use of available resources.

TEST YOUR KNOWLEDGE 8.6

(a) Why is it important to have an adequate balance of working capital?

(b) Explain how the liquidity ratio may be computed.

6.6.4 Additional solvency ratio indicators for Ludlow Ltd

				2011	2010	2011	2010
				£'000	£'000		
Working capital turnover	=	$\dfrac{\text{Turnover}}{\text{Working capital}}$	=	$\dfrac{7{,}000}{2{,}435}$	$\dfrac{6{,}000}{1{,}700}$	3 times	4 times
Total asset turnover	=	$\dfrac{\text{Turnover}}{\text{Total assets}}$	=	$\dfrac{7{,}000}{3{,}895}$	$\dfrac{6{,}000}{2{,}890}$	2 times	2 times
Stock turnover	=	$\dfrac{\text{Average stock}}{\text{Cost of sales/365}}$	=	$\dfrac{(1360+1500)/2}{5{,}530\,/365}$	$\dfrac{(800+1360)/2}{4{,}680\,/365}$	94 days	84 days
Receivables' turnover	=	$\dfrac{\text{Receivables}}{\text{Credit sales/365}}$	=	$\dfrac{1{,}560}{6{,}600\,/365}$	$\dfrac{960}{5{,}500\,/365}$	86 days	63 days
Payables' turnover	=	$\dfrac{\text{Payables}}{\text{Cost of sales/365}}$	=	$\dfrac{567.5}{5{,}530\,/365}$	$\dfrac{467.5}{4{,}680\,/365}$	37 days	31 days
ROCE	=	$\dfrac{\text{Profit for the period}}{\text{Shareholders fund} + \text{Non-current debt}}$	=	$\dfrac{177.5}{2{,}350}$	$\dfrac{172.5}{2{,}250}$	8%	8%
Gearing	=	$\dfrac{\text{Non-current liabilities}}{\text{Shareholders fund} + \text{Non-current debt}}$	=	$\dfrac{800}{3{,}150}$	$\dfrac{0}{2{,}250}$	25%	Nil

6.6.5 Other solvency ratios for Ludlow Ltd

1 The working capital turnover ratio is used primarily to indicate the ability of the company to generate sales on the basis of money used to fund operations. The ratio shows that Ludlow was more efficient in the use of working capital in 2010 (4 times) over 2011 (3 times). However, the difference is not too drastic; nevertheless managers may wish to check the reason for the small decline.

2 The total asset turnover ratio appears to be the same over 2010/11. However, while turnover did increase in 2011 so did additions to asset which is the main reason for the ratio to have remained the same over the two years.

3 The stock turnover ratio measures the investment in inventory. The aim is to minimise inventory holdings to minimise cash locked up in stock. In 2011 the company is taking 94 days to turnover stock as compared to 84 days in 2010. Managers may need to investigate why this is the case and ensure stock turnover is controlled, as this would have a knock-on effect on the overall cash operating cycle (i.e. the length of time it takes for cash to crystallise from purchase of goods eventually receiving money from customers).

4 The receivables turnover ratio measures the number of days receivables are outstanding. Obviously we are looking for a quickest turnaround in receiving money from outstanding receivables. In 2011 customers took 94 days, on average, to pay compared to 84 days in 2010. This means that together with stock turnover days, the company's cash is taking longer to materialise as cash.

5 The payables turnover ratio is similar to the receivables turnover ratio; however, here we are looking to the number of days the company takes to service its creditors. Again, due to increasing days being taken for cash to come in, the company is taking longer to pay its own debts.

6 The return on capital employed appears to be stable. This suggests company profitability appears to be stable; however, the ratio does not take account of liquidity. Companies can be profitable yet financially strapped for cash which could lead to company failure in the long run.

7   The gearing ratio indicates the company; having raised cash through debenture issue is geared by 25%. This may be a good thing for the company as a certain amount of debt capital used in operations can lead to a lowering of the overall cost of capital.

Overall, Ludlow appears to be in a stable condition while profitability is probably at an expected rate. However, some concerns arise on the liquidity issue. Managers may need to investigate and determine how to improve the liquidity position and not let it get any weaker.

Ludlow appears to have done the right thing by investing in the company through debt capital. However, this now raises the issue of servicing the debenture debt and gives rise to the calculation of the interest cover ratio:

$$\text{Interest cover} = \frac{\text{Operating profit}}{\text{Interest expense}} = \frac{435}{80} = 5 \text{ times}$$

The interest cover ratio suggests that Ludlow has sufficient operating profit to adequately meet its interest payment obligations.

STOP AND THINK 8.1

The real value in financial ratios lies in cash-flow-based ratios – accounting ratios do not show much. Do you agree or disagree?

END OF CHAPTER QUESTIONS

8.1   Explain the role of stewardship in managing a company's financial affairs.

8.2   Explain the principal features of ratio analysis.

8.3   State the primary accounting ratios and explain their purpose and usefulness in assessing a firm's performance.

8.4   An extract of balances for current assets and liabilities in respect of Roadster Ltd are presented below:

	2011	2012
	£'000	£'000
Current assets		
Inventory	240	180
Trade receivables	400	520
Cash and cash equivalents	55	60
	695	760
Current liabilities		
Account payables	425	320
Accrued expenses	80	40
	505	360

Required

(a) Calculate the liquidity ratios for the two years 2011 and 2012 respectively.

(b) Comment on the movements of the liquidity ratios and any issues of concern arising.

8.5   The following information relates to Brent Limited for the two years to 31 December 2011 and 2012. Brent Ltd – Income statement for the years to 31 December.

END OF CHAPTER QUESTIONS

	2011		2012	
	£'000	£'000	£'000	£'000
Sales (all credit)		1,500		1,900
Opening inventory	80		100	
Purchases	995		1,400	
	1,075		1,500	
Closing inventory	100		200	
Cost of goods sold		975		1,300
Gross profit		525		600
Less: Expenses		250		350
		275		250

Brent Ltd – Statement of financial position at 31 December

	2011		2012	
	£'000	£'000	£'000	£'000
Non-current assets (Net Book Value)		580		460
Current assets				
Inventory	100		200	
Trade receivables	375		800	
Cash and cash equivalents	25		–	
		500		1,000
Total assets		1,080		1,460
Equity and liabilities				
Ordinary shareholders fund		500		500
Retained earnings		300		550
		800		1,050
Non-current liabilities				
Debentures		200		1,050
Current liabilities				
Bank overdraft		–	10	
Trade payables	80	80	200	210
Total liabilities		280		410
Total equity and liabilities		1,080		1,460

Ignore taxation

Required

(a)   Calculate the following accounting ratios for the two years 2011 and 2012 respectively:
- gross profit margin;
- operating profit margin;
- return on capital employed;
- gearing;
- stock turnover days;
- current ratio;
- acid test;
- trade receivables collection period; and
- trade payables payment period.

(b)   Comment on the company's performance for the year to 31 December 2012.

8.6   Using the information from Brent Ltd in Question 8.5 above, carry out vertical and horizontal analysis for the company and comment on the figures.

Analysis and interpretation of accounts 2

■ **CONTENTS**

■ **LEARNING OUTCOMES**

This chapter continues with the part of the syllabus section entitled 'Analysis and Interpretation of Accounts'. After reading and understanding the contents of the chapter, working through *all* the worked examples and practice questions, you should be able to understand the purpose and explanations for gearings and company performance ratios and:

- the impact of debt on company profitability;
- the link between gearing and profitability;
- the impact of gearing on shareholders return;
- the impact of working capital on cash flow and company profit;
- explain company efficiency from asset usage ratios; and
- explain the pyramid of ratios.

1 Introduction

This chapter delves more deeply into ratio analysis and specifically addresses company performance from the perspectives of profitability and asset usage and efficiency. Particular ratios are used to evaluate company financial performance as well as measuring levels of financial commitment in relation to resources employed.

2 Subsidiary ratios

2.1 Gearing ratio

Capital is derived from two sources: shares and loans. It is quite likely for shares to be issued only when the company is formed, but loans are invariably raised at some later date. There are numerous reasons for issuing loan capital. For instance, the owners might want to increase their investment, but avoid the risk that attaches to share capital and they can do this by making a secured loan. Alternatively, management might require additional finance that the shareholders are unwilling to supply, so a loan is raised instead. In either case, the effect is to introduce an element of **gearing** or leverage into the capital structure of the company. There are numerous ways of measuring gearing, but the debt: equity ratio is perhaps most commonly used. An alternate form is debt: (equity + debt). For the purpose of calculating this ratio, debt may be measured in either of two ways:

(a) Debt defined as long-term loans:

$$\text{Debt : Equity ratio} \quad x \quad \frac{\text{Long-term loans}^{\star} : 1}{\text{Shareholders' equity}}$$

*This could includes any preference shares outstanding.

(b) Debt defined as total borrowing:

Lenders, when assessing risk, want to examine a business's full financial exposure. For this reason, they often find it useful to extend the definition of debt, used for the purpose of calculating the debt: equity ratio, in the following manner:

$$\text{Total debt : Equity ratio} \quad \text{x} \quad \frac{\text{Total financial debt}^{\star}}{\text{Shareholders' equity}} : 1$$

*Includes loans from directors and bank overdrafts that, although technically for the short term, are a permanent source of financing for many businesses.

The use of debt capital has direct implications for the profit accruing to the ordinary shareholders, and expansion is often financed in this manner with the objective of increasing, or 'gearing up', the shareholders' rate of return. This objective is achieved, however, only if the rate earned on the additional funds raised exceeds that payable to the providers of the loan.

 **WORKED EXAMPLE** **9.1**

The directors of Conway Ltd are planning to undertake a new project which calls for a total investment of £1 million in fixed assets and working capital. The directors plan to finance the investment with a long-term loan bearing interest at 12% per annum, and the financial controller forecasts an annual profit before finance charges of £150,000 from the new project.

Required
Calculate the surplus profit, if any, expected to accrue to shareholders from the new project (ignore tax).

Answer

	£
Additional profit contribution by new project	150000
Less: Interest charge, 12% of £1 million	120000
Surplus	30000

The existing shareholders benefit from the project to the extent of £30,000, because the new venture yields a return of 15%, whereas providers of the required finance have contracted for interest at the lower rate of 12%. Of course, profit may not come up to expectations and, if it is less than £120,000, the introduction of gearing will be detrimental to the ordinary shareholders, whose rate of return will suffer.

Returning to the case of Ludlow Ltd (see Worked Example 8.8), calculations of the debt: equity ratios are as follows:

2010   Zero gearing (no loans)

2011 $\dfrac{800000}{2350000} : 1 \;= 0.34 : 1$

A significant element of gearing was introduced in 2011 by the issue of an £800,000 debenture to finance an expansion of operations. The policy was not entirely successful and the rate of return on total assets declined from 12.3% to 11.5%. The shareholders' return suffered only a modest decline, however (see Chapter 10, section 10.2), and this suggests that, assuming 2010's results would otherwise have been repeated, the additional activity produced a return only marginally below the 12% interest payable on the debenture.

The shareholders of a highly geared company reap disproportionate benefits when earnings before interest and tax increase, because the interest payable on a large proportion of total finance remains unchanged. The converse is also true; a highly geared company is likely to find itself in severe financial difficulties if it suffers a succession of trading losses. It is not possible to specify an optimal level of gearing for companies but, as a general rule, gearing should be low in those industries where demand is volatile and profits are subject to fluctuation. The effect of profit fluctuations on the rates of return earned by companies with different levels of gearing is demonstrated in Worked Example 9.2 below).

WORKED EXAMPLE 9.2

Ponty Ltd and Pop Ltd are established companies engaged in similar lines of business. Trading conditions change significantly from year to year, and an analysis of past results achieved by companies in the same line of business as Ponty and Pop shows that operating profit before deducting interest charges can fluctuate by up to 50% above or below the following estimated results for the forthcoming year.

	Ponty	Pop
	£'000	£'000
Ordinary share capital (£1 shares) at 1 June 2010	1500	3200
Revaluation surplus at 1 June 2010	500	1000
Capital redemption reserve at 1 June 2010	–	800
14% Debentures at 1 June 2010	4000	1000
Operating profit before interest 2010/11	840	840

It is the policy of each company to pay out its entire profits in the form of dividends.

Required

(a) For each company, calculate:
   (i) the estimated rate of return on shareholders' equity;
   (ii) the gearing (debt: equity) ratio.

(b) A discussion of the relative merits of the capital structures of each of the two companies from the shareholders' point of view. The discussion should include calculations of *maximum* possible variations in the return on shareholders' equity.

Note

Ignore taxation.

(a)

	Ponty	Pop
	£'000	£'000
Operating profit	840	840
Interest charge	560	140
Profit before tax	280	700
Equity	2000	5000
Return on shareholder's equity	14%	14%

Debt: Equity – (See workings below)
4,000 : 2,000   2:1
1,000 : 5,000   1:5

Workings – Debt : Equity ratio

	Ponty	Pop
Debt	4000	1000
Equity	2000	5000
Debt/Equity	2	1/5
Answer:	2:1 or 200%	1:5 or 20%

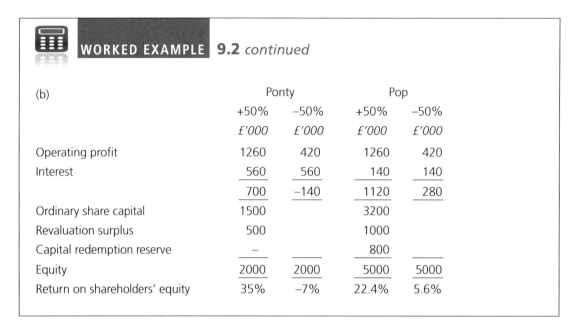

WORKED EXAMPLE 9.2 *continued*

(b)	Ponty		Pop	
	+50%	−50%	+50%	−50%
	£'000	*£'000*	*£'000*	*£'000*
Operating profit	1260	420	1260	420
Interest	560	560	140	140
	700	−140	1120	280
Ordinary share capital	1500		3200	
Revaluation surplus	500		1000	
Capital redemption reserve	–		800	
Equity	2000	2000	5000	5000
Return on shareholders' equity	35%	−7%	22.4%	5.6%

The following relevant comments might be made:

1   The capital structure of Ponty Ltd is highly geared, which means that there is a high ratio of debt to equity finance.
2   The main advantage of gearing is that the return to shareholders will be geared up when there is a rise in profits, because all additional profits accrue to the equity shareholders.
3   This can be seen above, with an increase in profits of 50% causing the return on shareholders' equity to increase 250% to 35%.
4   Conversely, when profits decline, the return on equity falls quickly due to the fact that the fixed interest charges, in the case of Ponty £560,000, must still be paid.
5   A fall in operating profit of 50% results in a figure for operating profit which is insufficient to cover interest charges and there is a reduction in shareholders' equity to the amount of £140,000.
6   The capital structure of Pop, by way of contrast, is low geared with a debt: equity ratio of 1:5 or 20%.
7   A 50% rise in profits results in an increase in the return on shareholders' equity but the rise is more modest to 22.4%.
8   Conversely, a fall in profits is not so detrimental to the equity shareholders who continue to receive a return of 5.6% on their investment.
9   A further drawback of a high level of gearing is that the company may face acute financial embarrassment if there is a significant fall in profits. Whereas dividends can be reduced when profits are low, if necessary to zero, interest charges are a legal obligation, which must be paid irrespective of profit levels.

TEST YOUR KNOWLEDGE 9.1

What is the purpose of gearing?

2.2 Proprietorship ratio – a brief discussion

Before discussing subsidiary liquidity ratios, it may be helpful to touch upon a longer-term financial ratio related to how a company is financed.

The total assets belonging to a company are financed by a combination of resources provided by shareholders and lenders. The proportion of business assets financed by the shareholders is measured by the **proprietorship ratio**, which is conventionally calculated by expressing the shareholders' investment, or equity, in the company as a percentage of total sources of finance.

$$\text{Proprietorship ratio} = \frac{\text{Shareholders' equity}}{\text{Total sources of finance}^\star} \times 100$$

*Total *sources of finance* include both non-current and current liabilities.

This ratio, conventionally expressed as a percentage, is a measure of financial stability, since the larger the proportion of business activity financed by shareholders, the smaller the creditors' claims against the company. This produces two advantages:

1   Equity finance is normally repaid only when the company is wound up. Even then, repayment occurs only if sufficient cash remains after all other providers of finance have been refunded the amounts due to them. Where an excessive proportion of total finance is provided by short-term creditors, management is likely to be under continuous pressure to finance repayments falling due. In these circumstances any withdrawal of, or reduction in, a source of finance causes the company acute financial embarrassment.
2   Dividends are payable at the discretion of management, whereas interest payable on loan capital is a legally enforceable debt. A company with a large proportion of equity finance is therefore more able to survive a lean period of trading than a highly geared company that is legally obliged to make interest payments irrespective of profit levels.

It is difficult to specify an appropriate percentage as this depends a great deal upon trading conditions within the industry. In general, a higher percentage is expected in those industries where there are large fluctuations in profitability, because reliance on overdraft and loan finance gives rise to heavy interest charges that a company may find it difficult to pay when results are poor. In any event, one normally expects shareholders to provide at least half the finance, and the implications of significant changes from one year to the next should receive careful investigation.

The proprietorship ratio, viewed from the creditor's standpoint, provides a useful indication of the extent to which a company can stand a fall in the value of its assets before the creditor's position is prejudiced. Carrying values are not the same as current values, of course, but a proprietorship ratio of say, 75% would indicate that there exists a significant cushion for creditors, and the resale value of assets would have to fall to less than one-quarter of their carrying value before the creditors' position on liquidation would be jeopardised.

Calculations for Ludlow Ltd (see Worked Example 8.8) are:

$$2010 \qquad \frac{2,250,000}{2,250,000 + 640,000} \times 100 = 78\%$$

$$2011 \quad \frac{2,350,000}{2,350,000 + 800,000 + 745,000} \times 100 = 60\%$$

Shareholders provide a healthy 78% of total finance at the end of 2010, but this declines to 60% by the end of the following year. The main reason for this change is the debenture issue that had a significant effect on the financial structure of the company. Shareholders remain the dominant source of funds, but there is now a much greater reliance on external finance and a corresponding need to meet annual interest payments.

3   Liquidity ratios

The primary liquidity ratios, current and quick ratios, have been demonstrated in section 8.5.6. We will now discuss subsidiary ratios related to working capital.

3.1 Interest cover

The fact that a company is legally obliged to meet its interest charges was referred to when examining the proprietorship ratio (see section 2 above). There is no legal restriction on sources of cash that may be employed by management to meet its interest payments; it may even make an additional share issue with the intention that part of the proceeds should be used for that purpose. Nevertheless, interest payments are a business expense and, in the long run, all such costs must be met out of sales revenue if the company is to remain viable. **Interest cover** stresses the importance of a company meeting its interest charges out of revenue, and it does this by expressing net profit before interest charges (operating profits) as a multiple of the interest charged.

$$\text{Interest cover} = \frac{\text{Profit before interest and tax}}{\text{Interest charged}}$$

The purpose of this calculation is to indicate the ease with which a company meets its fixed interest obligations out of profit. A low figure indicates that interest payable imposes a heavy burden on the company's finances, thereby increasing the risk of insolvency. It should be recognised, however, that interest cover would be expected to fall immediately after a loan issue. For example, debentures may be raised with two to three years' capital requirements in mind, but a full utilisation of the additional resources made available is unlikely to be achieved straight away. In this situation, current earnings have to bear the full weight of the additional charges, but the extra revenue, which is expected to result from an expansion programme, takes longer to materialise.

Interest cover is a ratio which receives a significant amount of attention from analysts in general and lenders in particular. Traditional measures of asset utilisation and asset cover for advances are of little relevance in service-based industries where tangible assets are at a low level. In these circumstances, it is particularly important to measure a company's ability to generate enough revenue to cover finance charges and leave a sufficient balance for dividends and to finance eventual loan repayments. The ratio of earnings: finance charges helps a great deal in this situation.

Calculations for Ludlow Ltd (see Worked Example 8.8) are:

2010   No interest charged

2011 $\dfrac{435,000}{80,000} = 5.4$ times

The interest cover for Ludlow Ltd appears to be adequate.

TEST YOUR KNOWLEDGE 9.2

(a) Why is it important to have a high proprietorship ratio?
(b) What is the reason for the growing importance of the interest cover calculation?

4   Asset turnover ratios

The ratios calculated in this section are designed to examine how fully management is utilising the resources placed at its disposal by shareholders and creditors. These ratios help to explain any improvement or decline in the solvency of a business. They also provide clues to underlying changes in profitability (these are measured by the accounting ratios contained in section 8.5.5).

4.1 Rate of inventory turnover

The term 'ratio' is used loosely in accounting to cover all the calculations that measure the relationship between two financial totals. We have already seen that net profit is conventionally expressed as a percentage of sales and that interest cover is presented as a simple multiple (i.e. *n* times). The **rate of inventory turnover**, which measures the speed with which a company turns over its inventory, may also be expressed as a single figure. The calculation is made as follows:

$$\text{Rate of inventory turnover} = \frac{\text{Cost of goods sold}}{\text{Average inventory level}}$$

Two typical queries asked about the above formula are as follows: Why use the cost of goods sold rather than sales? Why use the average inventory level rather than closing inventory? The reason is the same in both cases – to ensure that both the numerator and the denominator are computed on a comparable basis. Inventory, which makes up the denominator, are valued at cost for accounting purposes and the numerator must be computed on a similar basis. The sales figure *can* be used to produce a ratio that enables users to make helpful inter-period comparisons, when cost-of-sales figures are not available. However, there is a risk that incorrect conclusions may be drawn if there are changes in the gross profit margin from one accounting period to another.

Turning to the reason for using average inventory levels, the numerator measures the cost of goods dispatched to customers *during* an accounting period, and the denominator must therefore represent the investment in inventory *during* the same time period. In practice, inventory levels are likely to fluctuate a great deal; they are often built up during relatively quiet times and subsequently run down when the level of activity increases.

For this reason, it is important to calculate the average investment in inventory rather than use the inventory level at a particular point in time. The average is usually based on the opening and closing figures. A more precise calculation makes use of inventory levels at various dates during the year, perhaps at the end of each month (for similar reasons, average figures are used in the calculation of a number of other ratios considered below).

Many analysts prefer to present this ratio in terms of the number of days which have elapsed between the date that goods are delivered by suppliers and the date they are dispatched to customers (i.e. the stockholding period). This is done by modifying the formula so as to achieve the desired result in the following single step.

$$\text{Rate of inventory turnover days} = \frac{\text{Average inventories level}}{\text{Cost of Sales}} \times 365$$

Companies strive to keep the stockholding period as low as possible to minimise associated costs. An increase in the stockholding period from say, 30 to 60 days causes the investment in inventory to double. Extra finance then has to be raised, handling costs increase and the potential loss from damage to inventory and obsolescence is much greater. But although management aims to keep inventory to a minimum, it must at the same time ensure that there are sufficient raw materials available to meet production requirements (in the case of a manufacturer) and enough finished goods available to meet consumer demand. It is, therefore, management's job to maintain a balance between conflicting objectives.

Calculations for Ludlow Ltd (see Worked Example 8.8) are:

$$2010 = \frac{(1{,}340{,}000 + 1{,}360{,}000) \times 1/2}{4{,}680{,}000} \times 365 = 105 \text{ days}$$

$$2011 = \frac{(1{,}360{,}000 + 1{,}500{,}000) \times 1/2}{5{,}530{,}000} \times 365 = 94 \text{ days}$$

There has been a significant reduction in the average period for which inventory is held; this suggests that the management has streamlined the purchasing, selling and distribution functions. A comparison of the two statements of financial position reveals an increase in the figure for inventory, but this is to be expected as there has been a significant increase in the level of sales during the year. Indeed, a higher level of business activity normally calls for an equivalent increase in inventory to ensure that additional consumer requirements can be met without delay. It is because Ludlow's management has succeeded in increasing sales without a commensurate increase in inventory, means that money that would otherwise be tied up in inventory remains available for use elsewhere in the business.

The above presentation of the rate of inventory turnover produces a satisfactory measure for wholesalers and retailers, but only a rough approximation for manufacturing companies.

Manufacturers have three categories of inventory: raw materials, work-in-progress and finished goods. Ideally, each of these should be accounted for separately to compute the total stockholding period. The calculations are demonstrated in section 5 below, which examines the 'cash operating cycle'.

TEST YOUR KNOWLEDGE 9.3

Why is it usual to use cost of goods sold rather than sales for the purpose of computing the rate of inventory turnover?

4.2 Rate of collection of trade receivables

The period of credit taken by customers varies between industries but, as a general rule, companies extract the maximum amount of credit from suppliers since, in the absence of discounts for prompt payment, accounts unpaid represent a free source of finance. At the same time, undue delays should be avoided, as these have a harmful long-term effect on the company's credit rating. In practice, it is quite usual for customers to take six to eight weeks to pay their bills. The **rate of collection of trade receivables** is calculated *in days*, as follows:

$$\text{Trade receivables days} = \frac{\text{Average trade receivables}}{\text{Sales (or turnover)}} \times 365 \text{ days}$$

$$2010 \quad \frac{(800,000 + 960,000) \times 1/2}{550,000} \times 365 = 58 \text{ days}$$

$$2011 \quad \frac{(960,000 + 1,560,000) \times 1/2}{660,000} \times 365 = 70 \text{ days}$$

It should be noted that the denominator is confined to credit sales since only these give rise to receivables outstanding. Where the split between cash and credit sales is not given, the total sales figure may be used to calculate a ratio that gives useful comparative information provided there is no significant change in the proportion of total sales made for cash.

It takes Ludlow Ltd on average nearly two weeks longer to collect its debts in 2011. The result is that a disproportionate amount of money is tied up in trade receivables; these resources are yielding no return and are also losing value to the business during a period of inflation. The reasons for the change should be investigated (e.g. it may be the result of a conscious policy decision to offer customers additional credit to make the company's products more attractive). This can be a sound business tactic particularly when credit is tight, but management must make arrangements to finance the much higher level of trade receivables as a result.

An alternative explanation for the slower rate of debt collection may be slackness in the credit control department, whose functions include confirmation of new customers' creditworthiness before goods are supplied and the task of following up overdue accounts. Failure to discharge both these duties efficiently results in an unduly large figure for trade receivables and a substantial increase in the risk of bad debt.

4.3 Rate of payment of trade payables

This **rate of payment of trade payables** measures the average period of time taken by companies to pay their suppliers. The result must be interpreted with particular care as not all suppliers grant similar terms of credit but, provided there are no significant changes in the mix of trade creditors, the average payments period should remain stable.

$$\text{Rate of payment of trade payables days} = \frac{\text{Average trade payables}}{\text{Credit purchases}} \times 365$$

We are not given Ludlow's balance for trade payables at the beginning of 2010, so we cannot make the above calculation for that year. We can make the calculation for 2011 but, without a comparative figure for 2010, this is of little interpretive value. Comparable figures may be obtained, however, by basing each year's calculation on the *closing* figure for trade payables rather than the average figure for the year. This tells us the approximate numbers of days' purchases represented by the closing balance of trade payables. It does not, of course, follow that a similar credit period was obtained throughout the year, unless purchases were made at a uniform rate.

Calculations for Ludlow Ltd based on closing trade payables balances are:

$$2010 \quad \frac{467,500}{4,700,000} \times 365 = 36 \text{ days}$$

$$2011 \quad \frac{567,000}{5,670,000} \times 365 = 37 \text{ days}$$

A change in the rate of payment of suppliers may well reflect an improvement or decline in a company's liquidity. For instance, if a company is short of cash, it is likely that suppliers will have to wait longer for the payment of amounts due to them. This may be an acceptable short-term strategy, particularly where suppliers are familiar with their customer's temporary predicament. Management should, however, take prompt steps to arrange additional finance, otherwise supplies of goods will eventually be curtailed. The short-term solvency ratios show that Ludlow Ltd has no cash problems and, as might therefore be expected, the average period of credit taken from suppliers remains fairly stable at just about five weeks.

TEST YOUR KNOWLEDGE **9.4**

(a) What are the possible reasons for an increase in the rate of collection of trade receivables?
(b) Is an increase in the rate of payment of trade payables a good or a bad thing?

5   The cash operating cycle

A period of time elapses between the payment for goods or raw materials received into inventory and the collection of cash from customers in respect of their sale. The gap is known as the **cash operating cycle.** During this period of time the goods acquired, together with the value added in the case of a manufacturer, must be financed by the company. The shorter the length of time between the initial outlay and ultimate collection of cash, the smaller the amount of working capital that needs to be financed.

To estimate the length of the cash operating cycle, it is necessary to:

1   Calculate the time that the product spends in each stage of its progression from acquisition to sale and subsequent cash receipt.
2   Deduct from the length of time found in step 1, the period of credit received from suppliers.

The various elements in the calculation are described below and illustrated in Worked Example 9.3 which shows that Wing Ltd's cash operating cycle has 145 days in 2010 and 192 days in 2011. For a trading company that buys and sells goods without processing them, omit stages 1(a) and 1(b).

5.1 Inventory

Items are purchased or produced, held for a period of time and then used or sold. We have previously seen that estimates of the length of time for which various categories of inventory that are held must be based on a comparison of the average inventory levels with the issues of inventory during the period under consideration. In the case of a manufacturing company, separate calculations must be made for each of the following three categories of inventory:

- *Raw materials* – These are acquired, held in stock, and then transferred to production. Stocks of raw materials are related to raw materials consumed to find the average length of time for which they are held.
- *Working in progress* – Raw materials are taken from stock and processed, which involves additional manufacturing costs. The average production time is found by relating the value of work in progress to the cost of goods manufactured.
- *Finished goods* – When production is complete, the finished goods are transferred from the factory to the warehouse. (In the case of a trader, finished goods, stored in the warehouse, are purchased from outside.) The average length of time for which items are held can be found by relating the stock of finished goods to the cost of goods sold during the accounting period.

5.2 Trade receivables

The average age of debts is found from the values of trade receivables and sales (see section 4.3).

5.3 Trade payables

These finance the production and selling cycle from the time raw materials or goods are received into stock until they are paid for. The period of credit is found from the values of trade payables and purchases (see section 4.3).

The length of the cash operating cycle is obtained by aggregating the periods of time calculated for each of the above items.

WORKED EXAMPLE 9.3

The cash balance of Wing Ltd. has declined significantly over the last 12 months. The following financial information is provided.

Year to 31 December	2010	2011
	£	£
Sales	573000	643000
Purchases of raw materials	215000	264000
Raw materials consumed	210000	256400
Cost of goods manufactured	435000	515000
Cost of goods sold	420000	460000

Balances at 31 December	2010	2011
Trade receivables	97100	121500
Trade payables	23900	32500
Inventory:		
Raw materials	22400	30000
Work in progress	29000	34300
Finished goods	70000	125000

All purchases and sales were made on credit.

Required

(a) An analysis of the above information which should include calculations of the cash operating cycle (i.e. the time lag between making payment to suppliers and collecting cash from customers) for 2010 and 2011.

(b) A brief report on the implications of the changes that have occurred between 2010 and 2011.

WORKED EXAMPLE 9.3 *continued*

Notes

Assume a 365-day year for the purpose of your calculations and that all transactions take place at an even rate.

All calculations are to be made to the nearest day.

Answer

(a)

		2010 days			2011 days
Raw materials	$\dfrac{22400}{210000}$	× 365	39	$\dfrac{30000}{256400}$	43
Credit from suppliers	$\dfrac{23900}{215000}$	× 365	$\dfrac{-41}{-2}$	$\dfrac{32500}{264000}$	$\dfrac{-45}{-2}$
Production period	$\dfrac{29000}{435000}$	× 365	24	$\dfrac{34300}{515000}$	24
Finished goods	$\dfrac{70000}{420000}$	× 365	61	$\dfrac{121500}{460000}$	96
Credit to customers	$\dfrac{97100}{573000}$	× 365	62	$\dfrac{125500}{643000}$	71
Cash operating cycle			$\overline{145}$		$\overline{192}$

(b) The cash operating cycle has increased by 47 days or 32%. The increased investment in working capital may be calculated as follows:

	£	£
Inventory	121400	189300
Receivables	97100	121500
Less: Payables	−23900	−32500
	194600	278300

The increased period for which raw materials are held has been balanced by an equivalent increase in the period of credit taken from suppliers. Furthermore, the production period has remained constant at 24 days, suggesting no change in the efficiency with which resources are moved through the factory. The areas of concern are the significant increase in the period of credit taken by customers and the massive increase in the holding of finished goods that has grown from the equivalent of two months' sales at the end of 2010 to more than three months' sales at the end of 2011.

The company has achieved a significant growth in its gross profit percentage; more information is needed to discover whether any resulting increase in profit sufficiently compensates for the likely cost of the increase in capital employed.

5.4 Non-current asset turnover ratio

A new business first needs to arrange for the provision of accommodation and the installation of any necessary plant and equipment. It is unusual for these facilities to be used to their full capacity immediately but, as business builds up, the level of utilisation increases. The **non-current asset turnover ratio** measures the degree of non-current asset utilisation and is computed as follows:

$$\text{Non-current asset turnover ratio} = \frac{\text{Sales}}{\text{Average non-current assets}} : 1$$

The ratio is likely to reveal excess capacity from time to time during the life of a business, and it may be unavoidable. Possible reasons include:

- temporary inconveniences, such as a strike or a fire that destroys essential equipment;
- the collapse in demand for a product line, unless steps are promptly taken to dispose of the equipment or transfer it to an alternative use;
- the acquisition of additional non-current assets. The point is eventually reached where existing non-current assets are used to their full capacity and any further increase in business activity first requires the acquisition of additional plant. It is some while before demand increases sufficiently to absorb the extra capacity, however, and meanwhile non-current asset turnover declines.

Note – as non-current assets (NCA) depreciate and sales are constant – NCA turnover rises. Also – sales increase with inflation – NCA do not – NCA turnover rises.

 **WORKED EXAMPLE 9.4**

During 2008, Rhyl Ltd operated at full capacity and 1,000 units of output were produced and sold for £50 each using plant that cost £20,000. On 1 January 2009 management purchased for £20,000 additional plant with a capacity to produce a further 1,000 units. Output for the years 2009/11 is as follows:

2009	1,200 units
2010	1,500 units
2011	2,000 units

The selling price remained unchanged at £50 per unit.

Required

Calculate the non-current asset turnover ratio for each year ignoring depreciation.

Answer

$$2008 \quad \frac{50000}{20000} = 2.5{:}1$$

$$2009 \quad \frac{60000}{40000} = 1.5{:}1$$

$$2010 \quad \frac{75000}{40000} = 1.9{:}1$$

$$2011 \quad \frac{100000}{40000} = 2.5{:}1$$

The new plant is working at only 1/5th of its capacity during 2009, and the result is that non-current asset turnover declines to 1.5:1. Only when both new and old plant are working at full capacity in 2011, is the ratio restored to 2.5:1.

 **WORKED EXAMPLE 9.4** *continued*

Using the example for Ludlow Ltd (whose accounts are given in Worked Example 8.8), the calculations are:

$$2010 \quad \frac{6,000,000}{(550,000 + 550,000) \times 1/2} : 1 = 10.62 : 1$$

$$2011 \quad \frac{7,000,000}{(715,000^* + 550,000) \times 1/2} : 1 = 10.89 : 1$$

*The additional warehouse facilities become available on 1 January 2011 at a cost of £200,000.

The ratio has declined, which suggests that the additional warehouse facilities may not have been used to their full capacity during 2011.

 TEST YOUR KNOWLEDGE 9.5

Give three possible reasons for a decline in the non-current asset turnover ratio.

5.5 Total asset turnover ratio

It is management's job to make the fullest use of available resources, because only if this objective is achieved will profits be maximised. The inventory turnover, non-current asset turnover and trade receivables collection ratios are designed to measure management's ability to control the level of investment in certain selected areas, whereas the **total asset turnover ratio** has the broader aim of assessing the extent to which management utilises *all* available resources.

It is computed as follows:

$$\text{Total asset turnover ratio} = \frac{\text{Sales}}{\text{Average total assets}} : 1$$

A high ratio indicates that management is using the assets effectively to generate sales; most probably the company is working at near-full capacity. A decline in the ratio suggests that assets are underutilised and should either be used more fully or sold. One drawback of the calculation is that it benefits companies using older assets. This is partly the effect of inflation, but also because company accounts show non-current asset at a net carrying value that declines each year.

Calculations for Ludlow Ltd. are:

$$2010 \quad \frac{6000000}{(2,710,000 + 2,890,000) \times 1/2} : 1 = 2.14 : 1$$

$$2011 \quad \frac{7000000}{(3,690,000^* + 3,895,000) \times 1/2} : 1 = 1.85 : 1$$

*Assets at the end of 2010 totalled £2,890,000, but cash of £800,000 was received from a debenture issue made on 1 January 2011. This is included in the opening balance for the purpose of computing average total assets during 2011.

The ratio may be expressed either in the above form or as an amount of sales per £1 invested (i.e. sales were £2.14 per £1 invested in 2010 and £1.85 per £1 invested in 2011). It is therefore apparent that a significant reduction in asset utilisation has occurred; earlier calculations suggest that this is principally due to the much longer period of credit allowed to customers in 2011.

5.6   Profit ratios

The purpose of profit ratios is to help assess the adequacy of profits earned by the company and also to discover whether profitability is increasing or declining. A proper appreciation of the significance of the gross profit margin and the net profit percentage (examined below) is dependent upon a thorough understanding of the different ways in which business costs respond to changes in the levels of production and sales.

5.6.1 Gross profit margin

The calculation is made as follows:

$$\text{Gross profit margin} = \frac{\text{Gross profit}}{\text{Sales}} \times 100$$

Using the Ludlow Ltd example again, the calculations are:

2010 $\dfrac{1{,}320{,}000}{6{,}000{,}000}$ = 22%

2011 $\dfrac{1{,}470{,}000}{7{,}000{,}000}$ = 21%

The reduction from 22% to 21% appears small, but the effect is to reduce gross (and net) profit by 1% of £7 million (i.e. £70,000).The reason for the decline is implied by note 2 to the accounts, which tells us that the product range and buying price were unchanged over the period 1 January 2010 to 31 December 2011. Assuming the inventory was properly valued, the lower margin may, therefore, be attributed to lower selling prices.

The expectation that the gross profit margin should remain unchanged, irrespective of the level of production and sales, is based on the assumption that all costs deducted when computing gross profit are directly variable with sales. This is explored further in Worked Example 9.5 and the material that follows this example.

 WORKED EXAMPLE **9.5**

Chester is a trader who purchases frame tents for £40 each and sells them, through a mail order catalogue, at a price of £50 each. During 2010 and 2011 sales amounted to 1,000 tents and 2,000 tents respectively. There is no opening or closing stock.

Required
Prepare Chester's trading accounts for 2010 and 2011 and calculate the gross profit margin for each year.

Answer

Trading account	2010	2011
	£	£
Sales	50000	100000
Less: Cost of goods sold	40000	80000
Gross profit	10000	20000
Gross profit margin	20%	20%

Sales have doubled in 2011 and, because costs debited to the trading account are directly variable with sales, the gross profit is also twice the 2010 level. A gross profit of 20% continues to be earned, however, and the gross profit margin therefore remains unchanged at 20%.

A stable gross profit margin is quite usual for a trader like Chester, and also for a retailer, but less likely for a manufacturer. This is because the cost of goods sold figure for a manufacturing company includes fixed costs such as factory rent and rates, and semi-variable costs such as factory lighting and heating. Except in highly capital intensive industries, variable costs will nevertheless remain dominant and large fluctuations in the gross profit margin would be unexpected. A stable gross profit margin is therefore the norm and variations, which call for careful investigation, may be caused by any of the following events:

5.6.2 Price cuts

A company may need to reduce its selling price to achieve the desired increase in sales. For instance, assuming Chester had to reduce the selling price to £48 to sell 2,000 tents in 2011, the revised trading account would be as follows:

Trading account	2010
	£
Sales	96000
Less: Cost of goods sold	80000
Gross profit	16000
Gross profit margin	16.7%

5.6.3 Cost increases

The price which a company pays its suppliers, during a period of inflation, is likely to rise, and this reduces the gross profit margin unless an appropriate adjustment is made to the selling price. Assume Chester had to pay £44 for her tents in 2011 and the company keeps its selling price at £50.

Trading account	2011
	£
Sales	100000
Less: Cost of goods sold	88000
Gross profit	12000
Gross profit margin	12%

5.6.4 Changes in mix

A change in the range or mix of products sold causes the overall gross profit margin to vary, assuming individual product lines earn different gross profit percentages.

5.6.5 Under- or over-valuation of inventory

If closing inventory are under-valued, cost of goods sold is inflated and profit understated. An incorrect valuation may be the result of an error during a stock take, or it may be due to fraud. For instance, a business person might intentionally undervalue inventory to reduce the amount of tax payable. It must, of course, be remembered that the closing inventory of one period is the opening inventory of the next, so the effect of errors cancels out unless repeated.

5.6.6 Net profit percentage

The ratio is calculated as follows either before deducting interest (using operating profit as the numerator) or after deducting interest (in which case profit before tax is used as the numerator):

$$\text{Net profit percentage} = \frac{\text{Operating profit}}{\text{Sales}} \times 100$$

This ratio is designed to focus attention on the net profit margin arising from business operations. When examining the gross profit margin, we saw that an increase in sales is expected to produce an equivalent increase in gross profit and that gross profit expressed as a percentage of sales normally remains stable. Similarly, net profit increases with sales but, in this case, the increase occurs also as a percentage of sales.

The different response of the two profit figures to an increase in sales is explained by the fact that, whereas most of the costs debited to the manufacturing and trading accounts are variable, the majority of the remaining costs are fixed. The result is that an increase in sales causes cost per unit to decline because the fixed costs are spread more thinly over a larger volume of output. It is often useful to express each item of cost as a percentage of sales to help illustrate changes in their relative impact over time.

Calculations for Ludlow Ltd are:

$$2010 \quad \frac{345,000}{6,000,000} \times 100 = 5.8\%$$

$$2011 \quad \frac{435,000}{7,000,000} \times 100 = 6.2\%$$

There has been a small increase in the net profit percentage, but rather less than might have been expected in view of the fact that sales increased by one-sixth and expenses debited to the income statement were kept under tight control. (This could be confirmed by expressing the expenses individually or in total as a percentage of sales.) The main problem is the fall in the gross profit margin, since this caused gross, and consequently net, profit to be approximately £70,000 lower than would have been the case if the 22% margin achieved in 2010 had been repeated in 2011.

 **WORKED EXAMPLE** **9.6**

Assume the same facts as for Worked Example 9.5. In addition, Chester pays rent and rates of £3,000 each year while other overhead expenses, including the salary of a part-time employee, stationery and electricity, amount to £4,000 in 2010 and £6,000 in 2011.

Required
Prepare Chester's Income Statement for 2010 and 2011, and express costs and profit balances as a percentage of sales. Comment on the results.

Answer

	2010		2011	
	£	%	£	%
Sales	50000	100	100000	100
Less: Cost of goods sold	40000	80	80000	80
Gross profit	10000	20	20000	20
Less: Rent and rates	3000	6	3000	3
Other overhead expenses	4000	8	6000	6
Profit	3000	6	11000	11

The net profit percentage has risen from 6% to 11% because of the reduced impact of fixed costs as sales increase. The rent and rates have remained unchanged and have therefore fallen from 6% to 3% of sales, while other overhead expenses have increased by just 50% and, therefore, declined from 8% to 6% of sales.

The point will eventually be reached where output cannot be increased further without incurring a significant addition to fixed costs. For instance, if Chester's business grows further, she may have to rent new premises, thereby causing a large increase in overheads. This will cause a temporary reduction in the net profit percentage until full use is made of the increased capacity.

TEST YOUR KNOWLEDGE 9.6

(a) Why would you expect the net profit percentage to increase when sales increase?
(b) Outline three possible reasons for an increase in the gross profit margin.

5.6.7 Rate of return on gross assets

The **rate of return on gross assets** is often alternatively described as the rate of return on capital employed.

The problem with the latter description is that the term capital employed is used, in accounting, to signify at least two different financial totals:

■ shareholders' equity; and
■ gross or net assets.

To avoid potential confusion, the term 'rate of return on capital employed' is normally avoided in this text. Depending on the version of capital employed under investigation, we use the term 'rate of return on shareholders' equity' or 'rate of return on gross (or net) assets'. This section focuses on the rate of return on gross assets which is calculated as follows:

$$\text{Rate of return on gross assets} = \frac{\text{Profit before interest}}{\text{Average gross assets}} \times 100$$

It is management's job to ensure that the most effective use is made of available resources. The rate of return on gross assets measures the extent to which this objective has been achieved and, for this reason, is often described as the 'primary accounting ratio'. Calculations for Ludlow Ltd are:

$$2010 \quad \frac{345,000}{(2,710,000 + 2,890,000) \times 1/2} \times 100 = 12.3\%$$

$$2011 \quad \frac{435,000}{(3,690,000 + 3,895,000) \times 1/2} \times 100 = 11.5\%$$

6 Pyramid of ratios

6.1 Relationship between accounting ratios

An analysis of corporate performance made by students and even by trained accountants is often unsatisfactory. A common weakness is the failure to explore the relationship between the various ratios that have been calculated. A particularly important relationship is expressed in the following so-called **du-Pont formula**:

Secondary ratios   *Primary ratios*

Total asset turnover × Net profit %   =   Rate of return on gross assets

Management endeavours to maximise the return earned on gross assets, and it can accomplish this objective in two ways: it can increase the net profit percentage and/or it can achieve a higher rate of asset utilisation. It may well happen that greater asset utilisation, for instance more sales, can be achieved only by lowering prices; management has to judge whether the larger volume of activity is sufficient to justify the lower gross and net margins which result from implementing a policy of price reduction.

WORKED EXAMPLE 9.7

Holly and Head run separate businesses in different geographical areas, marketing a similar product for which there exists a ready market. They meet at a conference and are interested to discover that, whereas Holly keeps prices low in order to keep her business operating at full capacity, Head supplies goods only at 'normal prices for the industry'. They decide to compare their results and extract the following information from recently published accounts:

	Holly	Head
	£	£
Profit before interest (i.e. operating profit)	50000	100000
Sales	600000	750000
Average gross assets	200000	500000

Required

Calculate the 'primary' and 'secondary' ratios of Holly and Head.

Answer

Applying the formula:

$$\frac{\text{Total asset turnover}}{} \times \frac{\text{Net profit percentage}}{} = \frac{\text{Return on gross assets}}{}$$

$$\text{Holly} = \frac{600000}{200000} \times \frac{50000}{600000} \times 100 = \frac{50000}{200000}$$

$$3 \times 8.3\% = 25\%$$

$$\text{Head} = \frac{750000}{500000} \times \frac{100000}{750000} \times 100 = \frac{100000}{500000}$$

$$1.5 \times 13.3\% = 20\%$$

The above calculations show that Holly achieves the greater asset utilisation (£3 of sales per £1 invested as compared with the £1.50 achieved by Head), but her net profit percentage is lower (8.3% compared with Head's 13.3%). Overall, Holly's policies seem to be more successful (i.e. the greater asset utilisation more than compensates for the lower margins, and she achieves a rate of return on gross assets of 25%).

The formula may also be used to shed further light on the performance of Ludlow Ltd by extracting, from sections Total Assets Turnover Ratio, Net Profit Percentage and Rate of return on Gross Assets, the following ratios previously calculated:

	Secondary ratios Asset utilisation	Primary ratio Profit margin	Rate of return on gross assets
2010	2.14	× 5.75% =	12.3%
2011	1.85	× 6.20% =	11.5%

The asset utilisation is much lower in 2011, and the explanation for this is that much of the money raised through issuing a £800,000 debenture has been absorbed by increasing the period of credit allowed to customers by nearly two weeks. The directors have, however, succeeded in increasing the net profit percentage. Sales have been increased and, although price cuts have reduced the gross margin by one point to 2.1%, overhead expenses have been kept under tight control and a small reduction in the total cost per unit has been achieved. The higher net profit margin does not sufficiently compensate for the lower asset utilisation, however, and the primary ratio suffers a significant decline.

TEST YOUR KNOWLEDGE 9.7

Explain the nature and purpose of the du-Pont formula.

STOP AND THINK 9.1

Do you think companies should publish financial ratios rather than leaving the user to calculate them?

END OF CHAPTER QUESTIONS

9.1 The minority-shareholding in Merino Ltd is 20%. The company manufactures kitchen implements that are sold to retail chains and through a cash sales outlet from the company's factory premises. The minority shareholders are unsure whether this company is being well managed and has asked for your help in studying the accounts.

The minority shareholders tell you that the mark-up is usually 100% on cost in this type of business of which about two-thirds goes in overheads. The minority shareholders have also discovered that external liabilities are normally about one quarter of equity and that interest normally comprises about 20% of operating profit. The following financial information is available:

The following financial information for Merino Ltd:

Income statement for the year to 31 December 2012

	£'000
Sales	5500
Cost of sales	2700
Gross profit	2800
Administration expenses	375
Distribution costs	1175
Operating profit	1250
Interest costs	300
Profit before tax	950
Tax	220
Profit for the year	730

Statement of financial position at 31 December 2012

	£'000	£'000
Non-current assets		6000
Current assets		
Inventory	235	
Trade receivables	235	
Cash and cash equivalents	230	700
Total assets		6700

END OF CHAPTER QUESTIONS

Equity and liabilities
Share capital		1835
Retained earnings		1230
		3065

Non-current liabilities
Debentures		3000

Current liabilities
Trade payables	405	
Taxation	230	635
Total liabilities		3635
Total equity and liabilities		6700

Required

(a) Calculate:
   (i)   three ratios based on the above accounts which examine the management of working capital;
   (ii) three ratios based on the above accounts which examine the profitability of the company; and
   (iii) two ratios based on the above accounts which examine the capital structure of the company. Wherever possible, the ratios calculated should be those in respect of which comparative data is available.

(b) A discussion of the financial position and performance of Merino Ltd based on the results of your calculations under (a) and the information provided in the question.

9.2 The following information is provided for Tanner Ltd and Spanner Ltd, which supply a similar range of products but are located in different geographical areas and are not in competition with one another.

	Tanner	Spanner
	£'000	£'000
Operating profit	1000	1200
Turnover	7200	9000
Average investment in gross assets	2400	6000

The following accounting ratios are provided by the trade association to which they each belong. The ratios are averages for members of the association.

Gross asset turnover	2
Operating profit percentage	14%
Operating profit on gross assets	21%

Required

(a) Separate calculations for Tanner Ltd and Spanner Ltd of the accounting ratios equivalent to those provided by the trade association.

b) An explanation of the relationship between the three ratios and advice about how the relationship might be explored in greater depth.

(c) An analysis of the performance of Tanner Ltd and Spanner Ltd by comparison with members of the trade association and with each other.

Note

Calculations to one decimal place

END OF CHAPTER QUESTIONS

9.3 You are given the following financial information for XYZ Ltd in the table below:

£'000	2010	2009	2008	2007
Sales	290	190	160	90
Net assets	420	340	280	190
Total assets	1140	950	880	680

Using the following ratios:
- Net asset turnover ratio
- Total asset turnover ratio

Calculate the ratios and comment on the efficiency of asset usage of the company.

9.4 A company has 90 days inventory outstanding, 60 days sales outstanding and 70 days payable outstanding.

Cash Operating cycle = Days sales outstanding + Inventory days outstanding – Payable days outstanding

Required

Calculate the cash operating cycle of the business.

10 Analysis and interpretation of accounts 3

■ CONTENTS

■ LEARNING OUTCOMES

This chapter discusses further topics related to ratio analysis. After reading and understanding the contents of the chapter, working through *all* the worked examples and practice questions, you should be able to understand the purpose and explanations for segmental and cash flow ratios and:

- how to analyse and interpret cash flow ratios;
- discuss the importance attached to cash flows;
- analyse using various investor ratios;
- carry out inter-company comparison;
- discuss and calculate various measures of earnings per share; and
- discuss the limitations of accounting ratios.

1 Introduction

Accounting ratios enable users and analysts to assess company financial performance. We will discuss further uses of ratios by looking at segmental analysis of ratios, and investor ratios that caste light on shareholder returns and the efficiency of company finances by looking at various measures of cash flow ratios.

2 Segmental accounting and analysis

The primary purpose of all profit-making businesses is to make profit. The continued success of a business is due to sustained and satisfactory levels of income. This requires good decision-making and performance evaluation. The income statement, while serving many purposes, is a primarily a tool for performance evaluation by the varied stakeholders.

Businesses make financial disclosures on a number of items in the financial reports. While financial results can be reported in a number of ways, IFRS 8 and IAS 14 provide the basis for financial disclosure of segmental activity of a business. IFRS 8 defines reportable and operating segments, while IAS 14 defines the requirements for financial disclosure.

IAS 14 basically defines reportable segments on the basis of:

- geographical segments; and
- product segments.

Segmental accounting has been discussed in chapter 4. The purpose here is to perform analysis of segmental accounting to evaluate the performance of geographical/product segments.

Two primary ways of analysing segments are:

- full cost approach; and
- marginal contribution approach.

The two techniques are basically borrowed from management accounting but serve their purposes in terms of performance analysis.

2.1 Full cost approach

It would appear that the full cost approach may be the logical method to use due to the fact that ultimately a business cannot be successful without profit (net income). However, when we try to evaluate net income arising from a segment, some problems present themselves that are not encountered when we measure overall business performance. From a segmental perspective, there are two types of expenses incurred by a business: direct expenses and indirect expenses.

Direct expenses are those expenses of a segment that are directly traceable to a business segment. The closure of a segment would mean those costs would then not be incurred. Indirect expenses are common expenses to the overall business entity. These expenses are not directly caused by any one particular segment, but arise due to the overall functioning of a business entity.

The key characteristic of indirect expenses from a segmental viewpoint is that they must be allocated in order to measure the net income of a segment. Examples of indirect expenses include the following:

- salaries of senior management (e.g. the CEO);
- head office operating expenses;
- insurance on head office and head office equipment; and
- salaries of head office staff.

The underlying theoretical consideration for the full cost approach is that all expenses, regardless of where and why they have incurred, must be charged to the segments that benefit directly and indirectly. As such, these types of expenses must be allocated using some basis. Because various methods of allocation are available and because different methods result in different allocation percentages, the allocated cost may be perceived to be somewhat arbitrary. Some of the methods used to allocate indirect expenses include the following:

- sales by value;
- number of employees;
- assets employed; and
- floor space occupied.

The method(s) used should be based on a logical apportionment on an equitable basis. Inappropriate use of methods would tend to give the wrong impression of financial performance of segments of a business. The basic principles of the full cost approach are summarised as follows:

(a) the objective is to measure net income of each operating segment;
(b) overall net income of the business is the sum of the segmental net income;
(c) all indirect expenses must be allocated across each segment; and
(d) allocation of indirect expenses involves selecting bases of allocation.

The segmental net income approach may be defined mathematically as follows:

Segmental net income = segmental sales – direct expenses – allocated indirect expenses, or in more symbolical terms:

$$SNI = S - DE - AIE$$

Direct expenses are those expenses that can be traceable to a business segment. Variable expenses are activity-based expenses and are directly traceable to a segment. Fixed expenses may either be direct or indirect and can also be allocated or otherwise to a segment depending on their nature. The contractual nature of fixed expenses must be examined carefully to determine whether or not the expense is direct.

2.2 Segmental contribution approach

The major problem of the full cost approach is that it is technically possible for a segment to show an operating loss yet at the same time be making a positive contribution to net income. In other words, if the seemingly unprofitable segment is closed, then the overall net income of the business will decrease. The paradox will be examined more closely later in this section. To overcome this adverse feature of the full cost approach, many businesses prefer to use the contribution approach to measuring segmental profitability.

The segmental contribution approach as indicated by its name measures segmental contribution. Segmental contribution may simply be defined as sales less direct expenses. As a student, you should be careful to distinguish between segmental contribution and contribution margin. Contribution margin is sales less variable expenses. As some fixed expenses can be direct expenses, segmental contribution and contribution margin are not the same.

The basic principles of assessing segmental contribution are outlined below:

(a) Only the contribution of each segment is computed. No attempt is made to compute the net income of the segment.
(b) Indirect expenses of each segment are not allocated.
(c) Indirect expenses, however, are usually deducted from total segmental contribution in order to arrive at overall business net income.
(d) A segment is considered profitable if sales of the segment exceed the direct expenses of the segment.

The segmental contribution approach may be presented mathematically as follows:

Segmental contribution (SC) = Segmental sales (SS) – Direct expenses (DE)

In more symbolical terms:

1 $SC = SS - DE$
2 $DE = V(Q) + F\,D$
3 $S = P(Q)$

Where:
DE – direct expenses
P – price of the product in the segment
V – variable cost rate for the segment
Q – units of sales in a specific segment
FD – direct fixed expenses of the segment.

Therefore, equation (1) may be restated as follows:

$SC = P(Q) - V(Q) - F\,D$

It is apparent from equation (2) that the principles of cost–volume–profit analysis apply to segmental decision making. Variable costs are always direct costs. When activity ceases, variable costs cease. When activity increases, variable costs by definition increase. Indirect expenses are almost always fixed expenses.

The indirect expenses of a segment will continue to be incurred regardless of whether the segment is continued or not continued. Therefore, as long as the segment is making a contribution towards indirect fixed expenses, continuing operations at least in the short run makes the business better off.

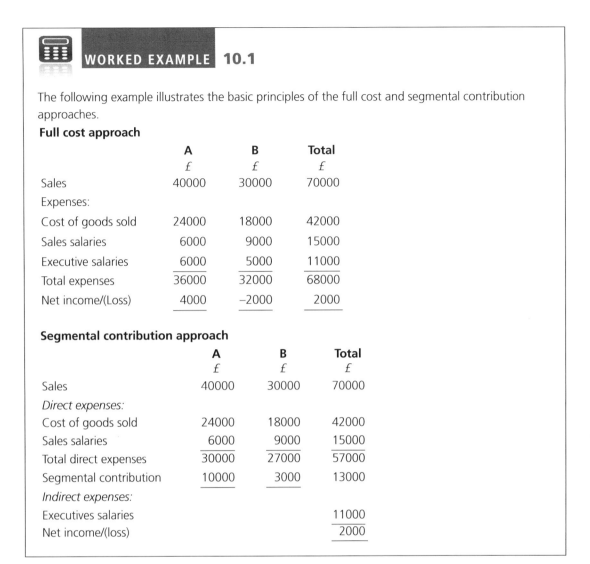

WORKED EXAMPLE 10.1

The following example illustrates the basic principles of the full cost and segmental contribution approaches.

Full cost approach

	A	B	Total
	£	£	£
Sales	40000	30000	70000
Expenses:			
Cost of goods sold	24000	18000	42000
Sales salaries	6000	9000	15000
Executive salaries	6000	5000	11000
Total expenses	36000	32000	68000
Net income/(Loss)	4000	–2000	2000

Segmental contribution approach

	A	B	Total
	£	£	£
Sales	40000	30000	70000
Direct expenses:			
Cost of goods sold	24000	18000	42000
Sales salaries	6000	9000	15000
Total direct expenses	30000	27000	57000
Segmental contribution	10000	3000	13000
Indirect expenses:			
Executives salaries			11000
Net income/(loss)			2000

In the above example, cost of goods sold and sales salaries are direct expenses of each segment. Executive salaries, an indirect expense, consequently are charged to the segments by being allocated on some basis. However, in the segmental contribution approach, executive salaries are not allocated.

Let's consider from the above example how allocations have been made. First, the full cost approach shows that segment B is operating at a net loss of £2,000. It may seem logical to close down segment B as the business would be better off by £2,000. However, the segmental contribution approach shows that segment B is making a contribution of £3,000. Secondly, it can be seen that executive salaries were allocated in the ratio of 57:43. The allocation percentages were determined by dividing segmental sales by total sales.

Segmental analysis provides management with the tools to analyse the contribution made by each sector either on geographical basis or product basis. By carefully examining trends and results in each segment, management is able to gain considerable insight into the company's operations viewed from different perspectives. And advanced computer-based information systems are making it easier to construct such statements for continuous monitoring purposes.

3 Rate of return on shareholders' equity

The factor that motivates shareholders to invest in a company is the expectation of an adequate return on their funds and, periodically, they will want to assess the rate of return earned in order to decide whether to continue with their investment. The rate of return expresses earnings as a percentage of the carrying value of shareholders' equity:

$$\text{Rate of return on shareholders' equity} \quad \frac{\text{Earnings}^* \text{ for equity shareholders}}{\text{Average shareholders' equity}} \times 100$$

*The ratio may be computed on a pre- or post-tax basis but, whichever basis is used, any preference dividends payable must be deducted since they reduce profits available for ordinary shareholders. An argument for using the pre-tax basis is that the resulting ratio can be related more meaningfully to the other calculations demonstrated in this chapter. On the other hand, corporation tax must be deducted to arrive at the balance available for distribution to shareholders and the post-tax basis implies full recognition of this fact.

Calculations for Ludlow Ltd (Worked Example 8.8) are:

$$2010 \quad \frac{345,000}{(2,155,000 + 2,250,000) \times 1/2} \times 100 = 15.7\%$$

$$2011 \quad \frac{355,000}{(2,250,000 + 2,350,000) \times 1/2} \times 100 = 15.4\%$$

$$2010 \quad \frac{172,500}{(2,155,000 + 2,250,000) \times 1/2} \times 100 = 7.83\%$$

$$2011 \quad \frac{177,500}{(2,250,000 + 2,350,000) \times 1/2} \times 100 = 7.7\%$$

There has been a modest decline in the return earned for shareholders, but rather less than might have been expected in view of the fairly sharp decline in the primary ratio from 12.3% to 11.5%. The reason for this difference is that the return earned for shareholders is dependent on three key factors:

- profit margins;
- asset utilisation; and
- capital structure.

We saw in an earlier section that the rate of return on gross assets is a function of profit margins and asset utilisation. However, it takes no account of the company's capital structure (this can be confirmed by observing the fact that the numerator comprises net profit *before* deducting any interest charges). The significance for the equity shareholders of financing a part of a company's activities with loan capital is examined in the section on gearing.

4   Inter-company comparison

Ratio analysis plays a crucial role by enabling inter-firm comparison by providing necessary data that shows differences and similarities between firms and between sectors. An inter-firm comparison indicates relative position. It provides the relevant data for the comparison of the performance of different firms/departments. Variances can soon be identified by using inter-firm comparisons by seeking out trends over time and/or over shorter periods. If a company's ratios suggest vast differences, say, within a sector, management can take action to remedy the situation.

Ratio analysis can assist management to reach conclusion regarding several aspects of the financial health, profitability and operational efficiency of the company through inter-firm comparisons. Ratio such as the asset turnover, points out the operating efficiency of the firm (i.e. whether the management has utilised the firm's assets correctly, to increase the investor's wealth).

Ratios by themselves help in empowering management with the tools to take corrective actions so that a fair return to its investors is made and secures optimum utilisation of a company's assets. The table below offers some comparisons of the food retail sector and indicates the top retailers with their respect results in the form of Return on Assets (ROA) and After-Tax Profit margins.

TABLE 10.1 Ratios for Tesco and Sainsbury's – 2011

Company	Business sector	ROA	Profit margin	EPS	ROCE
Tesco	Retailer clothing, food and financial services	4.00%	5.72%	33.3p	12.90%
J Sainsbury	Retailer clothing, food and financial services	5.90%	3.61%	34.4p	8.00%

Note:

ROA = Return on assets

EPS = Earnings per share

ROCE = Return on capital employed

The table above provides some level of inter-company comparison for two UK retail giants. Both have similar levels of ratios; however Tesco in comparison provides better results than J Sainsbury. If we look at the ROA, this is lower for Tesco than J Sainsbury, nevertheless, the Profit Margin suggests Tesco has been more efficient with costs and hence a higher profit margin than J Sainsbury. Whilst Tesco shows a higher profit margin, however, J Sainsbury shows a higher EPS. The ROCE for Tesco indicates much higher return on capital employed.

This comparison shows a mix of results, however, management of J Sainsbury may want to investigate why their profit margin is lower than Tesco and take remedial action. Similarly J Sainsbury's ROCE is also much lower than Tesco's and this warrants close inspection as to why the ROCE is so low.

5   Cash flow-based accounting ratios

The usefulness of financial statements is enhanced by an examination of the relationship between them; also by comparison with previous time periods, other entities and expected performance. We have seen that value can be further added through the calculation and interpretation of accounting ratios. An examination of accounting textbooks and the pages of accounting periodicals reveals an enthusiasm for rehearsing the potential of 'accounting ratios', demonstrated through calculations of the net profit margin, return on capital employed, current ratio and a host of other 'traditional' measures based on the contents of the income statement and statement of financial position. None of these focus on cash flow.

Traditional ratios suffer from the same defect as the financial statements (the income statement and statement of financial position) on which they are based. Such ratios are the result of comparing figures that have been computed using accounting conventions and 'guestimates'. Given the difficulty of deciding the length of the period over which a non-current assets should be written off, whether the tests which justify the capitalisation of development expenditure have been satisfied, the amount of the provision to be made for claims under a manufacturer's 12-month guarantee (to give just a few examples), ratios based on such figures are also bound to have limited reliability.

This is not to suggest that the traditional ratios are irrelevant. Clearly this is not so, as they reveal important relationships and trends that are not apparent from the examination of individual figures appearing in the accounts. However, given the fact that cash flow ratios contain at least one element that is factual (the numerator, the denominator or both), their lack of prominence in the existing literature is puzzling.

 **TEST YOUR KNOWLEDGE 10.1**

In what way might cash-based accounting ratios be considered superior to traditional accounting ratios?

The principal focus for informed investment decisions is cash flows, whether the capital project appraisal method is 'pay-back' or one of the more sophisticated discounted cash flow-based techniques, namely 'net present value' and 'internal rate of return'. Turning to performance evaluation, however, the emphasis usually shifts to techniques such as return on capital employed. The inconsistency between the two approaches is highlighted by the use of depreciation cost allocation procedures for the purpose of computing the ROCE; a calculation that has no place whatsoever in the above project appraisal methods.

Below are presented:

1   Ratios that link the cash flow statement with the income statement and statement of financial position.
2   Ratios based entirely on the contents of the cash flow statement.

To illustrate these calculations, the results of Tamari plc for 2011 and 2012 are shown in Figure 12.0. For each ratio both the calculation and a discussion of its significance are presented. Inevitably, there will be some overlap in the messages conveyed by the various ratios presented. This may be due to similarities in the nature of the calculations or to the fact that the results of just one company are used for illustration purposes. The application of the same ratios to different financial facts might well yield additional valuable insights.

Cash flow statement (using indirect method)	2012	2011
Cash flows from operating activities	£'000	£'000
Operating profit	501	420
Depreciation charges	660	600
(–)Increase/decrease in inventory	–305	250
(–)Increase/decrease in receivables	–184	220
Increase in payables	420	120
Cash generated from operations	1,092	1,610
Interest paid	–150	–50
Dividends paid	–160	–160
Taxation paid	–130	–110
Net cash generated from operating activities	652	1,290
Cash flows from investing activities		
Purchase of property, plant and equipment	–1,620	–900
Cash flows from financing activities		
Proceeds from issue of loan	1,000	100
Net increase in cash	32	490
Income statement extracts		
Operating profit	501	420
Interest paid	–150	–50
Profit before tax	351	370
Taxation	–125	–115
Profit for the year	226	255
	–175	–175
Extract from statement of changes to equity		
Dividends paid		
Retained profit for year	51	80
Statement of financial position at 31 December		

	2012	2011
	£'000	£'000
Assets		
Property, plant and equipment at cost	5,220	3,600
Less: accumulated depreciation	–2,360	–1,700
	2,860	1,900
Current assets (including cash)	1,893	1,372
Total assets	4,753	3,272
Equity and liabilities		
Called up share capital (£1 ordinary shares)	1,400	1,400
Share premium account	250	250
Retained earnings	333	282
	1,983	1,932
Non-current liabilities		
10 per cent loan repayable 2013–22	1,350	500
Current liabilities	1,350	500
Loan repayment due	150	–
Tax	125	115
Payables	1,145	725
	1,420	840
Total liabilities	2,770	1,340
Total equities and liabilities	4,753	3,272

FIGURE 10.1 Draft accounts of Tamari plc for 2012 and 2011

The following information is provided as at 31 December 2010:

- property, plant and equipment at cost, £2,700,000;
- current assets, £1,802,000;
- payables and taxation, £838,000; and
- called-up share capital, £1,400,000.

Note: Tamari raised a loan of £1 million during 2012. This, together with the already existing loan, is repayable by ten equal instalments over the period 2013–2022.

5.1 Ratios linking the cash flow statement with the two other principal financial statements

Cash generated from operations to current liabilities

$$\text{Cash generated from operations to current liabilities} = \frac{\text{Cash generated from operations}}{\text{Average current liabilities}} \times 100$$

Where:
   Cash generated from operations is taken directly from the cash flow statement published to comply with IAS 7.
   Average current liabilities are computed from the opening and closing statement of financial position.
   This ratio examines the liquidity of the company by providing a measure of the extent to which current liabilities are covered by cash flowing into the business from normal operating activities. The ratio is thought by some to be superior to the statement of financial position-based ratios such as the liquidity ratio as a measure of short-term solvency. This is because statement of financial position ratios are based on a static positional statement (the 'instantaneous financial photograph') and are therefore subject to manipulation by, for example, running down

inventory immediately prior to the year-end and not replacing them until the next accounting period. Statement of financial position-based ratios may alternatively be affected by unusual events that cause particular items to be abnormally large or small. In either case, the resulting ratios will not reflect normal conditions.

Calculations for Tamari plc

	Calculation	2012	Calculation	2011
Cash generated from operations to current liabilities	$\dfrac{1092}{\frac{1}{2}[1{,}420 + 840]}$	96.6%	$\dfrac{1610}{\frac{1}{2}[840 + 838]}$	191.9%

There has been a startling decline in this ratio between 2011 and 2012, falling to one-half of the previous level. This has been caused by a combination of a reduction in the operating cash flow and a rise in average current liabilities. Nevertheless, the current liabilities (which include taxation which may not be payable until the next financial year) remain adequately covered by cash flow on the assumption that this aspect of Tamari's financial affairs is repeated in the year 2010.

5.2 Cash recovery rate

$$\text{Cash recovery rate (CRR)} = \frac{\text{Cash flow from operations}}{\text{Average gross assets}} \times 100$$

Where:

Cash flow from operations is made up of 'cash generated from operations' together with any proceeds from the disposal of non-current assets. Gross assets (current and non-current assets) is the average gross value (before deducting accumulated depreciation) of the entity's assets over an accounting period. However, the statement of financial position usually shows the carrying value of non-current assets. A search of the notes is needed to find the gross value.

Assets are required to generate a return that is ultimately, if not immediately, in the form of cash. The CRR is, therefore, a measure of the rate at which the company recovers its investment in non-current assets. The quicker the recovery period, the lower the risk. You may have noticed that the CRR is, broadly, the reciprocal of the pay-back period used for capital project appraisal purposes assuming projects have equal (or roughly equal) annual cash flows.

Calculations for Tamari plc

	Calculation	2012	Calculation	2011
CRR	$\dfrac{1092}{\frac{1}{2}[7{,}113 + 4{,}972]}$	18.1%	$\dfrac{1610}{\frac{1}{2}[4{,}972 + 4{,}502]}$	34.0%

The CRR has also fallen to about one-half of the figure of the previous year. The implication is that the company is now recovering its investment in business assets over twice the period that was previously the case. It should be borne in mind, however, that the 2011 ratio benefited from the release of investment in working capital which was not, and probably could not, be repeated in 2012.

5.3 Cash flow per share

$$\text{Cash flow per share} = \frac{\text{Cash flow}}{\text{Weighted average no. of shares}}$$

There are two definitions of cash flow each reflecting different applications of the cash flow per share calculation. We will deal with the version

Where:

Cash flow = net cash generated from operating activities (see cash flow statement).

This version recognises the fact that cash is available for long-term investment only after working capital requirements, tax and dividends have been met. It indicates the ability of the company to fund long-term investment out of resources generated internally. The number of shares used as the denominator should be the weighted average of the number in issue during the year. However, the average needs to be weighted only if there is an issue of shares involving an inflow of resources; in the case of a bonus issue (where no extra resources are generated), the number of shares post-bonus issue should be used without weighting and the number in issue the previous year made comparable.

Calculations for Tamari plc

	Calculation	2012	Calculation	2011
Cash flow per share =	$\dfrac{652}{1,400 \times 100}$	46.6p	$\dfrac{1,290}{1,400 \times 100}$	92.1p

There is a marked decline in cash flow per share reflecting, again, the significant disinvestment in working capital that occurred in 2011.

5.4 Capital expenditure per share

Where:

Capital expenditure = cash flows from investing activities.

This ratio, in conjunction with cash flow per share can be used in order to obtain a broad indication of whether a business is a net generator of cash or whether it is cash-hungry.

Calculations for Tamari plc

	Calculation	2012	Calculation	2011
Capital expenditure per share =	$1,620 \div 1,400 \times 100$	115.7p	$900 \div 1,400 \times 100$	64.3p

The capital expenditure per share has risen dramatically and it is patently obvious that the company has had to look elsewhere to fund a much greater proportion of that investment in 2012 (115.7p − 46.6p = 69.1p per share) compared with 2011.

5.5 Debt service coverage ratio

$$\text{Debt service coverage ratio (DSCR)} = \frac{\text{EBITDA}}{\text{Annual debt repayments and interest}}$$

Where:

EBITDA = Earnings before interest, tax, depreciation and amortisation (i.e. profit before non-cash adjustments).

The purpose of this ratio is to help assess the ability of a company to meet debt repayments and interest out of the above amended version of cash generated from operations. A feature of this ratio is that it is forward looking with the denominator representing expected future cash flows. (If available, the numerator should also be prospective.) It is seen to be superior to traditional methods used by lenders to analyse risk of exposure to debt finance such as interest cover. A drawback of interest cover is that, as conventionally applied, it is backward-looking. Also, it takes no account of the level of capital repayments that, of course, can vary considerably depending on the period of the loan repayment.

Calculations for Tamari plc

	Calculation	2012	Calculation	2011
DSCR	$501 + 660 \div [150 + 150]$	3.9x	$420 + 600 \div [50 + 150]$	5.1x

The DSCR for 2011 is strong, with EBITDA 5.1x based on the prospective interest charges for 2012; there is no loan repayment in 2012. For 2012, the ratio declines to 3.9x but still shows debt commitments to be comfortably covered out of internally generated cash flow. The multiple also suggests that there is surplus cash available to meet working capital requirements and for tax and dividend payments and capital expenditure.

5.6 Ratios based entirely on the contents of the cash flow statement

It is possible to add to the interpretative value of the cash flow statement by expressing some of the financial totals contained in the cash flow statement presented in Figure 12.0 as ratios of one another. As is always the case with ratio analysis, the usefulness of a ratio depends on the existence of an expected relationship between the financial magnitudes being compared. A number of valid ratios could be computed and two are presented below to illustrate of the possibilities available.

5.7 The internal: external finance ratio

The relationship between internal finance and external debt finance may be examined by expressing net cash generated from operations as a ratio of external financing (cash flows from financing activities). A low ratio shows that the company is increasing its reliance on external funding, perhaps for the purpose of further investment, and deterioration in the gearing position of the company would be likely to result.

Calculations for Tamari plc

	2012	2011
Internal : external finance ratio	$652 : 1,000 = 0.65 : 1$	$1,290 : 100 = 12.9 : 1$

We can see that Tamari placed very little reliance on external finance in 2011, but this has changed dramatically during 2012 with external finance raised significantly in excess of that generated internally. This will be reflected in the statement of financial position by a revision of the long-term capital structure of the company, which could be interrogated further by computing leverage ratios.

5.8 The shareholder funding ratio

The extent to which the equity shareholders have funded business investment during the year can be examined by expressing free cash flow available to shareholders (net cash generated from operating activities) as a percentage of expenditure on non-current assets.

Calculations for Tamari plc

	2012	2011
Shareholder funding ratio	$652 : 1,620 = 0.40 : 1$	$1,290 : 900 = 1.4 : 1$

The shareholders of Tamari comfortably funded the entire business investment in 2011, leaving a significant surplus to improve the company's liquidity position. In 2012, by way of contrast, the directors have decided to rely heavily on debt to fund the substantial investment programme undertaken during the year.

5.9 Review

The purpose of the cash flow statement is to improve the informative value of published financial reports. The sections above have demonstrated the contribution of two types of calculation:

(a) ratios that link the cash flow statement with key related items appearing in the statement of financial position; and
(b) ratios that explore the inter-relationship between items within the cash flow statement.

As usual, it should be noted that different ratios are expressed in different ways, as percentages, as multiples or in pence, as well as in the classic form. The interpretative value of individual ratios will depend upon the nature of the financial developments at a particular business. It is also the case that the messages conveyed by certain ratios may be similar for a particular company covering a particular year, but in a different time and place the same ratios may yield different insights.

Finally, one must remember the importance of not attaching too much weight to any single ratio but to use a representative range of ratios that combine cash flow ratios with traditional ratios to build up a meaningful business profile.

TEST YOUR KNOWLEDGE 10.2

Explain how ratios can be used to improve the informational value of the cash flow statement.

6   Earnings per share

The basic purpose of the **earnings per share** (EPS) calculation is to discover the amount of profit accruing to the holder of one share in a company. EPS is widely used due to:

- the belief that earnings are an important determinant of share price. They set an upper limit for dividends, and, by comparing earnings with dividends, a measure of likely future growth from retained earnings can be obtained;
- the popularity of the Price/Earnings Ratio as an indicator of financial performance and also a method of business valuation; and
- the determination of financial commentators to reduce the complexities of corporate activity to a single figure.

6.1 Definition of EPS

The nature, purpose and calculation of EPS is dealt with in IAS 33 'Earnings Per Share'. EPS may be defined as the earnings, in pence, attributable to each equity share, and is calculated using the formula:

$$\text{EPS} = \frac{\text{Earnings}}{\text{No of equity shares in issue}}$$

Where:
Earnings = the profit (or in the case of a group the consolidated profit) of the period after tax, minority interests and extraordinary items and after deducting preference dividends and other appropriations in respect of preference shares
Shares = the number of equity shares in issue and ranking for dividend in respect of the period
   Further points to note:

- IAS 33 applies only to listed companies.
- When a loss is suffered, the EPS is a negative figure.
- The importance attached to EPS is reflected by the requirement for the current year's figure, together with the comparative for the previous year, to be displayed *on the face of the income statement*. It cannot be 'tucked away' in the notes.

A company is permitted to disclose, in addition to basic earnings per share, a second calculation, the fully diluted EPS, based on a different figure for earnings. This further disclosure is likely to occur where the directors consider that earnings have been affected by a non-recurrent transaction, so that exclusion of its effect produces a more useful indication of the projected performance of the enterprise. The revised figure is often referred to as the underlying earnings per share. The accounts should disclose how the revised earnings figure has been computed and the 'underlying' EPS must be given no greater prominence than the basic EPS. An illustration of how the two figures might be reported is given in Figure below taken from the accounts of Tesco plc.

	2011	2010
Full Year 26 Feb 2011	52 weeks	52 weeks
Revenue	67573	62537
Underlying profit from operations	3754	3424
Underlying operating margin	6.0%	5.9%
Joint ventures and associates	57	33
Profit from operations	3811	3457
Underlying profit before tax *	3813	3395
Profit before tax	3535	3176
Underlying EPS *	27.10p	29.31p
Basic EPS	27.14p	29.33p

* Underlying profit excludes the impact of non-cash elements of IAS 17, 19, 32 and 39 (principally the impact of annual uplifts in rents and rent free period, pension cost, and the mark-to-market of financial instruments); the amortisation charge on intangible assets arising on acquisition, acquisition costs and the non-cash impact of IFRIC 13. It also excludes costs relating to restructuring (US and Japan), closure costs, (Vin Plus) and the impairment of goodwill in Japan. *Source*: www.tescoplc.com/investors/financials/five-year-summary/; http://ar2011.tescoplc.com/pdfs/tesco_annual_report_2011.pdf

6.2 Calculation of EPS

We start with the basic calculation where no shares have been issued during the year.

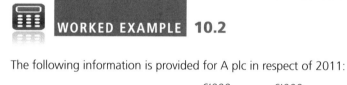

WORKED EXAMPLE 10.2

The following information is provided for A plc in respect of 2011:

	£'000	£'000
Profit before taxation		300
Taxation (30%)		90
Profit for the year		210
Dividends paid during the year:		
Ordinary shares	1000	
Preference shares	35	135
		75

The company has in issue £1 million ordinary shares of 50p each and £500,000 7% convertible preference shares.

Required
Calculate the EPS for 2011.

Answer

$$\text{EPS} = \frac{(£210,000 - £35,000^*) \times 100}{£1,000,000 \times 2} = 8.75\text{p}$$

* £500,000 × 7% = £35,000

6.3 Share issues during the year

We now introduce the complication of a share issue being made during the current year. There are three possibilities: issue at full market price; bonus issue during the year; and rights issue during the year.

6.3.1 Issue at full market price

This increases both the number of shares in issue *and* the earnings capacity of the company. The earnings for the period must, therefore, be spread over the increased number of shares in issue. However, where the issue takes place part of the way through the year, it is necessary to calculate the average number of shares in issue during the year, on a weighted time basis, as the extra shares only increase earnings *after* they have been issued.

 WORKED EXAMPLE 10.3

A plc (see Worked Example 10.2) issues a further 600,000 ordinary shares on 1 May 2012. Profits for the year for 2012 are £280,000.

Required
Calculate the EPS for 2012.

Answer

$$EPS = \frac{(\pounds280,000 - \pounds35,000) \times 100}{(\pounds1,000,000 \times 2) \times (600,000 \times 2/3)} = 10.2p$$

6.3.2 Bonus issue

A bonus issue of shares to current shareholders of a company produces no cash and so will not increase the available resources nor affect earnings capacity. The effect of the issue, therefore, is to spread the earnings over a greater number of shares. Because the bonus issue does not increase earnings capacity, there is no need to calculate a weighted average for the shares in issue during the year. Therefore, the date of the bonus issue, if given in a question, is irrelevant and can be ignored. However, it is necessary to restate the comparative EPS figure, for the previous year, in order to place it on a 'like' basis.

 WORKED EXAMPLE 10.4

The results of A plc for 2011 are as in Worked Example 10.2. During 2012, A plc makes a bonus issue of one additional ordinary share for every two shares presently held. Profits for the year for 2012 are £280,000.

Required
(a) Calculate the EPS for 2012.
(b) Calculate the revised EPS for 2011.

Answers
Calculation for 2012:

$$EPS = \frac{(\pounds280,000 - \pounds35,000) \times 100}{(\pounds1,000,000 \times 2) \times 3/2} = 7.2p$$

Revised calculation for 2011: EPS = 8.75 × 2m/3m = 5.8p. This adjusts for the fact that there are 50% more shares in issue in 2012 compared with 2011.

6.3.3 Rights issue

A **rights issue** occurs when new shares are issued to existing shareholders, usually at *below the existing market price*. This increases the number of shares in issue, but does not increase the earning capacity of the company *proportionally*. After a rights issue, the market price should therefore fall. The dilution in the value of pre-rights issue share capital, in such circumstances, can be demonstrated as follows:

WORKED EXAMPLE 10.5

	£
Four shares in circulation before rights issue at a market price of £2 each:	8.00
Rights issue of, say, one for two at an artificially low price of 50p each for illustrative purposes:	1.00
Six shares then in issue will have theoretical post-rights issue worth of:	9.00
Theoretical ex-rights price will be, £9 ÷ 6 shares	1.50

Diluted post-rights equivalent of pre-rights issue shares:

Four shares worth £2 each (pre-issue) = 4 × (£2 ÷ £1.5) = 5.3 shares (post-issue)

Proof:	£
Four shares at pre-issue market price of £2:	8.00
5.3 shares at theoretical ex-rights price of £1.5:	8.00

The above adjustments are incorporated in the calculation of EPS in the following manner:

1 Calculate total value of equity before rights issue: market price×number of shares.
2 Calculate proceeds of new issue.
3 Calculate *theoretical* price after issue:

$$\frac{1 + 2}{\text{Number of shares after rights issue}}$$

4 Calculate the post-issue equivalent of the number of shares outstanding pre-issue:

$$\text{Number of shares} \times \frac{\text{Actual pre-issue price}}{\text{Theoretical post-issue price}}$$

5 Calculate the number of shares in issue during the year on the weighted average basis.
6 Compute EPS.
7 Obtain corresponding comparative figure for previous year:

$$\text{Last year's EPS} \times \frac{\text{Theoretical post-issue price}}{\text{Actual pre-issue price}}$$

The following information is provided for B Ltd:

■ B plc has earnings of £16,640 for 2012.
■ There were 120,000 ordinary shares in issue at the start of the year.
■ 40,000 further shares were issued on 31 August 2012 at £1.50 each.
■ The market price of each share immediately before the rights issue was £2.

Required
Calculate the EPS for 2012.

Answer
Procedure to calculate EPS:

1 Calculate total value of equity before issue: market price×number of shares:
   £2 × 120,000 = £240,000

WORKED EXAMPLE 10.5 *continued*

2 Calculate proceeds of new issue:
£1.50 × 40,000 = £60,000
3 Calculate *theoretical* price after issue:

$$\frac{£240,000 - £60,000}{120,000 + 40,000} = £1.875$$

4 Calculate the post-issue equivalent of the number of shares outstanding pre-issue:

$$120,000 \times \frac{2}{1.875} = 128,000$$

5 Calculate the number of shares in issue during the year on the weighted average basis:
(128,000 × 2/3) + (160,000 × 1/3) = 138,667
6 Compute EPS:

$$\frac{16,640 \times 100}{138667} = 12p$$

TEST YOUR KNOWLEDGE 10.3

(a) Define earnings per share.
(b) What is meant by a weighted average EPS?

6.3.4 Diluted earnings per share (DEPS)

IAS 33 describes **diluted earnings per share** as:

> Dilution: A reduction in earnings per share or an increase in loss per share resulting from the assumption that convertible instruments are converted, that options or warrants are exercised, or that ordinary shares are issued upon the satisfaction of specified conditions.

On occasions, a company, whose shares are traded on a stock exchange, can issue shares that in effect are below the market price of those shares had they been available to interested parties ordinarily. The impact of offering shares at less than market price is the same as offering all or a portion of shares for free. Consequently this has a diluting effect on EPS.

WORKED EXAMPLE 10.6

The results of A Ltd for 2011 are as in Worked Example 10.2. During 2012, the entire 7% convertible preference shares of £1 each totalling £500,000 are converted at four ordinary shares for one convertible preference share. Profits for the year for 2012 are £280,000.

Required
Calculate the diluted EPS for 2012.

Answer

	No of shares in thousands	Earnings £'000	Pence
Basic EPS (W1)	2000	280–35	12.25p
Convertible Preference Shares (W2)	2000	35	
Diluted EPS	4000	35	7.00p
Diluted EPS	7.00p per share		

WORKED EXAMPLE 10.6 *continued*

The net effect of the preference shares converting to ordinary shares is that basic EPS
has reduced from 12.25 pence per share to 7.00 pence per share.
(W1)
For basic EPS purposes, profits available would have been:
(£280,000 – £35,000)/2,000 shares = 12.25p per share
(W2)
Preference share conversion:
2 ordinary shares × 1 (£1 preference share)
2×500,000 = 2 million ordinary shares.

TEST YOUR KNOWLEDGE 10.4

Explain the difference between basic and diluted EPS.

7 Limitations of accounting ratios

The various calculations illustrated in this and the last two chapters suffer from a number of
limitations that should be borne in mind by anyone attempting to interpret their significance.
The main limitations are:

- Accounting ratios can be used to assess whether performance is satisfactory, by means of
  inter-company comparison, and also whether results have improved, worsened or remained
  stable, by comparing this year's results with those achieved last year. The ratios do not provide *explanations* for observed changes, however, and the external user's ability to obtain
  further information varies considerably. The shareholder may ask questions at the annual
  general meeting, while a financial institution may demand extra information when an
  advance is requested, but only management has direct access to the information needed to
  provide the right answer.
- Deterioration in an accounting ratio cannot necessarily be interpreted as poor management.
  For example, a decline in the rate of inventory turnover initially appears undesirable, but
  further investigation might reveal the accumulation of scarce raw materials that enable the
  plant to continue working when competitors are forced to suspend production.
- Too much significance should not be attached to individual ratios (e.g. a rate of return on
  gross assets of 30% might indicate that all is well, but this conclusion might be unjustified if
  further analysis revealed a liquidity ratio of 0.4:1).
- Changes in many ratios are closely associated with one another and produce similar conclusions (e.g. the ratio of total debt to total assets (not illustrated in this chapter) and the debt:
  equity ratio). Care should therefore be taken when selecting ratios to be used as the basis for
  the analysis; a representative selection should be made and duplication avoided.
- Company financial statements are usually based on historical cost and, therefore, accounting
  ratios based on these figures would be expected to improve, irrespective of efficiency during a
  period of rising prices (e.g. total asset turnover of £3 per £1 invested might be computed from
  historical cost accounts, whereas a figure of £1.80 per £1 invested might be obtained if assets
  were restated at current values).
- Differences in accounting policies may detract from the value of inter-company comparisons,
  (e.g. the valuation of inventory on the LIFO basis (now banned) rather than the FIFO basis
  would probably produce a much lower working capital ratio).
- Financial statements and accounting ratios can be distorted as the result of one-off large
  transactions such as the credit purchase of plant, which will significantly increase current

liabilities until payment is made, or a profit on the sale of a non-current. Analysts should similarly be on their guard for evidence of window-dressing, perhaps designed to conceal a deteriorating financial position.

- Where a company undertakes a mix of activities, it is important to calculate separate ratios for each section wherever possible.
- Particular care must be taken when interpreting accounting ratios calculated for a seasonal business. Where sales are high at a particular time during the year (e.g. at Christmas) stock might be expected to increase and cash to decline in the months leading up to the busy period. In these circumstances, deteriorations in both the liquidity ratio and the rate of inventory turnover, compared with the previous month, are not necessarily causes for concern.
- Consideration must be given to variations in commercial trading patterns when assessing the significance of accounting ratios computed for particular companies. For example, a retail chain of supermarkets would be expected to have a much lower liquidity ratio and a much higher rate of inventory turnover than a constructional engineering firm. In this context, accepted 'norms' such as a working capital ratio of 2:1 must be used with care.

TEST YOUR KNOWLEDGE **10.5**

Discuss three limitations of accounting ratios.

END OF CHAPTER QUESTIONS

10.1 Gamma plc makes up its accounts on the calendar year basis. The profit for the year to 30 September 2011, attributable to the ordinary shareholders, is £20 million after deducting interest on £40 million 12% debenture stock. The ordinary share capital presently amounts to 100 million shares of £1 each, but the debenture holders have the right to convert their holding into ordinary shares at any date after 1 January 2015. The terms of the conversion are 120 ordinary shares for every £100 of debenture stock.
Assume a tax rate of 30%

Required
Calculate the basic and fully diluted earnings per share.

10.2 The following information is provided in respect of Roxon plc:

   (a)   *Income statement extracts, year to 31 December*

	2012	2011
	£m	£m
Operating profit	132	108
Interest payable	36	36
Profit before tax	96	72
Taxation (33%)	32	24
Profit for the period	64	48
Extract from statement of changes in equity		
Dividends: ordinary shares	–32	–16
8% Preference shares	–8	–8

   (a)   The ordinary share capital consisted of 30 million shares of £1 each in 2011 and through to 30 April 2012 when a bonus issue was made of one new ordinary share for every five shares presently held.

   (b)   The 8% preference share capital amounted to £100 million throughout 2011 and 2012.

   (c)   The interest payable is in respect of 12% debenture stock. The debenture holders have the right to convert their stock into ordinary shares at any time after 1 January 2012. The terms of the conversion are 20 ordinary shares of £1 each for every £300 of debenture stock.

END OF CHAPTER QUESTIONS

Required

(a)   Define earnings per share in accordance with standard accounting practice.

(b)   Explain what is meant by a *bonus issue* of shares and indicate its likely effect on the market price of the shares.

(c)   Compute the figures for EPS, including re-stated EPS for 2011, to be disclosed in the accounts of Roxon for 2012.

(d)   Outline the circumstances in which the obligation to compute the fully diluted earnings per share arises.

(e)   Compute the figures for fully diluted earnings per share to be disclosed in the accounts of Roxon for 2012.

10.3 The du-Pont Analysis is a technique for analysing the three components of return on equity (ROE):

(a)   Net Margin = Net Income/Sales. How much profit a company makes for every £1 it generates in revenue. The higher a company's profit margin the better.

(b)   Asset Turnover = Sales/Total Assets. The amount of sales generated for every £'s worth of assets. This measures the firm's efficiency at using assets. The higher the number the better.

(c)   Leverage Factor = Net Income/Shareholder's Equity. The higher the number, the more debt the company has.

The du-Pont Analysis uses the following formula:

$$\frac{\text{Net income}}{\text{Sales}} \times \frac{\text{Sales}}{\text{Assets}} \times \frac{\text{Assets}}{\text{Equity}} = \frac{\text{Net income}}{\text{Equity}}$$

Given the following information, in £'000, calculate firm efficiency for Alpha plc:

Net income	=	3,300
Sales	=	19,600
Assets	=	135,000
Equity	=	9,500

10.4 The following information appeared under equity in the statement of financial position of Anfield Ltd at 31 December 2010:

Equity	2010	2009
	£'000	£'000
Issued share capital (£1 ordinary shares)	45000	25000
Share premium account	13500	6000
Retained earnings	16200	19000
	74700	50000

You discover that the directors of Anfield arranged a bonus issue of one new ordinary share of £1 each for every five shares held on 31 March 2010. This was followed by a rights issue at £1.50 per share on 1 May 2010. The directors of Anfield paid an interim dividend for 2010 of 15p per share on 31 July 2010.

Required

Compute the following items for inclusion in the cash flow statement and related notes of Anfield for 2010, so far as the information permits:

■ proceeds from rights issue; and
■ profit for the period (2010).

Notes:

Ignore taxation.
Anfield neither received nor paid any interest during 2010.

Limitations of published accounts, current issues and overview

■ LIST OF CHAPTERS

11 Limitations of published accounts
12 Current issues
13 Overview

Part 4 covers the syllabus section entitled 'Limitations of published accounts', 'Current issues' and an 'Overview'.

■ OVERVIEW

There are limitations as to the value of information presented and disclosed in financial statements. The underlying economic reality can only be ascertained to a certain extent on the basis of financial report. Published accounts, therefore, have their limitations as only historic costs are reported and even where 'fair value' treatment of financial instruments are disclosed, these are managerial judgements and are prone to manipulation.

Chapter 11 discusses some weaknesses inherent in financial reports and how the accounting standards attempt to mitigate aspects of managerial behaviour in financial reporting that could have an economic impact on investor decision-making.

Chapter 12 discusses the social and ethical aspects of business and the impact of reporting on issues that have a bearing on society as a whole and the environment in which companies exist and carry out economic transactions. Since modern corporations are vast, they have economic, social and political implications in the wider world. Some of these implications are discussed here.

Chapter 13 provides an overview in to aspects of businesses affairs that are highly relevant to the chartered secretary. These aspects reflect on the chartered secretary's role in providing advice to directors and management on the legal and business aspects of the company.

Each chapter ends with practice questions that require application of knowledge gained.

11 Limitations of published accounts

■ CONTENTS

1 Introduction
2 Subjectivity and earnings management – impact on reported figures
3 Inventory management
4 The audit
5 Leases
6 Creative accounting or earnings management
7 Role of audit in mitigating creative accounting
8 Substance over form
9 External auditor – principles and practices
10 Auditors and non-audit services

■ LEARNING OUTCOMES

Chapter 11 covers the syllabus section entitled 'Limitations of Published Accounts'. After reading and understanding the contents of the chapter, working through all the worked Examples and Practice Questions, you should be able to:

■ understand and explain subjectivity and earnings management and how managers can take opportunity to meet their own aims;
■ demonstrate and show how inventory is calculated and its economic impact on profits;
■ discuss the role of audit in modern businesses;
■ explain and demonstrate lease types and the economic impact of accounting for leases;
■ appreciate and demonstrate how creative accounting occurs and the various means by which managers manipulate accounting numbers such as debt factoring, consignments, sale and repurchase agreements;
■ discuss and apply the principal of substance over form; and
■ discuss the role of the external audit and the implications of audit and non audit services for corporate governance.

1   Introduction

The IFRSs, with their latest updates, provide guidance to those who prepare financial reports as well as reflect on their presentational aspects. In so doing, the IFRSs and IASs, cover the general format of financial reporting that occurs on a regular basis. When an accounting issue arises, the framework provides guidance on how to report a matter that is transparent and useful to users. However, financial reporting standards cannot cover all factors that may be relevant to users of accounting information. These factors are discussed below.

As financial statements are based on historical costs, the impact of price level changes is almost completely ignored. The basic nature of financial statements is historic. These statements are based on past estimates, and the judgement of the management team who prepare the financial information. Only monetary transactions are reported in the financial reports. Some of the limitations are discussed below:

1   The financial position of a business is affected by several factors: economic, social and financial, but only financial factors are presented in the financial statements. Economic and social factors are left out. Thus, the financial position disclosed by these statements is not

entirely accurate. However, a trend towards reporting on social and environmental impact by businesses is becoming common practice, particularly with large listed UK companies.

2 The profit revealed by the statement of comprehensive income and the statement of financial position is not exact. They are essentially interim reports presented on an annual basis.

3 Facts which have not been recorded in the financial books are not depicted in the financial statement. Only quantitative factors are taken into account. Qualitative factors, such as reputation and the prestige of the business with the public, the efficiency, and loyalty of its employees, the integrity and skill-set of management etc. do not appear in the financial statement.

4 The past 'buying power' of a national currency does not mean that the currency has the same buying power in 2012. Existing historical accounting is based on the assumption that the value of the monetary unit (e.g. sterling) remains constant. Assets are recorded by the business at the price at which they are acquired and liabilities are recorded at the amounts at which they are contracted for. A monetary unit is never stable, especially under inflationary conditions. This factor has resulted in a number of distortions in the financial statements and is the most serious limitation of historical accounting.

5 Many items (e.g. provision for depreciation, inventory valuation, bad debts provision etc) depend on the personal judgement of management.

6 The convention of accounting conservatism: the income statement may not disclose the true income of a business entity as probable losses are considered, while probable income is not reported.

7 The non-current (fixed) assets are shown at cost less depreciation on the basis of the 'going concern concept' (one of the accounting concepts). But the market value of non-current assets may not be the same on disposal. The disposal of a non-current asset may give rise to a loss or gain which will be reported through the comprehensive income.

8 The financial figures disclosed in the financial statements are historical values of the items. Financial data must be analysed and evaluated in some way to give some sort of indication of the future prospects of a business entity. Management judgement is always involved in the preparation of financial statements. It is the analyst or user who gives meaning to financial information.

2 Subjectivity and earnings management – impact on reported figures

Modern accounting methods are based on the accruals (or matching) concept in which revenues and expenses are reported in the period they are incurred, irrespective of when physical cash transactions take place. IAS 1 requires business entities to prepare accounts on accrual.

There are many reasons why those preparing financial information may not present a completely accurate picture. This was discussed earlier with regard to Agency Theory. Managers, typically, use accounting techniques that either enhance actual earnings or defer earnings to future periods. One reason why managers may enhance earnings figures is self-interest (e.g.

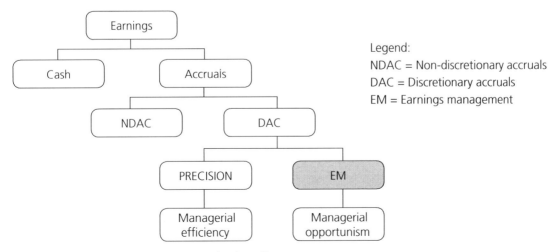

FIGURE 11.1 How managers manipulate figures

meeting bonus and remuneration targets). Before we discuss **earnings management** any further, it would be useful to understand how it works. The figure below demonstrates how managers are able to manipulate certain accounting figures for their own interests.

The figure suggests that earnings have two components: cash and accruals. In an accruals-based accounting system, revenues, and expenses are matched in the period they are incurred. Accruals, however, are a **subjective** measure of revenue and expenses. Nevertheless, the non-discretionary accruals (NDAC) element of total 'accruals' can be shown to be accurate, for instance, sales at the end of the year. Here the invoices relating to end of year sales are raised in the new financial year and matching cash is received from customers. However, in certain cases, managers will use their judgement to accrue revenues and expenses that are not clearly definable. They use their inside knowledge to communicate this information to the outside world. For example, a contract for services straddles more than one financial year. The value of the contract is £10 million and the contract runs for five years. Management may decide that the bulk of the contractual income (say 60%) will be in the first two years.

They will thus reflect 60% of the contractual income in the first two years in reported financial figures. This is acceptable if managers can explain their reasoning to the external auditors.

Conversely, managers may sometimes manage earnings for their own purposes to meet certain targets. This is known as managerial opportunism. As mentioned earlier, the only mechanism for managing reported earnings is through accruals manipulation. The nature of accruals is such that they reverse in the next accounting period. This has repercussions for reported figures. Any unassigned accruals will not be matched by the eventual receipt or payment of cash. This has an impact on current and future reported earnings.

Apart from meeting earnings expectations to achieve bonus targets, managers may increase, by various means, reported earnings to meet market expectations (e.g. by reducing gearing levels, increasing Earnings per Share (EPS)) hence strengthening the statement of financial position.

TABLE 11.1: Some actions managers can take to increase earnings

Managerial action	Purpose of action	Impact on earnings		Impact on balances		Related Standard
		Increase	Decrease	Increase	Decrease	
Assets classified as being held for sale	Decrease depreciation expense	Higher	No	CA	NCA	IFRS 5
Changes accounting policies	Reduction of reported expense	Higher	No	NCA	Depn	IAS 8
Misclassification of finance lease	Possible no effect	No	No	OBT	OBT	IAS 17
Revenues	Increase earnings	Higher	No	Rec	None	IAS 18
Research expenditure	Increase assets	Higher	No	NCA	None	IAS 38

CA   Current assets
NCA   Non-current assets
OBT   Off-balance sheet transaction
Depn   Depreciation
Rec   Receivables

Managerial opportunism is intended to increase reported earnings. This in turn motivates managers to meet certain targets such as gearing. A formula for gearing is:

$$\text{Gearing} = \frac{\text{Long-term Liabilities}}{\text{Equity Shareholders' Funds}} \text{ or Debt:Equity}$$

Another version of the gearing ratio is stated as:

$$\text{Gearing} = \frac{\text{Long-term Liabilities}}{\text{Equity Shareholders' Funds} + \text{Long- term liabilities}} \text{ or Debt:Equity} + \text{Debt}$$

 WORKED EXAMPLE **11.1**

The following are the financial figures of Raymond Ltd. In exercising its judgement, management has been over-optimistic about the amount of revenue it believes should be reported.

The pre-accruals column shows the actual figures as they should be reported. The post-accruals column shows the figure after managers have accrued an extra £8 million revenue. The impact of this is demonstrated below:

	Pre-accruals 2011 £'000	Post-accruals 2011 £'000
Sales	52000	60000
Cost of goods sold	36000	36000
Gross margin	16000	24000
Operating expenses		
Selling expenses	7000	7000
Administrative expense	5860	5860
Total operating expenses	12860	12860
Net operating income	3140	11140
Interest expense	640	640
Profit before tax	2500	10500
Income taxes (30%)	750	3150
Profit for the year	1750	7350
Non-current assets		
Property, plant and equipment	16000	16000
Current assets		
Inventory	8000	8000
Receivables	6000	14000
Prepaid expenses	300	300
Cash and cash equivalents	3700	3700
Total current assets	18000	26000
Total assets	34000	42000
Equity and liabilities		
Share capital (£1 shares)	6000	6000
Share premium	1000	1000
6% Preferred shares	2000	2000
Retained earnings	8000	15400
	17000	24400
Non-current liabilities		
8% loan	10000	10000
Current liabilities:		
Accounts payable	5800	5800
Accrued payable	900	900
Taxation	300	900
Total current liabilities	7000	7600
Total liabilities	17000	17600
Total equity and liabilities	34000	42000

WORKED EXAMPLE **11.1** *continued*

Required

Raymond Ltd is a manufacturer of machine parts. To assist in the cash management and expansion of the business, Raymond secured a £10 million long-term loan from its bankers. The terms and conditions of the loan stipulated that Raymond should not exceed a 50% debt: equity ratio (see formula given above). However, at the end of 2011, the debt covenant with the lender appears to have been breached. Managers at Raymond Ltd decided to increase revenue sales figures by an extra £8 million. The premise for this increase is based on over-optimistic expectation of revenues from contracts with certain customers.

Calculate the gearing ratio pre- and post accruals for Raymond Ltd and make relevant comments on the change in gearing.

Answer

	Pre-accruals figures 2011	Post-accruals figures 2011
	£'000	£'000
Sales	52000	60000
Earnings	1750	7350
Long-term finance	10000	10000
Shareholders' funds	17000	24400
Gearing	$\dfrac{10000}{17000}$	$\dfrac{10000}{24400}$
Gearing	59%	41%

 WORKED EXAMPLE **11.2**

Given the above information the consequence of actions taken by Raymond Ltd would have repercussions on other aspects of the company's financial figures.

Required

Calculate the change in earnings per share and any expectations by shareholders and potential investors.

Answer

	Pre-accruals figures 2010	Post-accruals figures 2010
	£'000	£'000
Sales	52000	60000
Earnings	1750	7350
Shares in issue	6 million	6 million
EPS	$\dfrac{1750}{6000}$	$\dfrac{7350}{6000}$
EPS	0.29	1.23

It would appear that from the pre-accruals, Raymond Ltd would have defaulted on the debt covenant agreed with the lender. The pre-accruals gearing ratio is 59%, way above the agreed level. Managers at Raymond Ltd have accrued an extra £8 million in revenue, which has increased the Total Shareholder's fund by about 44%. This appears to be drastic action by Raymond's managers for the current year. However, the impact of this £8 million extra accrual will have consequences for the following financial year as revenue will be reduced by £8 million in 2011. Unless Raymond Ltd increases its actual revenue by an equal amount in 2011, the company will face the same difficulties (i.e. default on the debt covenant).

The action taken by Raymond Ltd has meant an increase in earnings from the pre-accruals position to the post accruals position of 320%. Similarly, the change in EPS has also risen by 320% from pre-accrual EPS of 29p per share to £1.23 per share. This would cause great difficulties for the company, as shareholders may expect a dramatic rise in dividends to be announced. When this does not materialise, this may give cause for concern not just to the shareholders and lenders of Raymond, but to other stakeholders.

Taking the example from Raymond Ltd (above), discuss any further impact the action of management will have on the statement of financial position for Raymond.

 **WORKED EXAMPLE** **11.3**

The table below indicates the impact of change in ratio measuring company performance:

	Pre-accruals figures 2010	Post-accruals figures 2010	% Change Post Accrual
Current ratio	2.57	3.42	33%
Acid test	1.43	2.37	66%
Total asset turnover	1.53	1.43	−7%
ROE – (W1)	11%	32%	191%
ROCE – (W2)	6%	21%	250%

	Pre-accruals 2011 £'000	Post-accruals 2011 £'000
(W1)		
Return on equity (ROE)		
Equity (excludes preference shares):		
Share capital	6000	6000
Share premium	1000	1000
Retained earnings	8000	15400
	15000	22400
Net income	1750	7350
Dividends to preferred share holders	−120	−120
Income attributable to equity shareholders	1630	7230
Pre-accruals ROE = 1,630/15,000	11%	
Post accruals ROE = 7,230/22,400		32%
(W2)		
Return on Capital Employed (ROCE):		
Profit for the period	1750	7350
Capital employed:		
Pre-accruals 34,000 – 7,000	27000	
Post-accruals 42,000 – 7,000		35000
Pre-accruals ROCE = 1,750/(34,000 – 7,000)	6%	
Post-accruals ROCE = 7,350/(42,000 – 7,000)		21%

Evidently, the post-accruals figures indicate substantial strengthening of the statement of financial position for Raymond Ltd.

- *Current ratio*: Suggests that the liquidity position of the company has improved substantially. However, this is mainly due to the increase in receivables after the increase through accruals management.
- *Acid test*: The acid test ratio, a more stringent version of the current ration that excludes inventory in its calculation, again suggests that the liquidity of the company has strengthened due to the increase in revenue through accruals management.
- *Total asset turnover ratio*: suggests that the company efficiency has fallen even though revenues have increased substantially. This is due to the corresponding increase in total asset increase since the accruals effect has also increased receivables.
- *Return on equity*: The figures indicate that an increase of 191% has taken place due to the effects of increase in revenues and hence earnings. The increase in earnings is not, however, matched by any level of increase in shareholder's equity. Hence, a sharp rise in the ROE ratio is indicated.
- *Return on capital employed*: This ratio takes into account the total shareholders fund that includes reserves and retained earnings. The figures suggest an increase in ROCE by 250% due to increased earnings and increased total shareholders' fund.

It would be interesting to see how the company manages its revenues in 2012. An actual rise in revenue, without accruals management, would cancel out the effects of the use of accruals in 2011. However, if no action is taken and no accruals management occurs in 2012, we would expect a sharp and substantial fall in the ratios indicated. This would have repercussions on stakeholders and confidence in company performance may fall.

 TEST YOUR KNOWLEDGE 11.1

(a) Explain what is meant by subjectivity.
(b) Discuss the reasons why managers may engage in earnings management.

---

3   Inventory management

One method of inventory management is the valuation of inventory by the management. IAS 2 'Inventories', provides guidance for the accounting treatment of inventory valuation. The standard suggests that:

> The objective of IAS 2 is to prescribe the accounting treatment for inventories. It provides guidance for determining the cost of inventories and for subsequently recognising an expense, including any write-down to net realisable value. It also provides guidance on the cost formulas that are used to assign costs to inventories.

The accounting treatment of inventories, as governed by IAS 2, defines inventories as assets:

(a) held for sale in the ordinary course of business;
(b) in the process of production for such sale; or
(c) in the form of materials or supplies to be consumed in the production process or in the rendering of services.

IAS 2 requires companies to value inventories at cost, except where this exceeds net realisable value, in which case the latter figure should be used. The relevant terms are defined as follows:

- *Cost* comprises all costs of purchase, costs of conversion and other costs incurred in bringing the inventories to their present location and condition.
- *Net realisable value* (NRV) is the estimated selling price in the ordinary course of business less the estimated costs of completion and the estimated costs necessary to make the sale.

To ensure that full provision is made for foreseeable losses, IAS 2 requires the comparison between cost and NRV to be based on individual items of stock, with the proviso that groups of similar items may be compared where the comparison of individual items is impractical.

IAS 2 only permits the use of first-in-first-out and the weighted average cost formula as the two bases for measuring inventory. IAS 2 requires preparers of accounts to recognise inventory to NRV, but only if less than cost. NRV is the estimated selling price in the ordinary course of business, less the estimated cost of completion and the estimated costs necessary to make the sale. In the process of recognising NRV, it is clear the NRV has fallen; this must be recognised as an expense in the statement of comprehensive income.

 WORKED EXAMPLE 11.4

The following information is provided in respect of a group of items of inventory belonging to Banbury Ltd:

Item of inventory	Cost	NRV
	£	£
A	500	580
B	300	370
C	250	330
D	760	600

Required

Calculations of the total value of Banbury's inventories, based on the lower of cost and NRV, assuming that cost is compared with NRV:

(a) on an individual item basis;

(b) on a group basis.

Answer

(a) Individual item basis:

Item of inventory	Cost	NRV	Lower of cost and NRV Individual item basis
	£	£	£
A	500	580	500
B	300	370	300
C	250	330	250
D	760	600	600
	1810	1880	1650

(b) Group basis:

Item of inventory	Cost	NRV	Lower of cost and NRV Group basis
	£	£	£
A +B +C + D	1810	1880	1650

Comparing cost with the NRV of individual items results in a lower inventory value (£1,650 as compared with £1,810) and therefore a lower profit figure because the comparison of total figures for cost and NRV results in a foreseeable loss of £160 on item D (£760 cost – £600 NRV) being offset by total unrealised gains of £230 on items A–C (£1,280 NRV – £1,050 cost).

The principal situations in which NRV is likely to be below cost are where there has been:

- a fall in selling price;
- physical deterioration of inventories;
- obsolescence of a product;
- a decision, as part of an entity's marketing strategy, to manufacture and sell products for the time being at a loss; and
- miscalculations or other errors in purchasing or production.

In practice, any one of the above is unlikely to apply to more than a small proportion of the company's inventories. For the remainder, NRV will exceed cost and can be ignored when valuing inventories for inclusion in the accounts. However, the problem of deciding how to compute cost remains.

There are two basic areas of difficulty:

1   Whether to value inventories on the marginal cost or the total cost basis (see below).
2   How to identify purchases with issues to production and match finished goods with sales, (i.e. inventory valuation).

TEST YOUR KNOWLEDGE 11.2

Identify the principal situations in which NRV is likely to be below cost and explain the appropriate accounting treatment of the discrepancy.

3.1   Inventory valuation – Further examples

The impracticality of physically measuring inventory requires a method of estimation that would allow inventory reporting. Managers usually estimate inventory in the following ways:

3.1.1   Retail inventory method (RIM)

This method uses a cost-to-retail price ratio. The physical inventory is valued at retail and multiplied by the cost ratio (or percentage) to determine the estimated cost of closing inventory. The RIM requires that a record be kept of:

- the total cost and retail value of goods purchased;
- the total cost and retail value of the goods available for sale; and
- the sales for the period.

The RIM requires that the sales for the period are deducted from the retail value of the goods available for sale, to produce an estimated inventory-at-retail value. The ratio of cost to retail for all goods is then determined by dividing the total goods available for sale at cost by the total goods available at retail. The inventory valued at retail is converted to closing inventory-at-cost by applying the cost-to-retail ratio. Use of RIM is very common.

However, RIM is subjective and requires managerial judgement. Managers can manipulate retail prices to under or overstate inventory. As a result, earnings figures can be over or understated. The example below demonstrates the subjectivity of the retail inventory method.

 **WORKED EXAMPLE** **11.5**

Fresco plc is a nationwide chain of retail stores and measures it closing inventory on the Retail Inventory Method. The company also keeps record of actual cost of purchases, which in 2012 amounted to £120,000 with a retail equivalent of £240,000. Opening inventory was £220,000 at cost and £240,000 at retail. Net sales for the period amounted to £308,000

Required
Calculate the closing inventory for Fresco using the RIM and offer comparison with actual cost of purchase. Comment on the likely impact on earnings.

Answer

	Cost £	Retail £
Opening inventory	220000	240000
Purchases	120000	158000
Goods available for sale	340000	398000
Deduct: Sales		308000
Closing inventory at retail		90000
Ratio of cost to retail (£340,000 ÷ £398,000)		85%
Closing inventory at cost (85% of £90,000)		£76500
Sales	308000	308000
CoGS: bases on actual prices		−90000
CoGS: Retail Method	−76500	
Estimate of profits	231500	218000
Profit to Sales ratio	75%	71%
(CoGS Cost of goods sold)		

The RIM is a highly subjective method which can be used either to inflate or deflate profits. In a highly competitive trading environment, managers can deflate profits to exercise lower levels of tax liability. This can result in an increase in the distribution of retained profits in the form of lower dividends.

3.1.2 Gross margin (or gross profit) method

The gross margin method (GMM) (also known as the gross profit method (GPM)) uses the previous year's average gross profit margin (i.e. sales minus cost of goods sold divided by sales). Current year gross profit is estimated by multiplying current year sales by that of gross profit margin. The current year cost of goods sold is estimated by subtracting the gross profit from sales; the final inventory is estimated by subtracting the cost of goods sold from goods available for sale. The following example demonstrates the GMM:

WORKED EXAMPLE 11.6

	2011 Actual £	2012 Actual £	2012 GMM* £
Sales	480000	558000	558000
Beginning inventory	140000	82000	82000
Purchases	310000	400000	400000
Goods available for sale	450000	482000	482000
Closing inventory	–82000	-63000	–52340
CoGS	368000	419000	429660
Gross profit	112000	139000	128340
Gross margin on sales	23%	25%	23%

Workings:

Step 1	Cost of goods available	=	Beginning inventory	+	Net purchases
	Cost of goods available	=	£82000	+	£400000
	Cost of goods available	=	£482000		
Step 2	Gross profit	=	Gross Profit %	×	Sales
	Gross profit	=	23%	×	£558000
	Gross profit	=	£128340		
Step 3	Cost of goods sold	=	Sales	–	Gross Profit
	Cost of goods sold	=	£558000	–	£128340 (step 2)
	Cost of goods sold	=	£429660		

Cost of goods sold can also be calculated as 77% × sales of £56,000 = £44,800.

Step 4.	Ending inventory	=	Cost of Goods Available	–	Cost of Goods Sold
	Ending inventory	=	£482000	–	£429660
	Ending inventory	=	£52340		

GMM bears some similarity with the RIM; however, the GMM method does not rely on keeping retail price records. It is simply a ratio of gross profit to sales. This ratio is then multiplied by the sales value for the current year to arrive at gross profit figure. The current year cost of goods sold is estimated by subtracting the gross profit from sales, and the closing inventory is estimated by subtracting cost of goods sold to goods available for sale.

Worked Example 11.6 shows that had the company used the actual price of cost of purchases, the closing inventory figure could have been slightly higher than the estimated closing inventory under GMM. In this particular example, under GMM, the gross margin is the same in 2012 as it was in 2011. However, the GMM yields a lower profit amount. The GMM lends itself to manipulation and closing inventory could be managed to yield particular profit results.

4   The audit

The **audit** provides a mechanism by which corporate governance can monitor managerial action. All listed companies must subject their annual financial reports to verification. This is done through the external audit process. Limited companies, however, whose turnover is less than £6.5 million are exempt from an external audit. The audit quality in relation to external audit is defined as the joint probability of detecting and reporting material errors or misstatements in financial reports. The probability of detection relates to the level of auditor competence, however, the auditor's ability to reveal errors or misstatements depends on their independence (i.e. their willingness to face the pressure exerted by the producers of financial statements).

The auditor conducts the audit in accordance with International Standards on Auditing (UK and Ireland) issued by the Auditing Practices Board. An audit includes an examination of evidence relevant to the amounts and disclosures in the financial statements. It also includes an assessment of the significant estimates and judgements made by the directors in preparing the financial statements.

Generally, however, auditors express an opinion of the true and fair view of the financial figures being reported. In so doing they must have regard to the level of audit risk presented and the level of audit work that must be carried out to enable a view to be expressed.

An external audit process ensures that a company's internal controls, processes, guidelines and policies are adequate, effective and comply with the legal and accounting standards in force, industry standards and its own policies and procedures. The external audit also ensures that reporting mechanisms prevent errors in financial statements. Those who use audit reports include investors, company management, regulators and business partners such as lenders, suppliers and creditors.

The external audit provides reassurance to all user groups who have a vested interest in the financial affairs of a company (e.g. company management, regulators and investors). The audit enables both the senior management and the audit committee (see below) of a company to review the audit report to determine operating breakdowns and segments showing higher risks of loss and, where necessary, to take appropriate action to safeguard the assets of the company. An auditor's job is not to comment on the efficiency and proficiency of a company's financial performance, but to verify that the financial statements are free from material error and to question management on their judgment in various matters.

Regulators use audit reports to detect business trends and corporate practices and to ensure that such practices comply with the law. Investors read audit opinions to gauge a company's economic standing and management's short-term initiatives or long-term strategies.

Note
An audit committee is an aspect of the board of directors of a company. It has special responsibilities for both the internal and external audit functions. The audit committee has responsibility to provide the auditors with guidance, support and direction.

 **TEST YOUR KNOWLEDGE 11.3**

Describe what is meant by an audit and its role in business.

5 Leases

The purpose of IAS 17 'Leases' was to address the situation where loan capital remained off the statement of financial position (commonly referred to as off-balance sheet financing) as the result of a **leasing** arrangement. The standard is particularly notable because, within the international arena, it was the first to apply both the concept of substance over form and to incorporate the present value basis of measurement into the historical cost model.

The potential significance of the problem was brought starkly to the attention of the UK business community and the regulators as early as 1974 when the package holiday business Court Line Ltd collapsed. The directors had leased aircraft to operate the company's package holiday business, and the investigation of its affairs following the collapse showed there to be undisclosed obligations relating to leased assets of £40 million. The magnitude of this undisclosed financial obligation (equivalent to about £540 million in today's prices) was further demonstrated by the fact that it dwarfed the figure for shareholders' equity of £18 million reported in the last statement of financial position published before the company collapsed. Both the shareholders and the creditors whose entitlements *were* reported in the statement of financial position were astonished and dismayed to discover that contemporary GAAP permitted the omission of vast liabilities from the statement of financial position and, moreover, that such a company could get a clean audit report. Following their investigation of Court Line's affairs, the then Department of Trade and Industry's inspectors were certainly not overstating the position when they reported that 'the amounts involved were material and should have been disclosed'.

The fact was, of course, that the financial reporting procedures followed by Court Line were entirely justified on a strictly legal interpretation of its leasing agreements. The lessor's were the owners of the aircraft not Court Line. However, the *substance* of the arrangement was that Court Line had acquired the aircraft for its exclusive use with finance provided by the lessor; an arrangement which, in commercial terms, was no different from Court Line buying the aircraft outright on credit terms. In other words, there was a discrepancy between the legal *form* and the economic *substance* of the transaction, with Court Line choosing to comply with the former and ignore the latter.

It is an indication of the complexity of the topic (and probably effective lobbying from the leasing industry) that it was not until 1984, ten years later, that the problem was addressed through the issue of an accounting standard in the UK. IAS 17, with which we are concerned here, was modelled on the UK standard. It is worth mentioning at this point that the IASB has issued an Exposure Draft effectively classifying all leases as finance leases.

The standard-setters were faced with the need to:

- distinguish between leasing arrangements which resulted in off-balance sheet financing and those which did not; and
- determine the appropriate accounting treatment for each of them.

These objectives were achieved by devising and defining the terms finance lease and operating lease and specifying an accounting treatment for each of them. The key definitions contained in IAS 17 and elsewhere are as follows:

- *Finance lease*: A lease which transfers substantially all the *risks* and *rewards* incidental to ownership of an asset. Title may or may not be actually transferred at some stage.
- *Operating lease*: A lease other than a finance lease.
- *Risks and rewards:* These are presumed to be transferred from the lessor to the lessee where the *present value* of the minimum lease payments amounts, *substantially*, to the *fair value* of the leased asset.
- *Present value*: The current estimate of the present discounted value of the future net cash flows in the normal course of business.
- *Imputed interest:* The interest rate which equates the nominal amounts of the lease *rate* rentals with the leased asset's fair value.
- *Fair value:* The amount at which the leased asset could be exchanged in arm's length transaction.

The essence of IAS 17, therefore, is to draw a distinction between finance leases where the asset is leased to a particular party for all, or substantially all, of its useful life and operating leases where the asset is leased for a relatively short period to a succession of individuals (e.g. hire cars). The distinction is based principally on the concept of the 'risks and rewards' of ownership.

Risks and rewards normally attach to the owner of an asset. For example, a company buys an asset on the expectation that it will produce future financial benefits. The expectation is that the value in use of the future cash flows generated from the use of the asset will exceed the fair value of the asset at acquisition date. In the case of an arm's length transaction, this will be the amount actually paid. If these expectations are fulfilled, the rewards of ownership accrue to the owner. However, if the acquisition proves to have been a mistake (e.g. the market for the product disappears immediately the non-current asset is acquired) the risks and related loss are suffered by the owner. In an extreme case, therefore, the loss incurred will be equal to the entire cost of the asset.

In the case of a finance lease arrangement, however, the risks and rewards normally associated with ownership are instead transferred, through the lease contract, from the lessor to the lessee. For example, the contract may stipulate that, if the lessor wishes to end the leasing arrangement prematurely, a sum of money must be paid, as a penalty, equal to the amount of the lease rentals outstanding.

The essence of the *accounting* requirements relating to finance leases, therefore, is to oblige the lessee (i.e. the party possessing the risks and rewards and ownership) to report the asset in its statement of financial position, with the present value of the rental payments outstanding under the lease contract reported as a liability. At the date the lease contract is entered into, these amounts will be identical but, as time goes by, they will diverge as the asset is depreciated in accordance with the company's accounting policies and the liability is reduced by the value of the capital element of lease rentals paid.

In deciding where risks and rewards reside and, therefore, whether an arrangement should be accounted for as an operating lease or a finance lease, the lease contract must be examined. Typical matters that receive attention in the lease contract are:

- the period of the lease, which may vary from a day, or even less, to the entire life of the asset;
- the amount and timing of the lease payments;
- whether the lease can be cancelled;
- what is to become of the asset at the end of the lease period;
- whether the lessee is to be liable for the difference, if any, between the residual value of the non-current asset and the amount it is sold for;
- who is to be responsible for the payment of maintenance and repairs, insurance, taxes and other operating costs.

Arrangements that would suggest that the lease contract relates to a finance lease include: that the lease covers the entire life of the asset; the present value of the lease payments approximates the fair value of the asset; the lessee has no power to cancel the lease; the lessee has an option to purchase the asset for a nominal price at the end of the lease period; the lessee is liable for the difference between residual value and sales price; and the lessee is responsible for maintaining and insuring the asset.

 WORKED EXAMPLE 11.7

Alpha Ltd leases a machine to Beta Ltd on 1 January 2009.
Beta Ltd makes four annual payments of £35,000 commencing 1 January 2009.
Alpha Ltd sells the machine, also for cash, £108,728.
The life of non-current asset is estimated at four years and the residual value as zero.
The rate of interest implicit in the rental payments is 20%.

Required
Show how these transactions are to be recorded in the books of the lessee, Beta Ltd.

Answer
The rental payments may be split between interest and capital as follows:

		2009	2010	2011	2012
		£	£	£	£
1	Total outstanding 1 January	108728	88473	64167	35000
2	Rental paid 1 January	35000	35000	35000	35000
		73728	53473	29167	0
3	Interest expense for year, 20%	14745	10694	5833	0
4	Total outstanding 31 December	88473	64167	35000	0

Income statement entries

	2009	2010	2011	2012
	£	£	£	£
Depreciation charge	27182	27182	27182	27182
interest expense	14745	10694	5833	0

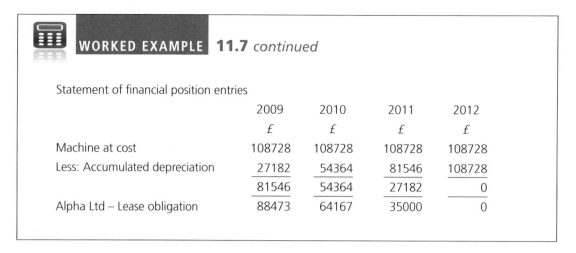

WORKED EXAMPLE **11.7** *continued*

Statement of financial position entries

	2009	2010	2011	2012
	£	£	£	£
Machine at cost	108728	108728	108728	108728
Less: Accumulated depreciation	27182	54364	81546	108728
	81546	54364	27182	0
Alpha Ltd – Lease obligation	88473	64167	35000	0

It is clear from the above calculations that an asset and a liability is disclosed which will have an impact on certain ratios of the company such as the gearing and return on asset ratios. The combined depreciation and interest charges arising due to finance lease recognition are higher in the early years of the lease than in the latter years. However, if the above lease was treated as an operating lease there would have only been a charge of £35,000 per annum to the income statement with no effect on the statement of financial position.

5.1 Debt factoring

A **factoring** arrangement involves the factor, perhaps a financial institution or specialist factoring company, buying some or all of an entity's accounts receivable or debt outright. The factor then administers the sales ledger, taking responsibility for sending out statements to customers and chasing up outstanding payments. The specific arrangements made (e.g. the amount advanced and responsibility for bad debts) can vary significantly. For example, the arrangement may involve an advance of 90% of the value of receivables with the remaining amount paid over, when collected, less a commission plus interest on the advance. The Scottish Enterprise website states that factoring is particularly attractive to businesses whose growth is sales-based and who need regular injections of working capital to buy materials, to increase production and to fund inventories purchase as sales rise. They continue:

> Late payment is the bane of most small businesses. Factoring substantially reduces the average payment period on invoices, something that can do wonders for the financial performance of a rapidly growing business. In particular, factoring can help avoid 'over-trading' and with a more predictable cash flow, your business can plan more effectively.

According to statistics released by the Factors & Discounters Association, factoring or invoice discounting in the UK is now (2012) being used by almost 42,000 companies, generating a combined turnover in excess of £212 billion.

The accounting treatment of a factoring arrangement naturally depends on who has the risks and rewards of ownership. If the total receivables are the subject of an outright sale, risks and rewards are transferred to the factor and the asset should be derecognised in the vendor's statement of financial position. If, at the other extreme, there are full rights of recourse in respect of bad debts, then the risks and rewards are not transferred and the receivables should continue to be reported in the entity's statement of financial position.

TEST YOUR KNOWLEDGE **11.4**

(a) Explain debt factoring.
(b) Describe how debt factoring can be useful for small companies.
(c) Discuss the potential to abuse the debt factoring method in relation to strengthening the statement of financial position.

6 Creative accounting or earnings management

Creative accounting can be defined in a number of ways. However, a working definition can be taken to mean: 'a process by which managers use their knowledge of accounting choices available to them to manipulate the figures reported in the accounts of a business.'

Creative accounting, or to use the more modern phraseology, earnings management, can occur in a number of ways both intentional and unintentional. Some basic reasons why creative accounting occurs and the role of audit in mitigating such practices are discussed below:

- *Accounting system* – the weaknesses inherent in the Anglo-Saxon method of accounting presents itself to manipulation by opportunistic managers.
- *Accounting choices* – Accounting rules allow companies to choose between relevant accounting methods. In many countries, a company can choose between a policy of writing off development expenditure as it occurs, or amortising it over the life of the related project. A company can, therefore, choose the accounting policy that gives its preferred image. In the UK and under IFRS development, expenditure must be written of to the income statement.
- *Accounting judgment* – By and large, the manner in which accounting rules and regulations are drafted demand management to deliver some level of estimates. Currently the IFRS requires management to provide some level of estimate where exact or accurate figures are either unavailable or inaccessible (e.g. pension costs). The defined benefits scheme (DB) is notorious for estimating pension costs to companies.

In some circumstances relevant experts are engaged to make estimates; for instance, an actuary would normally be employed to assess the prospective pension liability. In this case the creative accountant can manipulate the valuation both by the way in which the expert is briefed and by engaging an expert known to take either a pessimistic or an optimistic view. In either case, management may select the most favourable expert.

- *Accounting transactions* – Certain entries in the accounts involve an unavoidable degree of estimation, judgement, and prediction. In some cases, such as the estimation of an asset's useful life made to calculate depreciation, these estimates are normally made inside the business and the creative accountant has the opportunity to err on the side of caution or optimism in making the estimate.

Artificial transactions can be entered into both to manipulate the statement of financial position balances and to move profits between accounting periods. This is achieved by entering into two or more related transactions with an obliging third party, normally a bank. Supposing an arrangement is made to sell an asset to a bank, then lease that asset back for the rest of its useful life. The sale price under such a 'sale and leaseback' can be pitched above or below the current value of the asset, because the difference can be compensated for by increased or reduced rentals.

Genuine transactions can also be timed so as to give the desired impression in the accounts. As an example, suppose a business has an investment of £1 million at historic cost which can easily be sold for £3 million, being the current value. The managers of the business are free to choose in which year they sell the investment and so increase the profit in the accounts at a desired time.

7 Role of audit in mitigating creative accounting

The external auditor is increasingly viewed as a way to hold managers to account through an appropriate application of accounting policies and sound judgement when preparing financial reports. To this end an external auditor could help in mitigating creative accounting practices. This requires two fundamental perspectives; expertise in determining errors and misstatements in reported financial figures and the independence to report such errors or misstatements. These are discussed below:

The audit process, being a mechanism of corporate governance, is supposed to provide a measure of reassurance to users of accounts. In providing such assurance, the auditor must convey two primary characteristics:

- *Auditor expertise* – In being able to mitigate errors or misstatements (creative accounting), the auditor must have expertise both in their profession and in some cases in the industry that they specialise in. Faced with a new customer, or perhaps a new industry, smaller auditors may not have the acumen to conduct effective audits and therefore, offer reassurance to end users who may rely on their opinion.
- *Auditor independence* – Auditors depend on audit fees, in large part, to sustain their business. If an auditor has a small client base that makes up the bulk of their income this may compromise auditor independence. However, in the UK no more than 10–15% of fees income can arise from one client. Auditor independence is measured by the auditor's ability to demand correction to errors or misstatements made by management in financial accounts.
- *Audit quality* – Auditor expertise and independence together constitute what is called audit quality. Audit quality is the joint probability that an auditor will detect and report an error or a misstatement. The detection of an error or misstatement relates to auditor expertise. The auditor ability to report an error or misstatement relates to the auditor's independence.

TEST YOUR KNOWLEDGE 11.5

Explain creative accounting.

8 Substance over form

The principle of 'substance over form' allows a company to ensure that its financial reports offer a true and fair view of the economic realities of the business. In this way, the economic substance rather than the legal form is reported. The IASB has, in recent years, diverted its attention on the balance-sheet approach. Standards have been developed and either enhanced or amended to allow the substance of a transaction, rather than its legal form, to convey economic reality.

Some transactions present a window of opportunistic behaviour for managers. The 'substance over form' concept has addressed some of the mechanisms that were used (or in some cases may still be used, perhaps in smaller companies) to hide the true nature of a transaction. Some of these mechanisms are discussed below:

8.1 Sale and leaseback arrangement

A company that needs cash can enter in to a financial arrangement with a willing third party, such as a bank. The company sells its machinery to the bank and gets it back via a lease. This is called a 'sale and leaseback' arrangement. Under this arrangement, although the legal ownership has transferred, the underlying economics remain the same. Under the 'substance over form' principle, the sale and subsequent leaseback are considered to be one transaction. If two companies swap their inventories, they will not be allowed to record a sale because no sale has occurred, even if they have entered into a valid enforceable contract.

8.2 Consignment stock

Consignment sales are arrangement between two parties: the principal and the agent. In this arrangement the agent holds the goods on behalf of the principal with a view to selling on the good on behalf of the principal, thereby earning a fee or a commission.

In a *consignment* arrangement, the consignor (seller) ships goods to the consignee (buyer), which acts as the agent of the consignor in trying to sell the goods. There are many forms of consignment arrangements, however, the two main methods are:

- where the consignee receives a commission; or
- where the consignee 'purchases' the goods simultaneously with the sale of goods to the final customer.

Goods out on consignment are properly included in the inventory of the consignor and *excluded* from the inventory of the consignee. Disclosure may be required of the consignee; however, since common financial analytical inferences, such as days' sales in inventory or inventory turnover, may appear distorted unless the financial statement users are informed. However, IFRS does not explicitly address this.

8.3 Sale and repurchase arrangement

In effect, a sale and repurchase agreement is a loan. In this arrangement the sale of an asset takes place between two parties with a view to the assets subsequent repurchase at a higher price. The difference between the sale price and the repurchase price represents interest which is at times referred to as the 'repo' rate. The party that originally buys the securities effectively acts as a lender. The original seller is effectively acting as a borrower, using their security as collateral for a secured cash loan at a fixed rate of interest.

A sale and repurchase agreement is another arrangement that can be exploited to produce off-balance sheet finance. Its essential feature is that the company purports to have sold an asset, but has not relinquished all the risks and rewards associated with that asset in a manner which one would expect in the case of a normal sale. Fundamentally, therefore, it is a form of secured borrowing.

 **WORKED EXAMPLE 11.8**

A whisky blending company contracts to sell part of its stock of whisky to a bank for £10 million on 1 January 2010. The agreement makes provision for the whisky company to buy back the whisky two years later for £12.1 million. The whisky remains at the blending company's premises.

The market rate of interest for an advance to a whisky blending company is known to be 10%.

Required
Explain the substance of this transaction and how it should be accounted for in the books and accounts of the whisky company in 2010/11.

Answer
If the transaction was accounted for as a normal sale, inventory would be reduced by £10 million and cash would be increased by £10 million in the company's balance sheet. In such a case, the financing arrangement would remain off-balance sheet and the assets of the company would also be understated.

However, this is a financing arrangement rather than a normal sale. The company has transferred no risks and rewards of ownership to the bank and has merely borrowed money on the security of an appreciating asset.

The inventories should remain in the balance sheet of the whisky blending company, at the date of the initial advance (1 January 2010) at £10 million, with the cash received from the bank shown as a liability.

2010 accounts of whisky blending company	£m
Income statement – finance charge	1
Statement of financial position – 'loan'	11
2011 accounts of whisky blending company	
Income statement – finance charge	1.1
Statement of financial position – 'loan'	12.1

On 1 January 2012, the whisky blending company pays £12.1 million to the bank and the loan is removed from its statement of financial position.

This is a straightforward financing arrangement but additional provisions may be included which make it less easy to determine the substance of the transaction.

Examples include:

■ *The nature of the asset* – It is perhaps unlikely that a bank would want to retain ownership of a stock of whisky, but the position might be different in the case of property; the appropriate accounting treatment would then be different.

■ *The nature of the repurchase provision* – Is there an unconditional commitment by both parties or do either or both possess options concerning repurchase arrangements?

■ *The initial sale price and the repurchase price* – Do these look like artificial prices designed to operationalise a financing arrangement, or are they the actual market prices at one or both dates? If the figures used at each date are market prices, the arrangement begins to look more like a normal sale in which risks and rewards are transferred, particularly if either or both parties enjoy appropriate options (e.g. the 'purchaser' has the option to retain the asset rather than resell it to the initial vendor).

■ *The location of the asset and the right of the seller to use the asset whilst it is owned by the buyer* – Where the asset remains on the vendor's premises or the vendor retains a right of access to the asset, the transaction would appear not to possess the characteristics of a normal sale.

A sale and repurchase agreement often involves securities rather than tangible goods. See the arrangement disclosure in the following service offered by Arck Marketing Limited.

 CASE EXAMPLE 11.1

ARCK LLP is a management company with a number of business and controlling interests in a variety of companies.

This is a 'contracted' sale and repurchase agreement involving three parties. The FIRST party is ARCK Estrela Limited/ARCK LLP (The OWNER). The SECOND party is the SARP Client – Individual, Company, Self-Directed Pension, etc, (SARP) the THIRD party is The Fund – e.g. Integrity Alternative Asset Fund Protected Cell Company, and the associated Protected Cell Number (THE FUND).

The FUND enters into a Promissory Contract of Purchase with The OWNER to purchase a completed property – as an example, £150,000. The FUND has, prior to Notarisation of the completed property, to on-sell this Promissory Contract to any THIRD PARTY, but may only do so once they have undertaken their liabilities on the contract – i.e. FULL PAYMENT to the OWNER.

The OWNER always retains the Freehold of the Land and Property under development until final Notarisation. The FUND allows the OWNER to sell and repurchase (SARP) this contract to a third party, provided the third party never has any beneficial ownership, title or use to the land/property.

The FUND purchases individual units at a time depending on the inflows of money to that fund. Once it has sufficient invested funds, including any gearing it might take, the fund issues a Promissory Contract on a Specific Plot.

On doing so, the FUND will also sign a SARP contract on that specific plot thus guaranteeing the purchase for a specific amount at a specific fixed value.

The OWNER will then also sign the same contract allowing the sale to a specific SARP client selling it to them for a fixed price (£25,000 as an example) and also guaranteeing to purchase it back on the same day The FUND purchases the Plot from the OWNER. The purchase price to the SARP is listed on the contract.

Source: http://arckllp.com/uploads/Updated%20FAQ%20No.7.pdf

 TEST YOUR KNOWLEDGE 11.6

How do you decide whether a sale and repurchase transaction is a special purpose transaction?

9 External auditor – principles and practices

The external audit is a mechanism of corporate governance. Corporate governance has risen to prominence, particularly in the last 25 years, due mainly to high-profile corporate failures, some of which are listed below:

TABLE 11.2 Some high-profile corporate failures

Company	Year	Base	Impropriety
Maxwell Communication	2002	UK	False accounting
Polly Peck International	1990	UK	Dubious financial transactions
BCCI*	1991	Lux	Fraud and money laundering
Enron Corporation	2001	USA	Fraud and corruption
Worldcom	2002	USA	Loans and guarantees
Parmalat	2003	Italy	Financial fraud
Satyam Computers	2010	India	Falsification of accounts
*BCCI = Bank of Credit and Commerce International			

Amongst the companies listed above, Enron became synonymous with all that is bad in accounting and managerial opportunism. Lawsuits and criminal proceedings were instituted against the top management of the company with losses running in to billions of dollars.

At the time, Arthur Anderson, (once one of the 'big four') was Enron's auditor and was paid audit fees indicated to be around $23 million. The scandal led to the dissolution of Arthur Anderson and the company had to surrender its licence to practice.

The Powers Committee (appointed by Enron's board to look into the firm's accounting in October 2001) made the following assessment:

> The evidence available to us suggests that Andersen did not fulfil its professional responsibilities in connection with its audits of Enron's financial statements, or its obligation to bring to the attention of Enron's Board (or the Audit and Compliance Committee) concerns about Enron's internal contracts over the related-party transactions.

Section 11.4 (above) outlines some of the duties entrusted to, and expected from, external auditors. The reassurance provided by external audits has an economic impact on those who have vested interests in a company. It is, therefore, necessary that an effective audit has a role to play in the quality of corporate governance in a company as a mechanism to oversee managerial practices.

Some of the principal qualities expected of auditors are discussed below.

1 *Independence* from related parties who have an interest in the financial affairs of a company. In this respect auditors must not be swayed from their principal duty of being independent. Independence of mind is an additional pre-requisite. It is essential that the auditor not only acts independently, but also appears to be independent. If an auditor is in fact independent, but one or more factors suggest otherwise, this could potentially lead to stakeholders concluding that the audit report does not give a 'true and fair view'. The two types of independence threat can be summarised as:
   (a) *independence of mind:* freedom from the effects of threats to auditor independence that would be sufficient to compromise an auditor's objectivity; and
   (b) *independence in appearance:* no activities, relationships, or other circumstances that could lead well-informed investors and other users reasonably to conclude that there is an unacceptably high risk that an auditor lacks independence of mind. (The CPA Journal).
2 *Client–auditor relationship* – This refers to the level of professionalism in an audit engagement. The client is a source of income for the auditor. This could lead to a compromise on standards if the client puts pressure on the auditor to act in a specific manner.

3 *The size of the audit fee* – can be a mitigating factor on independence and professionalism in practice. The larger the fee the greater the probability that an auditor will relinquish his responsibilities and perform the audit without due diligence. If auditor fees are concentrated around a limited number of clients, this cold have a potential impact on auditor professionalism and independence.

4 *Repeat business* – an auditor needs to secure regular income and foster long-term client relationships. This may lead to lower fee quotations, so the auditor may reduce their level of substantive and due diligence work to cover costs.

5 *Familiarity* – requires auditors to be sceptical of information and representations made by their clients. Over-reliance on the client's word can compromise both independence and professionalism. For example, an auditor may become overly familiar with a client if they have a particularly close or long-standing personal or professional relationship with them.

6 *Non-audit services* – The long-standing debate on non-audit services has particular repercussions on auditor professionalism and independence. Many studies have suggested that to secure the more lucrative non-audit services contracts, auditors have tended to low-ball or undercut the audit price. Again, this practice may entice auditors to perform to a low standard by cutting corners in audit work.

The first substantive piece of guidance on corporate governance was published in 1992 and came to be known as the Cadbury Report. The report was the first to give a working definition of corporate governance and suggested that 'Corporate Governance is the means by which companies are directed and controlled'. The UK Code on Corporate Governance (2010) is the latest in a series of publications based on the work of the Cadbury Committee.

This requires a certain amount of disclosure as to how companies have complied with best practices as recommended in the code, referred to as the 'comply or explain' principle. One of the recommendations relates to the work of the Audit Committee *vis-à-vis* the external audit.

The committee has some specific duties in relation to external auditors. It recommends the appointment of auditors to the board and approves their fees and the other terms on which they are retained. The audit committee is tasked to engage or replace auditors as it sees fit. The board considers the views of the audit committee and will, in most circumstances, follow its advice. Auditor appointment or replacement is a serious matter and should be considered at the AGM.

The external auditor is responsible for assessing the implications of taking on a new audit engagement and should consider the following matters:

■ any professional relationships which the audit engagement partner or the audit firm has with a company;
■ non-audit services provided to a company (e.g. accounting, actuarial, administrative and risk management services); and
■ reputational risk to the auditor of such an engagement.

 TEST YOUR KNOWLEDGE **11.7**

Explain what factors can contribute to the independence and professionalism of auditors providing external audit services.

10 Auditors and non-audit services

Non-audit services provided by auditors to client companies have been a contentious issue in recent years. The issue mainly relates to auditors auditing their own work and the compromise to the quality of audit this presents. The Code on Audit Committee and Auditors provides a basis for the auditor–audit committee relationship:

> The board should establish formal and transparent arrangements for considering how they should apply the corporate reporting and risk management and internal control principles and for maintaining an appropriate relationship with the company's auditor.

In implanting the above principal of corporate governance practice the code further suggests that the task of the audit committee is:

> to review and monitor the external auditor's independence and objectivity and the effectiveness of the audit process, taking into consideration relevant UK professional and regulatory requirements.

There is currently no bar on auditors providing non-audit services for the same client; however, the code suggests that audit committees need:

> to develop and implement policy on the engagement of the external auditor to supply non-audit services, taking into account relevant ethical guidance regarding the provision of non-audit services by the external audit firm, and to report to the board, identifying any matters in respect of which it considers that action or improvement is needed and making recommendations as to the steps to be taken.

In this regard the code requires the audit committee to explain to shareholders, in the annual report, how auditor objectivity and independence is maintained if the auditor provides audit and non-audit services and the amount of payment for the non-audit services has to be disclosed in the published accounts.

The audit committee deliberates on auditor remit in relation to audit and non-audit services to ensure these do not impair the auditor's independence and comply with legislation. Under the code's guiding principles, the auditor's independence will be deemed to be impaired if the auditor provides a service where they:

- have a management role in the company; or
- audit their own work; or
- serve in an advocacy role for the company.

The three compromising actions above are not exhaustive, but are the main reasons for auditor compromise in due diligence. There needs to be a balance between the level of auditor involvement in a company's affairs and his/her independence and professionalism.

 TEST YOUR KNOWLEDGE 11.8

(a) Explain non-audit service
(b) Discuss how can directors can mitigate the impact of non-audit service on audit quality.

 STOP AND THINK 11.1

Auditors should warn shareholders of future risks to the company. Do you think this is an auditor's role?

END OF CHAPTER QUESTIONS

11.1 In 2010, Experia plc converted its 5% £20 million debt bonds to equity shares at 20% below market price of its share price.

Required

Explain the impact of this action on the Gearing, ROA, EPS ratios without any calculations.

During the year to 31 December 2011, Thomson plc entered into the two transactions described below:

  Having surplus cash available, Thomson made an investment in the securities of a listed entity in November. The directors intend to realise the investment in February 2018, in order to fund the planned expansion of Thomson's business.

11.2 Thomson lent one of its customers, Brent Ltd, £3 million at a variable interest rate pegged to average bank lending rates. The loan is scheduled for repayment in 2013 and Thomson has promised Brent that it will *not* assign the loan to a third party.

Required

(a)   Identify the appropriate classification of the two categories of financial assets detailed above, and briefly outline the reason for each classification.

(b)   Explain how the financial assets should be measured in the financial statements of Thomson at 31 December 2011.

This question requires students to consider the concept of 'substance-over-form' in their answer.

11.3 Fraser plc entered into a four-year lease agreement with Donut Ltd for the lease of a specialised machine on 1 January 2009. Fraser paid a deposit of £40,000 to Donut on 1 January 2009 and agreed to pay four equal annual lease rentals of £200,000 in arrears, starting on 31 December 2009. The initial direct cost incurred by Fraser in negotiating the lease amounted to £4,000.

  The machine had a fair value of £674,000 on 1 January 2009 and an estimated useful life of five years. Fraser is expected to insure and maintain the machine over the lease period. The firm's similarly owned assets are depreciated on a straight-line basis.

  The leased machine will be returned to Donut at the end of the lease period. The implicit interest rate within the lease is 10%.

Required

(a)   Using the information given above, calculate the amounts to be shown in the financial statements (Income Statement and Statement of Financial Position) of Fraser plc for the years ended 31 December 2009 and 2010.

(b)   Explain why Fraser plc might prefer to report the lease as an operating, rather than a finance, lease.

(c)   Identify and discuss six characteristics of a finance lease.

(d)   Discuss arguments advanced in IAS 17, 'Leases' for the capitalisation of finance leases in the books of the lessee.

11.4 The directors of Argo plc entered in to a bilateral agreement on 1 January 2010 with a local bank to borrow £25 million repayable over ten years. As collateral, Argo signed the rights to a certain group of tangible assets over to the bank.

  The terms of the agreement refer to the subsequent ownership of the assets reverting back to Argo after repayment of the loan. On 1 January 2010, Argo removed the assets from its books, arguing with the auditor that the assets now belonged to the bank. The auditors of Argo are under pressure to accept the case put forward by the management and audit the financial statements without the collateralised assets.

  The auditors have a few clients who generate the bulk of their business and revenue. The auditors have been promised lucrative fees if they audit Argo's records in the manner demanded by management.

Required

(a)   Describe the nature of the financial arrangement Argo has entered in to with the bank.

(b)   How should the transaction be recorded in the financial records of Argo plc?

(c)   Identify and explain the impact on the relevant ratios of Argo if the assets were removed from its financial records.

(d)   Identify the threats presented to the auditors of this audit assignment.

END OF CHAPTER QUESTIONS

(e)   On the basis of the UK Code on Corporate Governance, what action should be taken by Argo's auditors.

(f)   Discuss the economic impact if the auditors acceded to management demands.

11.5 Serendipity Ltd has been engaged in the manufacture of precision instruments for a number of years. The directors have decided to enter into leases as part of the financial structure of the company. The following information relates to a lease held by them. Lease payments are made in arrears.

Lease of plant:

Date of inception of lease	1 January 2005
Useful life of plant at 1 January 2005	30 years
Market value of plant at 1 January 2005	£400,000
Duration of lease	Ten years
Installments payable monthly in advance –	
2005	£3,000 per month
2006/10	£2,000 per month
2011/14	£800 per month

Required

1   State, with reasons, whether you would consider the lease to be finance or operating lease.

2   Assuming the lease should be correctly classified as an operating lease:

    (a)   calculate the annual rental expense under this lease.

    (b)   show how the lease would be reflected in the 2011 Statement of Financial Position of Serendipity Limited.

11.6 Luboil Ltd supplies a special type of machine oils to the manufacturing industry. On 1 January 2010 Luboil entered in to a contract with Seeder Ltd to supply £10 million worth of oil over five-year period. The contract stipulated price variation subject to market forces agreed in advance between the two parties.

As part of the contract, Seeder agreed to pay Luboil £10 million in advance subject to the price review. The supply of oil would be in equal instalments.

At 31 December 2010, Luboil's financial statements included the total £10 million in revenue invoiced to Seeder; however, only £1 million of inventory was disclosed in the cost of sales.

Required

(a)   As auditor of Luboil Ltd, explain to the management the accounting treatment that should have been disclosed.

(b)   Discuss the impact the impact on the ratios on Luboil after the necessary accounting changes.

(c)   Explain the disclosure notes that may be required in the notes to the accounts for such a contract.

11.7 What is consignment inventory?

11.8 A car manufacturer sells to a car dealer on the following terms:

■ Legal title passes either on sale of a car to the public, or when a car is used as a demonstration model. The car is paid for when legal title passes.

■ The price charged to the dealer is the price as at the original date of delivery.

■ The dealer is charged interest at 4% on cost during the period from delivery to payment.

■ The dealer has the right to return cars to the manufacturer at any time, but in practice this rarely happens.

At the balance sheet date the dealer has 15 cars in its showroom.

Required

How should the dealer account for these cars?

11.9 Sale and repurchase: One week before its year end, a whiskey distiller (WD) sells a consignment of its whiskey to a bank. WD has an option to repurchase at any time at cost plus 10% interest.

Discuss.

(a)   What services does a factor offer?

(b)   Explain factoring with, and without, recourse.

(c)   Company A sells £200,000 of its accounts receivables to a factor in return for an immediate 80% advance. Assuming debts are factored with recourse and a further advance of 10% will be received by Company A if the customer pays on time assuming the debts are factored without recourse, explain how the transaction will be accounted for in each of the two assumptions laid out above.

END OF CHAPTER QUESTIONS

11.10 The following data relates to Delta plc for year ending 2011 and 2012:

	2011	2012
	£'000	£'000
Net sales for the period	145000	167000
Opening inventories:		
at cost value	45000	52000
at retail value	54000	60000
Purchases: at cost	110000	135000
Purchases: at retail	127000	155000

Required

(a) Calculate closing inventory using Retail Inventory Method for 2011 and 2012.

(b) Calculate closing inventory using Gross Margin Method (to nearest £'000).

Current issues

■ CONTENTS

■ LEARNING OUTCOMES

Chapter 12 covers the syllabus section entitled 'Current Issues'. After reading and understanding the contents of the chapter, working through all the Worked Examples and Practice Questions, you should be able to:

■ explain the nature and purpose of subscription based databases and their relationship to company accounts;

■ discuss and demonstrate how XBRL business language fits in with, and applies to, accounting and financial reporting;

■ understand and appreciate the role of the accountant in a capitalist society and the implications of the role for reporting;

■ understand and explain what stand-alone environmental reports are;

■ appreciate the historical roots to environmental reporting and its development;

■ demonstrate the purpose and application of the Eco-management and Audit Scheme and its importance for business strategy;

■ understand and explain the main features of social accounting in Britain;

■ understand the purpose of corporate social responsibility reporting and the triple bottom line;

■ relate to the positivist and normative approaches to business ethics;

■ understand the relevance and importance of emerging role of ethics in business; and

■ understand the implications for accountants and the ethical dimension.

1 Introduction

This chapter discusses current issues relevant to the role of chartered secretaries in the modern business environment. The role of the chartered secretary is very demanding and requires a person to be knowledgeable generally, but particularly in the changing and diverse business setting.

Companies regularly share information with a number of organisations such as the stock markets on which they are listed. Companies also need to provide financial and related information to government agencies. The cost of information distribution can be high and, in some cases, is enormous. IT platforms such as eXtensible Business Reporting Language (XBRL) are the trend in business efficiency allowing companies to develop cost-effective data storage and retrieval system that allows flexibility in data analysis and data transformation.

Environmental concerns have raised the profile of companies that are proactive in social aspects in which companies operate. Many organisations such as Green Peace lobby governments to legislate against corporate action and make companies responsible more and more for their actions.

Companies are under pressure to report social aspects of their business activities and how they give back to the environment and society in which they operate. Reporting on corporate social responsibility is increasingly becoming common in the annual reports of listed companies.

2   Subscription databases and company accounts

The ever-increasing demand for information efficiency and cost-effective software for all aspects of human endeavour has led to the mushrooming of specialist and off-the-shelf database systems. Databases are software systems designed to store and retrieve data in the format an entity requires in the most cost-effective manner. If the costs of implanting data storage and retrieval systems outweigh their benefit, such systems are of little use to the user. **A subscription database** presents financial information in a standardised format, processes company-style financial information and transforms such data into a standardised form that facilitates comparability, analysis and usage. Some of these databases are described below.

2.1 Amadeus

Amadeus is a globally available database system that stores around 200,000 public and private companies in 36 European countries. This includes up to ten years of detailed information (consolidated statements are also provided when available) in a standardised financial format comprising 22 statements of financial position items, 24 statement of comprehensive income account items and 25 ratios.

The database provides descriptive information that includes:

- official national identification number, address, telephone, fax, website, legal form;
- year of incorporation;
- senior managers;
- auditors details;
- number of employees;
- quoted/unquoted indicator;
- industry and activity codes; and
- a trade description in the local language and English.

It offers company peer group analysis and ranked and formatted output.

2.2 Bloomberg

Bloomberg's database covers international companies and markets. The database system provides real time and historical financial market data and economic data, covering all sectors worldwide. It also features analytics, company financials, news, and customisable charting. Bloomberg provides company descriptions, five to ten years of financials, interest rates, time-series of statistics, company and industrial news.

A news report by the Reuters news agency, dated 28 February 2012, commentated on Bloomberg Corporation that:

> Executives demonstrated that, if a customer wanted to search for IBM's earnings before interest, taxes, depreciation and amortization in the fourth quarter of 1999, the user just had to type 'IBM EBITDA Q4 1999' into a search field and an answer would pop up. In the past, this would have required several key strokes.[1]

2.3 Datastream

Datastream is a database that stores financial information on international companies, markets and economic statistics. It includes company accounts and ratios, equity and capital market data, interest and exchange rates, economic and industrial statistics; long-time series for all data and downloads easily.

2.4 FAME

FAME is a global database and covers all UK registered companies including those that have recently formed and have yet to file their first set of accounts. FAME offers up to 10 years of detailed information for 1.6 million UK companies plus summarised information for a further 1 million companies. The detailed information includes:

- company profile;
- income statement;
- statement of financial position;
- statement of cash flows; ratios and trends;
- County Court Judgments and mortgage data;
- credit score and rating;
- complete lists of holding companies; subsidiaries and directors; shareholders (including enhanced shareholders option); and
- all 'site/trading' addresses, activity information including brand names and miscellaneous information.

It offers tailored output formats and can provide company peer group analysis.

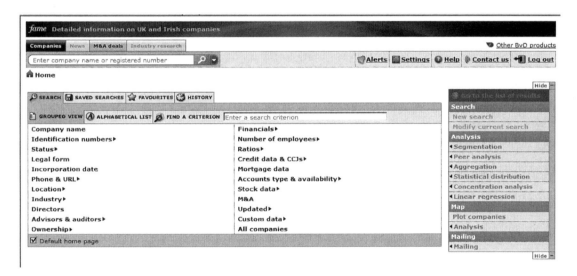

The dialog box presented above is a snapshot of FAME. The pictorial view of the after log-in sequence that presents the user with options to select relevant financial data such as ratios, company reports, number of employees and other aspects related to companies subscribed to FAME.

The demand from the user community to have access to web-based applications such as XBRL and inline XBRL or iXBRL-based databases is increasing at an alarming rate. XBRL and iXBRL is explained in section 3 below. Developers are constantly trying to keep pace with this ever- increasing demand. With the advancement of computer and wireless technology users can access information on the go.

A recent survey conducted by Thomson Reuters and published in *Accountingweb* online magazine reported the following on 1 February 2012:

> Accountants are hungry for applications that allow on-the-go access to the data they need to make decisions and run their practices, according to new research by Thomson Reuters Digita, a leading provider of accountancy practice software.

Digita, part of the Tax and Accounting business of Thomson Reuters, conducted the '12 Digita Days in December' poll to gauge attitudes and opinions on a wide range of technology-related issues. The survey comprised 12 questions on various topics including integration, iXBRL, time saving and how software adds value to the contemporary practice.

The survey attracted 432 responses from a cross-section of firms:

- 55% sole practitioners;
- 30% from mid tier firms with between two and five partners; and
- 15% from large firms with 6+ partners.

Many of the responses focused on the integration of practice software with mobile tools – confirming the view that tax and accounting professionals are increasingly adopting web-based and mobile applications in a drive towards greater efficiency and productivity.

Representative answers included:

- ability to use practice application software on an iPad;
- links with Outlook and BlackBerry;
- integration with Windows Messenger;
- integrated document capture;
- voice recognition capability;
- easier recording of client' phone calls.

Interestingly, only two respondents suggested a requirement for Cloud and online practice software, suggesting that accountants have still to be persuaded of the benefits. 'Our results suggest that accountants are increasingly looking for added integration with their day-to-day mobile applications to maximise efficiency,' said Andrew Flanagan, managing director, Digita for the Tax & Accounting business of Thomson Reuters. 'It is crucial to understand the changing needs of the profession and this survey is just part of an ongoing dialogue to ensure that Digital applications deliver the innovative functionality the profession demands.'[2]

Business entities, who wish to integrate their business processes are increasingly under pressure to formalise web-based application both in-house (i.e. within the company to integrate sharing of information on work practices and financial information) and externally to integrate with other applications such as subscription-based databases such as Bloomberg, or government departments such as HMRC for tax and related matters. Increasingly XML-based web languages are used to accommodate the switch to common web-based platforms for cost-effective data transfer and migration. The following an example of a common data transfer requirement:

 WORKED EXAMPLE **12.1**

An individual who is preparing financial reports has the following query:

> As a practice we only produce one set of accounts in Excel spreadsheet format so we are looking for a way of converting them into iXBRL without having to spend a fortune on software and without having to spend hours tagging everything ourselves. Some kind of Excel spreadsheet add-on would be the perfect solution. I'm sure there must be other practices facing the same problem, so I would appreciate any recommendations you could pass on to us.

Answer

Scenario 1 – by a respondent 1

You can indeed buy a 'tagging tool', which can be used to convert files from Word or Excel into XBRL. These are cheaper than a full software package, but as I understand it, are inevitably slightly more limited, so some manual tagging is necessary. Software developer, IRIS plc, provides such a tagging tool. I'm sure all of the big software companies do, as there are undoubtedly numerous firms who still use Excel and Word for preparing accounts. Alternatively, you could consider outsourcing the tagging function to a third party – which again is a solution offered by IRIS – but this can be fairly costly.

WORKED EXAMPLE **12.1** *continued*

Scenario 2 – by a respondent 2

You can use the VT[3] add-in to produce an iXBRL file from any set of accounts or tax computation in any Excel workbook. Views differ on how easy it is to self-tag a set of accounts. If you have to select tags from the full list (called *taxonomy*) then it is not easy at all. However, VT includes a special tagging dialog in which all the tags for a small company are laid out in the form of a sample set of accounts. It's easy to find the tag you want. It is possible, with experience, to self-tag a small set of accounts in 15 minutes. All the tagging data is saved in your own workbook (but is only accessible by the VT add-in).

Once your workbook is tagged you just have to click on the Generate iXBRL File button on the toolbar create by the add-in. VT will check you're tagging and tell you if there are any problems. If there are critical problems it will not generate an iXBRL file. In theory, it is not possible to generate an iXBRL file using VT that will be rejected by HMRC, but things can go wrong further down the line.

From April 2011 HMRC require company accounts to be submitted in the form of an iXBRL file. Paper and pdf files will no longer be accepted. An iXBRL file has the same format as a page on a website and the accounts it contains can be viewed in any web browser simply by opening the file. In addition, much of the data is specially tagged so that it can also be machine read.

TEST YOUR KNOWLEDGE **12.1**

(a) Explain the purpose and use of a subscription database.

(b) How can subscription databases help in communicating with relevant company stakeholders?

3 XBRL – Business reporting language and business application

The common language of the internet is Hyper-Text Markup Language (HTML) which enabled users to disseminate and share data and information on the internet in various ways and formats. Soon after the advent of the internet, many types of hypertext languages were developed specialising in the facilitation of various applications such as moving pictures, interactivity and sound and real time communication.

The business world, too, made headway in the development of hypertext languages that enabled users of financial information to exchange and store data in a re-usable format at minimal cost.

The development of **XBRL (eXtensible Business Reporting Language)** enabled the business community to electronically communicate economic and financial information in a manner that cut down costs, provides a greater level of efficiency of use and improved reliability to users and suppliers of information.

XBRL uses the XML (Extensible Markup Language) syntax and related XML technologies, which are the standard tools used to communicate information between businesses and the internet. Data can be converted to XBRL by appropriate mapping tools designed to convert electronic data to XBRL format, or data can be written directly in XBRL by suitable software.

XBRL works on a system of TAGS. Instead of treating financial information as a block of text, as in a standard internet page or a printed document, XBRL provides an identifying tag for each individual item of data. This is computer readable. For example, company revenues and items of expenses and net profit have their own unique tag. This enables manipulation by users, through query forms, to generate data and information in the required format.

The introduction of XBRL tags enables automated processing of business information by computer software, facilitating efficient re-use of data for comparison. Computers can treat XBRL data 'intelligently' enabling:

- *Storage* of data and information in XBRL enables selection, analysis, exchange and presentation in a variety of ways dependent on the end-users' requirements.
- *Speed* – XBRL greatly increases the speed of handling of financial data, reduces the chance of error and permits automatic checking of information.
- *Costs* – Companies can use XBRL to save costs and streamline their processes for collecting and reporting financial information.
- *Retrieval* – Consumers of financial data, including investors, analysts, financial institutions and regulators, researchers, can locate, manipulate, compare and analyse data much more rapidly and efficiently in XBRL than by other online facilities.
- *Data handling* – XBRL can handle data in different languages and accounting standards. It can easily be adapted to meet different requirements and uses.

 WORKED EXAMPLE **12.2**

(a) How do I generate an iXBRL file from Microsoft EXCEL spreadsheet?

Answer

- Make sure you are using a workbook created in the December 2010 edition or later
- Click on the *Generate iXBRL file* button on the VT toolbar in Excel
- In the *Generate iXBRL file* dialog just click OK. That's it!
- The Taxonomy setting should not normally be changed

(b) What file format is used by iXBRL files?

Answer

iXBRL files are written in HTML, the language used by web pages. An iXBRL file can be displayed in your web browser by double clicking on it. XBRL tags are also buried within the HTML, but are not visible in a standard web browser. These tags can only be seen in specialist software such as *VT Fact Viewer* or Corefiling's *Magnify* (Corefiling are HMRC's consultants).

HMRC's computers only see the tagged items that are shown with a yellow background in VT Fact Viewer. However, if your accounts or tax computation are ever reviewed by a human being at HMRC, they will see all the text that you normally expect to see in a set of accounts or computation (as shown on the *Document* tab of VT Fact Viewer or in a web browser).

 TEST YOUR KNOWLEDGE **12.2**

(a) What is XBRL?
(b) How can companies make use of XBRL in financial reporting and information sharing within the company and with outsiders?

3.1 XBRL metadata

Metadata terminology is fundamental to understanding the way in which XBRL works. It is not a term that is well understood in the business community, but technologist and developers are fully conversant with its meaning. Basically, metadata concerns an understanding of how data arises. This sounds convoluted but essentially, what it refers to is the localisation of programs to facilitate the use of different languages.

MS Word and Excel are used globally in most aspect of life, in education, financial analysis and business modelling etc. However, these applications are localised in national contexts and enable input and output and the design of dialog boxes and point-and-click buttons to be displayed in national languages around the world (e.g. English, Arabic, and Japanese etc). The use of metadata is demonstrated below.

An invoice may contain the following data:

- the invoice number   'S-50001'
- the invoice date   '1 Jan 2011'
- the quantity of each line item   '100 boxes'
- the amount of each line item   '£500'
- the total amount of the invoice   '£50,000'

The metadata are the values (not necessarily in number format) that must be attached to each item on the invoice (e.g. amount):

- the invoice number must start with the letter 'S', be followed by a dash and must be a 5-digit number;
- the invoice MUST contain an invoice number, an invoice date, at least one line item, and a total; and
- the sum of the amounts of each line item must agree to the total amount of the invoice, 'SUM (Amount for Line Item) = Total Amount'.

XBRL allows the development of syntax and tags that enables the development of the language on a localised or global basis such as the IASB and XBRL collaboration. A consistent development of metadata allows the reporting and sharing of financial report on a global basis. Additionally, the standardised collection of financial reporting information will facilitate the ease of use and automatic sharing between applications enabling manipulation of data in the required format.

Any aspect of the business process can be transferred to XBRL using the system of tags in the taxonomy dictionary. As is indicated from the answer in scenario 2 in Worked Example 12.2 above, many governmental returns will have to be submitted through some sort of XBRL formula-based technology.

3.2 XBRL taxonomy

XBRL taxonomies are the repositories that act as dictionaries containing assigned tags for specific individual items of financial data (e.g. profit). This enables the development of country- or company-specific taxonomies facilitating the application of accounting rules, regulations, standards and laws. From a users perspective there is no need to understand the technicalities of the language. It is a user-defined spectrum allowing for data migration, transferability, use and analysis.

XBRL supports an open standard of financial reporting. This means that it is flexible enough to support all the current ways of reporting in different countries and industries. The XBRL system is free; there are no license fees either to supply or to access the information. It is a non-profit venture primarily supported by XBRL International, which is a collaboration of around 550 major international companies, organisations and government agencies. XBRL has already been implemented and is regularly used in a growing number of countries and industries around the world.

3.3 IFRS and XBRL developments

The purpose of IFRS in the business community is to pave the way for global reporting processes that are common across countries. To facilitate and strengthen this process the IASB and XBRL entities are working together to develop a set of XBRL taxonomies that will enable the creation and use of common set of internet-enabled reporting formats throughout the world.

The following passages are from the IASB website:

Both IFRSs and XBRL are intended to standardise financial reporting in order to promote transparency and to improve the quality and comparability of business information, therefore, the two entities form a perfect partnership.

The **IASB XBRL Team** is responsible for developing and maintaining the XBRL representation of the IFRSs, known as the **IFRS Taxonomy**. The IFRS Taxonomy is used around the world to facilitate the electronic use and exchange of financial data prepared in accordance with IFRSs.

The IASB's XBRL activities include:

- *Taxonomy development* – for companies reporting in IFRS, the Foundation publishes tags for each IFRS disclosure. These tags are organised and contained within the IFRS Taxonomy.
- *Support materials* – the Foundation produces support materials to facilitate use and understanding of the IFRS Taxonomy.
- *Translations* – translations of the IFRS Taxonomy into key languages are provided to support users of both IFRS and the IFRS Taxonomy whose primary language is not English.
- *Global outreach* – the Foundation makes a concerted effort to promote the use of XBRL in conjunction with IFRSs around the world. The Foundation also encourages co-operation and communication with users of the IFRS Taxonomy.

The collaboration between IASB and XBRL is an important move towards harmonisation of financial reporting processes. This will have tremendous implication for the capital markets around the world enabling information capture, analysis and decision-making at greater speed than at any other time in history. In this regard the two entities i.e. IASB and XBRL held a discussion at a convention on 12 March 2012 with the emphasis on the development of IASB specific requirement for common electronic reporting.

---

4   The role of the accountant in a capitalist society

4.1 The modern corporation

To understand the role of accountants in a capitalist society we need to elaborate the concepts of 'accounting and **capitalism**' and examine how the two concepts merge to give a fundamental understanding of the modern corporation and its role in society.

At this point it would be prudent to mention the cause that gave rise to modern capitalism. The concept of the double-entry system allowed people to measure 'assets' and 'liabilities' in the thirteenth century. By doing this, the notion of 'profit' was established and, for the first time, business ventures could measure the profitability of their entrepreneurial activities. This allowed business activity to expand and become ever more complex in nature.

At its core, capitalism is the economic philosophy relating to the means of production with a view to profit. In a nutshell, capitalism is a society ruled by the profit motive. Capitalism as a system is built around trading in commodities and the means of production, which is how profits arise. Goods and services are produced using methods of production, raw material, labour, machinery etc. Capitalism in the modern world is defined by three factors:

- *Corporations* – huge businesses that create wealth through production and satisfying man's desire for material goods and services. It is through corporations that modern capitalism thrives and creates ever-increasing profits. Another view or sub-view to capitalism is that it exists in a state of competition. Businesses compete with each other to attract customers. The sale of products leads to profit; the distribution of these profits goes to investors.

- *Capital markets* – provide the means by which those with money can invest their wealth in profit-making ventures. The capital markets enable investments to be made both in and out of companies, thereby adjusting the value of corporations on the basis of information available to investors. In a perfect capital market all historic and current information is reflected in the price of the stock.
- *Markets for goods and services* – For corporations to exist they must be able to sell their goods and services. They do this through markets. Markets can be defined in many different ways (e.g. by geographical region). Western Europe and North America are the largest markets for consumer goods.

Free market economies such as the USA are typically defined by the three factors discussed above. However, weaknesses in rules and regulations leave room for manoeuvre – managers of corporations are able to manipulate profits and present an economic reality that is different from the truth. Ecological and social damage created by the production process is hidden from the consumer, who sees only the commodity and perhaps an upbeat advertisement. This has become a very topical subject in recent years and is discussed in the business ethics section more comprehensively.

4.2 The accountant

The contribution of accountants in the world of corporate reporting is profound. Accountants prepare the financial reports that are used by stakeholders in the capital markets and upon which they base their economic decisions. Accountants have a direct role in a capitalist society in which they communicate accounting and financial information. Estimation techniques and managerial judgement exercised in disclosing accounting figures require accountants to make faithful representations in financial reports.

 WORKED EXAMPLE 12.3

John is a newly qualified accountant and has just joined Paxo plc, a manufacturer of home furnishings, as an assistant financial controller. John's first task is to carry out an audit of the statement of financial position and appraise Peter, the financial controller, of any errors or changes that should be made.

On reviewing the lease agreements, John realises that the company has treated all its leases as operating leases. John brings this to Peter's attention. Peter, however, tells John that if they were to change the accounting procedure on leases it would impact on the balances and the financial characteristics of the company (i.e. its financial ratios would give an unfavourable view of the company to outsiders). This is particularly relevant as the company is in the process of negotiating a major loan agreement with a bank.

Required
Briefly discuss some ethical and professional dimensions the scenario presents specifically and more generally the impact of pervasive unethical behaviour by accountants in modern capitalist society.

Answer
This scenario demonstrates the ethical dimension of an accountant's role in making a faithful representation of financial figures.

- It is clear from the scenario that Paxo plc is engaging in accounting choices that paint a better picture of the company than actually exists. Certainly the changeover to financial lease accounting would disclose to the bank major weaknesses in the company and jeopardise the bank loan.
- John, being a newly qualified accountant, is ethically bound by his professional body to act in the best interests of the profession and, at the same time, not to bring his professional body in to disrepute.

- In going along with the company, John would be a party to the loan agreement being negotiated in as much the facts are not declared. John would need to ask himself if the bank knew of the facts would it still provide the loan?
- John would also need to do some soul searching and think about his actions. If all accountants behaved in an unethical manner, how would the capital markets react and how efficient would they be?

This example is indicative of the moral dilemma accountants often find themselves in. However, the economic impact of accountant's actions can be profound. Enron (USA) is considered to be one of the foremost examples of things going wrong with financial reporting. The collapse of Enron raised concerns for standards of behaviour in the corporate world and gave birth to the Sarbanes-Oxley Act (2002) and the Public Company Accounting Oversight Board in the USA. The Enron corporate debacle led to the demise of its auditor, Arthur Anderson.

The role of the accountant, and by extension, the accounting profession, in the modern capitalist society is interrelated and co-existential. Societies can be described in many forms, however, if we segment societies in terms of social, economic, organisation and political systems, a common form of communication must exist that is common to all segments. The role of accounting provides this function and enables different segments to communicate with each other. In its role as an intermediary, accounting information serves many important purposes, for example assisting users in making informed economic decisions, in relation to the effective allocation of scarce resources.

Accounting is a socially constructed phenomenon for society to organise itself and develop the means for production of goods and services. The last 50 years particularly have seen a huge rise in trade and transactions across the globe. The decline of trade barriers and protectionism policies in national states and the ability for corporations to cross-list in multiple capital markets has resulted in what appears to be markets without borders. The growth of global business and the emergence of new sectors such as e-commerce have lead to the development of complex financial transactions being undertaken.

The contributory role of accountants and accounting in the global capitalist market has been significant, but not without some problems. Rules, regulations and national laws have developed over the past few decades to deter accounting irregularities committed purposely or in error. For example, the nature and timing of financial instruments, changes to accounting policies and crystallisation of pension expenses, have created a lack of transparency and reliability in financial reporting.

Risk and risk-taking is seen as an integral part of business activity. However, when does risk-taking become unmanageable? The 2008 banking crisis had domino-effect repercussions for the whole world. Very few aspects of human life were untouched by the 2008 crisis and in 2012 we can still see the after-effects with the Royal Bank of Scotland still making losses running into billions of pounds. With the advent of IFRS improvements, corporate governance guidelines and the Sarbanes-Oxley Act, accounting misreporting still continued. When Lehman Brothers, a major bank in the USA went bankrupt, the New York Attorney General filed a law suit against Ernst and Young (one of the 'big four' auditors) accusing it of assisting Lehman Brothers in massive accounting irregularities.

The modern corporation is a complex organism enshrined with subjectivity and judgements that acts as a hindrance to the work of the accountant. This complexity often necessitates compliance to management's wishes due to pressure from the top. An accountant's primary responsibility is to the investor, to ensure that a level playing field is created to allow for informed economic decisions.

The development of GAAP and International Accounting Standards attempt to regularise accounting behaviour by mitigating or minimising accounting choices available to management. The development of theory in the accounting profession provided a platform for explaining corporate behaviour and a framework for application of accounting techniques thus providing and understanding of underlying effects.

TEST YOUR KNOWLEDGE 12.3

(a) Discuss and explain the meaning of a capitalist society
(b) How does the role of the accountant fit in with the capitalist society?

4.3 Accounting development and the markets

An intrinsic link exists between the capital markets and accounting. The figure below demonstrates this link and explains how accounting behaviour is regulated and its normative impact on the capital markets:

FIGURE 12.1 Accounting behaviour and its normative impact on the capital markets

This figure is one representation of how the role of the accountant is linked to the capital markets and the two main actors that have a bearing on, and implications for, financial reporting and the evolution of accounting standards.

Accounting choices that create financial misrepresentation will have an impact on investor decisions. This will be reflected in the capital markets, in short, in the movement of funds and how they are allocated. The capital markets absorb the financial information released to the wider world and reflect company financial performance in the price of the shares. The IASB and GAAP monitor company financial reporting and areas of contention that may arise in due course and issue new or revised standards when necessary.

It is clear that in an attempt to have a normative impact on corporate financial reporting, general accounting standards have a long way to go before complete or even substantial standardisation and harmonisation is achieved between companies and between countries when management can still make accounting choices that hinder clarity of purpose in financial reporting.

5 Stand-alone environmental reporting

Business activity, and the various methods by which corporations secure resources for production, by and large has an environmental impact, at least in the vicinity of their operations (e.g. the BP oil disaster in the Gulf of Mexico (2010)).

Despite the fact that corporate social reporting (CSR) has been evolving since the late 1980s, levels of disparity still seem to exist in CSR and, by extension, corporate environmental reporting as disclosed in various corporate publications. A number of surveys (e.g. KPMG's Biennial Survey on CSR) have suggested a growth in the number of companies that report CSR and environmental issues. Specific users have specific reasons for reading aspects of CSR reports.

The main reason for publishing environmental reports is to engage with particular audiences and enlighten them with relevant information.

Stand-alone environmental reporting is primarily web-based disclosure. It is usually separate from a company's annual report and other company publications devoted to issues on the impact of company operations on the environment. The quality and quantity of environmental reports partly depend on the nature of the business in which a company operates. Industries such as pharmaceuticals, chemical, petroleum and gas have attracted the most attention on environmental issues. These industries have led the way in environmental reporting. Some countries make it mandatory to publish environmental reports: Denmark, Sweden, Norway and Holland all require environmental reports by law, particularly from environmentally sensitive industries.

6 Historical roots to environmental reporting

6.1 Environmental Protection Act 1990

Environmental law can be traced as far back as the 1860s, where controls on air pollution from industrial units and factories necessitated legislation due to the release of harmful substances in the air. The Environmental Protection Act 1990 consolidated older laws into more relevant legislation. The Act gave rise to legal implications for directors of companies. They could be prosecuted if it could be proved that they had neglected their duty to protect the environment. The Act was a major development in environmental protection in the UK.

6.2 Industry initiatives

ISO 14000 (International Standards Organisation – Standard 14000) is a voluntary code which addresses environmental management and prevention. It is an industry-led standard that requires companies to abide by certain conditions relating to environmental issues. ISO 14000 requires companies to document and work towards reducing or eliminating pollution and processes that can be harmful to the environment. ISO 14000 was the basis by which the Environmental Management System (EMS) was developed. EMS is a management system designed to achieve organisational directives and policies regarding the environmental impact of an organisation's activities.

In 2009/10 the University of East Anglia published its environmental report stating:

> We published our IER and Aspects Register (a list of all activities at the University that have a potential environmental impact) in 2009. These are comprehensive documents (primarily compiled by a group of students on the University's EMS and Audit teaching module) and are important first steps in understanding our environmental impact. A summary of our environmental aspects and impacts ...

> By establishing a good baseline from which to develop our environmental and wider sustainability improvements, we have been able to *prioritise action, set objectives and targets for improvement, and strategies to achieve them*. We are now implementing these strategies, taking changes into account e.g. construction of the Thomas Paine Study Centre and University restructuring ...

6.3 Environmental reporting initiative: ACCA and Next Step Consulting (2001)

The Association of Chartered Certified Accountants (ACCA) published a best practice guide[4] that provides examples of best practices and indicates developments in CSR and Environmental trends over the years:

- Challenges from UK Prime Minister Tony Blair and other ministers for the UK FTSE350 to produce environmental reports (when the Labour Party was in power and Tony Blair was Prime Minster).
- Development of ethical indices (e.g. UK FTSE4Good Index Dow Jones/Sustainability Group Index)

- Mandatory reporting requirements in Denmark, Sweden, The Netherlands, Norway and France.

6.4 Economic consequences for environmental reporting

Pressures on corporations and the demand for environmental-related information have led to a plethora of disclosures on **environmental reporting**. However, environmental disclosures have economic implications for the company. Environmental reporting can be defined as:

> The process of communicating externally the environmental effects of an organisation's economic actions through the corporate annual report or a separate stand-alone publicly available environmental report.[5]

Invariably, disclosures would relate to the policy, procedures and processes and environmental audit in a company's environmental report. Consequently, users will assess, on the basis of information provided, the economic and reputational impact of such policies. Expenditure and benefits that transpire will be assessed for sustainability. A report by the ACCA on Singapore firms that disclose environmental matters looked at the impact of environmental reporting and identified ten important issues that have an economic impact on company environmental disclosures:

1 *Risk management* – in areas of financial, legal and reputation implications.
2 *Marketing strategy* – public image, brand enhancement such as through receiving environmental awards.
3 *Legal needs* – to keep in pace with/anticipate regulations.
4 *Competition* – to get ahead of/stay with competitors.
5 *Ethics* – individual commitment; commitment to accountability and transparency.
6 *Accounting requirements* – in compliance with financial reporting requirements and provide link between financial and environmental performance/reporting.
7 *Investors' interests* – demands of Green (ethical) investors.
8 *Employees' interests* – attracts right staff from the labour market.
9 *Value-add reporting* – to add value to corporate reports and communicate to a wider range of stakeholders, addressing their environmental concerns.
10 *Certification needs* – to indicate compliance with ISO 14000 and other environmental regulatory guidelines.

Various emerging regulations and the implications for financial reports indicate that there is a move towards 'integrated reporting' on CSR and environmental issues that allow interactivity on web-based publication of such reports. Web-based facilities would enhance the user perceptions and that of the company by allowing users to extract specific information to help them to make economic decisions.

TEST YOUR KNOWLEDGE 12.4

(a) Demonstrate your understanding of environmental issues in modern society.
(b) What are the consequences of environmental reporting?

7 Eco-management and Audit Scheme (EMAS)

7.1 What is an environmental audit?

An environmental audit is a tool that a company can use to identify the full extent of its environmental impact. It enables a company to determine its level of compliance with relevant legislation, thus enabling users of the report to understand achievements and shortcomings in company environmental practice.

7.2 Eco-management and audit scheme (EMAS)

The **EMAS** is an audit tool specifically designed for eco-management audits. It allows a company to determine both its environmental impact and determine ways to improve, or reduce, such impact. As greater numbers of companies realise that not taking part in environmental reporting has economic consequences, the EMAS assists companies to report in more or less a standardised fashion.

The EMAS was first made available as far back as 1995, with a particular emphasis on companies in the industrial sector. However, the scheme has now been extended to all businesses.

In 2009 the EMAS Regulation was revised and modified for the second time. Regulation (EC) No. 1221/2009 of the European Parliament and of the Council of 25 November 2009 on the voluntary participation by organisations in a Community eco-management and audit scheme (EMAS) was published on 22 December 2009 and entered into force on 11 January 2010.[6]

The main elements of the EMAS tool requires the disclosure of the following information.

---

a. **Conduct an environmental review**

The organisation needs to conduct a verified initial environmental review, considering all environmental aspects of the organisation's activities, products and services, methods to assess them, the organisation's legal and regulatory framework and existing environmental management practices and procedures.

b. **Adopt an environmental policy**

Registration to EMAS requires an organisation to adopt an environmental policy and to commit itself both to compliance with all relevant environmental legislation and to achieving continuous improvement in its environmental performance.

c. **Establish an EMS**

Based on the results of the environmental review and the policy (objectives), an EMS needs to be established. The EMS is aimed at achieving the organisation's environmental policy objectives as defined by the top management. The management system needs to set responsibilities, objectives, means, operational procedures, training needs, monitoring and communication systems.

d. **Carry out an internal environmental audit**

After the EMS is established an environmental audit should be carried out. The audit assesses in particular if the management system is in place and in conformity with the organisation's policy and programme. The audit also checks if the organisation is in compliance with relevant environmental regulatory requirements.

e. **Prepare an environmental statement**

The organisation needs to provide a public statement of its environmental performance. The environmental statement lays down the results achieved against the environmental objectives and the future steps to be undertaken in order to continuously improve the organisation's environmental performance.

f. **Independent verification** by an EMAS verifier. An EMAS verifier accredited with an EMAS accreditation body of a Member State must examine and verify the environmental review, the EMS, the audit procedure and the environmental statement.

g. **Register** with the Competent Body of the Member State. The validated statement is sent to the appropriate EMAS Competent Body for registration and made publicly available.

h. **Utilise the verified environmental statement**

The environmental statement can be used to report performance data in marketing, assessment of the supply chain and procurement. The organisation can use information from the validated statement to market its activities with the EMAS logo, assess suppliers against EMAS requirements and give preference to suppliers registered under EMAS.

Source: http://ec.europa.eu/environment/emas/pdf/leaflet/emasleaflet_en.pdf

---

7.3 Activities involved in an environmental audit

The format and procedural activities of an environmental audit will vary for different firms, depending on the nature of the business, its geographical location as well as the level of environmental impact of a company's business activity. The environmental audit will take into account external factors such as the target audience and level of disclosure.

Generally, environmental audits involve the collection, collation, analysis, interpretation and presentation of information. This information is then used to:

- assess performance against a list of pre-set targets, related to specific issues;
- evaluate and assess compliance with environmental legislation as well as corporate policies; and
- measure performance against the requirements of an environmental management system (EMS) standard.

To facilitate a successful environmental audit, the audit process requires the following steps:

- *Pre-audit stage*
  full management commitment;
  setting overall goals, objectives, scope and priorities; and
  selecting a team to ensure objectivity and professional competence.
- *Audit stage*
  on-site audit, well defined and systematic using protocols or checklists;
  review of documents and records;
  review of policies;
  interviews; and
  site inspection.
- Post-audit stage
  evaluation of findings;
  reporting with recommendations;
  preparation of an action plan; and
  follow up.

 STOP AND THINK **12.1**

What would be the economic impact for companies if they did NOT report on their environmental and social activities?

The three stages (i.e. pre-audit, audit and post-audit) provide the general basis for an environmental audit. However, depending upon the size and nature of the company, some areas may require a more in-depth investigation. This will, in most cases, involve specialist advice, independent verification and cooperation and action on any shortcomings identified during the audit stage.

 TEST YOUR KNOWLEDGE **12.5**

(a) Demonstrate your understanding of the eco-management and audit scheme.
(b) How can the eco-management and audit scheme help companies to identity strategies and policies and meet targets?

8 Main features of social accounting

Social accounting (also referred to as corporate social responsibility (CSR)) is the formal process by which business entities communicate the impact of their economic activity to stakeholders who have a vested interest in the entity. However, it is nowadays accepted that the greater society has an interest in CSR and social accounting. For example, the impact of the Deepwater Horizon oil spillage in 2010 has had a far-reaching effect on British Petroleum. It has cost the company billions of dollars in law suits and lost revenue.

Social accounting seeks to create a balance between a company's business activities and social and environmental objectives. However, it is a broad term which can mean different things to different people. In the example given above of BP and the Deepwater Horizon oil spillage in 2010, many different categories of stakeholders were, and continue to be, affected. Some have lost their livelihoods, while others have had to move out of their homes.

The range of reporting a company can engage in with a view to reporting on social accounting can include:

- recycling of waste;
- education;
- environment/pollution emission/chemicals;
- regeneration, social inclusion and community investment;
- workforce issues;
- responsible behaviour in developing countries;
- agriculture;
- pharmaceuticals/animal testing/drug development; and
- regeneration issues etc.

The process involves undertaking regular evaluation of what an organisation does through consultation/audit. Using feedback from relevant stakeholders, a company can monitor, adjust and plan its activities. Future performance can be more effectively targeted to achieve an organisation's objectives. From a broader perspective, social accounting is a mechanism that adds value to a company's financial report by providing information about non-financial activities and the related costs of business behaviour in society.

The Social Audit Network (SAN) is an entity that supports non-governmental organisations (NGOs) and charitable organisations both in the UK and internationally. SAN has well-defined objectives to help social organisations to attain an understanding of the environment in which these organisations operate. These should be:

- **multi-perspective:** encompassing the views of people and groups that are important to the organisation;
- **comprehensive:** inclusive of all activities of an organisation;
- **comparative:** able to be viewed in the light of other organisations and addressing the same issues within same organisation over time;
- **regular:** done on an ongoing basis at regular intervals;
- **verified:** checked by people external to the organisation; and
- **disclosed:** readily available to others inside and outside of the organisation.

When information is available, discernible and risk-averse investors can put pressure on companies to change or enhance their business practices to recognise the social agenda. This can only be achieved when there is a consistent flow of relevant and useful information over a sustained period of time.

Social accounting can be viewed from two competing perspectives: management control and accountability, allowing organisations to pursue profits as well as social objectives for a sustainable future.

Management exercises control over the resources and assets of a business. Social accounting can help management to facilitate internal corporate planning and objectives. Companies can benefit in a number of ways from implementing social accounting and reporting:

- commensurate sharing of information on business activities;
- precise transfer of costs to the consumer;
- reputational and corporate legitimacy;
- increased market presence and awareness;
- investor friendly; and
- awareness of social responsibilities.

Since the management control perspective is inward-looking, social accounting can be meaningful through external party participation who can verify organisational commitment to society. Some of these external parties include independent social audit, certification on standards and compliance and periodic and consistent reviews by independent persons or organisations.

9 History of social accounting in Britain – the corporate report

Social accounting is currently widespread practice amongst listed corporations. Major corporations (e.g. BP, BT, Royal Dutch Shell, The Body Shop) have a specific section in their annual report to address issues that have a social impact due to the company's business activities. These companies publish verifiable and independently audited reports on social accounting that include environmental and sustainability reports. The table below is an extract from The Body Shop targets:

UPDATE ON PROGRESS	
WHAT WE SAID WE WOULD DO	**WHAT WE DID**
30% reduction in store carbon emissions by year end 2008	Renewable sourcing increased in EMEA and UK We are unable to demonstrate a 30% reduction across our entire store estate
90% of car fleet to be hybrid vehicles by year-end 2008	93% of car fleet is hybrid
Carbon Neutral retailer by 2010	CO_2 emissions have reduced in some areas Renewable sourcing has grown in EMEA and UK
All air travel offset	All air travel was offset in 2007 and will be for 2008

Source: The Body Shop. Available at: www.thebodyshop.com/_en/_ww/values-campaigns/assets/pdf/
Values_report_lowres_v2.pdf

This clearly shows that The Body Shop has had mixed success in achieving set targets. However, the issue of transparency is as important as whether or The Body Shop achieved its aims.

9.1 Current trends

There is no single code on social accountability. A whole host of issues related to the impact of business activity has developed, essentially in the last two decades, with various organisations issuing guidelines and certifications for companies engaged primarily in industrial activity. The European Commission Green Paper on Corporate Social Responsibility (CSR) in 2001 suggested that the concept of CSR requires an enterprise to be accountable for its impact on all relevant stakeholders. Many more definitions exist; however, CSR, which includes social accounting, requires definitive guidelines that have global application and allow standardised reporting.

In the UK there are legal requirements for companies to adhere to (e.g. pollution levels in relation to land, air and water). These laws, together with the Health and Safety at Work etc Act 1974, were drafted out of a need to control dangerous activities in business practices in the UK.

In 2001 the British Government drew up a set of guidelines for environmental reports, together with key performance indicators (KPIs) called Integrated Pollution Control (IPC) to help companies to understand the environmental risks and consequences of their activities. The intention is for companies to establish environmental reports using information the companies already possess. The guidelines provide advice on how to draw up such documents and on how to measure the different indicators. These are then sent to FTSE companies and members of the Confederation of British Industry.

In 2005 the Operating and Financial Review (OFR) was abolished by the government. This required listed companies to disclose (in addition to financial information) disclosures on KPIs and business strategies that had a social and environmental impact. The Companies Act 2006 introduced the business review requirement for listed companies to report on environmental and social issues when they are relevant to stakeholders' understanding of business activities. This was less stringent than the previous OFR. However, s. 172 of the Companies Act 2006 still required directors to demonstrate due 'regard to their impacts on their employees, relationships with suppliers, customers and impact on environment'.

The removal of the OFR had implications for the Accounting Standards Board (UK). Since the OFR is now no longer a legal requirement, the ASB has published its 'Reporting Statement of Best Practice' which acts as a guideline rather than a mandatory requirement.

Since the 2006 Act makes it a regulatory requirement to disclose information related to social and environmental issues, procedures and processes must be in place to capture relevant information. This is in line with the European Union's Accounts Modernisation Directive 2003. The business review recognises that companies must provide information for investors and other stakeholders, together with a narrative explanation that expands on and complements increasingly complicated financial accounts.

Although a number of major reforms were contained in the new legislation, the two key reforms, were those in relation to directors' duties and the requirement for directors' reports to include a business review.

TEST YOUR KNOWLEDGE 12.6

(a) What is social accounting?
(b) How can social accounting be integrated as part of financial reporting?

10 CSR reports and the Triple Bottom Line (TBL)

Corporate social responsibility (CSR) goes by various names. In the corporate circle it is sometimes referred to as corporate citizenship. While CSR includes social accounting, it is a broader aspect of corporate reporting, integrating financial reporting with social and environmental perspectives.

Powerful multinational corporations touch peoples' lives in more ways now than at any time in the past. This necessitated a change in corporate attitude towards the environment and society in which they operate. CSR is a corporate tool that engages companies' self-assessment and self-regulation by integrating business functions with social needs, thereby taking account of ethical considerations as well as various stakeholder interests. Guiding principles and practices have developed from a number of perspectives:

10.1 ISO 26000

ISO 26000 (International Standards Organisation) is international standard, principle-based guidance on CSR practices and is designed to assist companies in implementing and integrating business practices with social awareness. This is not a certifiable standard and hence cannot be used as part of a social audit. The ISO website presents the following components of ISO 26000:

ISO 26000 will help all types of organizations – regardless of their size, activity, or location – to operate in a socially responsible manner by providing guidance on:
- Concepts, terms and definitions related to social responsibility
- Background, trends and characteristics of social responsibility
- Principles and practices relating to social responsibility
- Core subjects and issues related to social responsibility
- Integrating, implementing and promoting socially responsible behaviour throughout the organization and, through its policies and practices, within its sphere of influence
- Identifying and engaging with stakeholders
- Communicating commitments, performance and other information related to social responsibility.

ISO 26000 is developed on the basis of best practice from around the world and is seen as an important initiative in helping and guiding companies to integrate best practices in their business activity.

10.2   Triple bottom line framework

Initially developed for the public sector, this approach has become a dominant feature in providing the basis for reporting beyond profit figures. There are three components to the **Triple Bottom Line Framework** (TBL) approach: economic, ecological and social. However, TBL has not taken off significantly, although CSR has become an important issue in modern business practices. Freer Spreckley (1981)[7] argued for an extended version of the 'bottom' line in company financial reports. His idea of TBL was developed in '*Social Audit – A Management Tool for Co-operative Working*'.

The concept of the TBL encapsulates all stakeholders who are impacted by corporate behaviour and advocates an integrated approach to business activity that takes account of environmental, ecological and sustainability issues.

As an example, the Kjaer group (Denmark) deals in automotive parts in North Africa. In its 2012 Annual Report the Group makes the following statement:

The Kjaer Group Way of Management
The Kjaer Group Way of Management consists of the Group's mission, vision, key processes, policies and adoption of the '**Triple Bottom Line**' principle, which ensures that decisions are made with equal balance between financial results as well as social and environmental responsibility ...

The Kjaer Group shows the following logo on its website, indicating its areas of activity in relation to CSR.

> Entities operate with the lowest possible impact on the environment
> Environmentally friendly initiatives supporting or relevant to our business

ENVIRONMENTAL
SOCIAL
FINANCIAL

> Happy, healthy and safe workplace
> Fair and competitive compensation

> Sustainable and predictable growth
> Increased enterprise value
> Preferred partner
> Attractive company for investment

Source: www.kjaergroup.com/kcw.output/File/KGR%20aarsrapport%202010.pdf

As the bulk of the group's business is with North African countries, it maintains the highest of standards in dealing fairly with its customer base and links economic progress with social progress in a number of ways (e.g. it is involved in and contributes to NGO's work with poor people in North Africa).

10.3   Global Reporting Initiative (GRI)

This is a not-for-profit organisation that promotes both economic and sustainability issues. The GRI initiative is an important development and encompasses a number of issues for corporations and entities to take into account in both their business and non-business activities. These include ecological footprint reporting, TBL reporting, environmental social governance (ESG) reporting and corporate governance reporting. The idea behind GRI is to promote equal importance to social, environmental and governance matters with regard to economics.

10.4 Social, ethical and environment issues – a summary

All the initiatives discussed above demonstrate the relevance and global need for a greater quality of reporting above and beyond simple economic performance. The continuing integration of national processes within the greater global community now demands fairness for all. The developed world has to work hand-in-hand with the developing world, with a fair return for all. The Fair Trade initiative is a small but developing initiative which seeks to promote a better quality of life for workers in developing economies. Increasingly, retailers of consumer goods are disclosing how they source their raw material and finished and semi-finished goods from countries such as India, Pakistan and some African states.

Tesco plc is the largest food and retail chain in the UK with a turnover in 2011 of almost £61 billion and reported net profit of £2.7 billion. Tesco discloses its CSR policy very clearly on its dedicated corporate website. It specifically states its corporate dedication to fair-trade policies and publishes a separate stand-alone CSR policy. Tesco's 2011 CSR report indicates that the company:

- donated £64.3 million to various charities;
- provided employment for 4.2 million people in Thailand;
- created eight new regeneration pacts across the UK;
- procured £1 billion of locally sourced products in the UK; and
- was pro-active in both carbon disclosure projects and in environmental, climate change and waste issues.

The CSR policies pursued by Tesco enhance its corporate image with its worldwide customers. By integrating its economic aims with the social agenda, Tesco is at the forefront of CSR.

TEST YOUR KNOWLEDGE 12.7

Explain the purpose of the TPL concept and its usefulness to companies' corporate reporting.

---

11 Nature of business ethics

Ethics in general is founded on the philosophy of humanism. Ethics can mean different things to different people. At its core, ethics subscribes to human behaviour that provides a basis for fairness and socially acceptable conduct that does not allow one group of people to infringe on the rights of another. Some definitions of ethics are provided below:

- Ethics is fundamental to human behaviour and is related to good or bad practices in society.
- Moral conduct can be described as either being right or wrong, acceptable or unacceptable.
- Business ethics substantially relates to good or bad behaviour.

From the latter point we can expand on our understanding of business ethics as being a form of applied ethics that examines ethical principles and moral or ethical problems that arise in a business environment. It is a field of ethics that deals with moral and ethical dilemmas in many areas of human endeavour such as medicine, technology and the law.

In an ever-changing corporate landscape, business ethics has gained ground. Capitalism can no longer been seen as a simple case of making a profit. However, since capitalism requires people to make it work, societies and individuals demand fairness in their lives. Business ethics can provide benefits for companies through the efficient adoption of ethical practices that impact upon:

- the common good of society;
- a sense of ethical motivation and sustainability;
- a balanced approach to the needs of stakeholder groups;
- social and economical reputation;
- security from legal implications; and
- enhanced employee commitment and retention.

Ethical implications relate to all areas of a business including finance, marketing and operational, and management activity. By giving due regard to business ethics, companies can enhance their reputational capital and thus retain customer loyalty.

11.1 Ethical motivation

This protects a company's reputation by creating an efficient and productive working environment. In the current economic climate, promoting ethical principles gives employees greater sense of security.

11.2 Needs of stakeholders

This is a primary issue in business ethics. Stakeholder interest has a greater connotation in terms of societal pressures placed upon companies to be seen to be ethical. Company values and reputation are built not only on adopting ethical behaviour but also by applying, demonstrating and communicating that behaviour and its measurable impact on the environment and society.

11.3 Employee commitment and retention

Even in constrained times, businesses lose employees due to changes that are perceived as being unfair. This could prove to be a costly exercise when employees with good skills lose confidence in their employment. An ethical programme of employee engagement could prove to be a worthwhile exercise in which making the right decisions provides perceived benefits and rewards.

11.4 Legal implications of unethical behaviour

Legal implications can arise both from within a company and from external litigation. Employees who feel aggrieved by company's policies would not do so if robust policies were in place to deal with employee matters in a systematic and fair manner. Additionally, legal implications may arise if companies do not have robust detection and prevention measures in place to check and deal with legal issues that may cause reputational risk. For instance, if a company is fully compliant with legal requirements for health and safety, the possibility of legal liability would be greatly reduced.

Selected issues have been discussed above to demonstrate the nature of business ethics. Prior research has shown that unethical practices cost industry many millions in lost revenue. For example, work-related stress means employees are off work for many days or weeks resulting in lost revenue and production and the higher costs of employing temporary replacements.

 TEST YOUR KNOWLEDGE 12.8

Explain business ethics and the role it plays in modern corporations.

 STOP AND THINK 12.2

Consider the policies a petrochemical company based in North Scotland should consider in its ethical approach to business.

12 Positivist and normative approaches to ethical issues

Positivist or descriptive ethics relates to the description of an ethical problem and asks the question 'What is?' The emphasis is explaining the phenomenon of business ethics. The positivist approach to business ethics measures results against some control or quality targets. For example, research has looked into the impact of CSR on firm performance and the quality of reported earnings in financial reports.

The normative approach to business ethics is prescriptive in nature and relates to the provision of guidelines, rules and regulations in determining particular behaviour, for instance creation of standards that deter or encourage particular course of action (e.g. reporting ethical practices against targets in annual reports).

Positivist business ethics seeks objective explanations to moral and ethical issues and explains whether things are going right or wrong. For instance, unethical practices can entice reaction from very different quarters. The testing of animals for medical and industrial purposes has aroused a strong reaction from those opposed to animal testing who contest that it is unethical and inhumane to treat animals for the purposes of human consumption. Companies that demonstrate animal-free production techniques have benefited from increased revenues and the social reputation and commitment of employees and stakeholders who value such ethical commitment by companies.

Normative business ethics seeks to provide a prescription of 'how' businesses should behave ethically. The volume of standards and rules and regulations, some enshrined in national law, provide a basis for CSR and ethical responsibility.

However, normative and positivist ethics can complement each other. While normative business ethics prescribe moral and ethical behaviour, positivist business ethics can explain the impact of rules and regulations from a number of perspectives, such as impact in company reputation and earnings. Positivist business ethics provide quantifiable variables in describing the correlation between explanatory variables, such as the impact of ethical practices on firm profitability.

13 The role of ethics in modern business

Much of what comprises business ethics already been discussed. Increasingly the business community can no longer function efficiently unless it can demonstrate a commitment to ethical practices. To understand this concept further, let's look at some comments made by Charles Harrington of Parson Inc (USA) a mid-size company employing 11,200 workers:

> Our strong commitment to our six Core Values – Safety, Quality, Integrity, Diversity, Innovation and Sustainability – governs everything we do at Parsons. Our Core Values are the very beliefs that form the culture of our organization, that make us who we are, that form the basis for all of our decisions. We strive hard to create an atmosphere where the question of deviating from those Core Values, from doing what is right, whether for perceived individual or corporate gain, never even gets raised…

From the above commentary, important words used are:

- core values
- commitment
- safety
- quality
- integrity
- diversity
- innovation
- sustainability
- beliefs
- organisational culture
- doing what is right.

Some very important terminologies are used here, demonstrating that CSR and ethics are embedded in the business management processes of Parsons Inc. Similarly, in the UK, Tesco plc has embedded the ethical approach to its business processes as part of its business strategy, thereby enhancing company image, value and reputation. It is critical that the values, mission, and identity of the company come from the leaders and are implemented throughout the organisation so that it becomes second nature to the employees of the company.

In formulating participatory business ethics, applied ethics can assist companies to determine policies and processes that are developed from a shared perspective, offering stakeholders the opportunity to participate in the decision-making process. For example:

■ Tesco plc has a consultation process, where the company's suppliers are involved in its procurement policies. This gives some level of assurance to suppliers where Tesco may be their only, or main, customer.
■ The Body Shop has a comprehensive procurements policy for the sourcing of its products and is a member of the 'Fair Trade' initiative. The company tries to ensure that its overseas suppliers get a fair deal for their products and is also proactive in the context of illegal or socially unacceptable sourcing of its products (e.g. the use of child labour in the production of products).

Companies that attempt to create a balance between value maximisation and non-financial issues generally are trying to manage their businesses on a sustainable basis. The fact is that national and international accounting standards exist to regulate financial reporting, yet huge corporate collapses still occur (e.g. Satyam in India in 2009). This demonstrates that ethical malpractices abound in both developed and developing countries. However, many corporate collapses are simply down to economic factors or fail due to business strategy (e.g. Woolworths, Peacocks and Game).

Many examples, such as Tesco, have been provided in this section on business ethics. However, a recent development to hit the news relates to intellectual property rights (IPR). An intellectual property right is the ownership of an idea, thought, code, or information. For instance, protection of a particular drug developed over years of research ensures that the developing company has the right to any revenues that transpire. However, recent events indicate that patents are a company's way of monopolising a certain market. This suggests the stifling of competition in a capitalist market where competition is seen as good for the economy and protection for consumers. Competition forces companies to develop their business strategy to meet and manage competing forces.

Companies view IPR from a utilitarian perspective. However, a moral perspective has a counter argument in that utility is developed from societal needs and that a product that has universal application and provides relief for vast numbers of human beings cannot, by nature, be protected from value-maximising economic constrains; hence it must be shared universally. Some 39 pharmaceutical companies filed a lawsuit against South Africa's 1997 Medicines and Related Substances Control Amendment Act as its provisions aimed to provide affordable HIV medicines. This has been cited as a harmful effect of patents-based monopolisation by a handful of corporations.

British companies are seen as very proactive in ethical matters. Larger corporations have an integrated and embedded ethical approach to managing their business processes. Some companies have appointed ethics officers to manage the company's ethical affairs. Much ethical concern developed during 1980–2010, due to highly publicised corporate collapses mainly in the USA. With the enactment of the Sarbanes-Oxley Act 2002, ethics-related development formed a backdrop to unethical American business practices. Ethics is about setting boundaries beyond which it would be considered wrong to engage in activity that would damage a company's reputation.

14 Ethics and accountants in practice

Accountants have a fiduciary duty towards their employers as well as to their investors and to the larger world. This duty is based on both legal and ethical considerations. The past decade has seen some remarkable corporate collapses, mainly in the USA, with Enron, Worldcom Tyco etc. Methods of accounting, such as off-balance sheet finance and special purposes entities, were one of the main causes of financial irregularities coupled with, in some cases, unprofessional conduct by external auditors. These events have drawn attention to the professionalism of practicing accountants and levels of ethical standards.

The 'crisis' in the accounting profession that followed and the criticism it faced led to a stream of regulations emanating from both accounting bodies and governments to prevent further damage to the profession and bring a sense of stability and confidence to stakeholders.

In an article published in 2007 in the *Managerial Auditing Journal* mitigating factors were identified that contributed to ethical weaknesses for accountants. The article surveyed 66 members of the International Federation of Accountants (IFAC). The main factors that were identified included:

- self interest;
- failure to maintain objectivity and independence;
- inappropriate professional judgement;
- lack of ethical sensitivity;
- improper leadership and ill-culture;
- failure to withstand advocacy threats;
- lack of competence;
- lack of organisational and peer support; and
- lack of professional body support.

Above all, the main threat to an accountant's ethical behaviour is the self-interest that places personal consideration above ethical and professional judgement. For example, if an auditor questions the appropriateness of a particular accounting entry in an audit, the financial consideration in terms of fees being charged to the client may allow the auditor to act unethically and ignore the issue. In such circumstances, the accountant is faced with making professional decisions that include:

- reporting a particular matter or set of issues to an immediate superior both formally and informally; such issues could be related to lack of clarity on cash flows in and out of a company;
- whistle-blowing to an external and relevant agency – this would require careful consideration on the part of the accountant as it may involve exposure to possible litigation (e.g. illegal sourcing of products or trading with banned organisations or even countries);
- an unethical alternative, though not recommended, would be to ignore the issue and let the system catch up with it. However, there may be legal implications for 'not doing nothing', and in certain circumstances the law may require an individual to have deemed to have known certain facts and thereby taken some sort of an action to disclose a relevant issue; and
- consider resigning from their post on ethics grounds.

14.1 Professional ethics – regulations

After the notoriety of corporate scandals since the 1980s, new and enhanced regulations have emerged putting the onus on accountants to take ethical actions in circumstances that demand it.

14.1.1 Money laundering regulations

Money laundering has become a sophisticated venture for some organisations and persons. HMRC provides some guidance on this issue:

> The Money Laundering Regulations 2007 came into force in December 2007. All businesses that are covered by the regulations have to put suitable anti-money laundering controls in place. If the regulations apply to your business you must put these controls in place as soon as possible.

> As part of the anti-money laundering controls that you have to put in place, you need to appoint a nominated officer (sometimes called the money laundering reporting officer).[8]

Changes to the Money Laundering Regulations in 2007 recognised the same client–accountant privilege as exists with lawyers; this means that, since 2007, accountants are no longer required to report suspicious transactions to the National Criminal Intelligence Service. However, professional accounting bodies still retain an ethical dimension in their guidelines.

The ACCA and the ICAEW, as well as other UK professional accounting bodies, publish a code of conduct for its members in both industry and practice. In its Code of Conduct, the ACCA recommends that the ethical standards issued by the International Ethics Standards Board for Accountants (IESBA) should apply. Amongst its rules, the ACCA comments that accountants should give ethical consideration to:

- integrity;
- objectivity;
- professional competence and due care;
- confidentiality; and
- professional behaviour.

The ACCA Code of Conduct accepts that it is not possible to identify every situation that creates a threat to compliance; nevertheless it requires accountants to use their professional judgement when deliberating. The International Federation of Accountant's (IFAC) ethical standards require compliance by the professional accountant in managing conflicting situations that give rise to ethical concerns.

TEST YOUR KNOWLEDGE 12.9

Identify and explain the implications for the accountant with regard to business ethics.

Accountants, both in practice and in business, are seeing emerging trends for accountability and the requirement for ethical behaviour. The accountant in business comes under the scrutiny of the auditor. A conflict of loyalty may arise between the requirement to be transparent and management pressure to comply with its agenda. In such situations, ethical judgement needs to be exercised by accountants that may have professional and career implications.

 END OF CHAPTER QUESTIONS

12.1 Modern businesses seem to be in conflict between short-term profits and long-term sustainability.

Required
Consider the above statement and outline the main points managers should consider in relation to societies' needs and the long-term economic and social sustainability of a company.

12.2 Outline the steps companies should consider in developing an eco-management policy. In your answer make comments on policy procedures and monitoring and control.

12.3 A recently listed company on the FTSE 350, with a turnover of £550 million is receiving negative publicity as users of financial information are complaining that it is hard to use the company's financial information. HMRC has told listed companies that they require tax-related returns on a web-based system in XBRL format. The company's systems are antiquated and cannot be merged with web-based applications.

Required
(a) Explain to the company's CEO what action the company could take to avoid such bad publicity.
(b) Advise the company's CEO on the necessary steps the company needs to take to comply with HMRC's demands.

12.4 Abbey Group plc is a manufacturer of specialised machine parts and has a presence in most major growing economies such as China, India, Pakistan, Brazil as well as the European Union. Abbey maintains a divisionalised group structure where each country is a division. The group maintains a decentralised structure with divisions able to make decisions on a local basis; however, strategy is developed by Abbey HQ. Each division maintains its own IT policy with heterogeneous systems employed across the various divisions. Up to now the data sharing between divisions has been minimal as each division specialises in its own area of expertise and manufactures totally different machine parts. However, collecting the financial data is a laborious exercise and the annual group financial reports are badly affected. Financial and accounting data

END OF CHAPTER QUESTIONS

is collected in different formats and, in some cases, this information reaches the HQ in the form of e-mail attachments.

The Chief Finance Officer (CFO) of Abbey plc is unhappy about the length of time taken to collect and process financial and accounting data into a usable format for group purposes. The group is listed on the London and New York stock markets and has been previously warned by the listing regulators about the delay in submitting the group financial report.

The CFO calls a meeting of a working group to investigate the solutions to Abbey's IT problems. The Chief Systems Officer (CSO) suggests that the group could develop a common information sharing platform based on XBRL technology.

Required

From the information the case of Abbey plc:

(a)   Explain XBRL.
(b)   How can Abbey plc use XBRL to share financial information?
(c)   What would be the level of cost involved in setting up the new technology without going into the amounts in detail?
(d)   What platform would XBRL require?
(e)   Comment on the benefits of using XBRL to Abbey plc.

12.5 James is the environmental compliance officer for a medium-sized car parts manufacturing company. James has to decide whether or not the company should invest in new technology that would reduce toxic emissions from current technology being released into the atmosphere. The company's emission levels are within legal guidelines, however, James knows that environmental regulations for this particular toxin are lagging behind scientific evidence. A recent academic research paper suggests that if toxins of this type are not legislated for, it would impact on the health of people living near the company.

Required

(a)   Consider the ethical concerns that James is dealing with.
(b)   What action should the company take in assessing its environmental impact?
(c)   How should the company report such an impact?

12.6 Stakeholders are increasingly looking to the quality and quantity of corporate social reporting. In assisting users of corporate social reports, disclosures in the annual financial reports play an important role.

Required

(a)   Apart from a company's business performance, how can users of annual financial reports assess corporate social behaviour and a company's attitude towards its environment?
(b)   What other sources of information are available to ascertain corporate social behaviour?
(c)   Do 'green' organisations depict an accurate assessment of corporate impact on the environment?

Endnotes

1   See http://in.reuters.com/article/2012/02/27/bloomberg-idINDEE81Q0PL20120227.
2   See www.accountingweb.co.uk/press/thomson-reuters-research-highlights-accountants-need-mobile-integration.
3   VT is a suite of accounting and tax software that is iXBRL enabled which allows users great flexibility in data transfer between applications that are internet-based.
4   'ACCA Guide on Environmental and CSR reporting – Guide to Best Practice: 2001'. Available at: www.corporateregister.com/pdf/Guide.pdf.
5   The state of corporate environmental reporting in Singapore. Available at: www2.accaglobal.com/pubs/general/activities/library/sustainability/sus_archive/tech-ers-001.
6   European Commission Environment. Available at: http://ec.europa.eu/environment/emas/index_en.htm
7   Available at: www.locallivelihoods.com/Documents/Social%20Audit%201981.pdf.
8   Available at: www.hmrc.gov.uk/MLR/getstarted/intro.htm.

Overview

13

■ **LEARNING OUTCOMES**

Chapter 13 covers the syllabus section entitled 'Overview'. After reading and understanding the contents of the chapter, working through all the Worked Examples and Practice Questions, you should be able to:

■ discuss the role of the company secretary in analysing and interpreting accounting information;
■ understand and appreciate how the company secretary initiates and participates in meetings based on accounting information and decision making;
■ understand the role of the company secretary and the challenges presented by initiating changes to and improving the company accounting system;
■ appreciate contemporary accounting developments and the role of the company secretary; and
■ understand the significance of proposed published information for external users on regulatory and legal compliance.

1 Introduction

Financial accounting and reporting is central to modern entity management 'by the numbers'. The company secretary is regularly required to fulfil roles that are varied in nature and require an understanding of a range of legal, financial and social affairs. The company secretary is required to provide advice to senior management that allows them to discharge their fiduciary duty in an efficient and effective manner.

The company secretary is responsible for the efficient administration of a company, particularly with regard to ensuring compliance with statutory and regulatory requirements and for ensuring that decisions of the board of directors are implemented. The role of a company secretary has become more prominent in recent years, with ever-increasing numbers sitting the professional examinations of the Institute of Company Secretaries and Administrators (ICSA). Some primary and complimentary duties a company secretary is required to demonstrate include, but are not limited to:

■ Maintaining the statutory registers. These include:
  – the register of members;
  – the register of directors and secretaries;
  – the register of directors' interests;
  – the register of charges; and
  – for public companies only, the register of interests in shares.
■ Managing the company's premises and facilities.

- Participating in the following:
  - the financial accounting system;
  - strategy planning; and
  - the decision-making process related to changes in financial reporting.
- PAYE and payroll.
- VAT registration.
- Insurance and pensions.
- Dealing with social, ethical and corporate affairs etc.

As a senior officer of a company, the company secretary plays a significant role in providing relevant advice to the board and participating in the decision-making process. The work of the company secretary can be varied and in smaller companies, the role will fulfil a number various duties.

2   Accounting systems – output, analysis and interpretation

To be good in business, a company secretary has to be proficient with financial information and numbers. Success in any business comes back to the numbers. The board relies on them to make decisions and managers use them to evaluate both the company's performance and their own. That is true whether the job involves marketing, production, management, or information systems.

In business, accounting and financial statements are used to communicate the numbers. If a company secretary does not know how to read financial statements, they cannot really make any meaningful contribution to the board.

2.1 The role of the company secretary in financial reporting

The company secretary must be knowledgeable about finance and accounting matters and must be able to fill in for the company accountant as well as contribute to senior management meetings.

The table below demonstrates a hierarchical representation of financial reporting from the economic activity of the company to the publication of financial reports:

TABLE 13.1 The finance and accounting domain

Accounting function	Accounting components	The basic accounting equation	Using the accounting equation	Financial statement
Economic activities: Identification, recording, communication	Ethics in financial reporting	Assets	Transaction analysis	Statement of comprehensive income
Users of accounting information	Accounting standards	Liabilities	Summary of transactions	Statement of financial position
	Assumptions	Equity		Statement of cash flows
				Statement of changes to equity

Eventually, company actions must be demonstrated by accounting numbers. The company secretary will have a duty to ensure that both statutory law (e.g. the Companies Act 2006) as well regulatory standards (e.g. IFRS and UK GAAP) are reflected in the financial reports and the manner in which the audit trail is set up. In discharging their duties, the company secretary is involved in the analysis and interpretation of financial reports. A company's accounting system must be capable of delivering the required level of information to comply with various legislation and standards. The company secretary will be involved in the verification of such compliance through analysis and interpretation of financial reports. Three scenarios are presented below that requires the company secretary to call upon their skills to find solutions to existing problems:

2.2   Ethical considerations

At the last board meeting of Argentum plc, the non-executive directors (NEDs) complained that reported expenditure on environmental policy was well below the budgeted figures when, in fact, the company is robust on environmental issues. This has hindered the board in reporting substantial progress on environmental issues to external users of the corporate reports. The board has asked you, as the company's company secretary, to look into the matter and to report back to the board at their next board meeting in three month's time.

On inspection and after discussions with members of the accounting staff, it transpires that a lot of the expenditure for environmental purposes has been amalgamated with 'administration' costs. You, as the company secretary, have asked the company accountant to go back three years and audit the environmental expenditure. The accountant has reported that most of the environmental expenditure for the past three years has been recorded under various administration cost codes.

2.2.1   Action

You ask the company accountant to set up nominal codes specific to environmental expenditure under appropriate headings. You have agreed the audit trail with the accountant and have established where and how the various codes will be amalgamated and reported to back up the audit trail to the main nominal codes.

The accountant has created the new nominal codes and has reclassified past expenditure to ensure that environmental expenditure is both *recorded* and *reported* under appropriate nominal codes. The accounting procedures manual has been re-drafted and staff trained to follow appropriate recording procedures to ensure that relevant environmental expenditure is recorded under the correct nominal codes.

You have drafted a report and circulated it to board members prior to the next meeting for discussion. It explains the problem and the actions taken to correct it. The accountant, in conjunction with you as the company secretary, has drafted robust procedures for staff to follow.

The above example is a simple demonstration of how the company secretary gets involved in various issues that arise. Financial reporting is an important aspect of a company's procedure as there are interested parties both within and outside the company.

2.3   Regulatory reporting

At a recent meeting with the external auditors of Primrose Ltd, concern was raised about how the company is managing certain items on its statement of financial position. The chairman of Primrose Ltd has defended his company vigorously, stating that the company strives to ensure that there is complete transparency in its financial reporting.

The company's external auditor has raised the point that lease contracts appear to be recorded as operating leases, whereas the company has a long-term liability with the lessors. On investigation, the company secretary has confirmed the auditor's concerns and has drafted a report to the members of the board of Primrose Ltd explaining the nature of long-term lease contracts and how they should be implemented.

The company secretary also explained in his report that there are financial implications for recognising leases as financial leases and that this will impact gearing and increase the overall liabilities of the company. The board has approved the report and instructed the company secretary to ensure that:

- All leases are reviewed for appropriate recording and reporting action.
- The accountant/company secretary must discuss the nature of procurement of long-term assets and the manner in which these assets are financed and the implications for the board.
- Full disclosure is made in the financial reports with appropriate narratives explaining the nature of the company's assets and liabilities.

2.4 Regulatory reporting

The company secretary of Jones plc has noticed that the share price of the company is on a downward trend. The matter had been discussed at the last board meeting. The chairman of Jones plc tells you that he is not happy with the situation and asks you to make a preliminary investigation as to the cause of the downward slide of the company's share price.

The company secretary attends a meeting with the finance director in which the financial reports for the last five years were discussed. During the meeting, the company secretary raised the concern that, although Jones plc owns a substantial amount of land, mostly in city centres in the UK, and that land prices have risen tremendously, the financial accounts only record the original purchase price.

The finance director said the company has never re-valued its land simply because it did not have procedures and processes in place that automatically required an annual review of tangible and substantial assets.

2.4.1 Action

The company secretary, together with the finance director, took guidance from IFRS 13 'Fair Value Measurement' (effective on 1 January 2013) and IAS 8, IAS 16 and IAS 36. They drafted procedures to reflect the fair value of property, plant and equipment and the manner in which they are measured. The draft procedure manual recommends that fair value measurements should be applied to all tangible assets. In some cases, valuation should be sought from experts. Any changes to accounting measurements will need to be reported and disclosed on the basis of IAS 8 'Accounting Policies, Changes in Accounting Estimates and Errors', in the financial reports.

Other situations may arise in which the company secretary would need to coordinate with other staff members to discharge his duties. Some of these duties may entail legislative compliance. For example, the impact on the environment due to the nature of a company's business activities will require certain levels and types of disclosures in compliance with existing rules and regulations. In such cases, the company secretary must convey his opinion on the social, economic, and reputational impact this will have on the company.

3 Accounting information and decision making

As an officer of the company at the centre of the decision-making process, the company secretary has a major role to play in ensuring that good corporate governance is practiced. Accounting information provides the basis for decision making.

The impact of accounting information on the decision-making process and the capacity of the CS to lead from the front has already been discussed above. However, accounting information provides the basis for a formal and informal decision-making process.

The company secretary is the focal point for accounting information by facilitating legal and regulatory compliance. Initiating and participating in the decision-making process allows the company secretary to monitor and provide senior managers and the board with information on compliance matters. Accounting information defines the economic viability and performance of an economic entity. Companies need to investigate the past and plan for the future.

3.1 Board meetings

The strategic vision of major companies is provided at board level. The board considers the company's performance on the basis of accounting information and of planned activity and target levels. The job of the company secretary is to facilitate such meetings informing directors of when and where meetings they are scheduled, providing documents for consideration in advance, and ensuring the proceedings are minuted.

The board may well expect the company secretary to provide advice on legal and other matters or ask them to investigate the impact of a certain course of action.

3.2 The company

The board may make decisions about special and specific aspects of a company's progress. The company secretary may be tasked with ensuring compliance with, for instance, proper disclosure of financial information, that procedures are in place to allow this and they have been communicated to relevant personnel and staff.

3.3 The shareholders

The board makes some important decisions based on accounting information (e.g. a dividends policy). The job of the company secretary would be to initiate meetings with certain groups of shareholders and communicate to them company decisions and items of a strategic nature. This ensures that all shareholders receive equitable treatment.

3.4 Stock exchange rules

Some duties, even though they are deemed core to operations may not be legislated for specifically in relation to the company secretary (e.g. ensuring compliance with stock exchange rules and regulations). In practice, these duties are closely related to their other duties. As such, the company secretary will ensure proper working relationships are maintained with the stock exchange and that relevant and timely accounting information is provided in compliance with listing rules and requirements.

The role of the company secretary has changed enormously in recent years. The job now carries a lot of responsibility, and the company secretary is now expected to have a range of skills in various business-related matters.

4 Improving the accounting system and its output

The company secretary has a pivotal role in ensuring that:

- a company's accounting system is designed to reflect the information demanded;
- output from the system meets company requirements in the necessary format and on a timely basis; and
- the information is produced in the most cost-effective manner.

Changes are constantly taking place, not only from a legislative and regulatory perspective but also within the firm. New markets and new products need to be reflected in the accounting system. The accounting system needs constant changes, amendments and deletions to ensure that effective outputs are produced to facilitate decision making. Some important aspects of accounting information, its output and improvement are listed below:

(a) consider the company's business model in its current form;
(b) formulate a team tasked to develop, implement, test, and re-check against criteria for improvements;
(c) formulate a timeline for the project and consider responsibilities to particular personnel;
(d) agree when tasks are to be completed and when then next task should be initiated;
(e) implement changes and carry out test runs;
(f) assess and evaluate changes to specifications; and
(g) once criteria is met, report to senior management.

In the above process, the company secretary has a central role in facilitating the improvements needed and reporting to the board of progress and final implementation. See the example below of a business case requiring improvement to the accounting information system.

 **WORKED EXAMPLE** 13.1

Nector plc sells a wide range of herbal remedies and lately business has been booming. The following factors were recognised as impacting on the company's ability to deal with increased business:

- The company faced challenges in overseeing and controlling its accounting processes brought on by: accelerating growth; fragmented process ownership among accounting, finance, and the business units; and a complex corporate legal entity structure.
- The company wanted to implement business process improvements in accounting that better reflected state-of the-art accounting system strategies. The goal was to improve efficiency, reduce costs, and transform work processes.
- Additionally, the company wanted to establish appropriate controls to mitigate risk and comply with regulatory and legal requirements by improving the current accounting information system.

Required

As a company secretary, outline the steps that would be required to improve and meet the new demands.

Answer

As a company secretary, the following steps would assist in designing an improved accounting system:

(a) refer to the current system design;
(b) assess if improvements can be developed using the current system;
(c) evaluate alternative courses of action;
(d) select the most cost-effective and relevant option;
(e) draw up a plan of action and identify the tasks/changes needed;
(f) include new/improved internal control procedures;
(g) develop a time plan for when the project should be completed;
(h) initiate the improvement/changes;
(i) test the new/improved system;
(j) evaluate output; and
(k) finalise the improved system and run live.

Improvements to the accounting system would initially require identifying skilled and knowledgeable personnel who rise to the challenge of implementing the necessary changes.

The task would benefit from a mapping exercise to draw on people's experiences of the impact of implementing changes to the existing accounting system. This would mean looking to the current capabilities of the system and identifying if change is possible within the current framework, or whether technical improvements would be needed to meet specifications.

The task would call for an estimate of costs for improving the system, identifying if any outside help will be needed. In such circumstances, I would initiate a tendering process having previously obtained permission from senior management.

The design phase would identify tests that would need to be carried out to measure the efficiency of the improvements. Once improvement has been made to the system, tests would be initiated and the output evaluated. If further enhancements are required, these would be implemented and the system re-tested.

The company secretary, with the support of the accountant and perhaps the systems manager, may need to design and implement a new and improved system of internal control.

Once specifications are met in terms of the required output, 'live run' would commence. However, policy and procedure documents would need to be drawn up to assist staff in referring to new ways of entering data and running required output reports.

Staff should be trained in new procedures and the improvements regularly monitored to ensure compliance with new requirements.

In all circumstances, the company secretary will need to ensure that adequate measures of internal controls are embedded at user and system levels. The improved system must comply with regulatory and legal requirements. Duties should be segregated so that users can oversee and monitor any improvement in performance.

In the above example, certain systematic steps were recognised in developing and/or improving performance. However, over and above regulatory and legal compliance, there may be a need to integrate company accounting systems with internal and external requirements. In a company with divisions, for instance, a common platform may be required to integrate accounting processes and efficiency of data sharing. This aspect was discussed in chapter 12 where the need for XBRL was identified. More and more government agencies are demanding returns be filed using the XBRL platform.

A company's accounting system needs flexibility to be enhanced when necessary, or to facilitate additional changes to be made as and when the need arises. There has been a surge in migration to XBRL lately led by HMRC requirements. Companies in the UK are developing their accounting systems to meet this need. This provides an opportunity to initiate efficiency changes and to reassess current input/output needs.

 STOP AND THINK 13.1

In what ways can the company secretary act in a manner that impacts on decision making from an accounting system perspective?

5 Contemporary accounting developments

The pace of global business has increased tremendously in the last decade. National and international agreements (e.g. the globalisation initiative and World Trade Organisation protocols) mean that companies need to implement current technology that meets legal, regulatory and other obligations in a cost-efficient and timely manner.

The accounting profession has undergone major changes and accountants have transformed from primarily information processors to strategic business advisors. With the rapid pace of change in global business and the movement of finance across the world, the modern accountant needs to think in a strategic manner and not just as a provider of accounting information.

The role of the company secretary has also evolved from simply being a facilitator, to a more proactive provider of legal, financial and other services to the company. The global marketplace is based on ever-increasing complexity in technology that allows users to carry out transactions in a split second rather than in days or weeks.

The company secretary can advise the company on the significance of contemporary changes to the accounting profession. This can be seen from three important perspectives.

5.1 Legal changes

The accounting scandals of the past decade or so provided the impetus for change in legal compliance for companies. In the USA, the Enron case led to the Sarbanes-Oxley Act 2002. This demanded stringent compliance by listed companies and held the CEO and CFO directly responsible for any misreporting.

In the UK, the Cadbury Code 1992 was the impetus for listed companies to get their house in order and provided specific guidelines on responsibilities, disclosures and reporting. A number of other reports have been issued since the Cadbury Code looking at specific aspects of corporate governance practices. The Higgs Report (2003) reviewed the role and effectiveness of NEDs and made a number of recommendations about their role and their fiduciary duties and responsibilities.

The company secretary plays a pivotal role in providing specialist advice on the role of directors, their legal responsibilities and how these must be discharged. The UK Code on Corporate Governance (2010), which updates the Cadbury Code, provides extensive guidance on the role of directors, corporate structures, remuneration and internal and external relationships including the role of the external audit.

At times, cross-listed companies may need to abide by international legislation such as the Sarbanes-Oxley Act. Any UK companies listed on the London Stock Exchange which also have a presence on the New York Stock Exchange, must provide and disclose financial and non-financial information according to US law. The company secretary needs to be aware of the international dimension in discharging their duties.

5.2 Regulatory changes

The Financial Services and Markets Act 2000 requires public listed companies to disclose how they have complied with the UK Code on Corporate Governance and explain where they have not applied the code ('comply or explain'). This left the onus on companies to disclose their compliance or departure from recommended practice.

The UK Listings Rule, overseen by the Financial Services Authority (FSA)(soon to be replaced by the Financial Conduct Society (FCA)) This provides rules and regulations that listed companies must comply with to remain on the listings register. Here the company secretary would need to be at the forefront of knowledge in providing the board and relevant personnel with advice on compliance with UK listing rules. They would be active in this regard and ensure smooth communications between the Stock Exchange and the company. Compliance with submissions and directives of the FSA is a demanding task and changes to listings rules must be acted upon, or there are implications for the company which could lead to fines or other penalties.

The Companies Act 2006 codified the fiduciary duties of the board of directors. Not all directors are aware of their fiduciary duties and reply on the company secretary to advise them in discharging their duties. Again, the company secretary needs to be aware of current and forthcoming regulatory changes and be in a position to advise relevant personnel on actions, procedures and processes that need to be changed, amended, deleted or improved to facilitate compliance.

Company secretaries are required to be aware of current environmental law in the UK. As such, they must be involved in monitoring and providing advice on relevant issues relating to the way a company conducts its business activities. A breach of environmental law can mean financial penalties for a company but it may also impact upon its reputation.

5.3 Social changes

Many UK companies are proactive in social matters. Social accounting is increasingly seen as an integral part of corporate reporting. Users of financial information are increasingly demanding non-financial information to make investment decisions. Some companies have been criticised in the recent past for using child labour in the procurement process for finished and semi-finished goods. Activist organisations such as the 'People & Planet' campaign target UK companies that are involved, directly or indirectly, with sourcing products which use chld labour. On their website (http://peopleandplanet.org) the organisation made the following claim:

> People & Planet's Redress Fashion campaign is calling on UK companies to take responsibility for their whole supply chain – from seed to shirt – and guarantee that no forced child labour is used in the production of their garments.

The subject has become hot news – Sir Philip Green of the Arcadia Group made the following comment:

> Our companies buy garments and do not usually have visibility of the source of the raw materials. We rely on our suppliers to source all raw materials and to operate according to our detailed Code of Conduct which includes the statement that 'child labour must not be used' ... We would not be supportive of using cotton in products where the cotton has been picked in the manner you allege.

A company's reputation can be easily tarnished with such news leading to a consumer boycott of a company's products which could impact on profitability and corporate survival. In this respect the company secretary has a central role in advising implication of product procurement, particularly from developing nations.

TEST YOUR KNOWLEDGE 13.1

Identify some major changes to contemporary accounting developments.

6 Significance of (proposed) published information for external user groups

The Accounting Standards Board (UK) primarily advocates IFRS as the basis for reporting for listed companies. Small and medium-sized companies (SMEs) are also subject to accounting regulations, but their accounting treatment has been less stringent. The ASB currently adopts a three-tier system, categorised by company size. Tier 1 is for large public companies, while Tier 3 is for SMEs. In its circular in January 2012, the ASB mentioned that:

> The Accounting Standards Board (ASB) of the Financial Reporting Council has today published financial reporting exposure drafts (FREDs) 46 to 48 setting out revised proposals for the future of financial reporting in the UK and Republic of Ireland ...[1]

The revised proposals recommend:

a. **replacing all current accounting standards with a single FRS**. The ASB is proposing (consistent with its previous proposals) to use the IFRS for SMEs, as issued by the International Accountings Standards Board, as the base for FRED 48. This will reduce the volume of accounting standards from approximately 2,500 pages to 250 pages.

b. **introduction of a reduced disclosure framework**. The framework permits certain entities (mainly subsidiaries) to apply the measurement and recognition requirements of EU-adopted IFRS with reduced disclosures.

c. **retaining the financial reporting standard for smaller entities (FRSSE)**.

> As a consequence of feedback to its previous exposure drafts the ASB is proposing the following major changes:

d. **eliminate the tier system**. The ASB will not proceed with the tier system previously proposed. The application of EU-adopted IFRS will not therefore be extended beyond that required by Regulation[1] or by for example the rules of the Alternative Investment Market;

e. **introducing accounting treatments permitted under current accounting standards**. options to revalue land and buildings, capitalise borrowing costs or carry forward certain development expenses have been incorporated into the FRED 48. The ASB is proposing to retain accounting treatments permitted under current accounting standards and international accounting standards rather than its previous policy to make minimal changes to the IFRS for SMEs.

Source: ASB (UK) 30 January 2012: www.frc.org.uk/asb/press/pub2702.html

This would mean SMEs would need to adapt to the new ways of reporting. Accounting systems and information output would need to be considered in a manner that is relevant and incidental to regulatory requirements.

The company secretary would need to consider many of the changes and, in conjunction with the senior accounting officer and other relevant personnel, assess the impact of such changes and relevant costs. They would also need to appraise the board of the relevant changes required and the aspects of the business that would be affected and duration of time taken to effect changes.

6.1 SMESs and red tape

In addition to changes in regulatory requirements, the ASB further demonstrated simplification of red tape for SMEs. The ASB indicates that:

> The Department for Business, Innovation and Skills (BIS) has recently launched the company and commercial law theme under the Red Tape Challenge programme. The Red Tape Challenge gives the public an opportunity to comment on the regulations under each theme with a view to reducing and simplifying regulations. The theme's objective is to ensure that the UK has a company law framework that gives companies the flexibility to compete and grow effectively.

> The ASB has worked with BIS in developing its revised proposals and considers that it is in line with the Red Tape Challenge. The proposed framework allows entities the flexibility to prepare effective financial reports that are proportionate to the size and complexity of the entity whilst reducing significantly the volume of current UK and Irish accounting standards.

For larger business entities, regulatory changes to IFRS 10 'Consolidated Financial Statements' and IFRS 13 'Fair Value Measurement' provide specific meaning to procedures for the consolidation and measuring of fair value and what constitutes fair value measurement. Both standards are applicable on or after 1 January 2013.

The publication of IFRS 10 and 13 will have an economic impact on other aspects of reporting such as:

- IFRS 11 'Joint Arrangements'
- IFRS 12 'Disclosure of Interests in Other Entities'
- IAS 27 'Separate Financial Statements' (as amended in 2011)
- IAS 28 'Investments in Associates and Joint Ventures' (as amended in 2011).

The board would be interested in looking at the impact that these will have and what new arrangements, at least in the accounting system and procedures for recording, will be required. Here, the company secretary would act in an advisory role.

 STOP AND THINK **13.1**

Think about the various roles a company secretary performs. How has this changed over the years and to what extent do they act as a legal advisor to the board?

 END OF CHAPTER QUESTIONS

13.1 Discuss the areas that a company secretary would be knowledgeable in a modern corporate setting.

13.2 How has the role of the modern company secretary changed over the last decade and what caused these changes?

13.3 Discuss the role of the company secretary in relation to the board of directors.

13.4 In relation to published financial reports, what is the main role of the company secretary?

13.5 Consider the role of a company secretary and answer the following questions:

    (a)   Does every company need a secretary?

    (b)   Does a company secretary need any qualifications?

    (c)   Does the secretary have to be a UK citizen?

    (d)   Can a company secretary be held criminally liable over the affairs of a company?

    (e)   Does a company secretary have any powers?

    (f)   What rights does a company secretary have?

END OF CHAPTER QUESTIONS

13.6 Discuss how the company accounting officer and the company secretary roles complement each other from the company secretary perspective.

13.7 What consideration should the company secretary take into accounting when initiating accounting system improvements?

13.8 The company secretary was advised by the auditors of Ralph Ltd that there would appear to be discrepancies in the claims made by certain employees of the company for out of pocket expenses. In particular there two cases where employees have been making expenses claims that require an explanation.

CASE 1

John is being sponsored by the company to attend a course to become a qualified company secretary. The nearest college that provides tuition is ten miles away. John attends a twice-weekly session at the college. John makes his claim for 40 miles at 50p per mile and also claims subsistence of £20 and hotel charge of £80 for overnight stay. However, the college is a walking distance from John's residence and he goes home seven days a week.

CASE 2

Ralph Ltd cares a great deal about its employee's welfare. Apart from other facilities and support, the company provides interest-free loans to employees to purchase season tickets for travel to work. In some cases the loan can be substantial, ranging for £100 to £1,000. The loan is not available to those employee's who live within a two-mile radius of work. However, during the audit, it transpires that some employees living within the two-mile radius have been claiming the interest free loan for up to £1,000. Currently the head cashier only deals with approving and raising the payments through the payroll.

Required:

(a) Discuss the ethical issues that arise in both Cases 1 and 2.

(b) Discuss the role of the company secretary in dealing with the above matters.

(c) Define any policy contribution that should be developed together with measures of internal control.

Answers to end of chapter questions

Chapter 1 – The regulatory framework for the preparation and presentation of financial statements

1.1 Accounting rules provide a basis for recording and reporting financial performance. In assessing the periodic financial performance of the company, there should be a systematic set of procedures that all companies should follow to allow for:
- consistency of accounting estimation and treatment;
- consistency in recording of accounting information;
- comparability between periods and between companies;
- reliability of reported financial reports; and
- timeliness of financial reports.

Accounting rules and principles provide guidance in the treatment of accounting information calculated on an accruals basis. If every company in the world recorded accounting information in its own way, there would be no consistency or reliability in financial reports.

1.2 There are various organisations that directly or indirectly influence the quality and quantity of financial and non-financial information that should be provided:
- *Statutory information* – is required by law. Companies in the UK have to abide by the Companies Act 2006 and provide/disclose certain level of information such as the statement of financial position, statement of comprehensive income, statement of cash flows and the statement of changes to equity as well as explanations to these statements.
- *Regulatory information* – is required on the basis of UK GAAP or IFRS. The same information is provided as statutory law except that IFRS and UK GAAP provides the accounting treatment of certain items and how accounting numbers should be calculated and disclosed.

1.3 With globalisation issues and the cross-border listing of corporations, it is important that there is uniformity in reporting financial reports. The scandals of the past decade have demonstrated that accounting information needs to be regulated to bring about convergence, harmonisation and standardisation in financial reporting.

Investors and other stakeholders who have a vested interest in corporations demand transparency. Regulation of accounting information promotes consistency and reliability in financial reporting and makes companies accountable for their actions.

1.4 There is an argument for allowing market forces to prevail and letting the markets decide what information users require and what information should be provided. It is argued that those companies that provide higher quality of accounting information and are more transparent will attract greater investment. However, time and again history has shown that the market needs certain guidance and regulation to promote transparency and protection for the shareholder and other stakeholders. Simple market forces are not enough to give such protection to stakeholder groups.

1.5 The modern accounting profession is regulated by a mix of national and professional standards. Certain organisations are given legal credibility. Organisations such as the IASB which issues IFRSs have a legal credibility and companies that do not conform to their standards of accounting and disclosure would be in breach of their duties and responsibilities.

The law provides the legal basis for redress and the standards provide a level of protection for relevant stakeholders including those who prepare financial reports. Under EU law, listed companies must conform to IFRS, publish financial reports on the basis of IASB standards in force and make preparations for those standards yet to come into effect.

1.6 Principal–agent theory addresses issues of information asymmetry, which in the context of management of companies' regulation generally means that management knows more about its abilities and effort and about the company than stakeholders.

The development and technique of regulations has long been the subject of academic research. Two basic schools of thought have emerged on regulatory policy, namely, positive theories of regulation and normative theories of regulation.

Positive theories of regulation examine why regulation occurs. These include theories of market power, interest group theories that describe stakeholders' interests in regulation, and theories of corporate opportunism that describe why restrictions on corporate discretion may be necessary for markets to provide efficient services for stakeholders. In general, the conclusions of these theories are that regulation occurs because:

- corporations are interested in overcoming information asymmetries with the stakeholders and in aligning corporate and stakeholder interests;
- stakeholders' want protection from corporate power;
- corporations want protection from rivals; or
- stakeholders want protection from corporate opportunism.

Normative theories of regulation generally conclude that regulators should encourage competition where feasible, minimise the costs of information asymmetries by obtaining information and providing corporations with incentives to improve their performance, provide for price structures that improve economic efficiency and establish regulatory processes that provide for regulation under the law and independence, transparency, predictability, legitimacy, and credibility for the regulatory system.

1.7 Arguments for and against accounting standards

Standards:

- provide a systematic approach to the work of accountants in evaluating accounting numbers;
- help to improve published reports and increase consistency, reliability, comparability and transparency;
- supplement company law with clearer and more consistent figures;
- allow analysts and potential investors to compare and evaluate companies;
- force weaker companies to improve their work;
- provide a legal defence for accountants and strengthen resistance to 'corporate pressure on accountants and auditors';
- provide credibility to the accounting profession which might otherwise be undermined if there are continuing scandals over the extreme subjectivity of some companies' financial statements;
- provide discipline; although some believe that if companies were left to their own devices they would ultimately be disciplined by the financial markets; and
- attempt to alleviate the risk to investors.

Arguments against accounting standards:

- accounting standards are costly and bureaucratic;
- accounting figures (due to their very nature) do not lend themselves to standardisation; industries differ, so do firms; the needs of users vary. Standards may be suitable for the average user, but may not provide enough information for more particular requirements;
- standards can lead to tedious requirements;
- standard setters may bow to political pressure; thus the development of accounting standards may be merely consensus-seeking (e.g. accounting standards could be over-influenced by those parties with easiest access to the standard setters or the most vocal lobbyist);
- standards in themselves could actually reduce professional judgement and be bad for the academic education of accountants (e.g. they might be more interested in what is required to comply with the standard than in investigating the ideal accounting system);
- standards may lull users into a false sense of security (i.e. investors may believe that the accounts are all based on the same specific rules, when in fact, a standard principle may still leave room for different estimates);
- standards may result in adverse allocation effects if they do not take account of possible economic consequences. Accounting standards might result in sub-optimal behaviour to ensure that accounting earnings are not reduced; and

■ standards could result in overload (e.g. if there are too many standards; standards that are too detailed; or standards that are not specific enough).

What is public interest? (This is a normative issue)

The *public interest theory* of accounting is concerned with achieving publicly desired results which, if left to the market, would not be obtained. The main issue of public interest theory is to respond to the demands from the general public with regard to correcting market inefficiencies (i.e. accounting inconsistencies between firms). However, it is difficult to meet the demands of each individual because competition is not formally acknowledged by the regulator or is not coherent. Different stakeholder groups have different requirements.

1.8 In the stakeholder approach to the notion of the corporation, a corporation is seen as a nexus of contracts; hence regulations are needed to create desired behaviour. Regulations cannot capture all that is needed for the best interests of the wider public; however, incremental development in regulations enhances public accountability over time.

The last decade has seen a tremendous surge in financial regulations and the banking crisis in 2008 resulted in a whole host of regulations regarding risk taking and the risk appetite of banks. While some regulatory exercise has been related to past events (e.g. the Sarbanes-Oxley Act 2002 after Enron collapsed) some regulations are indicative of future requirements (e.g. the UK Code on Corporate Governance 2010 which has laid down specific guidelines on boardroom responsibilities and behaviour).

1.9 Arguments for and against regulation in accounting have been discussed in Question 1.7. However, the main themes in Questions 1–6 suggest that accounting as a social behaviour requires monitoring and control to protect various groups.

1.10 It cannot be said that regulators are disinterested parties; however, regulation can arise from a number of points of view and for a number of reasons. It could be argued that what was needed yesterday to regulate corporate behaviour may not be needed today. Nevertheless, the development of accounting standards and the harmonisation and standardisation exercise and globalisation issues suggest regulation is developed for social benefit and on an ad hoc basis. However, a certain amount of regulation is borne out of past events that have had a public bearing.

The need for regulation can at times emanate from within a profession representing different aspects of social behaviour. Interested parties that have a stake in the efficient running of a profession develop, or work towards, systematic procedures that account for the majority of stakeholder interests.

Chapter 2 – The conceptual framework for the preparation and presentation of financial statements

2.1 (a) Statement of income and comprehensive income.
(b) Statement of financial position.
(c) Statement of cash flows.
(d) Statement of changes to equity.

2.2 (a) Assets.

2.3 (c) Equity.

2.4 (d) Historical cost, fair value, and recoverable amounts.

2.5 (a) Goodwill.
(b) Intellectual property.
(c) Patents.

2.6 The term net realisable value (NRV) refers to the net amount that a company expects to realise from the sale of inventory. Net realisable value is the estimated selling price in the normal course of business less estimated costs to complete and estimated costs to make a sale.

Chapter 3 – Financial accounting and the preparation of financial reports

3.1 There are four principal statements that a company is required to publish and include:
- statement of comprehensive income;
- statement of financial position;
- statement of cash flows; and
- statement of changes in equity.

The purpose of the statement of comprehensive income is to show the financial performance of the company based on inputs and outputs and the profits that transpire.

The statement of financial position demonstrates to the user the assets and liabilities and equity of a company at any particular moment in time usually the year end.

The statement of cash flows shows the cash flow in and out of the company through three main headings: cash flow from operating activities; cash flow from investing activities and cash flow from financing activities.

The statement of changes in equity shows all changes in owner's equity for a period of time.

3.2 (a) The carrying amount of retained earnings at the beginning and the end of the period.
(b) The carrying amount of total equity at the beginning and the end of the period.
(c) The carrying amount of each component of equity at the beginning and the end of the period separately disclosing changes resulting from:
(i) profit or loss;
(ii) each item of comprehensive income; and
(iii) the amounts of investments by, and dividends and other distributions to, owners.

Answer: (c).

3.3

Sigma plc

Statement of financial position as at 31 December 2011

Assets	£'000
Non-current assets	
Property, plant and equipment	900
Brand	100
Capitalised development expenditure	200
Investments in subsidiaries	200
Other receivables (due to be received 2014)	300
Goodwill	400
	2,100
Current assets	
Inventory	300
Trade and other receivables	950
Derivative financial assets (short-tem)	100

Cash and cash equivalents		200
		1,550
Total assets		3,650
Equity and liabilities		
Equity		
Ordinary share capital (£1 ord. shares) *(see W1)*		2,390
Capital redemption reserve		80
Revaluation reserve		150
Retained earnings		300
Total equity		2,920
Non-current liabilities		
10% Bonds – 2015		60
Deferred tax		100
Provision for decommissioning of nuclear plant in 2015		50
Retirement benefit obligations		120
		330
Current liabilities		
Trade payables		300
Taxation		100
		400
Total equity and liabilities		3,650
(W1)		
Total assets		3,650
Non-current liabilities		330
Current liabilities		400
(A)		730
Equity items:		
Capital redemption reserve		80
Revaluation reserve		150
Retained earnings		300
(B)		530
Total equity and liabilities (excluding share capital)		1,260
Share capital – £1 ordinary shares: £3,650 – £1,260		2,390

3.4 Opal Ltd

Statement of comprehensive income for the year ended 31 December 2012

	£'000	
Revenue	5,100	
Cost of sales	–2,480	
Gross profit	2,620	
Distribution costs	545	
Administrative expenses	971	W1 = 924 + 60 – 13
Profit from operations	1104	
Interest payable	12	W2 = 200 x 6%
Profit before tax	1092	
Tax	300	Note 9
Profit for the year	792	

Opal Ltd

Statement of changes in equity for the year ended 31 December 2012

	Share Capital	Share premium	Retained Earnings	Total
Balance 1/1/2012	1750	250	850	2850
SOCI			792	792
Dividends			–35	–35
New issue of shares	250	200		450
	2000	450	1607	4057

Opal Ltd

Statement of financial position at 31 December 2012

	£'000	£'000	
Non-current assets			
Equipment		4,310	W2 = 3890 + 600
Current assets			
Inventory	270		Note 6
Trade receivables	208		
			Note 3 (W4 = 26,000 / 2 =
Prepayments	13	491	13,000)
		4,801	
Equity and liabilities			
Share capital	2,000		Note 7 & 8 (W5 = 2,200 - 200)
Share premium	450		Note 7 & 8 (W6 = 250 + 200)
Retained earnings	1,607	4,057	
Non-current liabilities			
6% Debenture Loan	200	200	
Current liabilities			
Trade and other payables	229		W8 = 212 + 12 15
Income tax	300	544	Note 9
		4,801	

(a) IFRS 3 defines fair value as: 'the amount for which an asset could be exchanged, or a liability settled, between knowledgeable, willing parties in an arm's length agreement'.

(b) Measurement and recognition of revenues – IAS 18 prescribes the measure and recognition of revenue. The measurement of revenue is provided in IAS 18 as:

Revenue should be measured at the fair value of the consideration received or receivable. An exchange for goods or services of a similar nature and value is not regarded as a transaction that generates revenue. However, exchanges for dissimilar items are regarded as generating revenue.

Recognition of revenues – IAS 18 provides an explanation of revenue as:

Recognition, as defined in the IASB Framework, means incorporating an item that meets the definition of revenue (above) in the income statement when it meets the following criteria:

■ it is probable that any future economic benefit associated with the item of revenue will flow to the entity, and
■ the amount of revenue can be measured with reliability.

(c)   Other comprehensive income is defined as gains or losses on non-current assets that have yet to be realised. These items may include:
   –   gains or losses on foreign currency translations;
   –   changes in the fair value of available-for-sale financial assets;
   –   actuarial gains and losses arising on a defined benefit pension plan;
   –   revaluations of property, plant and equipment; and
   –   changes in the fair value of a financial instrument in a cash-flow hedge.

(d)   Reporting entities – An entity that carries on business and conducts financial transaction is classified as a reporting entity and is required to file accounts with at least the tax authority (HMRC). These include, sole traders, partnerships, clubs and societies and limited companies. In the latter case there may be other requirements such as publication of annual reports (for listed companies) and the submission of accounts to Companies House.

Chapter 4 – Income statement analysis and accounting policies

4.1   An entity shall present its total comprehensive income for a period either:
   (a)   in a single *statement of comprehensive income*, in which case the statement of comprehensive income presents all items of income and expense recognised in the period; or
   (b)   in two statements; an *income statement* and a statement of comprehensive income; in which case the income statement presents all items of income and expense recognised in the period except those that are recognised in total comprehensive income outside of *profit or loss* as permitted or required by this IFRS.

Example:

Profit for the year	500,000
Other comprehensive income:	
Gain on currency translation	20,000
Change in the fair value of hedging instruments, net of tax	3,000
Other comprehensive income for the year, net of tax	23,000
Total comprehensive income for the year	523,000

4.2   Due to quantity or value, not all operating segments need to be separately reported. Operating segments only need to be reported if they exceed quantitative thresholds.
Quantitative thresholds (IFRS 8 para 13)
Information on an operating segment should be reported separately if:
■   Reported revenue (external and inter-segment) is 10% or more of the combined revenue of all operating segments.
■   The absolute amount of the segment's reported profit or loss is 10% or more of the greater of:
   –   the combined reported profit of all operating segments that did not report a loss, and
   –   the combined loss of all operating segments that reported a loss;
■   The segment's assets are 10% or more of the combined assets of all operating segments.
Two or more operating segments may be combined (aggregated) and reported as one if certain conditions are satisfied. The objective of this Standard is to establish principles for reporting financial information by segment to help users of financial statements:
■   better understand the enterprise's past performance;
■   better assess the enterprise's risks and returns; and
■   make more informed judgements about the enterprise as a whole.

4.3   For the year to 31 December 2010, Radar plc's depreciation charge should be calculated by dividing the carrying amount of the asset at the date of the change in estimate by the remaining useful life of the asset as below:

	£'000
Carrying amount at 1 Jan 2010	30,000
Depreciation for 2010 (W1)	−5,000
	25,000

W1: £30,000,000/4 = £7,500,000

The PPE is six years old – with a new unexpired life of ten years = four years left.

4.4 Buffalo

Statement of comprehensive income of Buffalo Ltd as at 31 December 2010

	Copiers	Paper	Printing	HO	Total
	£'000	£'000	£'000	£'000	£'000
Revenue	611	395	104	–	1,110
Less: Cost of sales	384	146	44	–	574
Administration expenses	47	9	18	22	96
Distribution costs	101	17	24	–	142
Finance costs	6	1	1	2	10
Net profit	73	222	17	−24	288

Statement of financial position of Buffalo Ltd as at 31 December 2010

Assets	Copiers	Paper	Printing	HO	Total
Non-current assets at book value	1012	767	432	232	2,443
Current assets					0
Inventories	31	14	12	–	57
Receivables	23	12	9	–	44
Bank	148	46	31	–	225
Total assets	1,214	839	484	232	2,769
Equity and liabilities					
Equity					
Share capital				1,000	1,000
Retained earnings				1,449	1,449
					0
Non-current liabilities					0
Long-term borrowing	210	–	–	–	210
Current liabilities					0
Payables	32	20	16	10	78
Short-term borrowing	13	7	4	8	32
Total equity and liabilities	255	27	20	2,467	2,769

4.5 An entity must change its accounting policy only if the change is:
- required by standard accounting practice; or
- results in the financial statements providing more relevant and reliable information about the entity's financial position, financial performance or cash flows.

Usually, a change in accounting policy is applied *retrospectively* to all periods presented in the financial statements as if the new accounting policy has always been applied. This means that the brought-forward carrying value of the asset or liability and retained profits must both be appropriately adjusted.

4.6 (a)   IAS 8 defines an item as material in the following circumstances. Omissions or mis-statements of items are material if they could, by their size or nature, individually or collectively influence the economic decisions of users taken on the basis of the financial statements. Materiality depends on the size and nature of the omission or misstatement judged in the surrounding circumstances. The size or nature of the item, or a combination of both, could be a determining factor

(b)   Income statement for Hawkestone Ltd for year to 30 June 2012

	£'000
Revenue	74,400
Cost of sales (Note 1)	−50,240
Gross profit	24,160
Distribution costs	−7,200
Administrative expenses	−12,400
Profit from continuing operations	4,560
Closure of manufacturing division (note 2)	−14,600
Loss for period	−10,040

Statement of changes in equity of Hawkestone Ltd for year to 30 June 2012

	Share capital	Share premium account	Retained Earnings	Total
	£'000	£'000	£'000	£'000
Balance at 1 July 2011	20,000		25,200	45,200
Prior period error (note 3)			−4,280	−4,280
Changes in equity during the year				
Loss for the period			−10,040	−10,040
Issues share capital				
Balance 30 June 2012	10,000	18,000		28,000
	30,000	18,000	10,880	58,880

4.7   A non-recurring item is a gain or loss found on a company's income statement that is not expected to occur regularly (e.g. litigation costs, write-offs of bad debt or worthless assets, employee litigation costs, and repair costs for damage caused by natural disasters).

Analysts seeking to measure the sustainable profitability of a company typically disregard non-recurring items, as these items are not expected to affect the company's future net income. If non-recurring items have a significant effect on the company's finances, they should be listed, net of tax, on a separate line below operating profit from continuing operations. Additionally, narratives to the accounts should provide further analysis and explanation as to the nature of the non-recurring items.

4.8   IFRS 5 determines the basis for classification for an asset held for sale and suggests that, in general, the following conditions must be met for an asset (or 'disposal group') to be classified as held for sale:

■ management is committed to a plan to sell;
■ the asset is available for immediate sale;
■ an active programme to locate a buyer is initiated;
■ the sale is highly probable, within 12 months of classification as held for sale (subject to limited exceptions);
■ the asset is being actively marketed for sale at a sales price reasonable in relation to its fair value; and
■ actions required to complete the plan indicate that it is unlikely that plan will be significantly changed or withdrawn.

In essence, once an asset has been declared as held for sale; it must be transferred to current assets and disposed off during the next 12 months.

4.9 Discontinued operations represent divisions within a business that have either ceased operations due to a lack of profitability or have been sold. This may be due to the fact that the operation is unprofitable, or a change of business direction. IFRS 5 requires listed companies to report earnings per share of all divisions in its business, including discontinued operations.

IFRS 5 indicates the definition of discontinued operations as:

A discontinued operation is a component of an entity that either has been disposed of or is classified as held for sale, and:

- represents either a separate major line of business or a geographical area of operations, and
- is part of a single co-ordinated plan to dispose of a separate major line of business or geographical area of operations, or
- is a subsidiary acquired exclusively with a view to resale and the disposal involves loss of control.

4.10 IFRS 8 defines an operating segment as a component of an entity:

- that engages in business activities from which it may earn revenues and incur expenses (including revenues and expenses relating to transactions with other components of the same entity);
- whose operating results are reviewed regularly by the entity's chief operating decision maker to make decisions about resources to be allocated to the segment and assess its performance; and
- for which discrete financial information is available.

Chapter 5 – Valuing assets and liabilities, differences in accounting policies, fair presentation and the directors' report

5.1 An *asset* is defined as a resource controlled by the entity as a result of past events and from which future economic benefits are expected to flow. Assets may be tangible physical items or intangible items with no physical form and include:

- *Plant and machinery* – tangible assets typically with more than one year of economic use.
- *Land and buildings* – tangible resources typically held by an entity for many years.
- *Investments* – could be short- or long-term such as investments in other entities with a view to adequate returns.

A *liability* is defined as a present obligation of the entity arising from past events, the settlement of which is expected to result in an outflow from the entity of resources embodying economic benefits. On a company's statement of financial position, a liability may be a legal debt or an accrual, which is an estimate of an obligation. Examples of liabilities are:

- *Short and long-term bank loans:* These are an obligation on the entity which must be settled sometime in the future.
- *Taxation:* A present obligation by the entity to settle a legal requirement.
- *Trade payables:* Amounts due to suppliers which must be settled normally in the current financial year or which in a short period of time according to agreed terms.

5.2 The recognition of revenue is the process of recording revenue in an accounting period under one of the various methods. In the period of revenue recognition, related expenses should be matched to revenue. Revenue is recognised at the time of sales; however, other methods of recognising revenue are provided in IAS 18 as:

Recognition, as defined in the IASB Framework, means incorporating an item that meets the definition of revenue in the income statement when it meets the following criteria:

- it is probable that any future economic benefit associated with the item of revenue will flow to the entity; and
- the amount of revenue can be measured with reliability.

5.3 The term *impairment* is usually associated with non-current assets that have a market value that has decreased significantly. For example, a packaging plant may have a carrying value of £20m after five years of a ten-year useful life. However, new technology may have caused the market value of the packaging plant to drop by 10% of the closing carrying value. Hence the fair value should be reflected in the statement of financial position as:

- £20m x 90% = £18m; Hence the new carrying value of the packaging plant in the sixth year is £18m. On the basis that the undiscounted future cash flows from the asset (including the sale amount) are less than the asset's carrying amount, an impairment loss must be reported.
- The amount of the impairment loss is measured by subtracting the asset's fair value from its carrying value. IAS 36 provides comprehensive guidance on impairment of assets.

5.4 (a) Going concern

This is the idea that a company will continue to operate for the foreseeable future and will not go out of business and liquidate its assets. For this to happen, the company must be able to generate and/or raise enough resources to stay operational. However, as an accounting concept, auditors will usually issue a going concern assessment for the next 12 months. In the next period audit the going concern will be re-tested by the audit and a new view disclosed.

(b) Accruals

Cash is a very weak measure of company's performance. The accruals method requires that revenue and expenses be matched in the period they are incurred irrespective of when cash is received or payments made.

5.5 Sales or revenue should only be recognised on a 'faithful representation' basis. The faithful representation concept states that profits should not be recognised until a sales transaction has been completed (but cash need not have been transferred). In addition, a cautious view is observed for future problems and costs of the business. Revenue should be provided for as soon as a transaction has occurred, not on the basis that a transaction is expected to occur.

Liabilities should be recognised and provided for in the accounts as soon as there is a reasonable indication that such liabilities will be incurred.

5.6 Directors are solely responsible to the shareholders. The role of directors is one of stewardship. Directors are responsible for managing or, under some statutes, supervising, the management of, the corporation. If the board of directors is dissatisfied with company's management, its recourse is through the company's CEO. If the CEO is not performing as expected, the board may replace him.

Shareholders make a financial investment in the corporation, which entitles those with voting shares to elect the directors. Shareholders do not normally have any right to be directly involved in company management. Their connection to company management is typically via the board of directors. If shareholders are not satisfied with the performance of the directors, they may remove the directors or refuse to re-elect them.

Directors have a duty to publish financial reports that depict the underlying economic reality of the company. This allows shareholders to make informed economic decisions and vote at the annual general meeting how they see fit. This signals either their satisfaction or dissatisfaction with the progress of the company.

5.7 (c) Recognise the reduction as an impairment indicator and carry out an impairment test.

5.8   Lease payments

Year	Loan	Repay	Capital	Interest	Loan O/S
0	38,211	0	38,211	0	761,789
1	761,789	230,010	169,067	60,943	592,722
2	592,722	230,010	182,592	47,418	410,130
3	410,130	230,010	197,200	32,810	212,972
4	212,972	230,010	212,972	17,038	0

Depreciation charge

Year	Opening value	Depn charge	Closing value
1	804,000	201,000	603,000
2	603,000	201,000	402,000
3	402,000	201,000	201,000
4	201,000	201,000	0

The opening balance of lease charges are: £800,000 - £38,211 = £761,789
In the each year of the lease the company will make a depreciation charge of £201,000; however, in the first year, the procurement cost of £4,000 will be capitalised, hence the total cost of purchase of the lease will show a balance of £761,789.

5.9   (a)   The initial cost of tangible non-current assets should be measured according to the provisions of IAS16:

An item of property, plant and equipment should initially be recorded at cost. Cost includes all costs necessary to bring the asset to working condition for its intended use. This would include not only its original purchase price, but also costs of site preparation, delivery and handling, installation, related professional fees for architects and engineers.

(b)   The circumstances in which subsequent expenditure on those assets should be capitalised are:

- that expenditure provides an enhancement of the economic benefits of the tangible non-current asset in excess of its previously assessed standard of performance;
- a component of an asset that has been treated separately for depreciation purposes is replaced or restored; or
- subsequent expenditure relates to a major inspection or overhaul that restores the economic benefits that have already been consumed and reflected in depreciation.

IAS 16's requirements regarding the revaluation of non-current assets and the accounting treatment of surpluses and deficits on revaluation and gains and losses on disposal provide that:

Depreciation should be on a systematic basis over the useful economic life of the asset. However, a periodic review of the fair value of an asset must be carried out by the directors and disclosed in the financial reports.

If on fair value inspection an asset appreciates in value, the difference between the fair value and the carrying value must be credited to reserve and debited to property, plant and equipment or another class of non-current assets.

Any subsequent loss in value should first debit against the revaluation reserve. If the whole amount can be charged to the revaluation reserve, no entry is needed in the statement of income.

If the revaluation reserve is less than the impaired value, the revaluation reserve is depleted first, then any difference is charged to the income statement.

On disposal of an asset, any gains or losses on disposal are charged to the income statement.

5.10 The Companies Act 2006 places a fiduciary duty on company directors to discharge their duties in a faithful manner. The UK Code on Corporate Governance 2010 provides extensive guidance on boardroom behaviour and ostensibly places a detailed burden on the board to act in a transparent manner and to have in place processes and procedures of internal control that secure the asset of the firm and provide basis for transparent reporting.

Directors have a primary responsibility to prepare the accounts and report to the shareholders, who own the business, on how well the company has performed financially in the accounting period.

The *auditors'* responsibility follows on from this; they must check these accounts and report to the same shareholders whether or not the directors have accounted fairly and truthfully. In the event of inconsistency between the director's report and the auditor's financial review, the auditor has the right to report the inconsistency to the directors under the Companies Act 2006, and require the situation to be corrected.

5.11

Year	Loan	Repay	Capital	Interest	Loan O/S
1	1,500,000	160,000	85,000	75,000	1,415,000
2	1,415,000	160,000	89,250	70,750	1,325,750
3	1,325,750	160,000	93,712	66,288	1,232,038
4	1,232,038	160,000	98,398	61,602	1,133,640
5	1,133,639	160,000	103,318	56,682	1,030,321
6	1,030,321	160,000	108,484	51,516	921,837
7	921,837	160,000	113,908	46,092	807,929
8	807,929	160,000	119,604	40,396	688,326
9	688,326	160,000	125,584	34,416	562,742
10	562,742	160,000	131,863	28,137	430,879
11	430,879	160,000	138,456	21,544	292,423
12	292,423	160,000	145,379	14,621	147,044
13	147,044	154,396	147,044	7,352	0

The final instalment payment is reduced to £154,396 as per the question.

Chapter 6 – Purpose of the cash flow statement

6.1 (b) Taxation paid.

6.2 (a) Managing activities.

6.3 Cash flows are not a measure of a company's profit, but represent the cash flow in and out of a company due to its revenues and expenses and cash flow from investing and financing activities. Company profit takes into account all goods and services received but not paid for. These are recorded under the accruals concept thus facilitating a profit.

Cash flow indicates a company's ability to meet its financial obligations. Positive cash flow enables a company to meet payroll, pay suppliers, meet debt repayments and make distributions to owners. Cash can be generated by operations, or provided by lenders or owners. Profits provide the basis for a company to measure firm performance against set criteria and expectation and plan investment activity or rationalise operations to meet economic environment.

6.4 (a) Increase in inventory leads to a cash outflow since payment has been made for the increase in inventory.
  (b) Decrease in payables also leads to a cash outflow since the creditors have been paid.
  (c) Decrease in receivables means an inflow of cash as we have reduced our debtors.
  (d) The increase in market value of a company's shares directly does not have any effect on in/outflow of cash unless new shares are issues by the company.
  (e) A gain is an accounting entry and does not have an impact on the cash flow per se; however, cash inflow will be realised on disposal of assets.
  (f) When shares are issued, these represent financing activity; hence cash inflow will be recorded under this activity.

6.5

	£m	
Opening receivables	20	
Credit sales for the year	75	
	95	
Cash received from debtors	83	Balancing figure
Closing receivables	12	

Cash received from trade receivables is: £83 million during the year.

6.6

	£m	
Opening payables	12	
Credit purchases for the year	36	
	48	
Cash paid from debtors	30	Balancing figure
Closing Payables	18	

Cash paid to creditors: £30 million during the year.

6.7 (a) Depreciation – this is a calculated charge over the useful life of an asset.
  (b) Impairment charge – this is a non-cash charge to the income statement this does not have a cash flow impact.
  (c) Gains and losses – are also non-cash movements as these are computed profit or loss on disposal of an asset

6.8 Irrespective of the gains or losses incurred on disposal of the asset, the only item that will be recorded in the cash flow statement under investing activity is the £120,000 received on disposal of the asset.
  However, the statement of comprehensive income will record the following profit or loss:

	£'000
Cost of purchase	500
Accumulated depreciation	400
	100
Cash on disposal	120
Profit made on disposal	20

The profit made on disposal of the asset is £20,000.

6.9

	£'000
Profit	20,000
Add: depreciation	500
	20,500
Decrease in inventory	800
Increase in Receivables	−200
Decrease in Payables	−400
Cash from operating activities	20,700

6.10 Sarah Ltd – Statement of cash flow to 31 December 2011

Cash flow from operating activities	Item	£
Profit before tax		302,000
Add: depreciation	1	50,000
Increase in inventory	2	−117,000
Increase in trade receivables	3	−24,000
Decrease in trade payables	4	−83,000
Tax paid	5	−24,000
Net cash flow from operating activities		104,000
Cash flow from investing activities		
Purchase of property, plant and equipment		0
Disposal of property, plant and equipment		0
Net cash flow from investing activities		0
Share issue	6	48,000
Dividends paid (per note 1)		−137,000
Repayment of long-term loan	7	−18,800
Net cash flow from financing activities		−107,800
Net increase/(decrease) in cash and cash equivalents		−3,800
Opening cash and cash equivalents		−3,200
Closing cash and cash equivalents		−7,000

Calculations:

Item			
1	Depreciation:		
	Opening depreciation	180,000	
	Balancing charge	50,000	
	Closing depreciation	230,000	
2	Inventory:		
	Opening inventory	45,000	
	Balancing movement	30,000	
	Closing inventory	75,000	
3	Trade receivables:		
	Opening Trade Receivables	120,000	
	Balancing movement	24,000	
	Closing Trade Receivables	144,000	
4	Payables:		
	Opening Payables	170,000	
	Balancing movement	−83,000	
	Closing Payables	87,000	

5	Tax paid:	
	Opening tax	18,000
	Tax charge to income statement	36,000
	Balancing movement	24,000
	Closing tax	30,000
6	Share issue:	
	Shares issue: £1.20 x 40,000	48,000
7	Loan:	
	Opening loan balance	84,800
	Balancing movement	–18,800
	Closing loan balance	66,000

6.11 (1)   Plumbus Ltd – Statement of Cash Flow to 30 September 2011

Cash from operating activities	£
Profit for the year	136,000
Depreciation	102,000
Inventory	4,000
Receivables	7,000
Loss on disposal	2,000
Payables	–48,000
Tax charge to IS	54,000
Tax paid	–43,000
Interest expense	8,000
	222,000
Cash from investing activities	
Property, Plant and Equipment (PPE)	–132,000
	–132,000
Cash from financing activities	
Share issue	54,000
Long-term loan	59,000
Dividends paid	–113,000
	0
Cash flows for period	90,000
Opening cash and cash equivalents	54,000
Closing cash and cash equivalents	144,000

Calculation:	
Depreciation	
Opening	188,000
Disposal	–30,000
Depreciation for the year	102,000
	260,000
Property, Plant and Equipment (PPE)	
Opening PPE	418,000
Additions	132,000
Disposal	–40,000
Revaluation reserves	10,000
Closing PPE	520,000

PPE disposal	
Book value	40,000
Depreciation	−30,000
Net Book Value	10,000
Sold	8,000
Loss on disposal	2,000
Taxation	
Opening	11,000
For the year	54,000
	65,000
Paid	43,000
Closing	22,000
Dividends	
Opening retained profit	33,000
Profit for the year	136,000
	169,000
Dividends paid in cash	113,000
Closing retained profit	56,000

(2)   The company appears to be in a stable financial condition. However, the debt: equity ratio (£224,000: £248,000) appears to be close to the company's debt capacity. This means any further borrowings may see costs of borrowing rise.

The company appears to be managing its payables and receivables well. However, it seems this company is an SME and in its growth stage, so it should review its supplier and customer policy on credit received and allowed to increase working capital and liquidity in the company.

The company could also consider raising both its shareholding and further long-term capital through a new share issue to private investors. Plumbus is a small limited company and may not be able to offer its shares to the general investor.

Chapter 7 – Group accounting

7.1	Consolidated statement of financial position	£'000	£'000
	Goodwill on acquisition	6,000 − [1,000 + 1,720 + 1,200]	2,080
	Other net assets at book value	7,200 + 3,700 + 1,200	12,100
			14,180
	Financed by:		
	Ordinary share capital (£1 shares)		10,000
	Retained profit at 1 November 2009		2,940
	Net profit for 2009/10	260 + 980	1,240
			14,180

7.2

Goodwill	£'000	£'000
Consideration		2,500
Share capital	1,800	
Pre-acquisition profits 1 Oct 2010: 600 x 2/3	400	
Goodwill		300
Minority interest: 3,600 x 1/3		1,200
Post-acquisition profits: 300 x 2/3		200

7.3 Club holds 100% of the equity shares of Diamonds and 75% of the shares of Hearts

Workings	Total equity	At acquisition	Since acquisition	Minority interest
	£	£	£	£
Diamonds				
Share capital	80,000	80,000		
Retained profits:				
At acquisition date	33,200	33,200		
Since acquisition	11,400		11,400	
	124,600	113,200	11,400	
Hearts				
Share capital	40,000	30,000		10,000
Retained profits:				
At acquisition date	7,200	5,400		1,800
Since acquisition	–13,600		–10,200	–3,400
	33,600	35,400	–10,200	8,400
Totals (Diamond and Hearts)	158,200	148,600	1,200	8,400
Total price paid, £126,000 + £44,000		170,000		
Goodwill on acquisition		21,400		
Retained profits, Clubs Ltd			43,000	
Goodwill impairment				
(21,400/4)		–5,350	–5,350	
		16,050	38,850	

Consolidated statement of financial position Clubs Ltd and Subsidiaries at 31 December 2010

	£	£
Goodwill		16,050
Non-current at carrying value		488,200
Current assets	171,000	
Less: Current liabilities	178,000	
Net current assets		−7,000
Total assets less current liabilities		497,250
Less: 15% debentures		250,000
		247,250
Financed by:		
Share capital (£1 shares)		200,000
Retained profits		38,850
		238,850
Minority interest		8,400
		247,250

7.4 In the process of preparing consolidated financial statements, it is necessary to eliminate intra-group balances and transactions such as plant and machinery, purchase and sales of inventories and other assets between parent and subsidiary. In many cases, the separate financial statements of a parent company and a subsidiary include amounts of inter-company items that should be offset or eliminated. Before preparing the consolidated financial statements, accounting entries should be prepared to bring the balances up to date and to eliminate the inter-company balances.
Company A will have to adjust its profits figure by following the accounting treatment for UNREALISED profits:
- Reduce the retained earnings of Company A by 25% (the mark-up) or 20% of the selling price.
- Reduce the inventory of Company B by 25% (the mark-up) or 20% of the price.
The above adjustments ONLY apply to unsold inventory

7.5 Step 1: Group structure: 70% Parent, 30% NCI.

Step 2: Calculate the consideration transferred
Given in the question   265,000

Step 3: Calculate fair value of net assets at the date of acquisition and at the reporting date

	Fair value of net assets	
	£	£
	39,814	40,178
Share capital	100,000	100,000
Share premium	50,000	50,000
Retained earnings	50,000	100,000
Fair value adjustment	20,000	20,000

Intangible non-current assets written off	−10,000	−30,000
	210,000	240,000

Step 4: Calculate the post acquisition profit of Beta

Fair value of NCI assets at the reporting date	240,000
Less fair value of NCI assets at the date of acquisition	210,000
Post-acquisition profit	30,000

This will be shared between the group and the NCI as follows:

Group (70% x 30,000)	21,000
NCI (30% X 30,000)	9,000
	30,000

Step 5: Calculate the goodwill at the date of acquisition and at the reporting date

Consideration transferred	265,000
Fair value of NCI (30% x 100,000 x 2.5)	75,000
	340,000
Less fair value of net assets at acquisition date (from step 2)	210,000
Goodwill arising on acquisition	130,000
Less goodwill impairment	65,000
Goodwill at 31 December 2009	65,000

Goodwill impairment will be split between the group and the NCI as follows:

Group (70% x 65,000)	45,500
NCI (30% x 65,000)	19,500
	65,000

Step 6: Calculate the NCI at the reporting date

Fair value of NCI at the date of acquisition	75,000
Add NCI's share of the post acquisition profit of Beta (step 4)	9,000
Less NCI's share of goodwill impairment	−19,500
NCI at the reporting date	64,500

Step 7: Calculate the consolidated retained earnings

Alpha's retained earnings	100,000
Add group's share of the post acquisition profit of Beta (step 4)	21,000
Less unrealised profit on inventory (20/120 x 20,000 x 1/2)	−1,667
Less group's share of goodwill impairment (step 5)	−45,500
	73,833

Alpha Group

Consolidated statement of financial position at 31 December 2011

	£	£
Non-current assets		
Goodwill	65,000	
Property plant and equipment (500,000 + 70,000 + 20,000)	590,000	
Investments (290,000 + 60,000 − 265,000)	85,000	
	740,000	

Current assets

Inventory (100,000 + 50,000 – 1,667)	148,333	
Trade receivable (150,000 + 100,000 – 15,000)	235,000	
Bank (30,000 + 20,000 + 5,000)	55,000	
		438,333
Total assets		1,178,333
Equity and liabilities		
Share capital		700,000
Share premium		140,000
Consolidated retained earnings		73,833
		913,833
Non-controlling interest		64,500
		978,333
Current liabilities		
Trade payables (90,000 + 60,000 – 10,000)	140,000	
Accruals	60,000	200,000
		1,178,333

7.6 The parent entity concept considers the group to consist of the net assets of the parent and all its subsidiaries with the non-controlling interest being a liability of the group.

The effects of the preparation of consolidated financial statements are:

- the non-controlling is classified as liability; and
- the effects of intra-group transactions are proportionally adjusted for.

According to IFRS 10: 'Control of an investee arises when an investor is exposed, or has rights, to variable returns from its involvement with the investee and has the ability to affect those returns through its power over the investee'.

An investor controls an investee if, and only if, the investor has *all of* the following elements: [IFRS 10:7]

- power over the investee (i.e. the investor has existing rights that gives it the ability to direct the relevant activities (the activities that significantly affect the investee's returns));
- exposure or rights to variable returns from its involvement with the investee; and
- the ability to use its power over the investee to affect the amount of the investor's returns.

7.7

Profit	26
Add:	
Depreciation	33
Taxation	12
	71
Working capital movement:	
Inventories: 107 – 101	6
Receivables: 86 – 99	–13
Payables: 72 – 52	20
Tax paid during the year	–5
Cash flow from operating activities	79

The item of purchase of non-current asset will come under 'investing activities' and will not be disclosed in cash flow from operating activities.

7.8 Under the gross equity method the joint ventures should receive the same treatment as that set out for associates. The investor's consolidated cash flow statement should include dividends received from associates as a separate item between operating activities and returns on investments and servicing of finance. Any other cash flows between the investor and its associates should be included under the appropriate cash flow heading for the activity giving rise to the cash flow. None of the other cash flows of the associates should be included.

Therefore, an entity which reports a joint venture interest using the equity method includes in its consolidated cash flow statement the cash flow in respect of its investments in the jointly controlled entity, and distributions and other payments or receipts between it and the jointly controlled entity. For example 'Distributions from joint ventures' should be included under the heading 'Cash flow from investing activities'.

Chapter 8 – Analysis and interpretation of accounts 1

8.1 Alternative theories exist that attempt to explain the nature and characteristics of the modern corporation. However, in contrast to the agency theory, stewardship theory suggests that, left to their own devices, managers will act responsibly to maximise shareholder wealth.

Stewardship, therefore, has a pivotal role in managing the affairs of a company. Management will select the best strategies given the limited resources of the firm and, within the context of those limited resources managers will attempt to increase the value of the firm. This basically means managers have custody of the firm's assets and in the presence of competing demands will select the options that maximise returns.

8.2 Ratio analysis is a form of financial statement analysis that is used to obtain a quick indication of a firm's financial performance in several key areas. The ratios are categorised as short-term solvency, debt management, asset management, profitability, and market value.

As a tool, ratio analysis possesses several important features. The data, provided by financial statements, is readily available. The computation of ratios facilitates the comparison of firms which differ in size. Ratios can be used to compare a firm's financial performance with the industry average. They can also be used as a form of trend analysis to identify areas where performance has improved or deteriorated over time.

Because ratio analysis is based on accounting information, its effectiveness is limited by the distortions which arise in financial statements (e.g. historical cost accounting and inflation). Therefore, it should only be used as a first step in financial analysis, to obtain a quick indication of a firm's performance and to identify areas which need to be investigated further.

8.3 Top of Form

Bottom of Form

There are three main ratios that can be used to measure the profitability of a business:

1   The gross profit margin.
2   The net profit margin.
3   Return on Capital Employed (ROCE).

The gross profit margin

This measures the gross profit of the business as a proportion of the sales revenue.

The net profit margin

This measures the net profit of the business as a proportion of the sales revenue.

Return on Capital Employed (ROCE)

This is often referred to as the 'primary accounting ratio' and it expresses the annual percentage return that an investor would receive on their capital.

8.4 The liquidity ratios are measured using the current ratio and the quick ratio. The current ratio is current assets divided by current liabilities. The quick ratio measures liquidity in a company by excluding inventory (stock) from the current ratio:

(a)

	2010	2011
Current ratio	695	760
	505	360
Current ratio	1.4	2.1
Quick ratio	695 − 240	760 − 180
	505	360
Quick ratio	0.9	1.6

(b) The two ratios suggest that Roadster Ltd has improved its liquidity position over the two-year period from 2010 to 2011. The current ratio has gone up from 1.4 to 2.1 suggesting the company has been efficient in its use of current assets.

The quick ratio has also gone up from 0.9 to 1.6, an increase of 78%, suggesting that the company has been highly efficient in current asset management.

8.5 (a) Ratio workings

Ratio	2011	2012
Gross profit margin	35%	32%
Operating profit margin	18%	13%
Return on capital employed	34%	24%
4 Gearing	25%	19%
5 Stock turnover days	37 days	56 days
6 Current ratio	6.3	4.8
7 Acid test	5.0	3.8
8 Trade receivables collection period	91 days	154 days
9 Trade payables payment period	29 days	51 days

(b) Comments on company performance – Brent Ltd

The highlights from the ratio analysis suggest the company has not performed as well in 2012 as it did in 2011.

The gross profit and operating profit ratios indicate a decline in profitability. This argument is strengthened by the fact that ROCE has declined from 34% in 2009 to 24% in 2012.

It appears the business has seen a decline in 2012. The inventory/turnover ratio suggests that in 2012, the inventory replacement has been 6.5 times rather than the 9.75 times in 2011. This argument is supported by the current and quick ratio which has declined considerably over the two trading years.

Since the gearing ratio has declined from 25% in 2011 to 19% in 2012, this suggests that the company did not invest its profits in new investments as the earnings for 2012 have been transferred to its reserve with no reduction in the debentures liability.

The trade receivables collection period has significantly increased. This may cause the company some cash flow problems unless the situation is addressed and debtors are properly managed.

The payables payment period has also increased considerably and this may create issues with procuring purchases on credit term. Again, this needs to be managed efficiently otherwise problems may cause financial distress in the company in the future.

8.6   Vertical analysis – Brent Ltd.

Brent Ltd – Income statement for the years to 31 December

	2011		2012	
	£'000	%	£'000	%
Sales (all credit)	1,500	100	1,900	100
Opening inventory	80		100	
Purchases	995	66%	1,400	74%
	1,075		1,500	
Closing inventory	100		200	
Cost of goods sold	975	65%	1,300	68%
Gross profit	525	35%	600	32%
Less: Expenses	250	17%	350	18%
	275	18%	250	13%

The company appears to be making reasonable operating profits in both years. However, profitability has declined in 2012. This appears to be due to purchases and expenses. Horizontal analysis – Brent Ltd.

	Sales	CoGS	Gross Profit	Expenses	Op. Profit
2010	1500	975	525	250	275
2012	1900	1300	600	350	250
	Sales	CoGS	Gross Profit	Expenses	Op. Profit
2011	100%	100%	100%	100%	100%
2012	127%	133%	114%	140%	91%

CoGS = Cost of goods sold

The horizontal analysis clearly shows where problems have occurred during 2012. The CoGS and expenses during 2012 have contributed to the decline in 2012 profits. Management may wish to consider the above analysis and investigate why this has happened.

Chapter 9 – Analysis and interpretation of accounts 2

9.1 (a)   Working Capital Management

Current ratio	$=$	$\dfrac{CA}{CL}$	$\dfrac{700}{635}$	$=$ 1:1
Acid test ratio	$=$	$\dfrac{CA - Inventory}{CL}$	$\dfrac{700 - 235}{635}$	$=$ 0.73:1
Asset turnover ratio	$=$	$\dfrac{Turnover}{Total\ Assets}$	$\dfrac{5,500}{6,700}$	$=$ 0.8
Stock turnover ratio	$=$	$\dfrac{Stock}{Cost\ of\ sales} \times 365$	$\dfrac{235}{2,700} \times 365$	$=$ 32 Days

Profitability

Gross profit margin	=	Gross Profit	2,800	=	51%
		Turnover	5,500		
Operating profit margin	=	Net Profit	1,250	=	23%
		Turnover	5,500		
Return on assets	=	Net Profit	1,250	=	18%
		Total Assets	6,700		

Capital structure

Gearing 1	=	Long-Term liabilities	3,000	=	98%
		Total Equity fund	3,065		
Interest cover	=	Operating profit	1,250	=	4:1
		Interest expense	300		

(b) **Working Capital Management**

This ratio shows that the company is its working capital reasonably well. With the current ratio at 1.1 and the acid test ratio at 0.73, and the nature of the business being in retail, the level of liquidity is acceptable. However, this situation can change quickly and management must have sound plans to keep the current and acid test ratios at the same or higher levels.

Profitability

All the three profitability ratios show a healthy return to the investor. The gross margin ratio shows a 51% turnover which is due to the usual sector return. The net profit margin and return on asset ratios also seem to be in line with expectation. Nevertheless the kitchen appliance business is very susceptible to economic downturn; people will delay home improvements in austere times, so, while returns appear to be acceptable, there could be severe impact on the business in tough economic conditions.

Capital structure

The gearing ratios can be estimated in two ways: debt/equity or debt/(equity + debt). Lenders will usually set a debt covenant based on gearing levels. Some lenders may stipulate that a company's gearing may not go over say, 50% based on DEBT/DEBT + EQUITY estimation. However, the interest cover ratio, which is 4:1, suggests the company can meet its interest payments.

The ratio suggests the company is highly geared and any further increase in debt will risk a default on the debt covenant. The company needs to lower its debt and/or increase its profits and profitability to stay within agreed bounds.

9.2 (a)

	Tanner	Spanner	Trade
	£'000	£'000	
Operating profit	800	1,200	
Turnover	7,600	9,000	
Average investment in gross assets	2,400	6,000	
Gross asset turnover	3 times	1.5 times	2 times
Operating profit percentage	10.5%	13.3%	14%
Operating profit to gross assets	41.7%	20.0%	21%

(b) The three ratios are intrinsically linked to each other as they are all a different measure of company performance. The gross asset turnover and the operating profit ratios compare company performance in relation to sales. As gross asset turnover moves up or down this is reflected in the movement respectively in the operating profit percentage ratio. Again, the rate of return on gross assets is linked to gross asset turnover. As the gross asset turnover moves up or down, the rate of return on gross assets moves likewise.

(c) Both Tanner and Spanner seem to be in line with the trade association performance, however, tanner has seen its gross asset turnover three times as compared with the trade association and Spanner who have two times and 1.5 times gross asset turnover respectively. However, Tanner seems to be more efficient in its costs and expenses and has superior operating profits and operating profit to gross assets. This suggests tanner is more profitable than Spanner.

9.3 Net asset turnover ratio = Sales/Net assets
Total asset turnover ratio = Sales/Total assets

£'000	2010	2009	2008	2007
Sales	290	190	160	90
Net assets	420	340	280	190
Total assets	1,140	950	880	680
Net asset turnover	69%	56%	57%	47%
Total asset turnover	25%	20%	18%	13%

Asset usage efficiency:
The ratios indicate that the company has progressively become highly efficient in the use of its assets. By 2010 the company had increased sales by 222%, while having increased its asset base by 68%. It will be useful to consider why such efficiency has transpired due to the increase in the company asset base. This exercise will continue to enable the company to maintain and improve its operations and processes.

9.4

Cash operating cycle = Days sales outstanding +
Inventory days outstanding -
Payable days outstanding

Cash operating cycle = 60 + 90 - 70 = 80 days

Using the stated formula the company has an 80-day cash operating cycle. Depending on the nature of the business and possibly the industry the company is in, the 80-day operating cycle may be sufficient. However, the length of this cycle could impair the growth of the company, so it needs to investigate how it should reduce the cycle to enable it to grow and become more efficient in its operations.

Therefore, an entity which reports a joint venture interest using the equity method includes in its consolidated cash flow statement the cash flow in respect of its investments in the jointly controlled entity and distributions and other payments or receipts between it and the jointly controlled entity. For example, the heading 'Cash flow from investing activities' should include 'Distributions from joint ventures'.

Chapter 10 – Analysis and interpretation of accounts 3

10.1 Basic earnings per share (EPS)

	£
Earnings	£20,000,000
Shares issued	100,000,000
Basic EPS	20p/share

Diluted earnings per share (DEPS)

Earnings	20,000,000
Savings on interest (£40m x 12%)*	4,800,000
	24,800,000
Reduced tax savings on foregone interest	−1,440,000
Adjusted net earnings	23,360,000

(*£4,800,000 x 30% = £1,440,000)

Number of shares on conversion:

Shares issued	100,000,000
Conversion: £40m/100 x 12 =	48,000,000
Total shares:	148,000,000

DEPS after adjusted net earnings:

£23,360,000/148,000,000	16p/share

The debenture conversion has diluted the current shareholder wealth. The impact of the conversion would decrease current basic EPS from 20p per share to 16p per share.

10.2 (a) Earnings per share (EPS) represents the profit attributable to ordinary shareholders divided by the weighted average number of shares in issue during the year.

(b) A bonus share is essentially a free share given to current shareholders in a company, based on the number of shares that the shareholder already owns. While the issue of bonus shares increases the total number of shares issued and owned, it does not increase the value of the company.

Although the total number of issued shares increases, the ratio of number of shares held by each shareholder remains constant. An issue of bonus shares is referred to as a bonus issue. Depending upon the constitutional documents of the company, only certain classes of shares may be entitled to bonus issues, or may be entitled to bonus issues in preference to other classes.

(c)

	2012	2011
Basic earnings per share (EPS)	*£'000*	*£'000*
Profit for the year	64,000	48,000
8% Preference share (£100m x 8% = £8m)	−8,000	−8,000
Profit attributable to ordinary shareholders	56,000	40,000
Shares in issue		
Shares in issue	30,000	30,000
Bonus issue (1 for 5)	6,000	–
Total shares	36,000	30,000
Basic EPS	£1.56	£1.33
Re-stated EPS for 2011: £1.33 × 5/6 = £1.11		£1.11

(d)   Dilution to earnings per share (EPS) can arise due to a number of factors:
Conversion of debentures, preference shares and other financial instruments will
have an impact on wealth effects due to the number of shares issued if the conversion is offered at less than market value of the shares. However, there are other situations which may give rise to diluted earnings per share such as warrants and options.
Presently share ranking does not exist, but it may do in the future for dividend purposes. This may also lead to dilution of EPS if such share-ranking instruments had
conversion rights to ordinary shares

(e)

	2012
Diluted Earnings per share (DEPS)	*£*
Earnings	56,000
Savings on interest	36,000
	92,000
Reduced tax savings on foregone interest: £36m × 33% = £11.88m	−11,880
Adjusted net earnings	80,120
Calculation of debenture:	
£36,000,000 × 12%/100% =	300,000,000
Shares in issue	36,000,000
£300,000,000/£300 × 20 =	20,000,000
Total shares	56,000,000
Diluted EPS: £80,120,000/56,000,000 =	£1.43

10.3 The du-Pont Analysis is a technique for analysing the three components of Return on equity (ROE):

Net income		Sales		Assets
Sales	×	Assets	×	Equity
3,300		19,600		135,000
19,600	×	135,000	×	9,500
17%		15%		1,421%

Return on Equity = 35%

10.4 (a)

Rights issue price £1.50		
Premium per rights share:1.50 – 1.00		0.5
Closing share premium account		13,500
Opening Share premium account		6,000
Premium on rights issue		7,500
number of rights issue shares (7,500/0.50)		15,000
Proceeds from rights issue (15,000 × £1.50)		22,500

(b) Share issues

Opening shares in issue		25,000
Bonus issue: 25,000/5	5,000	
Number of shares under rights issue	15,000	
Total new share issues		20,000
Total weighted number of shares		45,000

Profit for 2010	£
Closing reserve (as stated in the question)	16,200
Add: Bonus issue	5,000
Add: Dividends paid	6,750
	27,950
Less: Closing retained earnings	–19,000
Profit for the period (2010)	8,950

Chapter 11 – Limitations of published accounts

11.1 Gearing

As the conversion of the 5% bond would result in decreased debt and a substantial rise in equity, this would have the effect of lowering the gearing ratio and hence facilitating further debt opportunity should the company need it. However, although the conversion of the 5% bond may lower the gearing ratio, it may have a negative impact on other aspects of the company finances.

Return on Equity (ROE)

Essentially the impact of the bond conversion will necessitate a substantial increase in the number of issued shares. If the net effect of the conversion results in issue of free shares, the bond conversion will dilute the earnings of the company. This means ROE will be lower after the bond conversion to equity. The ROE ratio compares earnings against the value of shareholder fund, not the number of shares issued.

Earnings per Share (EPS)

The impact of the bond conversion could be sharply felt on the EPS. The revised earnings figure will be divided by the new total number of shares in issue (this may be on a weighted-average basis). The EPS may be higher or lower after the bond conversion and may have an impact on shareholder wealth and the amount of capital invested. If new shares are issued below the market price of a company's share, this in effect amounts to a 'bonus' issue and a recalculation of previous year's EPS.

11.2 (a) *Investment in securities*

IAS 39 is the current effective standard for financial instruments. It will be superseded by IFRS 9 on 1 January 2013. The securities investment by Thompson plc comes under IAS 39 and will need to be disclosed at fair value in the statement of financial position as an asset together with the gain or loss shown in the income statement/statement of comprehensive income. Since this is a long-term investment, the nature of the investment should be disclosed in the narratives and a fair value measure should also be carried out to assess its present value. IFRS 7 gives guidance on how the disclosure should be made in the statement of financial position. Disclosures should state:

(a) information about the significance of financial instruments; and

(b) information about the nature and extent of risks arising from financial instruments.

Loan transaction

The loan to Brent Ltd is also classified as a financial instrument and, together with IAS 39 and IFRS 7 this will need to be disclosed in the financial statements. The loan will need to be measured at its fair value and disclosed as an asset with an estimation of its present value to maturity. The nature and purpose of the loan should also be disclosed, together with the relationship that Thompson has with Brent Ltd. A disclosure will also be made that Thompson has given an undertaken not to transfer the liability to a third party. Stakeholders should form a view as to the undertaking.

(b) The nature of the two financial instruments is long term. They will both have to be measured at fair value and disclosed in the financial statements. The most common form of measurement is the risk attached to the financial instruments. The rate of risk will determine the present value of the assets at maturity.

11.3 (a) *Lease calculations for disclosure*

Fair value of the lease asset	674,000
Periodic rental	200,000
Implicit rate of interest	10%
Frequency of lease rental	Annual
Lease period	4 years
Useful economic life of the asset	5 years

Lease Table

Year	Opening balance	Interest	Rental	Closing balance
0	674,000	0	40,000	634,000
2009	634,000	63,400	200,000	497,400
2010	497,400	49,740	200,000	347,140
2011	347,140	34,714	200,000	181,854
2012	181,854	18,146	200,000	0

Statement of comprehensive income for the year ended 31 December 2009

	2009	2010
	£	£
Depreciation	169,500	169,500
Interest	63,400	49,740

Havent plc statement of financial position as at 31 December 2010

	2009	2010
Non-current assets	£	£
Property, plant and equipment cost	678,000	678,000
Accumulated Depreciation	169,500	339,000
	508,500	339,000
Non-current liabilities		
Lease obligation	347,140	181,854
Current liabilities		
Lease obligation (497,400 - 347,140)	150,260	165,286
Total non-current liabilities	497,400	347,140

(b)   *Operating/finance leases*
Whether a lease is classified as a finance lease or an operating lease depends on the substance of the lease arrangement rather than the form of the contract. Thus, if 'in substance', substantially all of the risks and rewards incident with ownership are transferred from the lessor to the lessee the arrangement gives rise to a finance lease. Fraser may wish to report the finance lease as an operating lease for the following reasons:

1   A finance lease requires certain disclosures and these must be according IAS 17 requiring disclosure of the fair value of the lease and its obligation. Hence an asset and a liability may be set up at the same time.

2   Essentially, a lease agreement is a long-term debt and this has bearing on the gearing of the company and its return on equity. The finance lease agreement may cause Fraser to default on its current debt covenant, if any, and hence may be a cause for concern by its lenders.

(c)   *Characteristics of finance leases*
The lease transfers ownership of the leased asset to the lessee at the end of the lease period on payment of a nominal amount if, within the terms of the contracts:

■   the lease term covers most of the asset's useful economic life;

■   the lessee has an option to buy the asset at a nominal price at the end of the lease and it is reasonably certain that the option will be exercised;

■   at the inception of the lease, the present value of the minimum lease payments amount to substantially all of the fair value of the leased asset;

■   generally the leased asset is of specialised nature and only the lessee can use it without major modifications;

■   the lessee pays the lessor's losses if the agreement is cancelled during the primary lease period; and

■   the gains or losses resulting from the fluctuations in the residual value of the leased asset accrue to the lessee.

The lessee can lease the asset at a peppercorn rent after the primary lease period of the finance lease. This transfers risks and rewards of ownership hence they are responsible for repairs, insurance etc.

(d) *Recording leases in the books of the lessee*
The guidance provided in IAS 17 'Accounting for Leases' mainly focuses on the nature of the lease. If the nature of the lease is such that it transfers, substantially, all the rights and obligations to the lessee and that all future economic benefits will flow incidental to the lease to the lessee, then the lease is a finance lease.
This essentially means, for all intent and purposes, that the lessee is the owner of the asset and the argument that the nature of a lease contract should reflect the substance over the form is being propagated by IAS 17.
By requiring a lessee to recognise a finance lease in the statement of financial position, IAS 17 is demonstrating that the lessee has substantial long-term obligations far beyond the simple periodic payment and that, in law, the lessee is obligated to fulfil the terms and conditions of a lease contract.

11.4 (a) *Lease and buyback agreement*
The nature of the financial transaction Argo plc has entered in to with the bank is essentially a 'lease and buy back' agreement. The terms and conditions of the agreement basically suggest that the loan is collateralised against the assets of the company. The company still has control of the assets and will continue to use them for its purposes.

(b) *Accounting treatment of sale-and-lease-buyback agreements*
A sale-and-lease-buyback involves the selling of an asset by Argo to the bank. Companies adopt this type of approach to release cash.
The leaseback of the assets of Argo is for the major part of the asset's economic life. Therefore, this is a finance lease in accordance with IAS 17. Where the sale- and-leaseback transaction results in a finance lease, any profit over the carrying amount is not immediately recognised as income by the seller (lessee). The accounting treatment will be in accordance with IAS 17 for leases.

(c) *Impact on Argo's books on removal of assets*
- A decline in the assets of Argo will mean a decline in depreciation charges and hence an increase in reported earnings.
- If the transaction between Argo and the bank is not reported according to IAS 17, Argo would indeed have created off-balance sheet finance.
- As such, long-term lease obligations would not be recognised in the statement of financial position of Argo plc, giving the company a much improved statement of financial position. This could influence economic decisions made by the users of the company's financial report.
- The financial ratios of the company (i.e. ROA, ROE, EPS and gearing) would lead to a much improved indication of company performance.
- Argo would, in fact, be engaging in off-balance sheet activity, infringing on the substance-over-form concept.
- The level of transparency in the books of Argo would decrease.

(d) *Threat to auditors of Argo plc*
The UK Code on Corporate Governance and IFRS including UK GAAP, explain the roles and responsibilities of the auditor in great depth. The job requires independence, integrity, professionalism and responsibility.
The auditors of Argo would need to consider the due diligence process and assess the risk posed to their independence and professionalism by taking on such an engagement. It may be that Argo would be subject to substantive testing in other areas if it were to redefine the finance lease as an operating lease. The auditor may need to consider the threat to his independence, professionalism and his objectivity.
These may impact on the auditor's duty to be transparent. The UK Code on Corporate Governance places responsibilities on auditor conduct and the relationship he has with the board of directors and shareholders. In discharging his duties, the auditor needs to assimilate these threats prior to taking on an engagement, clarify his terms of reference and state how the audit will proceed.

(e) *Auditor conduct*
The auditor needs to ensure that he assimilates all relevant facts and has access to all relevant documents at least in the case of the financial arrangements Argo has entered into with the bank. He should seek representation from the directors and

elicit explanations for the transaction. In doing so he must ask for proper accounting procedures to be adopted in respect of the transaction and relevant disclosure made in the financial reports.

(f) *Auditor intimidation threat*

There are economic consequences if the transaction is not recorded according to IFRS rules which have been highlighted above. If the auditor fails in his duty to demand proper accounting because of intimidation from management, this will have an impact on the auditor's professionalism, integrity and due diligence.

- The books of Argo will appear to be far superior than they are in the absence of liability and long-term obligations being disclosed.
- Users may make economic decisions on the basis of a clean audit.
- Damage to the auditor's reputation which may have professional consequences from appropriate professional body as well as legal and regulatory implications.
- Damage to the company's reputation and the economic impact that may ensue as a result of earnings management or creative accounting.

There may be other implications both for the company and the auditor (e.g. listing rules may be infringed which will also have legal and regulatory consequences).

11.5 1 From the terms of the agreement, it appears that the lease is an operating lease as:
- about one-third (10 years) of the useful economic life of the asset (30 years) will be used under the terms of the lease by Serendipity;
- it appears that all the risk and rewards of ownership will NOT be entirely transferred to the company;
- the length and duration of the lease is unsubstantial in nature; and
- the value of the lease agreement is unsubstantial in nature.

2 The annual lease expense should look at the nature of the usage of the asset rather than the agreed monthly payment. As the duration of the lease is ten years, the following annual payments should be charged to the statement of income from 2005 to 2011:

(a)

	£
Lease agreement	194,400
Term	10 years
Annual rental	19,440
2011 – lease charge to IS to date	136,080
2011 – lease actually paid	165,600

Actual lease payments and charge to IS 2005–2011

Year	Actual lease amount paid	Lease charge to IS
2005	36,000	19,440
2006	24,000	19,440
2007	24,000	19,440
2008	24,000	19,440
2009	24,000	19,440
2010	24,000	19,440
2011	9,600	19,440
	165,600	136,080

The above book entries will create a prepayment in the year 2011, however, over time at the end of the ten-year lease, all the payments will equalise to zero.

(b) Extract from the statement of financial position

Current asset

Lease account (2011)	136,080
Less: Rental paid	–165,600
Prepayment on lease account	29,520

11.6 (a) Luboil has incorrectly credited to sales a £10 million contract entered into with Seeder Ltd. This is not the correct procedure. Luboil should divide the contract over five years and post, subject to price variation as agreed with the customer, Seeder Ltd, as to the price variation. Formal recognition of the agreement on price variation should be available to the auditor for inspection. Additionally, a fair value approach to price variation should be used and the contract should be explained in the narratives to the financial reports.

(b) There will be some impact on changes to sales having made the proper treatment of the account. As the contract is based on supply, there may be legal issues with stopping supply to Seeder Ltd. This has to be taken in to consideration.

However, performance ratios such as EPS, ROA, ROE and ROCE will fall, perhaps considerably once accounting adjustments are made and only £2 million revenue is accounted for rather than £10 million.

(c) The contract between Luboil plc and Seeder Ltd is substantial in nature and over a five-year period. Disclosure in the financial report will explain the nature of the contract, its duration and the price variation structure. The price variation will need to be explained as well as how this will be arrived at.

11.7 Consignment inventory is inventory that is in the possession of the customer, but is still owned by the supplier. Essentially, this is a principal–agent relationship, where by the seller acts as an intermediary to the owner of the consignment. Upon realisation (i.e. sale of the consignment) the cash is transferred to the principal and the agent charges a commission for his services. The consignment arrangement may take different forms; however, the title of the consignment remains with the consignor until such time as it passes to the buyer.

11.8 Goods out on consignment are properly included in the inventory of the consignor (the principal) and are *excluded* from the inventory of the consignee (the agent). Disclosure may be required from the consignee, as since common financial analytical inferences (e.g. as days' sales in inventory or inventory turnover) may appear distorted unless the users of the financial statement are informed.

The car dealer should follow the accruals concept in this regard. All expenditure should be assigned to commissions realised; this means that any costs involved directly related to particular consignment should be recorded appropriately. On the sale of such consignments, the agent will be entitled to his commission. Once the commission crystallises, the agent can recognise revenue and the related cost that has occurred.

The dealer should further disclose the co-signatory relationship with the car manufacturer, any assets in the possession of the dealer at the financial report date and other relevant facts pertaining to the consignment agreement at the reporting date.

11.9 The nature of the transaction between WD and the bank is one of sale and repurchase rather like a lease-and-buyback agreement. WD will need to reflect the substance of the transaction and record in the books the liability that arises out of the transaction as well as the asset.

The liability that arises is the capital repayment as well as interest at 10%. The transaction will be measured for present value. As the term expires (maturity) the capital will be repaid and the interest charge will be expensed.

The liability will have to be disclosed in terms of current and non-current and the interest charge can be expensed periodically according to the substance and the terms of the agreement.

(a) Factoring is a financial transaction in which a business can quickly raise cash against its invoices. The cash provider (the factor) becomes the owner of the debt outstanding and can pursue customers for payments. A factor will process and forward to a business, say, 80% of the face value of an invoice. Once the payment has been recovered, the factor subsequently transfers the other 20% and charges the business interest and perhaps other related charges for services provided.

(b)   Factoring without recourse means that the factor assumes all risk of customer non-payment. As there is more risk to the factor, factoring fees are usually higher and the advance rate is lower than factoring with recourse. When factoring is provided with recourse, the factor can seek compensation from the invoice issuer. Under this arrangement, factoring charges and fees are lower as there is some level of security for the factor.

(c)   Company A enters into a factoring agreement with a factor. With recourse, the factor will forward 80% of the invoice value with a further 10% when the customer pays. The remaining 10% will be the charges from the factor to Company A, for services. However, without recourse, the factor may impose a lower initial forwarding of invoice value, say, 70% and a higher charge for greater risk say, 12%. The factoring entity will assess the risks involved and offer its factoring services to a customer, such as Company A having assessed all risk

11.10 (a)   Closing inventory using Retail Inventory Method:

	2011		2012	
	Cost	Retail	Cost	Retail
	£	£	£	£
Opening inventory	45,000	54,000	52,000	60,000
Purchases	110,000	127,000	135,000	155,000
Goods available for sale	155,000	181,000	187,000	215,000
Deduct: Sales		−145,000		−167,000
Closing inventory at retail		36,000		48,000
Ratio of cost to retail (£155,000 ÷ £181,000)		86%		
Ratio of cost to retail (£187,000 ÷ £302,000)				87%
Closing inventory: £36,000 × 86% (Rounded to nearest £'000)		£31,000		£42,000

(b)   Closing inventory using Gross Margin Method:

	2012 Actual	2012 Actual	2012 GMM*
	£	£	£
Sales	145,000	167,000	167,000
Beginning inventory	45,000	52,000	52,000
Purchases	110,000	135,000	135,000
Goods available for sale	155,000	187,000	187,000
Closing inventory	−45,000	−55,000	−60,000
CoGS	110,000	132,000	127,000
Gross profit	35,000	35,000	40,000
Gross margin on sales	24%	21%	24%

Workings:

Step 1	Cost of goods available	=	Beginning inventory	+	Net purchases
	Cost of goods available	=	£52,000	+	£135,000
	Cost of goods available	=	£187,000		
Step 2	Gross profit	=	Gross profit %	×	Sales
	Gross profit	=	24%	×	£167,000
					(rounded to nearest £'000)
	Gross profit	=	£40,000		
Step 3	Cost of goods sold	=	Sales	–	Gross profit
	Cost of goods sold	=	£167,000	–	£40,000 (step 2)
	Cost of goods sold	=	£127,000		

Cost of goods sold can also be calculated as 76% × sales of £167,000 = £40,000.

Step 4	Ending inventory	=	Cost of goods available	–	Cost of goods sold
	Ending inventory	=	£187,000	–	£127,000
	Ending inventory	=	£60,000		

Chapter 12 Current issues

12.1 Companies have achieved notoriety by putting profits before social and ethical considerations. Business activity by companies can impact upon a whole host issues from environmental impact to social and ethical misbehaviour. The demand for raw materials like timber has in the past left vast tracts of land bare with no renewable actions taken.

In considering their economic activities companies need to consider sustainability issues as well as ethical concerns. The following measures need to be reflected in business policies and procedures that reflect societal and environmental needs:

- *Risk management* – in areas of financial, legal and reputation implications.
- *Marketing strategy* – public image, brand enhancement such as through receiving environmental awards.
- *Legal needs* – to keep pace with/anticipate regulations.
- *Competition* – to get ahead of/stay with competitors.
- *Ethics* – individual commitment; commitment to accountability and transparency.
- *Accounting requirements* – in compliance with financial reporting requirements and provide link between financial and environmental performance/reporting.
- *Investors' interests* – demands of green (ethical) investors.
- *Employees' interests* – attracts right staff from the labour market.
- Value-add reporting – to add value to corporate reports and communicate to wider range of stakeholders, addressing their environmental concerns.
- *Certification needs* – to indicate compliance with ISO14000 and other environmental regulatory guidelines.

The above considerations will enable companies to draft policies and procedures to implement, monitor, and control their corporate actions and report in a transparent manner. Many CSR tools are available to help companies to develop a company-wide system that reflects social as well as economical and sustainable business activity.

Companies could adopt the eco-management and audit scheme to determine the full extent of its environmental impact and enable them to determine the level of compliance with relevant regulation and laws that a company has to abide by, thus, enabling users of an environmental audit report to understand their achievements and shortcomings in company environmental practices.

The Triple Bottom Line approach could be reflected in a company's financial accounts. This gives users information on how a company is measuring up to its social and environmental commitments.

CSR reports provide an enhanced view of the company to stakeholders.

12.2 The EMAS is an audit tool specifically designed for eco-management audits. This allows a company to determine its environmental impact and determine ways to improve or reduce this impact. As greater numbers of companies realise that not taking part in environmental reporting has economic consequences, EMAS helps companies to report in more or less a standardised fashion. The main element of the EMAS tool requires companies to:

(a) *Conduct an environmental review*

The organisation needs to conduct a verified initial environmental review, considering all environmental aspects of the organisation's activities, products and services, methods to assess them, the organisation's legal and regulatory framework and existing environmental management practices and procedures.

(b) *Adopt an environmental policy*

Registration to EMAS requires an organisation to adopt an environmental policy and to commit itself both to compliance with all relevant environmental legislation and to achieving continuous improvement in its environmental performance.

(c) *Establish an EMS*

Based on the results of the environmental review and the policy (objectives), an EMS needs to be established. The EMS is aimed at achieving the organisation's environmental policy objectives as defined by the top management. The management system needs to set responsibilities, objectives, means, operational procedures, training needs, monitoring and communication systems.

(d) *Carry out an internal environmental audit*

After the EMS is established an environmental audit should be carried out. The audit assesses in particular if the management system is in place and in conformity with the organisation's policy and programme. The audit also checks if the organisation is in compliance with relevant environmental regulatory requirements.

(e) *Prepare an environmental statement*

The organisation needs to provide a public statement of its environmental performance. The environmental statement lays down the results achieved against the environmental objectives and the future steps to be undertaken in order to continuously improve the organisation's environmental performance.

(f) *Independent verification by an EMAS verifier*

An EMAS verifier accredited with an EMAS accreditation body of a member state must examine and verify the environmental review, the EMS, the audit procedure and the environmental statement.

(g) *Register with the competent body of the Member State*

The validated statement is sent to the appropriate EMAS Body for registration and made publicly available.

(h) *Utilise the verified environmental statement*

The environmental statement can be used to report performance data in marketing, assessment of the supply chain and procurement. The organisation can use information from the validated statement to market its activities with the EMAS logo, assess suppliers against EMAS requirements and give preference to suppliers registered under EMAS.

Generally, environmental audits involve the collection, collation, analysis, interpretation, and presentation of information. This information is then used to:

- assess performance against a list of pre-set targets, related to specific issues;
- evaluate and assess compliance with environmental legislation as well as corporate policies; and
- measure performance against the requirements of an environmental management system (EMS) standard.

12.3 Memo

From: IT Officer

To: CEO

Date: 1 May 2012

Subject: Company reputation and XBRL

(a) Company reputation

Listed companies need to issue financial and non-financial information to a whole host of users with different needs. Listed companies in particular have many stake-holders with vested interest in the affairs of a company. Modern reporting tools are available to companies that allow easy uploading and formatting of financial information that can be manipulated according to the user's requirements. By adopting modern Internet-based technology the Company can enhance its image by catering to the needs of external users and stakeholder. In achieving this Company needs to take account of how it can achieve this aim and how the relevant technology can assist in realising the aim.

XBRL is a web-based business language that uses HTML technology. By using XBRL, systems can be developed to be available both in-house and external to users. XBRL is easily developed and allows for internal sharing of company information in a cost-effective manner. Information can then be used as input to other information systems.

The use of XBRL tags enables automated processing of business information by computer software, facilitating efficient re-use of data for comparison. Computers can treat XBRL data 'intelligently' enabling:

Storage of data and information in XBRL format that enables selection, analysis, exchange and presentation in a variety of ways dependent on the end-user requirements.

Speed – XBRL greatly increases the speed of handling of financial data, reduces the chance of error and permits automatic checking of information.

Costs – Companies can use XBRL to save costs and streamline their processes for collecting and reporting financial information.

Retrieval – Consumers of financial data, including investors, analysts, financial institutions and regulators, researchers, can locate, manipulate, compare, and analyse data much more rapidly and efficiently in XBRL format than by other online facility.

Data handling – XBRL can handle data in different languages and accounting standards. It can flexibly be adapted to meet different requirements and uses.

Subscription-based databases allow companies to transfer their financial information that can be accessed by users for their own purposes. Bloomberg is a highly efficient real-time database system that allows subscribers access to financial and real-time information such as share prices and numerous facilities to manipulate and transform data according to need.

(b) XBRL

Companies now have to complete returns online to meet HMRC requirements (e.g. tax returns and other tax-related financial information). This necessitates companies developing in-house XBRL systems that can be interfaced with external parties' data collection software that will allow the efficient and timely transfer of data.

Using XBRL technology will enable our Company not only to comply with regulatory and/or legal requirements, but also enable the structural development of the Company allowing it to have an effective Internet presence where users can access information that is suitable for their purposes.

12.4 (a) XBRL is a web-based technology that facilitates the electronic communication of economic and financial information in a manner that cuts down costs, provides a greater level of efficiency of use, and improved reliability to users and suppliers of information.

XBRL uses the XML (Extensible Markup Language) syntax and related XML technologies, which are the standard in communicating information between businesses and the internet. Data can be converted to XBRL by appropriate mapping tools designed to convert electronic data to XBRL format, or data can be written directly in XBRL by suitable software.

(b) XBRL works on a system of TAGS. Instead of treating financial information as a block of text, as in a standard internet page or a printed document, XBRL provides an identifying tag for each individual item of data. This is computer readable. For example, company revenues and items of expenses and net profit have their own unique tag. This enables manipulation by users, through query forms, to generate data and information in the required format.

(c) Most companies employ the computer desktop and laptop systems as a means for data capture, analysis, and output. A company would need to ensure that its web technology is up-to-date or otherwise invest in new computer systems. XBRL works on the internet and hence, software tools would need to be procured that allow conversion between applications such as accounting software systems, Microsoft Doc files and Excel spreadsheets which can be used to transfer base data into a useable format for the XBRL system. Comparatively, costs are low; however, maintenance and dedicated staff may need to be employed to provide expert services to staff and employees.

(d) The common platform for XBRL is the internet. XBRL codes are embedded in HTML source codes and the system works from dedicated websites.

(e) XBRL is web-based, hence the running costs of XBRL are quite low and maintenance costs are relatively cheap. However, the functionality of XBRL-based system is very powerful allowing easy access and conformity to company requirements. Proprietary software can be used in conjunction with XBRL to manage changes, enhancements, and amendments.

12.5 Introduction

Pressure on companies to comply with modern business practices demands that they reflect upon and take appropriate action on environmental and social issues using a proactive approach to business activities management. Waste and toxic emissions are dealt with by law in the UK such as the Environmental Law Act 2006. It may be that current legislation does not require companies to disclose certain relevant information that may be useful to users; however, a company can demonstrate its proactive commitment to environmental issues by disclosing concerns and addressing them effectively. This has a positive impact on the credibility, integrity, and reputation of a company. In being proactive, companies can demonstrate to stakeholders their commitment to social and environmental needs.

(a) James is under an obligation as the environmental compliance officer to bring existing environmental issues to the attention of senior management. He needs to provide practical solutions as to how the toxic waste could be better managed by investing in new and improved technology.

By offering alternative courses of action and a carrying out a cost–benefit analysis, James could demonstrate the future benefits of the investment. Additionally, James needs to underline the ethical and environmental importance of taking proactive steps and disclosing this to stakeholders thereby adding reputational capital to the company.

(b) The company could take a series of practical steps to comply with environmental issue at hand. The company could:
- identify areas of concern and draw up policies relevant to the company using appropriate audit tools, such as GRI or TBL;
- use external experts to advise on best and future course of actions;
- have effective monitoring and audit policies in place that are regularly updated;
- provide training for relevant employees on environmental and social matters; and
- disclose systematically and regularly in annual reports the targets and achievements to date being clear and honest in doing so.

(c)   There are many ways a company can report its initiatives. The most common procedure is to disclose its green and social policies through its corporate report. The company should develop standalone reports that concentrate on social, environmental and ethical issues explaining how these are achieved or what processes are in place. This gives a clear indication of targets and timelines.

12.6 (a)   Company disclosure on listed companies usually features a report on corporate social responsibility (CSR). This report is separate from the financial report and indicates company policy towards social, environmental, and ethical issues. The CSR report will also indicate policy and procedure and line of responsibility. Additionally, it will discuss targets set and achieved, any deficiencies in policy and practice and the pragmatic steps taken to ensure the company complies with legal and ethical requirements.

(b)   Within the financial report, companies will report on product lines and geographical operations. This would indicate the exposure the company faces in sourcing its raw material and the markets to which it sells its products.

The directors and CEO reports will provide additional information as to the progress the company is making on CSR issues such as ethical trading and its impact on the environment. Reports from relevant third parties such as the external auditor will feature in the financial reports or as part of the wider CSR report giving independent verification.

Commitment to certification and standards and how they have been applied will also be indicators of company commitment to the social agenda.

(c)   'Green' organisations such as charities and expert entities may have their own views of green issues. However, these organisations are a good way of ascertaining the current issues that companies need to address and provide examples of best practice and recommendations.

13 Overview

13.1 There are competing demands placed upon the modern company secretary. In their capacity as the expert in company legal issues, the company secretary is expected to be knowledgeable in a number of areas including:
- company law and the changes to legal requirements;
- regulations and the changes to regulations;
- environmental, ethical and social issues;
- financial reporting issues;
- employee/staff issues;
- advisory capacity to the board;
- training of NEDs; and
- administration of boardroom procedures.

The above are some aspects of the work undertaken by the company secretary. However, these are core tasks that would be expected from a company secretary in a modern corporation.

13.2 Traditionally and to the wider public, the company secretary, to all intents and purposes, was simply a person who took care of the administration procedures of the board.

However, over the past decade, the role of the company secretary has become a more demanding and senior role requiring a proactive approach to company matters; acting in an advisory capacity as the company's expert on legal matters; ensuring that the company complies with its memorandum and articles of association; and drafting and incorporating amendments in accordance with correct procedures.

The financial debacles of the past decade or so have resulted in close scrutiny of board performance and their attitude towards the wider public. Corporate governance is the mechanism by which companies are directed and controlled; hence the company secretary provides guidance on governance issues that impact upon business matters. As ethical issues have gained prominence, the company secretary is required to advise the board on ethical concerns.

Environmental issues have also gained prominence in recent years, with large corporations being proactive about environmental matters, reporting on environmental issues and the impact of their business activity on the environment. Here the company secretary deals in a range of issues that have a bearing on the reputation of the company as well its economic impact.

13.3 The company secretary is responsible for the efficient administration of a company, particularly with regard to ensuring compliance with statutory and regulatory requirements and that the decisions of the board of directors are implemented.

The company secretary is responsible for keeping the board informed of their fiduciary duties and how best to discharge them in compliance with relevant statutory laws and regulations.

The company secretary has to deal with a number of issues that may eventually have legal implications (e.g. conflicts within and outside the company). Meeting with institutional investors may be a remit of the company secretary and it will be their job to negotiate between the board and the shareholders.

Other aspects of a company secretary's role may involve advising on legal matters in relation to employees and their rights. However, a company that has a proactive employee policy will wish to work for the welfare of its employees and it will be the job of the company secretary to ensure that all statutory and regulatory concerns are addressed with relevant people.

Company secretaries should also ensure that, if any of their responsibilities are delegated, these tasks are properly executed. They can still be held accountable in law for any failure by the company to comply with its obligations. The fiduciary duties of directors can apply equally to executives occupying senior management positions in the company and authorised to act on its behalf. This usually includes the company secretary who, in any event, as an officer of the company has the following fundamental duties:

- to act in good faith in the interests of the company;
- not to act for any collateral purpose;
- to avoid conflicts of interest; and
- not to make secret profits from dealings for or on behalf of the company.

In some countries, particularly the UK, the company secretary is a formal role. The Institute of Chartered Secretaries and Administrators admits members as a chartered secretary. The role of chartered/company secretary has achieved the status of executive officer and it is a highly paid vocation.

13.4 While the senior company accounting offer, such as the CFO, has the overall responsibility, the company secretary is involved in ensuring that regulatory and statutory compliance is met. The company secretary will be involved in ensuring the accuracy, consistency and reliability of published financial statements. In this regard they may well liaise on behalf of the audit committee to ensure that the external audit is carried out in an efficient and transparent manner and that the auditors have access to all required and relevant information.

The company secretary is responsible for coordinating the publication and distribution of the company's annual report and accounts and interim statements, in consultation with the company's internal and external advisers, particularly when preparing the directors' report.

13.5 (a) Does every company need a secretary?

No. The Companies Act 2006 amended the rules to allow private limited companies to exist with just one director as long as the company's articles did not expressly require a secretary.

(b) Does a company secretary need any qualifications?

The company secretary of a private limited company (Ltd) needs no formal qualifications. It is up to the directors to ensure that a person has appropriate knowledge and experience to act as a secretary of the company. In the case of a public limited company (Plc), the secretary will normally be expected to be professionally qualified as a lawyer, accountant, or company secretary, though previous experience as a secretary of a Plc may also be taken into account.

(c)   Does the secretary have to be a UK citizen?
No. Except for occasional restrictions imposed by the government on the activities of certain foreign nationals a director or secretary can be of any nationality and can live anywhere in the world.

(d)   Can a company secretary be held criminally liable over the affairs of a company?
As the secretary is an officer of the company, they may be criminally liable for defaults committed by the company (e.g. failure to file any change in the details of the company's directors and secretary and the company's annual return).

(e)   Does a company secretary have any powers?
No, but the Companies Act 2006 allows them to sign re-registration applications (e.g. the re-registration of a limited company as unlimited). The secretary is also allowed to sign most of the forms prescribed under the Companies Act.

(f)   What rights does a company secretary have?
That depends on the terms of their contract with the company. The secretary has no special rights under the Companies Act 2006.

13.6 The company secretary will have developed a detailed working knowledge of the company's internal control procedures. This includes having excellent knowledge of the financial procedures of the company and its various control processes. In conjunction with the company's accounting officer, the company secretary will ensure that proper levels of controls are in place to record and report financial figures in the accounting information system.
The accounting system must reflect both the accounting information needs of the company and the accounting cycle. The company secretary, together with the company accountant, will ensure that proper audit trials are available and that there is some flexibility to improve the accounting information system.
Additionally, the accounting system must reflect the proper system of hierarchy that captures and reflects information for reporting purposes on the basis of current statutory and regulatory requirements.

13.7 Changes are constantly taking place, not only from a legislative and regulatory perspective but also within the firm. New markets and new products need to be reflected in the accounting system. The accounting system needs constant changes, amendments and deletions to ensure that effective outputs are produced to facilitate decision making. Some important aspects of accounting information, its output, and improvement are discussed below:
(a)   consider the company's business model in its current form;
(b)   formulate a team tasked to develop, implement, test, and re-check against criteria for improvements;
(c)   formulate a timeline for the project and consider responsibilities to particular personnel;
(d)   agree when tasks are to be completed and when then next task initiated;
(e)   implement changes and carry out test runs;
(f)   assess and evaluate changes for specifications; and
(g)   once the criteria is met, report to senior management.
In the above process, the company secretary has a central role in facilitating the improvements needed, reporting progress to the board and final implementation.

13.8 The company secretary has a central role in ensuring that company internal control procedures are adequate and sufficiently efficient to mitigate any errors, mistakes or malpractice.
1   In both cases 1 and 2, the ethical dimensions arising relate to:
(a)   weaknesses in internal control and segregation of duties. Internal control procedures need to be strengthened to mitigate any weaknesses arising from one person having responsibility across a range of duties;
(b)   a proper level of approval. This needs to be in place to mitigate any misappropriation of company funds. In both cases, an independent staff member needs to verify existing rules, guidelines and employee details. These should then be passed to another member of staff to decide if a claim or portion of a claim is acceptable. The final decision should be made by a senior manager, perhaps even the company secretary where appropriate.

2   The company secretary will be involved in all stages of assessment with internal control procedures and mechanisms. They will involve relevant staff and/or managers to ensure and verify that controls are working efficiently.

The company secretary may require assistance and advice from external people or organisations in developing and improving internal controls. Once the internal control procedures are verified and/or improved, these should be communicated to appropriate personnel.

3   Training should be provided to employees relating to company procedures. If necessary, clear guidelines should be drawn up for employees who try to break company rules. Internal controls should be checked periodically to assess the efficiency of control mechanisms.

Glossary

Accounting equation The accounting equation is the basis for double-entry booking where Assets - liabilities = equity.

Accounting policies Accounting policies are the specific principles, bases, conventions, rules and practices applied by an entity in preparing and presenting financial statements.

Accruals Provisions for goods and services received but not yet paid for. Accruals are one of the main accounting principles.

Agency theory A theory concerning the relationship between a principal (shareholder) and an agent of the principal (managers).

Asset An asset is a resource controlled by the enterprise as a result of past events and from which future economic benefits are expected to flow to the enterprise.

Associate A business entity that is partly owned by another business entity in which the stake holding is at above 20% but below 51%.

Capital and capital maintenance Concept of financial and physical capital maintenance. Financial capital relates to equity, while the physical capital relates to the increase in capital at the end of the year.

Cash and cash equivalents The mostly liquid assets found within the asset portion of a company's statement of financial affairs. Cash equivalents are assets that are usually ready to cash within three months.

Chair's report A statement included in the annual report of large companies in which the chair of the board of directors gives an overview of the company's performance and prospects.

Companies Act A set of legal and regulatory requires that business entities, particularly limited liability entities, must adhere to in the course of business.

Consolidated accounts When a number of business entities belong to a parent either directly or indirectly, the parent entity prepares a set of consolidated accounts. This has the effect of showing the financial affairs of the group as though it was a single business entity hence intra-group transactions are cancelled out.

Convergence This means reducing international differences in accounting standards by selecting the best practice currently available, or, if none is available, by developing new standards in partnership with national standard setters.

Convertible loan Loan stock that can be converted into ordinary shares at a set date or dates at a predetermined price. The conversion price is the price of ordinary shares at which loan stock can be converted. The number of ordinary shares received by a loan stock holder on conversion of £100 nominal of convertible loan stock is £100 divided by the conversion price.

Convertible preference shares Preference shares that can be converted into ordinary shares. A company may issue them to finance major acquisitions without increasing the company's gearing or diluting the earnings per share (EPS) of the ordinary shares. Preference shares potentially offer the investor a reasonable degree of safety with the chance of capital gains as a result of conversion to ordinary shares if the company prospers.

Corporate governance The system by which companies are directed and controlled. In the UK the corporate governance system is based on the UK Code on Corporate Governance 2010.

Cost of capital The cost to a company of the return offered to different kinds of capital. This may be in the form of interest (for debt capital); dividends and participation in the growth of profit (for ordinary shares); dividends alone (for preference shares); or conversion rights (for convertible loan stock or convertible preference shares).

Current asset In the entity's normal operating cycle a current asset is held primarily for trading purposes. It is expected to be realised within 12 months of the statement of financial position. It can also be cash or a cash-equivalent asset.

Current cost Assets are carried at the amount of cash or cash equivalent that would have to be paid if the same or an equivalent asset were currently acquired. Liabilities are carried at the undiscounted amount of cash or cash equivalents that would be required to settle the obligation currently.

Current liability This is expected either to be settled in the normal course of the entity's operating cycle, or is due to be settled within 12 months of the statement of financial position.

Debentures A type of debt instrument that is not secured by physical asset or collateral. The loan may or may not be repayable. If a debenture is not repayable, it may be offered to debenture holders as a convertible loan (see convertible loan).

Debt Long-term capital consisting of money lent by investors. Can be called loan stock, loan notes or debentures. Return on debt consists of interest (usually at a fixed rate) which is payable irrespective of the financial performance of the company. Secured loan stock holders rank before ordinary shareholders for repayment of capital if the company goes into liquidation.

Directors' report An aspect of the annual financial report produced by the board of directors of a business entity required under UK company law. It details the state of the company and its compliance with a set of financial, accounting and corporate social responsibility (CSR) disclosures.

Discontinued operations A component of an enterprise that has either been disposed of, or is classified as 'held for sale'.

Discount rate Cost of capital used to define interest rates or to discount cash flows to find present values.

Dividends A portion of a company's earnings that is returned to shareholders.

Double-entry bookkeeping System of debits and credits that measures assets and liabilities (profit or loss).

Earnings management The manipulation of financial transactions to give a better perspective of a business' financial affairs (e.g. increased revenue or misrepresentation of certain type of expenses).

Earnings per share (EPS) The amount of earnings per each outstanding share in a company. In case of share movement in a period the EPS is stated on a weighted average shareholding basis.

Elements of financial statements Assets liabilities, equity, revenues and expenses.

Equity shares With equity shares the payment of dividends is not guaranteed, and the amount of dividends depends on the company's financial performance. Equity shareholders are last in line for payment of dividends and for repayment of capital if the company goes into liquidation. Equity shareholders accept these risks and disadvantages because they are the legal owners of the company, have voting rights and own any remaining funds after other claims have been met. They expect to benefit, through growth of dividends and share prices, from the company's future success.

External audit A verification process conducted by a third party on the verification of the financial reports. The external audit is carried out by a registered external auditor.

Fair presentation The faithful representation of the effects of transactions in accordance with the definitions and recognition criteria for assets, liabilities, income and expenses set out in the Framework and can be defined as 'Presenting information, including accounting policies, in a manner which provides relevant, reliable, comparable, and understandable information'.

Fair value The measurement of an asset or liability or a financial transaction that best reflects its price. The price may be on a market basis or other means acceptable to a body of users. Fair value must be based on IFRS guidelines.

Faithful representation The principle that reported financial figures that convey to the user the underlying economic reality of the business entity.

Finance lease A resource controlled by a business entity for the substantial part of its life from which future benefits will flow to the company.

Financial gearing Ratio of debt to equity (shareholders' funds). A measure of a firm's financial risk.

Financial ratios A means of evaluating a company's performance or health that uses a standard of comparisons of items on the company's financial statements. Ratios can be calculated in financial and non-financial terms (e.g. debtor days outstanding which is measured days).

Framework This conceptual framework sets out the concepts that underlie the preparation and presentation of financial statements for external users.

Gains or losses In the course of business, an entity will make gains or losses on certain types of transactions such as sale of items of PPE classified as being 'held for sale' or profit or loss on currency translations etc.

Generally Accepted Accounting Principles (GAAP) Refer to the standard framework of guidelines for financial accounting used in any given jurisdiction.

Going concern An accounting concept that under which financial reports are prepared on the assumption that a business will not be liquidated within the next 12 months.

Goodwill The difference between the consideration, price paid for an asset, and its carrying value.

Harmonisation Reconciles to a certain extent, with national differences and provides preparers of accounting information a common framework the opportunity to deal with major issues in a similar manner globally.

Historical cost The amount of cash or cash equivalents paid for an asset, or the fair value of other considerations given to acquire it.

International Accounting Standards Board (IASB) The body that sets IFRS. The IASB may make amendments to existing accounting standards or issue new standards with reference to new accounting issues or for better clarity for existing and new accounting matters.

International Financial Reporting Standards (IFRS) Set of accounting standards that provide the basis for reporting accounting and financial information.

Inventory Is the stock in trade of a business entity. Inventory is either raw material or finished goods. It must be valued at the lower of cost or net realisable value.

Liability Obligation of an entity arising from past transactions or events, the settlement of which may result in the transfer or use of assets, provision of services or other yielding of economic benefits in the future.

Net present value (NPV) The sum of the present values of all the cash flows associated with an investment project.

Non-controlling interest Where a parent company owns say 80% of another business entity, the other 20% belongs to minority shareholders. This is called the non-controlling interest.

Non-recurring profits and losses Unusual or infrequent transactions outside the normal business activities of a firm and reported separately in the income statement.

Offsetting The concept of reporting separately assets, liabilities, expenses and revenue to give users a clearer picture of a company's transactions.

Operating lease A lease whose term is short compared to the useful life of the asset or piece of equipment

Preference shares Non-equity shares, with a (usually fixed) dividend paid – subject to the availability of distributable profits – before ordinary share dividends can be paid. Preference shares do not normally have voting rights, but rank before ordinary shares for distribution of capital in the event of liquidation.

Present value The amount of money at today's date that is equivalent to a sum of money in the future. It is calculated by discounting the future sum to reflect its timing and the cost of capital.

Principal financial statements These include the statement of comprehensive income, statement of financial position, statement of changes to equity and the statement of cash flows.

Property, plant and equipment Items of non-current assets, land and buildings held for use are stated in the statement of financial position at their cost, less any subsequent accumulated depreciation and subsequent accumulated impairment losses.

Published annual report The corporate report published by business entities, particularly corporations, both public and private that includes, apart from financial information other aspects of a company's business activities such as social and environmental reporting.

Realisable value Assets are carried at the amount of cash or cash equivalent that could currently be obtained by selling the asset in an orderly disposal. Liabilities are carried at their settlement values, that is, the undiscounted amounts of cash or cash equivalents expected to be required to settle the liabilities in the normal course of business.

Relevance Accounting information should be able to influence the economic decisions of users. Relevant accounting information should have predictive and/or confirmatory value.

Reporting entities Business and some non-business entities that are required to prepare and submit to a relevant government agency results of their financial transactions (e.g. sole traders, partnerships and limited companies).

Retained earnings Profits reinvested in the business instead of being paid out as dividends. They belong to the shareholders and form part of shareholders' funds, together with equity capital subscribed by shareholders and reserves. The cost of retained earnings is the same as the cost of other forms of equity capital included in shareholders' funds.

Revenue The gross inflow of economic benefits (cash, receivables, other assets) arising from the ordinary operating activities of an entity.

Rights issue An issue of shares to existing shareholders, usually at a discount to the market price.

Segmental reporting Financial reporting of revenues generated based on either geographical or product basis.

Stakeholders Parties to a company who have a vested interest in that company (e.g. employees, management, customers, suppliers and lenders etc).

Standardisation The process by which rules are developed for standard setting for similar items globally.

Subsidiary A business entity wholly or partly owned (e.g. 51% or above) by another business entity, where the majority shareholding belongs to the 'parent' company.

True and fair override When a business entity does not want to follow a particular accounting standard, considering that if it follows the particular standard, the requirement of the basic accounting principle of 'fair presentation' may be compromised.

True and fair view Used to describe the required standard of financial reporting but equally to justify decisions, which require a certain amount of arbitrary judgement. It is the principle that is used in guidelines ranging from auditing and financial standards the Company's Act.

Value-in-use Is the discounted present value of the future cash flows expected to arise from the continuing use of an asset, and from its disposal at the end of its useful life

XBRL A web-based language that serves as a platform for business reporting using common Internet language tools. Referred to as eXtensible Business Reporting Language it is embedded in the HyperText Markup Language.

Directory

References

ACCA Ethical Framework for Professional Accountants – www.accaglobal.com

ACCA Guide on Environmental and CSR reporting – Guide to Best Practice: http://www.corporateregister.com/pdf/Guide.pdf

Accountingweb – www.accountingweb.co.uk/

Auditing Practices Board: Scope of an audit of the financial statements of a UK publicly traded company or group – www.frc.org.uk/apb/scope/UKP.cfm

Bebchuk, L., Cohen, A. and Ferrell, A., What matters in corporate governance? Unpublished working paper, Harvard Law School.

Becker, C., De Fond, M., Jiambalvo, J. and Subramanyam, K. R. 'The effect of audit quality on earnings management', in *Contemporary Accounting Research*, 15: 1–24 (1998).

Benedict, A and Elliott, B., *Practical Accounting* (Prentice Hall, 2001)

Berle A. A. and Means, G. C., *The Modern Corporation and Private Property* (Harcourt, Brace & World, [1932] 1968).

Blewitt, J., *Understanding Sustainable Development* (Earthscan, 2008)

Bloomberg: http://topics.bloomberg.com/database-software/

Blowfield, M., *Corporate Responsibility*, 2nd edition (Oxford University Press, 2011).

Bonner, S. E., 'A model of the effects of audit task complexity' in *Accounting, Organizations and Society* 19(3): 213–44 (1994)

British Standards Institute (BSI) – Certifications: www.bsigroup.co.uk

Cadbury Committee, *Report of the Committee on the Financial Aspects of Corporate Governance*, (Gee, 1992).

Calder, A., *Corporate Governance: A Practical Guide to the Legal Frameworks and International Codes of Practice* (Kogan Page, 2008)

Copeland, T. and Weston J. F., *Financial Theory and Corporate Policy*, 3rd edition (Addison-Wesley, 2008).

Deegan, C. and Unerman, J., *Financial Accounting Theory*, European edition, (McGraw Hill, 2008)

DeFond, M.L T., Wong, J. and Li, S. H., 'The impact of improved auditor independence on audit market concentration in China' in *Journal of Accounting and Economics*, 28: 269–305 (2000)

Deloitte IAS Plus – IFRS and IAS Standards: www.iasplus.com/standard/standard.htm

Dharan, B., 'Earnings management: Accruals vs. financial engineering' in *The Accounting World*, February 2003.

Dine, J. and Koutsias, M., *Company Law*, 7th edition (Palgrave McMillan, 2003).

Drobetz, W., Schillhofer, A., and Zimmermann, H., 'Corporate governance and expected stock returns: Evidence from Germany', in *European Financial Management*, 10(2): 267–93 (2004)

Drury, C. *Cost and Management Accounting: An introduction*, 7th edition (Cengage, 2011)

Eco-Management and Audit: http://ec.europa.eu/environment/emas/tools/index_en.htm

Elliott, B. and Elliott, J., *Financial Accounting and Reporting*, 13th edition (Prentice Hall, 2011)

Francis, J. R. 'What do we know about audit quality?' in *The British Accounting Review*, 36(4): 345–68 (2004)

Glautier, M. W. E. and Underdown, B., *Accounting: Theory and Practice*, 7th edition (Pitman Publishing, 2010)

HMRC *Money Laundering Guide*: www.hmrc.gov.uk/MLR/getstarted/intro.htm

Hopwood, A. J., 'Understanding financial accounting practice', in *Accounting, Organizations and Society*, 25(8): 763–66 (2000).

IASB *Part A & B: International Financial Reporting Standards* (2011)

Institute of Chartered Accountants of England and Wales (ICAEW) *Code on Ethics* www.icaew.com/en/technical/ethics/icaew-code-of-ethics/icaew-code-of-ethics

Jensen, M. C. and Meckling, W.H., 'Theory of the firm: Managerial behavior, agency costs, and ownership structure', in *Journal of Financial Economics*. 3(4): 305–60 (1976)

Kaur, R., *Lease Accounting: Theory and Practice* (Deep and Deep, 2004)

Khan, Y., Cash flows as determinants of dividends policy in mature firms: Evidence from FTSE 250 and AIM-listed firms. Available at SSRN: http://ssrn.com/abstract=1365367 (2009)

Khan, Y. and D'Silva, K. E., Audit Fee Modelling and Corporate Governance in a South Asian Context, Making Corporate Governance Work: Towards Reforming the Ways We Govern Conference, January 2010. Available at SSRN: http://ssrn.com/abstract=1942393 (2010)

Kothari, J. and Barone, E., *Advanced Financial Accounting*, (Prentice Hall, 2011)

Li, Y. and Stokes, D., 'Audit quality and the cost of equity capital', Second Workshop of Audit Quality, EIASM 2008.

Libby, R. and Luft, J., 'Determinants of judgment performance in accounting settings: Ability, knowledge, motivation and environment' in *Accounting, Organizations and Society*, 18(5): 425–50 (1993).

Lloyd, B., 'The influence of corporate governance on teaching in corporate finance' in *Long Range Planning*, 39: 456–66 (2006).

Meek, G. K. and Saudagaran, S. M., 'A survey of research on financial reporting in a transnational context', in *Journal of Accounting Literature*, 9: 45–182.

Melville, A., *International Financial Reporting: A Practical Guide*, 3rd edition (Prentice Hall, 2011)

Myers, S. C., *Principles of Corporate Finance*, 10th edition (McGraw Hill, 2010)

Nobes, C and Parker, R., *Comparative International Accounting*, 11th edition (Prentice Hall, 2010)

Nobes, C. W., 'Towards a general model of the reasons for international differences in financial reporting', *Abacus* 34(2): 162–87 (1998)

Reynell, C., 'Corporate governance: Killing capitalism?' in *The Economist*, Vol. 367, Issues 8318–8330 (2003)

Soloman, J., *Corporate Governance and Accountability*, 3rd edition (Wiley & Sons, 2010)

Spreckley, F., 'Social Audit: A management tool for co-operative working', see www.locallivelihoods.com/Documents/Social%20Audit%201981.pdf (1981)

Stickney, C. P., Weil, R. L. , Schipper, K. and Francis, J., *Financial Accounting: An Introduction to Concepts, Methods, and Uses*, 13th edition (Cengage, 2009)

Tricker, B., *Corporate Governance: Principles, Policies and Practices*, 2nd edition (Oxford University Press, 2012)

Weetman, P., *Financial Accounting – An Introduction*, 5th edition (Prentice Hall, 2011)

Whittington, G., 'The adoption of international accounting standards in the European Union' in *European Accounting Review*, 14(1): 127–153.

Further Reading

L. Scott, Adomako, A. and Oakes, D., *International Accounting: A compilation* (Pearson, 2011)

Holmes, G., Sugden, A. and Gee, P., *Interpreting Company Reports and Accounts*, 10th edition (Prentice Hall, 2008)

Basioudis, I. G., *Financial Accounting – A Practical Guide*, (Prentice Hall, 2010)

Magazines, Journals and Newsletters

Accountancy

This is the monthly journal of the ICAEW. It covers a wide range of topics.

CA Magazine

This is the monthly magazine of the ICAS.

Accounting and Business
This is the monthly magazine from ACCA. It covers business and professional developments worldwide.

Financial Management
This is CIMA's professional magazine. It focuses on management accounting methods and technology, and has good coverage of some of the topics in the ICSA course (e.g. capital investment appraisal). It is available from the magazine department at CIMA's headquarters.

Public Finance
This is the monthly magazine on public sector financial management from CIPFA.

Financial Times newspaper

Professional bodies and useful organisations

The specialist financial accounting bodies in the UK are the Institute of Chartered Accountants in England and Wales (ICAEW) and the Institute of Charted Accountants of Scotland (ICAS). Other professional accounting bodies are the Association of Chartered Certified Accountants (ACCA), the Chartered Institute of Management Accountants, (CIMA) and the Chartered Institute of Public Finance and Accounting (CIPFA).

All these accounting bodies include financial management elements in their examination schemes and many of their members are employed in financial management roles in industry, commerce and the public sector.

All the organisations listed below post additional information and resources on their websites. Many of the professional bodies also have international sites and offices that can provide students with additional local or regional material.

Association of Chartered Certified Accountants (ACCA)
29 Lincoln's Inn Fields
London WC2A 3EE
Tel +44(0)20 7396 5700
www.accaglobal.com

Chartered Institute of Management Accountants (CIMA)
26 Chapter Street
London SW1P 4NP
Tel +44(0)20 7663 5441
www.cimaglobal.com

The Chartered Institute of Public Finance and Accountancy (CIPFA)
3 Robert Street
London WC2N 6RL
Tel +44(0)20 7543 5600
www.cipfa.org.uk

Index